Introduc

CENTRAL AMERICAN Studies

Second Edition

EDITORS

Beatriz Cortez
Douglas Carranza Mena
California State University, Northridge

Kendall Hunt
publishing company

Cover image © Beatriz Cortez

Kendall Hunt
publishing company

www.kendallhunt.com
Send all inquiries to:
4050 Westmark Drive
Dubuque, IA 52004-1840

ISBN 978-1-4652-5105-3

Printed in the United States of America

CONTENTS

CHAPTER ONE

CENTRAL AMERICAN IDENTITIES

CHAPTER TWO

LITERATURE

CHAPTER THREE

HUMAN RIGHTS

CHAPTER FOUR

GENDER

CHAPTER FIVE

ENVIRONMENT

CHAPTER SIX

DIVERSE ETHNIC AND CULTURAL PRACTICES

CHAPTER SEVEN

IMMIGRATION

CHAPTER EIGHT

GLOBALIZATION

ACKNOWLEDGMENTS

A transnational and long list of influences, friendships, and role models too numerous to name here have impacted the academic trajectory we have chosen to follow and our perspectives on community, immigration and the place of this particular program in the redefinition of the role of our immigrant community. The Central American Studies Program has grown into an independent, B.A. degree granting program, thanks to the work of the faculty, students and community organizations linked to the program, as well as to the continued institutional support that we have received at California State University, Northridge. In particular, we wish to thank Dean Dr. Elizabeth Say at the College of Humanities and Provost Dr. Harry Hellenbrand. We are deeply grateful for their support. We thank the editorial team at Kendall/Hunt Publishing for their diligent work in the coordination of this project, especially, Beth Trowbridge, Senior Production Editor and Christine Bochniak, Author Account Manager. This book includes the publication of many articles and texts that informed and inspired us. We are indebted to the authors of all the academic texts included in this volume as well as all the courageous testimonials that bring to light a long list of injustices and inequalities in Central American daily life. We wish to also thank the literary authors whose work reproduced here illustrates the prolific and rich Central American literary production. In addition, we have benefited from the discussions and work with the students who have taken this course with us since we redesigned it nine years ago. Our experience working with them has helped us further transform this text. We are indebted to Beatriz Flores de

Cortez for reading the final version of our manuscript and for improving its clarity. Finally, and more importantly, we thank our families for their love, support, encouragement and unwavering interest in our work.

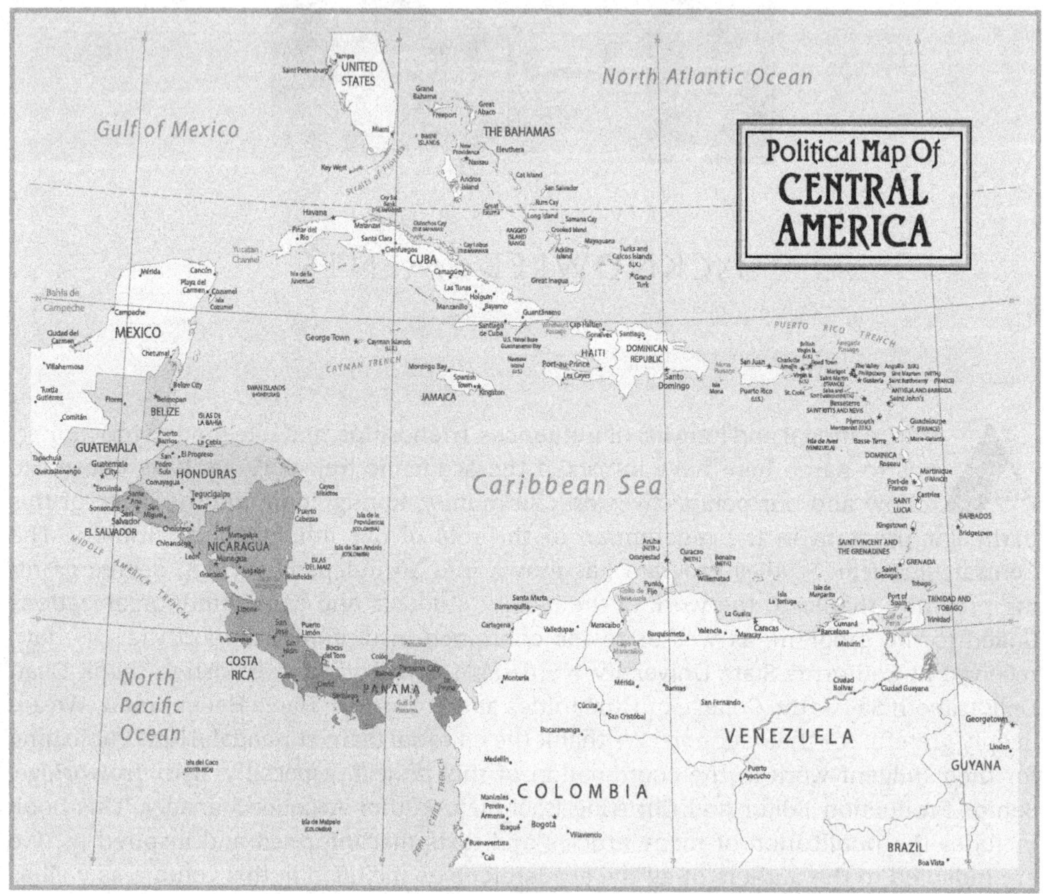

Image © ekler, 2014. Used under license from Shutterstock, Inc.

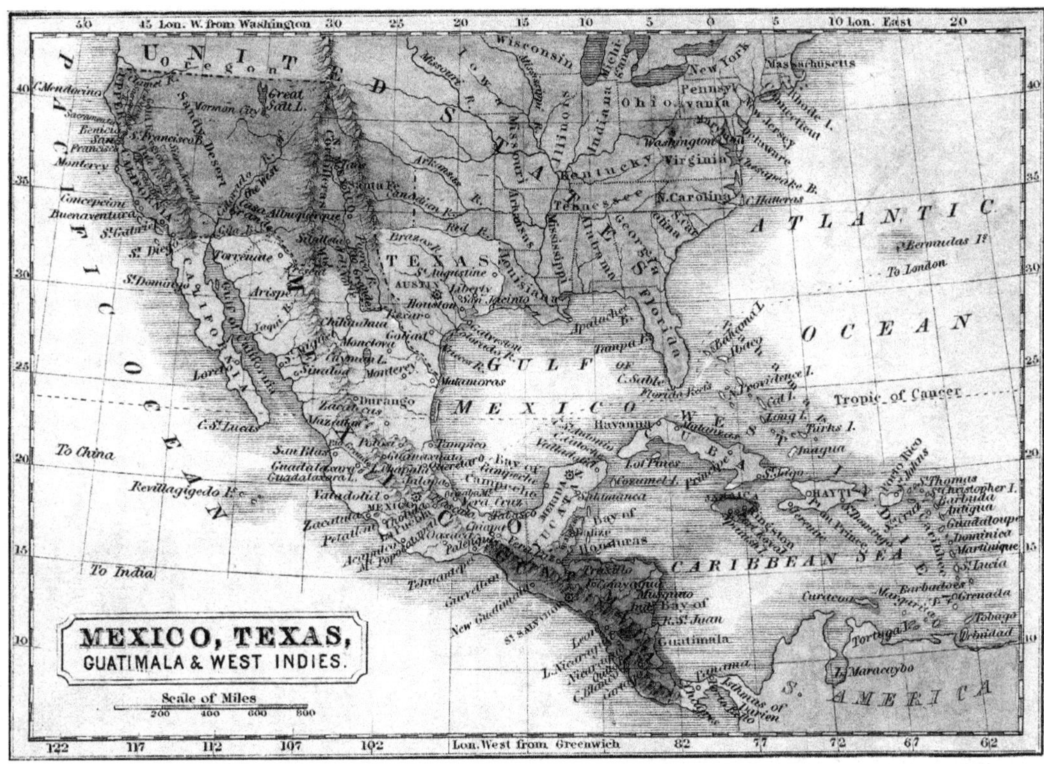
MEXICO, TEXAS,
GUATIMALA & WEST INDIES.
Scale of Miles
200 400 600 800
Lon. W. from Washington
Lon. East
Lon. West from Greenwich
Tropic of Cancer
To China
To India
To London
ATLANTIC
OCEAN
GULF OF MEXICO
CARIBBEAN SEA
TEXAS
AUSTIN
Houston
Ohio
Pennsylvania
New York
Massachusetts
Virginia
Washington
Kentucky
Tennessee
N. Carolina
Illinois
Indiana
Wisconsin
Florida
Louisiana
Havanna
Matamoras
Durango
Valadolid
Monterey
Bermudas Is.
Revillagigedo Is.
Guatimala
Barbadoes
Martinique
Trinidad
Tobago
Curacoa
Honduras
Campeche
S. AMERICA

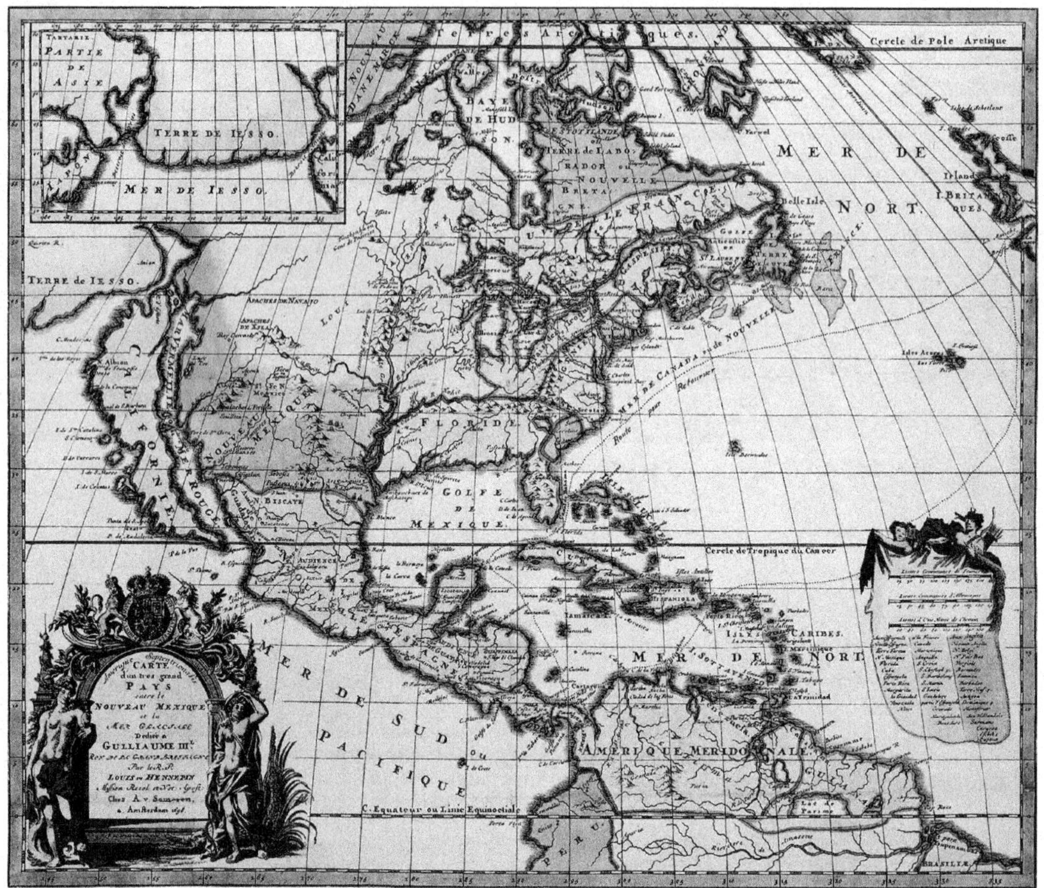
Cercle de Pole Arctique
TERRE DE IESSO.
MER DE IESSO.
TERRE de IESSO.
MER DE NORT.
Belle Isle
FLORIDE.
GOLFE DE MEXIQUE.
Cercle de Tropique du Cancer
MER DE NORT.
ISLES CARIBES.
MER DE SUD ou PACIFIQUE
AMERIQUE MERIDIONALE.
C. Equateur ou Linie Equinoctiale
PERU
BRASILIÆ

INTRODUCTION

Central American Studies is an emerging field of studies. It is an interdisciplinary academic space that emphasizes the transnational character of Central American communities in the diaspora. This reader was designed as a tool to teach the Introduction of Central American Studies at California State University, Northridge, which established the first program of Central American Studies in the United States in August, 2000, as well as at any other university that offers a similar interdisciplinary course. The courses that fall under the category of Central American Studies offer a variety of perspectives and approaches, including the study of politics, gender, art, culture, identity and literature. This reader includes an overview of this emerging field of studies while presenting students with the diverse issues, perspectives and worldviews relevant to Central American peoples.

The Central American Studies Program at California State University, Northridge is valuable for students seeking to understand their own heritage, as well as for those who plan to work with the ever-growing Central American community in the United States and those who have a scholarly interest in understanding the character of this active and expanding transnational community.

A Brief History of Central American Studies at California State University, Northridge

California State University, Northridge has a long history of activism on campus. The Latino presence on campus is quite significant, qualifying it as a Hispanic-Serving Institution, or HSI, which the U.S. Department of Education defines as "a non-profit institution that has at least 25% Hispanic full-time equivalent (FTE) enrollment, and of the Hispanic student enrollment at least 50% are low income" (n.p.). In addition to its growing enrollment of Latino students, the university has expanded its ethnic studies programs. In Fall 1990, twenty years after the establishment of the Chicana/o Studies and the Pan-African Studies Departments at California State University, Northridge, "the Asian American Studies Department was established with the objective to serve an estimated 3,700 Asian students on campus at the time" (Pyle, 3). Today, it is estimated that the so-called Minority populations at California State University, Northridge constitute more than half of the university's student population. This history of activism and the cultural spaces established by other ethnic studies programs paved the way for Central American students, faculty and the community at large to lobby within the California State University system and within the California legislature for a Central American Studies Program.

Prior to the establishment of the Central American Studies Program, the Central American United Student Association (CAUSA) formed as a subcommittee of MEChA in 1993. Dr. Alberto García, the only professor in the Chicana/o Studies Department of Central American origin at the time and an immigrant from Nicaragua, served as the first faculty advisor for CAUSA and continued to do so for several years. He injected the organization with his passion and invested his time and even his own funds in its projects and publications. Just as had happened with the student organization, at the time of its creation the Central American Studies Program was inscribed within the realm of the Chicana/o Studies Department with the support of its faculty.

However, it is important to recognize a fundamental fact: Central American Studies emerged as the representation of an identity that exists in contention with and is different from the Chicano identity. This difference makes it necessary to establish a cultural space that allows for the construction, study and visibility of the Central American identity on its own. This applies as well beyond the university context, particularly since the celebration of difference has not been a characteristic of Central American national cultures. On the contrary, in Central America, both from a perspective of nationalist state discourse and from that of revolutionary culture, unity has been at the heart of the formation of national culture and, as a result, of the erasure of difference. Nevertheless, difference is necessary, as it has been stated from quite diverse spaces of discussion.

Dr. Alberto García was also the first coordinator of the Central American Studies Program while it was a minor program under Chicana/o Studies from August 1999 until the time of its inauguration as an independent minor program in August 2000. As the program grew, part-time professors Roberto Lovato and Aquiles Magaña, as well as Chicana/o

Studies full-time professors Gerald Resendez and Dr. David Rodriguez also served as program coordinators from August 2000 to June 2004. Dr. Beatriz Cortez served as Program Coordinator from August 2004 until June 2010. Dr. Douglas Carranza has served as Program Director from August 2010 until the present.

After several years developing the curricula, student enrollment and program resources, in August 2007 the Central American Studies Program inaugurated the first Bachelor of Arts in Central American Studies in the country. This was possible due to student, faculty and community support, as well as to the institutional support that our program received, particularly from Dean Dr. Elizabeth Say from the College of Humanities. At this time, more than 115 students have graduated with a Bachelor of Arts in Central American Studies, and have moved on to graduate school or professional life serving their communities.

The Emphasis on Ethnic and Cultural Diversity

As the modern nations emerged influenced by European liberalism, the concepts of unity and equality in Central America were applied to the region through a practice that maintained difference by making it invisible and natural even while it promoted a discourse of equality and inclusiveness. As a result, the discursive need to transform the national multitude into a people of uniform qualities under the identitarian affiliation of the *Ladino,* that is, the non-Indigenous, or the *Mestizo,* that is, mixed European and Indigenous, as the modern national subject was established. The writings of Central American intellectuals during different historical moments of the modern nation express this *Ladino/Mestizo* consciousness. As an example we might look at Miguel Angel Asturias in Guatemala, who in 1923 argued in his university thesis for the eradication of Indigenous people from the national landscape, since he considered them "degenerate" (89–90). He argued for a process of *mestizaje* that would allow a uniform national subject to take the place occupied by Indigenous people (101–06). Asturias does celebrate the ancient Indigenous component of national culture and national identity, in part because it provides specificity to it, and in part because he is convinced that the process of the Spanish conquest eradicated the ancient Indigenous cultures. Nevertheless, he goes to great lengths to express his dissatisfaction with the contemporary Indigenous cultures and peoples that are part of the modern nation's landscape:

> It is easy to observe the psychic degeneration that has overcome the Indian, from the time when he was the indomitable race that died or fled to the mountains in its majority rather than surrender, or bravely fought unequaled heroic battles for his independence, to the condition he is found in today: yesterday courageous, today cowardly. Between these two parameters an entire lifespan is made painful and sorrowful by the Castilian spur that drew blood on his flanks, by the bellicose bites the conquerors ground into his mouth and by the cacaxtes, the packmule harnesses worn by men. (Asturias 420)

As a result, the articulation of difference as a central dimension of the identitarian space that Central American Studies seeks to establish is fundamental. It is not only the case that, as Homi Bhabha states, "[t]he social articulation of difference, from the minority perspective, is a complex, on-going negotiation that seeks to authorize cultural hybridities that emerge in moments of historical transformation" (2), but also that difference functions as the basic right on which we claim this academic and cultural space.

Central American Studies in the Twenty-First Century

Walter D. Mignolo, discussing the role of the Humanities in the twenty-first century, argues that global citizenship requires the dismantling of global racism, and that the decolonial shift in the humanities brings with it a body of knowledge of experiences and memories that were previously disqualified (314). Also, Mignolo doesn't encourage the liberal ideal of unity and commonality, whose basis he believes is the white European heterosexual male's paradigm; rather, he argues for the exploration of difference. As he considers the claim that "because we all are equal, we have a right to be different" (quoted by Mignolo, 314), he invites those of us who work in the humanities to help "acknowledge that global citizenship is a myth while global racism is not overcome and to work toward the decolonization of imperial knowledge that engendered the coloniality of being" (Mignolo, 329).

It is significant for Central American Studies as an emerging area of studies to be able to recognize and celebrate difference. While it is difficult to classify this field of studies under the umbrella of Chicana/o Studies, there are fundamental points of coincidence between the Chicana/o Studies and the Central American Studies perspectives. One of these points of coincidence is the lack of investment that both of these perspectives place on their *Latino* background; quite to the contrary, they both emphasize their *Indigenous* heritage. In fact, our vision of Central American Studies is one that deconstructs the *Ladino/Mestizo* identity, that rejects the vision of the Central American identity as *Hispanic,* and that seeks to open spaces for the knowledge and understanding of Central America's diverse cultural and ethnic identities. Of course, one must also make a distinction between the Chicano construction of identity with a foundation on an Indigenous distant past and the Central American identity that our community's reality demands—one constructed by diverse cultural and ethnic Indigenous and Afro-Caribbean identities coexisting with the *Ladino/Mestizo* and European consciousness not only in our distant past but also in our present. Another difference in the construction of the Chicana/o and the Central American identities is that Chicana/o Studies as a field does not share the marked transnational experience of the Central American peoples, nor their refugee status, nor their battle for legalization and immigrant rights.

Along the same lines, it is difficult to classify the field of Central American Studies under the umbrella of Latino Studies, that is, under a classification that runs the risk of blurring the Central American identity within the context of Latino identities in the U.S., and that would particularly represent a force that eradicates the myriad of Indigenous and Afro-Caribbean experiences that are part of the Central American identity and experience as a whole.

Because most Central American people in the United States and in Southern California are recent immigrants who arrived in large numbers starting in the 1980s, this is a newly established population with the need to generate visibility for its insertion in the cultural debate for identity and self definition. As a result, the Central American experience in the U.S. requires some sort of strategic essentialism; that is, it needs the visible definition of its identity and of its spaces. This is not because its identity cannot be flexible and malleable, able to transform itself throughout the years; and it is not because for strategic political reasons it can also be affiliated and part of the Latino community in the U.S. Rather, it is because it is an emerging identity that requires its own space for its inscription, its own space for the celebration and knowledge of its cultures and its definition in its own terms, be it from a cultural, popular or academic perspective.

The National vs. the Regional

To further add to the problematic erasure of ethnic and cultural diversity in Central America throughout the process of the emergence of this field of studies, we were faced with the need to address the question of the national vs. the regional. Central America is not a cultural region united by any type of regional or cultural shared identity. Rather, the marked presence of nationalistic cultures within the Isthmus maintains identities often separated in opposition to or in competition with one another. These national identities follow the traditional modern construction of national identity based on territoriality, on the eradication of difference, on the formulation of a uniform national subject, in the case of the state apparatuses and on the construction of the idea of national unity, in the case of revolutionary cultures. Outside the Central American territory, from the cultural and identitarian spaces of immigration represented by the diasporic communities that, in this case, have settled in the United States, the Central American identity functions best outside of the Central American territory, and it exists as an umbrella term composed by difference. In other words, in spite of the fact that the experience of immigration and the nostalgia that it produces presents the nation and nationalism as the foundations of identity, for our field of studies it is fundamental to deconstruct nationalism. As Hardt and Negri state:

> In cases of diasporic populations, [. . .] the nation seems at times to be the only concept available under which to imagine the community of the subaltern group. [. . .] It may be true, as Benedict Anderson says, that a nation should be understood as an imagined community—but here we should recognize that the claim is inverted so that the *nation becomes the only way to imagine community!* Every imagination of a community

> becomes overcoded as a nation and hence our conception of community is severely impoverished. (107)

Therefore, Central American Studies strives for the visibility of the Central American cultural and ethnic diversity and its experiences of transnationalism, post-nationalism and immigration. It is a positioning no longer affiliated with the colonial dimensions of a nation or a territorial region, but with a more permeable and malleable understanding of this cultural region and of the movements of its displaced peoples. As Hardt and Negri state, the colonial civilizing project that defined the nation in clear terms and that viewed disease (understood in the broadest way) as "a sign of a lack of civilization" (135) can no longer stand in this age of globalization when "[t]he boundaries of nation-states . . . are increasingly permeable by all kinds of flows. Nothing can bring back the hygienic shields of colonial boundaries. The age of globalization is the age of universal contagion" (136).

As traumatic and significant as the experience of immigration has been for Central Americans, it is evident that the issues that our communities consider fundamental struggles define our identities: the revolutionary experience of the 1980s and 1990s; the history of economic oppression during most of modern history of the Central American region; our contention with an imperialistic U.S. foreign policy, particularly marked by episodes such as the William Walker invasion of Nicaragua in the 1850s; the arbitrary formation and occupation of Panama during most of the twentieth century; and the U.S. support of the Contras during most of the Sandinista government in Nicaragua and its support and counter-insurgency training of the Guatemalan and Salvadoran military dictatorships during the recent civil wars. Nevertheless, one must also acknowledge that these are struggles linked to the experience of the modern nation, which relate to the construction of the idea of a cohesive national identity, to the economy that sustained national and international political relations.

In Central America, nevertheless, there are other identities that coexist with these, and they do not necessarily relate to the modern economic and nationalistic dimensions of Central American experience. These are identities that exist outside of the space of the modern nation and that struggle against the efforts launched by the modern nation to erase them: These are the diverse ethnic and cultural identities that are also a fundamental part of the Central American experience. These are the populations massacred and persecuted in the name of nationalism and in the name of modernity. Furthermore, it is important to realize that these are identities and communities that, in the diaspora, are no longer defined *in absentia,* as the national dominant culture within the Central American region relegates them to silence. This is particularly evident as we approach our classrooms and we realize that we will not be speaking and defining Indigenous and Afro-Caribbean peoples in their absence, but rather, we will often be speaking of the Indigenous and Afro-Caribbean experiences and identities to a body of students that includes members of their communities. It is a dynamic that requires that our in-class discussions generate a space for the active participation of the students who are themselves representatives of the diverse identities that constitute the Central American experience.

Teaching Central American Studies from the Space of the Diaspora

On a similar note, teaching Central American Studies outside of the Central American territory is an experience unlike any other at the university level within the Central American region. Whereas, within the Central American territory a university education is accessible to a limited percentage of the population and is marked by a middle class *Ladino/ Mestizo* sensibility that requires the acculturation of members of other communities who seek access to higher education, in the diasporic communities the Central American population is markedly working class and diverse.

At California State University, Northridge the official numbers of Central American enrolled students do not include a large percentage of the student population of Afro-Caribbean heritage. These students are forced to choose in their application for admission to the University between a Central American (Hispanic) and an Afro-Caribbean (Black) identitarian affiliation. It is estimated that the Central American population ranges from 3,500 to 4,000. In other words, Central American student enrollment at California State University, Northridge constitutes an approximate 9 percent of the student population.

The Central American Studies Program at California State University, Northridge has a tri-fold mission: to empower the large and growing Central American community in the United States by promoting academic excellence, community involvement and cultural diversity; to open spaces of global citizenship and dialogue between academia and society at large that contribute to the construction of a Central American transnational identity; and to promote an understanding and appreciation of the diverse Central American cultures, ethnicities and worldviews from an interdisciplinary perspective.

Currently, the students enrolled in the Program come from diverse backgrounds. The majority come from Central American immigrant communities that link them to the urban experience in Los Angeles and to the rural experience in Central America. Our students, as well as the Central American community at large, come from an experience marked by undocumented immigration and/or refugee status. A large percentage of the Central American students enrolled in the program have lived in the Pico/Union Westlake area of urban Los Angeles and have studied in over-populated high schools where they lacked the encouragement to move on to the university setting. As a result, our Program's objectives include being advocates for our students and the Central American community, and making up for the work and opportunities that many of our students were not able to have access to; that is, to offer interdisciplinary courses that allow them to develop their critical thinking, writing and reading skills and that motivate them to become independent, self-driven lifelong learners.

With regards to the Central American experience and identities, our courses seek to provide students with an awareness of the complexity of the historical, social and cultural developments in Central America. Our program strives to help them develop a greater understanding and appreciation of the transnational Central American community's experiences and cultures and its contributions to the United States. We strive to develop the intellectual and social foundations, and the leadership skills, necessary for promoting social change in the United States and its society, especially in relation to the Central American community that has settled in this country. Furthermore, as global citizens, our Program seeks to prepare students to recognize, understand, evaluate and change the culture of exclusion that has been prevalent in both Central America and the United States, as well as to instill in students an understanding and appreciation of the diverse Central American cultures, ethnicities, experiences and worldviews.

Fortunately for the Program, the Central American student population at California State University, Northridge is diverse, and it includes not only immigrants originating from a number of Indigenous and Afro-Caribbean communities in Central America, but also from immigrant families that have formed across national identities: Nicaraguan-Salvadoran, Guatemalan-Panamanian and so forth, as well as Anglo students. In other words, our vision of the program corresponds to our student population's characteristics: transnational, diasporic, culturally and ethnically diverse, and from interdisciplinary academic backgrounds.

Introduction to the Central American Studies Reader

The Introduction to the Central American Studies course presents an overview of our program. Even when some of our courses explore the realm of traditional disciplines such as literature, art, music, history and film, they do so from the interdisciplinary perspective of an ethnic/area studies program. Furthermore, most of our courses are fully interdisciplinary, such as the Central American Diaspora; Urbanization in Central America; Poverty, Development and the Environment in Central America; Violence and Culture in Central America; and Religious, Social or Revolutionary Movements. There are also courses that specifically explore the cultural and identitarian perspectives and experiences of particular populations, such as Afro-Caribbean Cultures and Identities, Contemporary Indigenous Peoples in Central America or the Changing Roles of Central American Women. Furthermore, our courses reflect the strong connection that our program has with the Central American community at large, particularly through the required Fieldwork in the Community course. The premise of this course is that students have valuable knowledge to share with their community, and, more importantly, that the community itself is an invaluable source of knowledge for the students. It is through service learning with the community that students can acquire this knowledge.

The Introduction to Central American Studies reader is meant to be a textbook for the introductory freshman class in this field. It is divided into eight different sections: Central American Identities, Literature, Human Rights, Gender, Environment, Diverse Ethnic and Cultural Practices, Immigration, and Globalization.

The Institutionalization of Central American Studies

California State University, Northridge has been at the heart of the institutionalization of Central American Studies. Of course, this process of consolidation comes with certain political benefits as it provides visibility for Central Americans and it is part of a wider process of recognition of Central American immigrants in the United States. Nevertheless, that the institutionalization of this area of studies has begun in Northridge, a place where large numbers of Central American students have access to the program, is significant. It has generated a space that has emerged within the contexts of an immigrant imaginary of transnationalism, interdisciplinarity, diversity and difference.

Works Cited

Asturias, Miguel Angel. *Sociología Guatemalteca. Guatemalan Sociology.* Trans. Maureen Ahern. Tempe, AZ: Arizona State University, Center for Latin American Studies, 1977.

Bhabha, Homi K. *The Location of Culture.* London: Routledge, 1994.

Hardt, Michael and Antonio Negri. *Empire.* Cambridge, MA: Harvard University Press, 2000.

Mignolo, Walter. "Citizenship, Knowledge, and the Limits of Humanity." *American Literary History* 18.2 (2006): 312–31.

Pyle, Amy. "Class Consciousness Education: The Founding of a CSUN Asian-American Studies Department Comes 21 Years after Chicano and Pan-African Studies." *Los Angeles Times* 19 September 1990: 3.

Rafael, Vicente. "The Cultures of Area Studies in the United States." Social Text 41 (1994): 91–111.
"Hispanic Serving Institution." *U.S. Department of Education.* 5 August 2006.

CHAPTER ONE

CENTRAL AMERICAN IDENTITIES

Central American identities are diverse, and the region's cultural production expresses this diversity. But what is culture? Culture is everything that is part of people's daily life. It includes culinary practices, dress codes, social relationships and ways of organizing, as well as expressions more formally associated with cultural production such as music, art, literature, film, architecture and sculpture, among others.

We cannot define culture in a permanent, rigid way. While there are elements in a certain culture that remain, there are other dimensions of it that are ever-changing, for every group.

In Central America today there are many different groups of people. These include the Maya, Nahuat (that includes Pipil people and Nicarao people, among others), Lenca, Miskito, Sumu, Rama, Matagalpa, Garifuna, Cuna, Talamanca, Cacaopera and many other Indigenous groups; peoples of mixed origin such as Mulattos and Mestizos, which are Spanish colonial names given to those people of African and Spanish descent and Indigenous and Spanish ancestry, respectively; Europeans of Spanish origin; Criollos, or Spaniards born in the Americas; and a variety of more recent immigrants.

Culturally speaking, there is also the definition of Indigenous or *Ladino/Mestizo,* which means a cultural affiliation that is non-Indigenous, and often, that exists in contention with the Indigenous identity.

Central American culture is not uniform. All the different groups of people that inhabit the region show significant variability in terms of social organization, religion and culture. Furthermore, the modern concept of Central America and the different nations that form the region are of recent formation. Guatemala, El Salvador, Honduras, Nicaragua and Costa Rica declared their independence collectively from Spain in 1821 and went through a process forming the modern nation as part of the Central American Federal Republic from 1824 to 1839, and later individually. As a result, these nations have not existed for more than 195 years. Prior to that, during the Spanish colony, the name of this region was the Kingdom of Guatemala. Before that, it did not have a name to unify it in the modern Western sense. However, each local area had a different name, a different culture, different types of social organizations and different religions and languages.

What we know now as Central America formed during independence with the emergence of the modern nations. When independence took place, the Spaniards and the Criollos, among all the different groups of people that lived in Central America at the time, had the political knowledge to establish the modern Central American nations. They were also Spaniards, except that they were born in the American colonies. They understood and followed the European pattern for modern nation formation. And they had the greatest investment in independence.

Starting in the year 711, groups of Arabs and Berbers moved from Northern Africa across the Mediterranean and slowly invaded Spain. These groups, also known as Moors, remained in Spain for approximately 800 years, greatly influencing Spanish culture, architecture, art, cuisine, music, literature and scientific knowledge. When Leon and Castilla united in the Spanish Peninsula to implement what was called the *Reconquista* or the Re-conquest of Spain, the Moors became defined as enemy invaders of the emerging nation and were eventually expelled in 1492. However, their influence remains in Spanish culture today.

In order to encourage people to take part in the wars for the re-conquest of Spain, the Spanish Crown offered those who recaptured territories titles of nobility, lands and often workers to work for them. Therefore, many people joined in the wars for the reconquest of Spain in search of the rapid elevation of their families' status. As a result, the emerging Spanish culture established working with one's own hands by one's own means as a sign of poverty and the lack of titles of nobility.

Furthermore, one of the ways in which the emerging powers were able to consolidate national identity in Spain was through the implementation of a purity of blood mandate that required people to demonstrate that they were pure blooded Spaniards, without any Muslim or any Jewish ancestry. Jewish peoples, in fact, were also officially expelled from Spain in 1492, in part because they were not Catholic, but also, in order to take away their possessions and replenish the empty coffers of the Spanish Catholic Crown.

Once the Spanish re-conquest was complete in 1492, those who had been unable to obtain titles of nobility during the re-conquest faced dark prospects for their future. The arrival of Christopher Columbus in the Americas that same year provided those who had been left out a new opportunity to attain titles of nobility and access to the world of privilege closed to them in Spain. Many of these adventurers set off to participate in the wars of the Spanish conquest of the Americas in hopes of changing their future prospects. Those who were successful did receive titles of nobility, lands and people forced to work

for them under diverse systems that included different forms of slavery, tax payment, labor tax and other bondages.

As a result, many Criollos, that is, Spaniards born in the Americas, were born to privilege. They inherited the titles of nobility obtained by their ancestors who had participated in the conquest. They came to the world in a context of racial prejudice where peoples were classified through a taxonomy that included many categories or *castas*. Criollos and Peninsulares, or Spaniards born in the Spanish peninsula, were at the top of the ladder in that taxonomical hierarchy: They were full blooded Catholic Spaniards who possessed titles of nobility and prestige and often financial privilege. So, why would the Criollos want to promote the cause for independence?

In spite of their privilege, there was something that the Criollos could not have: They did not have access to political power. The Crown had doubts about their political allegiance and considered them "contaminated" by the American landscape, food and society. As a result, political power belonged exclusively to Peninsular Spaniards during colonial times. This was one of the main reasons why the Criollos supported independence from Spain.

In order to achieve independence, the Criollos disseminated a discourse of equality borrowed from the French liberals who were participants in the French Revolution and who applied it to the European context of their nation (France) at the time. However, once independence was accomplished in the Americas, not all were considered equal because the colonial Eurocentric mindset largely remained after independence, and it continues to persist today. As a result, the symbols used to define the new emerging nations in Central America did not reflect the cultural diversity of the region but were linked to European tradition. These included the songs selected as the national anthems for these nations and other patriotic symbols.

The new nations in Central America were defined with an identity perceived as permanent, linked to the national territory and full of the desire to implement modernity. These symbols reinvented for the newly formed nations a narrative of their roots and elaborated the idea of a cohesive, uniform national subject and national identity that denied the Indigenous component to these nations. Furthermore, identity is not permanent as we might imagine from examples of our own lives. Identity is constructed through culture and through the daily practices of people and not through abstract, nation-building discourse. Nevertheless, in Central America, as the discourse of national identity after independence attempted to construct a permanent and immobile identity in daily life, the diverse identities that coexisted in the space of the nation continued to transform themselves through the daily practices of the people who inhabited these countries and who continue to do so today. Furthermore, these practices are also evident in the people who continue to be linked to these countries even though they have migrated to other areas, as in the case of Central American populations in the United States.

The other two nations that form Central America today, Panama and Belize, are of even more recent formation. Panama formed in 1903 after it separated from Colombia during a bloodless war for independence sponsored by the United States. After Panama's independence, the United States undertook the construction of the Panama Canal. Once the canal was inaugurated in 1914, Panama became a major international travel route and a key player in international trade. The canal brought modernization and further linked Central America to the emerging global capitalist economy. However, the canal also brought alienation and segregation for Panamanians, while it kept Panama's economy dependent on the United States and under colonial conditions throughout most of the twentieth century.

Belize, which was previously called British Honduras, was formally named a British colony in 1862. Slavery had been officially abolished since 1838; however, its society remained highly stratified throughout the colonial period. From mid-nineteenth century, the Belize Estate and Produce Company (BEC) initiated a monopoly in British Honduras and gained control of extensive territories, the labor force and trade in this colony. Later on, the United Fruit Company also began operations in British Honduras, bringing U.S. interests into play. Furthermore, as the colonial era came to an end for Belize, Guatemala saw Belize as a key territory for its access to the Atlantic Ocean and, therefore, as a possibility for developing alternative routes for transoceanic trade. Because of the struggles generated by all the interests at play, Belize did not obtain its independence from Britain until 1981. However, Belize's colonial legacy continues to be visible today.

Finally, in order to coexist in celebration and respect of diversity, it is important to establish that there are societies that are more complex than others; there are social groups that choose to live in both urban centers and in simpler villages; there are groups of people who believe in modernity and others who believe in simpler ways of organizing; but whatever the choice, no type of society is superior to others. Complex societies are able to achieve greater levels of distribution of labor, to develop scientific and complex knowledge and to build monumental architecture, but they are rarely able to meet the basic needs of all their people. Poverty, social problems and crime are often part of more complex forms of organizing. The more complex a society, the more inequality we find. Sometimes, a society that has achieved complexity can fall apart, or it can take on simpler ways of organizing, as in the case of the Maya of Guatemala and Southern Mexico today. The history of Central America illustrates the ways in which the construction of an empire requires the colonization and oppression of others, as happened during the colonial period in Central America.

The article titled "Colonial Policy and Slavery" by Héctor Díaz Polanco explores the colonial concept of Indigenismo as a practice designed by non-Indigenous peoples to apply to Indigenous peoples. This practice, which continues today in modern Latin American nations, assumes that Indigenous peoples lack the skills to define their own destiny. Díaz Polanco explains that the concept of Indigenismo is used in two very different ways. The definition of its more common use is the practice, by non-Indigenous people, of defending or expressing appreciation for Indigenous people through a variety of attitudes and practices. However, it is also a way of reproducing the definition of Indigenous peoples as *Others* by the modern subject, more importantly, as others who are unable to speak for themselves. According to Díaz Polanco, the more theoretical use of the concept "implies subordination and conflict" because it is the practice by which the dominators use the state institutions to "impose their will" on the dominated. It is a practice that serves as state policy and that continues to exclude Indigenous peoples from the realm of the nation even today. As a result, as Díaz Polanco states, Indigenism does not provide a solution to the ethnic problems in all these nations. Quite the contrary, it is an integral "part of the problem."

In addition to that, as Díaz Polanco explains, the contemporary integrationist indigenist policies seek to find ways to acculturate Indigenous people into a homogeneous national subject that would no longer reflect ethnic and cultural diversity but rather the modern and European worldviews. During colonial times, ethnic groups mixed. However, this process did not generate a homogenous society. On the contrary, the implementation of a *casta* system ensured the permanence of a hierarchical system of ethnic diversity and Eurocentric power. However, when the *casta* system was eliminated in order to implement the discourse of equality and liberalism that accompanied the process for independence, a new objective emerged: the implementation of a homogeneous modern national subject. Unfortunately, the perception continues that Indigenous peoples and ethnic diversity are obstacles in the formation of this homogeneous national subject.

Colonial Policy and Slavery

HÉCTOR DÍAZ POLANCO

The various indigenist policies that have operated throughout history are the reflection and, in many ways, the cause of the Latin American nation-states' unresolved heterogeneity. "Indigenism" as a common usage can be distinguished from "indigenism" as a theoretical concept. In its common usage indigenism includes attitudes, expressions, or practices vaguely associated with appreciating or even defending the Indian. In this sense, "indigenist" can be used to describe the fervor and frenetic activity of Friar Bartolomé de las Casas during the sixteenth century and of the people who defend Indians' human rights today, or the contemporary musicians, writers, or painters who are interested in the life or culture of indigenous groups. As a theoretical concept, in contrast, indigenism is a *sociological category* that refers to the relationship among sociocultural groups in given economic, social, and political contexts. In this sense it implies subordination and conflict. The presence of dominated (Indians) and dominators (non-Indians) within the framework of a state makes it possible for the latter to use the instruments and institutions of power to impose their will on the former. Such genism is often simultaneously an ideology, a more or less formalized anthropological topic, and a practice that tends to serve as state policy.

In reality, especially when state policy is paternalistic, indigenisms in the two meanings just explained tend to mix; that is, indigenism as state ideology and practice seeks to convey the positive connotations and the idealism of indigenism in its common usage. But since the former is, in fact, antithetical to the latter, it is useful to distinguish between them.

Therefore, the indigenism we are concerned with here involves policies that have been thought out and designed by non-Indians to be applied to others. It does not assume any consideration of the points of view and interests of those others. Rather, it assumes a more or less blatant denial that these others have anything to say about their own affairs and destiny. The various indigenisms of this kind are at once alien (with regard to ethnic groups) and extremely homogenizing. And when exclusionary sociocultural patterns become the platform of a given national organization, indigenism becomes a strategic vehicle for antidemocratic and conservative projects.[1]

Past indigenisms have often systematically and even deliberately precluded any kind of autonomy for distinctive sociocultural groups. Indigenism employed as state policy may go as far as genocide, ethnocide, ethnophagy, or a combination of these, or it may modify ethnic diversity and even make it more complex, but it never resolves the tensions and conflicts of diversity. In any event, the solution to the ethnic problem lies not in identifying "good" as opposed to "negative" indigenism but in escaping *the very logic of any indigenism*. Indigenism is not the solution to the ethnic-national question; it is part of the problem.

As we have seen, the colonial regime was in general an immense cauldron in which new mixtures formed from preexisting sociocultural ingredients as a consequence of a painful brewing. But the result was not an undifferentiated or homogeneous society. Later, during the nineteenth century and the first decades of the twentieth, policies deliberately sought the homogenization of society in the criollomestizo sociocultural mold. These policies did not meet their goal of extermination but did provoke transformations in the ethnic composition of the society. In the twentieth century, the question of persistent ethnic diversity remained a policy "problem" whose resolution lay in the hands of modern "integrationist" indigenists.

Three phases of indigenism can be distinguished:[2] (1) the indigenism of the first three centuries of the colonial regime, (2) the postindependence indigenism of the nineteenth and early twentieth centuries that liberals conceived and effected, and (3) the indigenism of modern Latin American states, developed particularly since the mid-twentieth century.[3]

Some researchers have identified the policy applied during the colonial phase,[4] with the "segregationist"—better described as corporatist—modality that was characteristic of nearly all of the Spanish dominions in America during the second half of the sixteenth century. Corporatist measures were designed to differentiate (though not properly to separate structurally) native groups from the rest of the population in the economic, sociocultural, and political spheres. During the sixteenth century the Spanish crown concentrated the scattered native populations in their original areas of settlement or, more frequently, in new places (called Indian towns). Religious and civil authorities often selected these sites with a view to facilitating direct control (ideological, political, economic, social, administrative) over the settlements. Structurally, this divided colonial society into two systems that, nevertheless, were kept closely articulated. The resulting "republic of the Indians and republic of the Spanish"[5] gave rise to a model of socioeconomic and ethnic barriers later called "castes."

Indian Slavery

Colonial policy toward ethnic groups did not simply take the form of segregationism or corporatism, although this modality dominated the more advanced phase of the regime. The enslavement of natives was widespread during the early colonial era. Indeed, it is sometimes forgotten that trafficking in slaves began not in the Old World-New World direction but in the opposite one. A few years after the Europeans arrived, the first contingent of Indian slaves, captured at Hispaniola, was sent to Spain.[6] In addition, Indians were used as slave labor on their own land after the invasion. Thus, it was the Indians and not the Africans who were the first to suffer the yoke of slavery in America. Later, as the native population quickly perished under the harshness of this exploitative regime and as a consequence of the illnesses brought by the Europeans, black slaves imported on a large scale began to supply labor for the heavy tasks of production in the new possessions.[7] Before that, however, the Spanish sought to provide labor for the islands by exploiting Indian slaves brought from other parts of America (natives of the so-called useless islands and the mainland coasts).

Because the islands of the Antilles, particularly La Española or Hispaniola,[8] were the initial site of the conquest and colonization of the Americas,[9] the indigenous peoples there were the first victims of slavery. Only four years after the "discovery," in 1496, a third of the indigenous population of Hispaniola had already perished).[10] Less than two decades later, in 1510, when the Spanish monarch was considering the introduction of Indian slaves into Castile, "the extraordinary decline of the Indians in Hispaniola forced the king to change his mind."[11] The rapid extermination of the island's indigenous peoples was merely a prelude to the regional demographic disaster that was to come: The autochthonous population of the other islands was also decimated in a short period. Already by this stage, slave labor was essential to the exploitation of the gold deposits or placers discovered in several parts of the new lands.

During the first third of the sixteenth century, Indian slavery had been broadly extended throughout subjugated America. Indians were enslaved in their own homelands and exploited in the process of Spanish production. Spanish troops in sailing vessels would capture the aboriginal people of the mainland and transport them to the Antilles, especially Hispaniola and Cuba. Because of transport conditions, ill-treatment, inadequate food, and so on, many prisoners died during these journeys. Some sources report that hundreds of corpses were thrown into the sea.

The Requerimiento and the "Just War" Against the Indians

Indian slavery required some justification that, at least according to the interpretations of those days, could resolve the conflict between the autochthonous population's captivity and the dominant culture's ethical precepts, particularly those of Catholicism. To construct such rationalizations and to define an adequate *modus operandi* compatible with Christian principles (all ironies apart), the most outstanding theologians, canonists, and legal experts were consulted. The so-called doctrine of the just war emerged from the thinking of these intellectuals.[12]

In essence, this doctrine declared that it was legitimate to capture and enslave Indians who forcefully "resisted" the conquerors and refused to accept the Catholic faith. According to the accepted precepts of "natural law," members of the human species were considered free, but in time of war, "the peoples' natural law" accepted captivity because it was more humane than killing defeated enemies. Thus, the general principle of human freedom was made compatible with the exception accorded cases of "just war."[13]

What was necessary, therefore, was to be sure that warfare was "just," giving the natives the opportunity to remain peacefully under Spanish rule. With this objective, at the beginning of the sixteenth century a renowned Castilian jurist, Doctor Juan López de Palacios Rubios, adviser to the king, Ferdinand the Catholic, wrote what Saco describes as "one of the most unusual and extraordinary documents ever produced by history. Before the Castilians took possession of the lands and the Indians, they were to read the document, the *Requerimiento,* written in the Castilian language which, if the Indians could ever understand in words, through interpreters, they would never be able to comprehend,"[14] since the document addressed questions completely foreign to the Indians worldviews and sociocultural systems.

The document "explained" that God created heaven and earth and made Saint Peter, the first pope, the lord of all humans, that Saint Peter had jurisdiction over all the world's people, that a successor of his had given the islands and mainland of the Atlantic Ocean to the king and queen of Spain, and that, therefore, all the inhabitants of those territories should submit to those monarchs and accept the Catholic faith without resistance.

Leaving no options and permitting no discussion of any of its premises, this unusual text ended with the following threat:

> If you would not be willing, and if with malice you would be slow to submit, I certify that with God's help we shall powerfully assail you and make war against you from every side and in every way, and we shall subject you to the yoke and obedience of the Church and Their Highnesses, and we shall take your persons and those of your women and children and enslave you and sell you and dispose of you at Their Highnesses' command, and take your goods and inflict upon you all the injury and hardship we can as vassals who neither obey nor want to receive their lord and resist and contradict him; and we declare that you shall be accountable for the death and injuries that ensue and that Their Highnesses, ourselves, or these knights who come with us shall not be culpable.[15]

One can easily understand that this *Requerimiento* served as a simple pretext for the Spanish army to take many Indians as slaves, arguing they had been captured under conditions of "just war" and for "just reasons." This is, without any doubt, one of best illustrations of the hypocritical use of religion to justify vile deeds.[16] Several centuries distant from us, this rambling may seem an exercise in black comedy, but it was quite seriously used to support horrendous excesses. There are many accounts of instances in which indigenous people, who could not comprehend the exact contents of the document, did not have to show that they would not comply with it or even display any sort of hostility toward the recently arrived foreigners for violence to fall upon them. Peaceful aboriginal groups who accepted the foreigners and who wanted to please them were assaulted, captured on the pretext of having "resisted," and, finally, enslaved.

Often the military did not even concern themselves with communicating the message (if such an address could be called a message, since, as Las Casas said, to the Indians it would have been the same if "it had been Latin or jabbering"). The Spanish read the document at a great distance from Indian villages and even in the loneliness of the fields, where they had no visible interlocutor. Afterwards, the army moved on to capture the malicious "rebels."[17]

The *bachiller* Anciso, sent to Cenú territory by Pedrarias de Avila, describes the reaction to the *Requerimiento* of two caciques:

> They answered that in that which I said, that there was not but one God and that he governed heaven and earth, and that he was the Lord of everything, that it seemed all right to them and that that was the way it should be, but that in what I said about the pope being the lord of the universe, in God's place, and that he had given that land to the king of Castile, they said that the pope must have been drunk when he did that, since he was giving away what was not his, and that the king, who asked for and took things at will, must be a lunatic, because he was asking for what belonged to others . . .

> and they said that they were lords of their lands and there was no need for another lord. I asked again for their submission; if not granted, I said, I would make war against them . . . we took their lands by force; . . . and later I captured another of their caciques in a different place and found him to be a man of truth who kept his word and who found wrong what was wrong and right what was right; and there, almost all wars are made in this way.

Las Casas, who transcribed this passage, thought that it also demonstrated how unjust warfare was initiated, but he considered what Anciso claimed to be the response of the Indian chiefs pure "fable," since they could not have comprehended the concepts of the *Requerimiento* and there was mutual ignorance of each other's language.[18] If so, the reported responses of the caciques are even more interesting, since they may be the expression of the doubts that plagued the conquerors about the legitimacy and rationality of their arguments and activities.

There were, of course, other "legitimate" means of enslaving Indians. Especially in New Spain (where, in contrast to Peru, capture played a large role), another cause for slavery was *rescate*—the "rescuing" of indigenous people who had been slaves under the pre-Hispanic system and in turn had become slaves under Spanish rule. The caciques and *principales* (indigenous authorities) also gave the Spanish indigenous people as slaves as part of their tribute payments.[19]

The Spanish conquerors argued that it was legal to enslave at least some Indians because in pre-Hispanic societies (particularly the highly developed groups of Mesoamerica) the institution of slavery already existed. However, there is reason to believe that in this case, as in others regarding contact between two cultures, there was misinterpretation, whether with malice or not, of an institution that did not precisely match its European counterpart.

Indeed, what the Spanish called "slavery" among the Indians was not slavery in the sense in which the relationship was understood in Europe. The Spanish chroniclers noted the substantial differences between the two institutions. It was mentioned, for example, that neither the existence of so-called pre-Hispanic slavery nor its causes could he compared with their European counterparts. In the indigenous societies the causes for slavery could be extremely trivial, and the condition of indigenous "slaves" in their own society was nearly identical to that of "free men" in the European system. Indigenous slaves could have possessions and even slaves of their own; service to the master was occasional and not fundamentally oriented toward production; "it often happened that male slaves married their women masters and female slaves their male masters," reported López de Gámara. Whereas in Europe the children of slaves were born into slavery, in the pre-Hispanic system they were born free.[20] Motolinía, who observed the Spanish practice of enslaving Indians who had been "slaves" under the autochthonous regime in exchange for tribute, considered that "according to [indigenous] law and truth, almost no one is a slave." And in relation to their condition in the communities, he clarified that

> these Indians do not use the services of their slaves with the servitude and labor that the Spanish do, because they have them as almost free, in their ranches and estates, where they farm a certain part for their masters and another portion for themselves, and they have their homes, wives, and children, in such a way that they do not have so much obligation that they would run away from their condition or from their masters.[21]

The Abolition of Indian Slavery

Beginning in the 1530s, measures were adopted to abolish the slavery of the American Indian population. This process was influenced in particular by the denunciations of slavery by the friars. The Spanish crown's attitude oscillated because of the contradictory considerations involved: It received income on the basis of slavery, but, from another perspective, slaves did not pay tribute to the monarch, and at the same time slavery reduced the Indian population. In time the arguments in opposition to Indian slavery became overwhelming. A document issued on August 2, 1530, prohibited the enslavement of Indians even if they were captured in the course of a "just war." The *rescate* was also abolished.

The colonizers opposed these measures, arguing that the military actions taken in America were a *private* matter paid for by captains and soldiers rather than by the state and the main benefit these men had from their incursions was the appropriation as slaves of the prisoners. Besides, it was said, it was no help to the natives themselves to forbid slavery, because more indigenous people would be killed in battle if the soldiers had no incentive to take men as prisoners. Slavery via *rescate* was justified, according to the colonizers, because in becoming slaves of the Spanish instead of the caciques the enslaved Indians would "benefit" by learning Christian doctrine and, eventually, avoiding being sacrificed in pagan religious rites. Partly because of these arguments but, more important, because of the effective pressure of the colonizers and the royal interests themselves, on February 20, 1534, Charles V abrogated the prohibition on enslaving Indians and allowed the resumption of enslavement by war and by *rescate.*

Nevertheless, protests against slavery continued to be raised. Now better situated to impose its will, the crown issued New Laws in 1542 of which chapter 21 prohibited Indian slavery in any form. The *Recopilación de Leyes de los Reinos de las Indias* (1681) incorporated this prohibition.[22]

In spite of these resolutions, certain forms of enslavement of natives persisted for a long time in several areas of the New World. One of these forms was a court sentence to forced labor. It was not uncommon for Spanish magistrates to condemn Indians to work in a mine or a mill for life. After the Indian rebellion in the province of Tehuantepec in 1660,[23] which expanded into other provinces and districts of the bishopric of Oaxaca (Villa Alta, Nexapa, and Ixtepeji), the punitive judge sent by the viceroy (the Count of Baños) sentenced the indigenous leaders to serve "all their lives in a mill whose service is sold" in favor of "His Majesty's court."[24] In fact, the Indians being sentenced were practically sold to Spanish entrepreneurs who kept them locked up under severe conditions that included excessive labor and little food.

Slavery also resulted from the constant warfare waged by the criollos against Indian villages that resisted colonial expansion, for example, the peoples generically called Chichimecas in the northern part of Mexico. The great Chichimec War took place from 1550 to 1600. The Chichimecs were nomadic groups of northern New Spain. Whereas the sedentary indigenous ethnic groups of the central New Spain were easy prey for the Europeans, the northern groups for decades resisted repeated attempts at conquest (or "pacification," as the crown preferred to call it). As in the central territories (where the Tlaxcaltec were used in the subjugation of Moctezuma's empire), in the north the Spanish astutely used the military strength of some indigenous groups to subdue others. In this case it was the Mexicas, Tarascos, and Otomís who spearheaded the annihilation of Chichimec resistance.[25]

The Caribs of the Antilles, the Araucanians (Mapuches) of the southern part of the continent, and the Mindanao in the Philippines also suffered warfare and slavery. Indian slavery gradually ceased to be a central method of domination of the autochthonous population as other mechanisms and institutions whose objective was to secure a stable labor force gained strength.

The Misery of the Indigenous Peoples

Discussion of the effects of slavery, the brutality of the *encomienda* (legalized in Hispaniola in 1503), and the cruelty of the conquistadores on the aboriginal population of the islands of the so-called West Indies continues to this day. in these passionate debates it has routinely been asserted that the true "executioners of the conquest were not the conquistadores" but the pathogenic microbes brought from Europe, which caused enormous mortality among the indigenous population. To deny the effect of the great epidemics would be absurd, but it cannot be overlooked that the microbes operated within the social framework created by colonization and that many other factors brought about by colonial relations were the direct and fundamental cause of the destruction of the autochthonous Caribbean population. These same conditions later put the survival of the mainland's native societies at risk.

During the initial phase of colonization in Hispaniola, as Frank Moya Pons stresses, natives "were put to work in the mines, and in Columbus's time they were treated as an inexhaustible natural resource that one need not feed or look after because there were always villages waiting to be conquered." After Columbus was dismissed, the Indians had it no better under Francisco Bobadilla and Nicolás de Ovando. The consumption of Indians that these governors allowed and even encouraged at the beginning of the sixteenth century "finally destroyed the island's aboriginal ecological balance." The shattering of their social system and subsistence as well as the harshness of the work imposed upon them made the desperate Indians commit mass suicide (eating the poison of the bitter cassava, killing their children, and provoking self-induced abortions).[26]

Silvio Zavala and José Miranda note the diverse and complex causes (among them, of course, epidemics) of the drastic decline of the Indian population of the Antilles.[27] The account of Friar Toribio Motolinia, a member of the Franciscan mission of "the twelve" that arrived in Mexico in 1524, of what he called the "ten work plagues" that fell especially upon the Indians is well known; (1) illnesses, (2) the "conquest of this New Spain;" (3) the famine that followed the capture of Mexico City, (4) the excesses imposed upon the *calpixques* or servants that the conquistadores placed in their *repartimientos* and towns, (5) "the great tributes and services that the Indians rendered," (6) work in the gold mines, because the Spanish treated this metal "like another lamb adored by God," (7) the building of Mexico City, during which "many Indians" perished, (8) slavery, a plague that "is not taken to be the lesser of them," (9) the effects of providing labor for the mines (especially carrying the cargo long distances), and (10) dissent among the Spanish that had as a consequence the execution of many Indian nobles (Cuauhtémoc among them).[28]

According to Sempat Assadourian, the chroniclers of Peru emphasize as causes of the population's collapse "the indigenous mortality produced by the wars of conquest and, among the members of the Spanish army themselves, the periods of hunger resulting from those wars and from the greedy disorder of the Europeans in their struggle to obtain gold and silver. To these we could add death brought about by the war of succession between Huáscar and Atahualpa. A recent analysis of indigenous sources has confirmed these demographic observations."[29]

Regarding the Antilles, several elements, including the aforementioned epidemics, coalesced in what has been called the "Antillean demographic disaster." The aboriginal population in the Antilles was relatively small compared with that in other territories (e.g., the central part of Mesoamerica and the Andean regions and the Caribbean social groups were relatively fragile (hunter-gatherer societies or, at most, egalitarian or cacique-stage tribal systems) and collapsed soon after the early colonial impact.[30] These peoples had not reached the degree of political and productive organization or the sociocultural complexity characteristic of other regions at the moment of the clash with the invaders. Thus, this population was even less well prepared to face the exhausting labor regime, the new productive relations, and the destruction of communal order introduced by the Europeans.

The Antillean region, being the first center of European settlement in the New World and a strategic point from which the conquest radiated toward the mainland during the crucial first phase, bore the heavy burden of contributing the goods and capital necessary to finance much of the rest of the colonizing enterprise. Thus, its indigenous population was literally exploited to the point of exhaustion, especially in mining but also in food production and in the provision of certain services."[31]

Within a few decades the indigenous population of the islands had been practically annihilated. For example, it is estimated that when the Europeans arrived there were about 1 million Indians in Hispaniola,[32] but by 1508 only some 60,000 survived, and this figure had diminished to about 11,000 by 1518. As Carl Sauer points out:

> [Alonso] Zuazo correctly foresaw the end of the aboriginal people by the last years of the century's second decade, a date valid for Jamaica and Puerto Rico, too, and closely approximate for Cuba as well. Occasionally small groups survived in scattered mountain refuges, perhaps to disappear by mixing with future immigrants. In less than twenty years from the founding of La Isabela (the first city, established by Columbus toward the end of 1493], the imminent extinction of the aboriginal people was evident, and within ten more years it had been fully accomplished.[33]

The final result was total extinction: by 1570 only some five hundred indigenous people had survived the devastating impact of the conquest.[34] The extent of the catastrophe cannot be measured by the initial population of natives in the scholars' estimates. There is no difference, in principle, between a process that causes the elimination of hundreds of thousands of human beings and one that causes the extinction of millions. Speaking of the controversies surrounding the original number of Indians in the various American regions, Nocolás Sánchez-Albornoz asserts that this alters only in relative terms the question of the abrupt decline in the population. Thus, "by 1570 there were several hundred Indians in Hispaniola. What is being discussed, then, is whether they had diminished from an original population of several million or several hundreds of thousands," but whatever their initial number, the result is "equally catastrophic."[35]

During the first half of the sixteenth century, the Spanish colonizers attempted to deal with the increasing scarcity of labor by immigrating themselves and importing indigenous people captured in other areas of America. The first option was a failure, and the second had no future because it soon became clear that the real problem lay in colonial policy with regard to the indigenous labor force, a policy characterized by incredible clumsiness. Given the increasing difficulty in introducing Indian slaves from other parts of the continent and the scarcity of labor in the Antilles, the introduction of black slaves acquired momentum.[36] It began on a small scale at the beginning of the sixteenth century, when Africans were brought in first from the peninsula itself and, later, massively, from the African coast.[37]

The Antillean drama was extraordinarily important for the ensuing stages of colonization in the vast and densely populated territories of the mainland. The holocaust that resulted from the first large-scale colonizing experience in American lands "was so horrifying and unproductive for the Spanish themselves that they tried to create more orderly and judicious systems of exploitation on the mainland!"[38] In their own way, they achieved this goal. When it seemed that the Europeans were about to repeat the same disaster in the new colonies (killing the indigenous population on whose tribute and labor they fundamentally depended), the example of the Antillean experience prompted them to mend their ways.

The case of New Spain illustrates the process. Cook and Borah estimate that by 1518 there were in central Mexico alone some 25 million Indians; thirty years later (in 1548) the autochthonous population had diminished to a fourth of that (6.3 million) and two decades later (in 1568) to a tenth of its original size (approximately 2.5 million).[39]

The combination of the reckless exploitation of the Indian communities and the frequent epidemics they suffered was decimating the native population much as it had in the Antilles.[40] During the first years of the sixteenth century there continued to be a significant reduction of the native population, which had decreased to less than 1 million by 1620. Cook and Borah conclude that "by 1620–1625, the Indian population of central Mexico, under the effects of the arrival of the Europeans, had diminished to approximately 3 percent of the size it was when the Europeans first landed on the beaches of Veracruz."[41]

The Spanish were heading toward a second total destruction of aboriginal peoples, but this time they had the experience, the conditions, and the time to make the goals of colonization and the survival of sufficient numbers of autochthonous people compatible. As a matter of fact, Borah explains;

> On the mainland, in contrast to what happened in the West Indies, there was time to experiment. In spite of the serious decline suffered by the Indians during the decades following the conquest, considerable nuclei survived in the majority of regions, especially in the highlands. They lasted long enough for the conquerors to realize that these problems existed and, by a process of experimentation and reexamination, try to implement solutions.[42]

Thus, by mid-sixteenth century the collapse had been averted and a certain stability had been achieved; then, by the end of the century, there was a perceptible increase in population that continued throughout the eighteenth century. The moment at which the Indian population of central Mexico reached its nadir is debatable, but regional and local variations were evident and must not be overlooked.[43] Apparently, the inflection point in the demographic curve must be located around 1650.[44]

Demographics influenced the course of the colonial process. The organization and management of Indian communities, together with the gradual consolidation of the European system of domination and exploitation, had perceptible effects on the demographic tendencies that prevailed for more than one and a half centuries.

The various measures adopted by the crown, especially during the second half of the sixteenth century, shaped the colonial regime's indigenist policy. Meticulous legislation, not always rigorously observed, and the creation of a series of economic, administrative, and judicial institutions were enough to allow the colonial government to work with a modicum of effectiveness (which, of course, says nothing about the fairness of the system) in avoiding the destruction of the Indian population.

It is important to clarify that the goal was not to impose any constraint on the exploitation of indigenous people; rather, it was to regulate and rationalize this exploitation in such a way that the wealth created by the native population and their labor could be appropriated in the most orderly way possible by the various sectors involved in colonization. Colonial policy toward Indians, precisely because of the drastic decline in the autochthonous population and the parallel increase of the non-Indian population and its demands for tribute and services, caused a relative increase in the burden on these

How the indigenous people were treated in the Americas.

communities, particularly during the seventeenth century. In other words, disorderly exploitation and senseless destruction was avoided while, at the same time colonial indigenism sought to exact the most out of the surviving Indian population. Exactions did not, however, decline in proportion to the decline in the Indian population.[45] What has been called "the economic benefit policy" meant, in brief, the extraction of the largest possible amount of wealth from the New World.[46]

Since a great variety of sectors were fighting over much diminished booty, it was necessary to refine the methods of political and ideological control. Although sporadic outbursts of indigenous rebellion were not avoided, the Spanish were able to prevent an explosion that would totally undermine the system. Certainly, all the non-Indian social groups (excluding slaves and other workers) and even the indigenous "nobility" that was incorporated into the colonial system of domination, depended on the natives' labor. The *encomenderos,* the settlers, the clergy, the growing bureaucracy, and the Indian caciques and *principales* all participated in an organization that offered each and every one of them the space and opportunity to exploit, to the same degree, the bulk of the indigenous people.[47] The Spanish crown, favored by the arrangement and the system's new cohesiveness, was in charge of regulating its functioning so that the common source of benefits would not be extinguished.

Notes

1. Elsewhere I have pointed out that "indigenist variants have the common feature of being essentially politically alien conceptions with regard to the ethnic groups themselves. They are aimed at understanding or justifying the policies (the practice) imposed upon 'others' by non-Indians. From the point of view of their goals, these indigenist variants are definitions of what must change so that everything (or, at least, everything important for maintaining the logic of the system) will remain the same." Héctor Díaz Polanco, *Etnia, nación y politica,* 2nd edition, Mexico City, Juan Pablos Editor, 1990, p. 28.
2. My intention is to provide a broad survey of the main issues that frame these indigenist policies, and thus forces me to omit many details and peculiarities, doubtless important, that go beyond my purpose.
3. The indigenist anthropologist Gonzalo Aguirre Beltrán has called the policies that correspond to these phases *segregation, incorporation,* and *integration.* Cf. Gonzalo Aguirre Beltrán, "Un postulado de politica indigenista," in *Obra polémica,* Mexico City, Secretaría de Educación Pública/Institato Nacional de Antropologiá e Historia, 1975, pp. 21–28.
4. I shall continue this analysis in the following chapter and will leave the nineteenth and twentieth centuries for chapter 4.
5. Enrique Semo, *Historia del capitalismo en México,* Mexico City, Era, 1973, pp. 69 ff.
6. On February 24, 1495, Christopher Columbus sent to Seville in four ships 500 Indian slaves that he had captured at Hispaniola. In June 1496 another cargo of 300 Indians left for Spain. Silvio Zavala, "Los trabajadores antillanos en el siglo XVI," *Revista de Historia de América,* no. 2, 1938, p. 32.
7. José Antonio Saco, *Historia de la esclavitud de los indios en el Nuevo Mundo, seguida de la historia de los repartimientos y encomiendas,* Havana, Editora Cultural, 1932, p. 112.
8. Now Santo Domingo Island, shared by the Dominican Republic and Haiti.

9. "During this period [1492–1520], America's economic and political center was at Hispaniola, and Santo Domingo was for many years its capital. The island became a real laboratory for relationships between the Europeans and the American Indians, as well as an experimentation center for the acclimatization of the Europeans and their animals and plants. . . . From 1492 to 1518, the majority of the Spanish emigrants passed through Santo Domingo; very important individuals (Fernández de Enciso, Hojeda, Francisco Pizarro, Diego Velázquez, Vasco Núñez de Balboa, Juan Ponce de León, Hernán Cortés, Pedro de Alvarado) and also people who became not only chiefs or soldiers but writers or critics of the conquest (Las Casas) went there." Francisco de Solano, "El conquistador hispano: Señas de identidad," en Francisco de Solano et al., *Proceso histórico al conquistador,* Madrid, Alianza Editorial, 1988, pp. 21–22. The Spanish learned to name many American things in these islands before going on to the mainland, which explains why some terms of the extinct *Taino* language (of the Arawakan family) spoken by those aboriginal people are among the most abundant in Castilian today.
10. Saco, *Historia de la esclavitud,* p. 113.
11. Ibid. p. 157.
12. Silvio Zavala, *La colonización española en América,* Mexico City, SepSetentas, 1972, chap. 4.
13. Ibid.
14. Saco, *Historia de la esclavitud,* p. 149.
15. Fray Bartolomé de las Casas, *Historia de las Indias,* vol. 3, 2nd edition, Mexico City, Fondo de Cultura Económica,1965, pp. 26–27.
16. Lewis Hanke, "The 'requerimiento' and its interpreters," in *Revista de Historia de América,* no. 2, 1938, pp. 25–34.
17. In chap. 58 of his *Historia* Las Casas refutes each of the arguments included in the document I am discussing, as well as the "great and reprehensible deceit" in it that shows "how unjust, impious, scandalous, irrational, and absurd such *requerimento* was."
18. Ibid., p. 46.
19. Zavala, *La colonización,* p. 77. More information can be found in the book by the same author, *Los esclavos indios en Nueva España,* 2nd edition, Mexico City, El Colegio Nacional, 1981.
20. Francisco López de Gómara, *Historia general de las Indias,* vol. 2, *Conquista de México,* Barcelona, Ediciones Orbis, 1985, p. 313; Zavala, *La colonización,* pp. 79–80.
21. Fray Toribio Motolinía, *Historia de los indios de la Nueva España,* ed. Edmundo O'-Gorman, 4th edition, Mexico City, Editorial Porrúa, 1984, pp. 17 and 94.
22. See Alberto Sarmiento Donate (ed.), *De las leyes de indias (Antología de la recopilación de 1681),* Mexico City, Secretaría de Educación Pública, 1988, book 6, title 2, law 1. Cf. Silvio Zavala, "Los trabajadores antillanos en el siglo XVI" *Revista de Historia de América,* no. 2, 1938, pp. 37–39; see also *La colonización,* vi.
23. There is detailed information about this rebellion, credited as being the most important Indian uprising against the government of New Spain during the seventeenth century, in Héctor Díaz Polanco and Carlos Manzo (eds.), *Documentos sobre las rebeliones indias de Tehuantepec y Nexapa* (1660–1661), Mexico City, Centro de Investigaciones y Estudias Superiores in Antropología Social, 1992.
24. Two chronicles written by Spanish officials (that of Juan de Torres Castillo about the Nexapa, Ixtepeji, and Villa Alta revolts and that of Cristóbal Manso de Contreras about the rebellion in Tehuantepec) may be found in Genaro García, *Documentos inéditos o muy raros para la historia de México,* 3rd edition, Mexico City, Editorial Porrúa, 1982, pp. 273–368.

25. Phillip W. Powell says, "As in almost all phases of the Spanish conquest of Mexico, the Indians were the bulk of the belligerent forces against the Chichimec warriors from north of the viceregal capital. As warriors, interpreters, explorers, and messengers, the pacified aboriginals of New Spain performed important, often indispensable, roles in subduing and civilizing Chichimec country. Sometimes armies made up entirely of other indigenous warriors (particularly Otomís) marauded the war zones to seek out, conquer, and help Christianize the hostile northern nomads. . . . Afterwards, as the penetration of the Great Chichimeca advanced, the recently pacified chichimeca joined the belligerent effort of the white men and were used to conquer other tribes." Philip W. Powell, *La guerra chichimeca (1550–1600),* Mexico City, Secretaría de Educación Pública, 1984, p. 165; see also *Capitán mestizo: Miguel Caldera y la frontera norteña; La pacificación de los chichimecas (1548–1597),* Mexico City, Fondo de Cultura Económica, 1980.
26. Frank Moya Pons, *Historia colonial de Santo Domingo,* Santiago, Universidad Católica Madre y Maestra, 1974, pp. 61–62.
27. "Most notable about this course or evolution was the great [population] decline that took place between the time of the conquest and the twilight of the sixteenth century, a decline mainly determined by the following factors: (a) the conquest itself, during which many Indians were sacrificed, and, in addition to warfare, during the exhausting expeditions to faraway lands such as those of Cortés and Nuño de Guzmán, in which Indians had to carry cargo or perform other auxiliary services; (b) slavery, which enormously harmed the Indians, the mining and transportation tasks being terribly harsh and the nourishment given them very deficient; (c) personal service, for the sana reasons as slavery; (d) epidemics, above all those of 1545 and 1546, which caused great devastation in almost all the indigenous villages, and (e) famines (whether or not they coincided with epidemics) in years of poor harvest and under the initial economic disorganization. The mortality rate increased considerably among the natives." Silvio Zavala and José Miranda, "Instituciones indígenas en la colonia," in Alfonso Caso et al., *La política indigenista en México: Métodos y resultados,* 3rd edition, Mexico City, *Instituto Nacional Indígenista,* 1981.
28. Motolinía, *Historia de los indios,* pp. 13–18.
29. Carlos Sempat Assadourian, "La despoblación indígena en Perú y Nueva España durante el siglo XVI y la formación de la economía colonial," *Historia Mexicana,* 38, no. 3, January–March 1989, p. 420.
30. For an approach to these social systems, see Luis F. Bate, "El modo de producción cazador recolector o la economía del salvajismo," in *Bolean de Antopología Americana,* no. 13, July 1986; Iraida Vargas, "La formación económica social tribal," in *Boletín de Anapologia Americana,* no. 15, July 1987; Mario Sanoja, *Los hombres de la yuca y el maíz,* Caracas, Monte Ávila Editores, 1981, pp. 195ff.
31. Rolando Mellafe, *Breve historia de la esclavitud en América Latina,* Mexico City, SepSetentas, 1974, pp. 21–22.
32. Estimates vary with the author, but the most common version of those days was that Hispaniola had over a million inhabitants." Carl Ortwin Sauer, *Descubrimiento y dominación española del Caribe,* Mexico City, Fondo de Cultura Económica, 1984, p. 106. Cook and Borah's studies consider the island's population to have been much larger. "For Hispaniola island we found that, in 1492, there was a population of approximately eight million people. This huge human reserve was reduced, in ten years, to less than a tenth, and within three decades it was virtually extinct. W. Borah, "La Europa renacentista y la población de América," in Sherburne F. Cook

and Woodrow Borah, *El pasado de México: Aspectos sociodemograficos,* Mexico City, Fondo de Cultura Económica, 1989, p. 416.

33. Ibid., p. 307.
34. Mellafe, *Breve hisotría,* p. 22.
35. Nicolas Sánchez-Albornoz, "Las migraciones anteriores al siglo XIX," in Brigitta Leander (ed.), Europa, *Asia y Africa en América Latina y el Caribe: Migraciones "libres" en los siglos XIX y XX y sus efectos culturales,* Mexico City, Siglo XXI/UNESCO, 1989, pp. 63–64.
36. With elegant irony Jorge Luis Borges wrote, "In 1517 Friar Bartolomé de las Casas took pity on the Indians who were languishing in the arduous hells of the Antillean gold mines and proposed to the emperor, Charles V, the importation of black people to languish in the arduous hells of the Antillean gold mines." Jorge Luis Borges, "Historia universal de la infamia," in *Obras completas,* vol. 1, 1923–1972, Buenos Aires, Emecé Editores, 1989, p. 295.
37. On the enslavement of Africans, see José Antonio Saco, *Historia de la esclavitud de la raza africana en el Nuevo Mundo y en especial en los paises américo-hispanos,* 2 vols. Havana, Editora Cultural, 1938; Javier Malagón Barceló, *Código negro carolino (1784),* Santo Domingo, Ediciones de Taller, 1974; Fernando Ortiz, *Los negros esclavos,* Havana, Editorial de Ciencias Sociales, 1988; Hugo Tolentino, *Raza e historia en Santo Domingo: Los orígenes del prejuicio racial en América,* vol. 1, Santo Domingo, Universidad Autonoma de Santo Domingo, 1974; Carlos Esteban Deive, *La esclavitud del negro en Santo Domingo (1492–1844),* 2 vols., Santo Domingo, Museo del Hombre Dominicano, 1980; José L. Franco, *Historia de la revolución de Haití,* Santo Domingo, Editora Nacional, 1971; Rubén Silié, *Economía, esclavitud y población,* Santo Domingo, Universidad Autónoma de Santo Domingo, 1976; Franklin Franco, *Los negros, los mulatos y la nación dominicana,* Santo Domingo, Editora Nacional, 1969; Jean Price-Mars, *La República de Haiti y la República Dominicana,* vol. 1, Puerto Príncipe, 1953; Ricardo Alegría, "Notas sobre la procedencia cultural de los esclavos negros de Puerto Rico durante la segunda mitad del siglo XVI," in *Encuentro,* no. 2, San Juan, Comisión Puertorriqueña para la Celebración del Quinto Centenario del Descubrimiento de América y Puerto Rico, 1990; Miguel Acosta Saignes, *Vida de los esclavos negros en Venezuela,* Caracas, Hespérides, 1967; Luis A. Diez Castillo, *Los cimarrones y la esclavitud en Panamá,* Panama, Editorial Litográfica, 1968.
38. Woodrow Borah, *El juzgado general de indios en la Nueva España,* Mexico City, Fondo de Cultura Económica, 1985, p. 37.
39. Sherburne F. Cook and Woodrow Borah, *Ensayos sobre historia de la población: México y California,* 3, Mexico City, Siglo XXI, 1980, p. 13.
40. A record of the major epidemics suffered by the population of the Valley of Mexico can be found in Charles Gibson, *Los aztecas bajo el dominio español,* Mexico City, Siglo XXI, 1975, pp. 460–463.
41. Cook and Borah, *Ensayos sobre historia de la población* p. 100.
42. Borah, *El juzgado general,* p. 37.
43. For example, Miranda asserts that population growth began well before 1650 (between 1620 and 1630) in the bishoprics of México, Michoacán, and Puebla. These estimates are based on the settlement (or liquidation of debts) of the *medio real* that the Indians paid those jurisdictions to build cathedrals during the second half of the seventeenth century. José Miranda, "La población indígena de México en el siglo XVII," in *Historia Mexicana,* 30, no. 4, April–June 1981, pp. 569–570.
44. José Carlos Chiaramonte, "En torno a la recuperación demográfica y la depresión económica novohispana durante el siglo XVII," *Historia Mexicana,* 30, no. 4, April–June 1981, pp. 569–570.

45. W. Borah, *El siglo de la depresión de la Nueva España,* Mexico City, Ediciones Era, 1982, p. 19.
46. Sempat Assadourian, "La despoblación indígena," pp. 425ff.
47. For a description of this situation, particularly during the sixteenth and seventeenth centuries, see Jonathan I. Israel, *Razas, clases sociales y vida política en el México colonial (1610–1670),* Mexico City, Fondo de Cultura Económica, 1980, introduction and chap. 1.

In the previous article, Díaz Polanco discussed the process through which the project of the Spanish conquest elaborated a discourse that defined the European attack on Indigenous peoples as a just war. Along these same lines, in the article "The Discourse of Concealment and 1992" Guatemalan Maya scholar Enrique Sam Colop exposes the use of discourse that conceals the violence inflicted through the conquest on the Indigenous population. He calls our attention to the ways in which renowned Latin American authors speak matter of factly today of the conquest while schools teach children that Indigenous peoples were "pacified" as if they were "violent" peoples. He also provides examples of textbooks that refer to the conquest as the "encounter of two worlds," as in the friendly encounter of two groups of people under equal conditions. This article brings to our attention our need to reflect on the language that we have been taught to use with regards to the conquest of the Americas, one of the most violent wars in history, a war that resulted in millions of Indigenous people losing their lives through violence, torture, overwork and illness. The author also discusses the publications that appeared on the occasion of the quincentennial of the arrival of the Spaniards in 1992, when the press in Guatemala provided numerous examples of the racist discourse that further conceals the oppression, violence, injustice and exclusion that Indigenous peoples in the Americas have endured and continue to endure. This language, which has become naturalized in modern school systems, perpetuates the legacy of colonialism and contributes in present times to the exclusion and oppression of Indigenous peoples.

The Discourse of Concealment and 1992

ENRIQUE SAM COLOP

Colonial Discourse of the Twentieth Century

In the sixteenth century the initial impact of European expansionism was concealed by the euphemisms "pacification" and "liberation"; in the twentieth century the preferred terms are "cultural contact" and "encounter of two worlds," implying the union of two societies for mutual understanding and respect. This discourse shuns honest reflection and tries to justify the colonization that continues today: current economic, political, cultural, and social structures that place the worst burden on native peoples are effectively derived from initial European colonialism. At an ideological level, colonialism is manifested through a discourse that idealizes the sixteenth-century invader and justifies his aggression, a discourse that rationalizes the extinction of Maya culture and languages and justifies the imposition of Hispanic culture and the Spanish language. This is a racist discourse, a discourse of negation of the other.

About what happened five hundred Gregorian years ago, the recipient of the 1990 Nobel Prize for literature, Octavio Paz, writes that the original peoples of Mesoamerica were vulnerable before the Spaniards due to a "technical and cultural inferiority" and that they could not imagine the Spaniards due to their lack of intellectual and historical categories in which to place them. Thus, the Spaniards, says Paz, were considered "gods and supernatural beings" (Paz 1987).

Spanish cultural superiority is interpreted by some as "manifesting itself in a greater capacity for flexible. and rational thought, and a pragmatic allocation of energy and material resources," and yet in the case of Yucatán "it is difficult to see much of either in the Spanish campaigns" (Clendinnen 1988: 32). Other authors, such as Severo Martínez Peláez (1970), argue for a Hispanic "superiority" associated with technological development. As an example of this "superiority," Martínez Peláez cites Alvarado's remarks to Cortés about the Indians' ignorance that "the horses were ineffectual on steep and rough terrain" and that the Indians "easily fell in the traps that the horsemen set for them" (1970: 28). Nevertheless, contrary to the view of Martinez Peláez, the *Annals of the Kaqchikels* states: "Xb'an je k'otoj, xb'an k'a jul kej simaj xekamisab'ex . . . Je k'a k'i kastilan winaq xekan, kere k'a kej xkam pa jul kej. (The Kaqchikels. . . . dug holes and pits for the horses and scattered sharp stakes so that they should be killed. . . . Many Spaniards perished and the horses died in the traps for the horses)" (Recinos and Goetz 1953: 125). This version is collaborated by Pedro de Alvarado himself: "They made many holes and pits with stakes covered with earth and grass into which many horses and Spaniards fell and died" (Recinos 1950: 129–130). Such arguments of "cultural superiority" are, at best, partial interpretations. Military strategies, bacteriological warfare, and violations of codes of war do not determine cultural "superiority" or "inferiority."[1] If technological development equated "cultural superiority," then the United States, since it is technologically more developed, would be more culturally developed than Latin America.

The opinion that the Maya regarded the Spaniards as "gods" is, as Victor Montejo has documented, a Spanish invention repeated to this day (Montejo 1991). The books of Chilam B'alam, for example, do not speak of the Spaniards as "gods" but rather as agents of misery, and the *Annals of the Kaqchikels* bluntly states: "K'ere k'a tok xul Kastilan winaq ri ojer, ix nuk'ajol. Kitzij tixib'in ok xeul, mani etaam wi kiwach, je kab'owil xekina' ajawa'. (Thus it was that the Spaniards arrived here long ago, my children. Truly they inspired fear when they arrived, we did not know their faces, the lords took them for icons)" (Recinos and Goetz 1953: 121; Warren, chap. 5).

The term in question is *kab'owil* or *kab'awil,* which Brinton (1969), Recinos and Goetz (1953), and others translate as "god" or "gods." *Kab'awil* in fact means "icon" (good or bad, depending on the point of view, like the Statue of Liberty, the cross, the swastika, or the Virgin of Guadalupe). In the *Calepino Kaqchikel* (Varela n.d.), *kab'awil* is translated as "statue," "idol," "hoax," and "image." Francisco Hernandez Arania, one of the authors of the *Annals of the Kaqchikels,* associated the Spaniards with "statues" and "idols" that instilled fear because of their unknown faces and their human callousness; he had earlier described the tragic consequences of the Spaniards' arrival among the K'iche': the torture and sacrifice of their leaders and the destruction of their city. The books of Chilam B'alam of Chumayel and Tizimín say that the soldiers of the "true god" (the Spaniards) are inhuman; and elsewhere, Jesus Christ was associated with one of the "dreaded Lords of death" (Bruce 1983: 275). Thus, what was divine for the Christians was not necessarily so for the Maya.

Cardoza y Aragón states that "actually, there exist two cultures in Guatemala, that of the indigenous and that of the West" (1990: 16). He describes neither "a tranquil coexistence" nor a cultural dilemma, because "the hegemonic culture has almost torn apart the great Indian culture, and the 'ruins of the Indian culture' are what are being revamped by Indian revolutionaries and the dominant culture, which obligates the creation of a culture that, because of all the historical and geographic reasons, will slowly become Mestizo" (1990: 16). Cardoza y Aragón then asks, "Is this ethnocentrism? Is this a racist tone?"

It has been suggested that the roots of Guatemalan *mestizaje* spring from the *Popol Wuj* because this sacred Mayan text was copied and translated by a Spanish priest. Even a university vice chancellor wrote that the *Popol Wuj* is not a Maya work but a mestizo one: "The author or authors were already Mestizos. They already knew Spanish, although not well" (Juárez-Paz 1992: 69). The original *Popol Wuj* was a hiero-. glyphic book. It was transcribed in K'iche' with Latin characters in the late sixteenth century by K'iche's who recounted the difficult circumstances under which the transcription was made.[2] This manuscript remained hidden for the next century and a half, until Francisco Ximénez was permitted to copy and translate it into Spanish. Since then the first K'iche' alphabetic version has disappeared (see Carmack 1973, who suggests that the original text still exists).

Theories of authorship of the *Popol Wuj* have changed over the centuries, following a telling sequence: for Friar Ximénez, the author was Satan; for René Acuña, he was a Spanish priest; for others, the text was mestizo because Ximénez transcribed it; and finally, some believe the K'iche' authors were not Maya but mestizos since they transcribed it into Spanish. In this attempted usurpation of symbols, it is curious to note that those who draw on the *Popol Wuj* to ground their *mestizaje* do not propose the same with the *Xajoj Tun,* an indigenous text that was also copied and translated by a priest—a French priest. Cardoza y Aragón says: "We have deprived [the Indians] of even their past, exploiting it as our past, and on ending my sentence I discover that I am speaking as a mestizo" (1990: 14). The *Popol Wuj* is, to use a metaphor of Dante Liano (1984), "a birth certificate" of the Maya, not of the mestizos.

The Guatemalan press speaks of a mestizo homeland and of an "inevitable Hispanic integration" through the confluence of Indian and Hispanic blood. The press appears to sympathize with both the celebrators and the detractors of the quincentenary celebration, calling for mutual cultural and linguistic respect as well as a "national unity" based on Spanish. Some journalists, in a spasm of racism, say that their *mestizaje* is a reason for pride and that "genetic destiny" advocates the move toward the Hispanic. Thus wrote a columnist: "*Mestizaje* is indispensable for certain backward peoples of decadent races; they have to be considered from the point of view of anthropology, culture, and other rubrics of progress and the betterment of man and, therefore, of the races. This brings us to eugenics" (Wyss 1992a: 9, 1992b). Rafael Burgos Figueroa, a columnist who claims to know the "true history," writes that five hundred years ago the Spaniards were "ferociously attacked by poisonous snakes, mosquitos, impenetrable jungle, and savage tribes that enjoyed the practice of human sacrifice" (1991a: 9); that by the of contact Maya culture had already been "taken away by extraterrestrials" (1991b: 11); and that no proof of cannibalism remains because "the gluttons left no scraps or waste behind to prove it" (1991c: 25). Carlos Manuel Pellecer, who asserts that he is a protector of the Indians, writes that the Maya are on the "margin of life, of creative and generous action" (1991a: 12); that they are "furious, vindictive exterminators" (1991b: 12); and that their culture is "elemental" and "there is no evidence that it could advance the interest of tourism" (1991c: 12). Pellecer also equates, Maya demands for the recognition of their rights with the death of the Ladino state and the recognition of Maya common law with "returning to the practice of human sacrifice, servitude, slavery, and of course, to the use of splints to shape the head" (1991d: 12, 1991e).

Nevertheless, the Guatemalan press also publishes opinions such as the following: "While the massacres that the Spaniards committed upon arriving to our land are considered a pardonable neglect, ethnic animosity is not recognized as one of the principal causes of an undeclared thirty-year war in which the participation of indigenous groups is minimized because they are deprecated to the point that they became rebels" (Mejia 1992: 12); or the following: "It has been a long time since the Spaniards were protagonists of our history. The protagonists are, in contrast, the Ladinos who have the Indian and Guatemala in a situation that has to be recognized as feudal" (Liano 1992: 61). Finally, the following editorial questions Ladinos who refer to the Maya as their property:

> I have wondered and asked, when some idiot refers to indigenous Guatemalans as "our" little Indians, if it is true that they have inherited "a herd of Indians" among the multiple properties that their parents or grandparents have left them. At every opportunity, I am asked to clarify this innocent question . . . and I do: How many little Indians did your parents leave you? Have you inherited them already or are you going to inherit them? How jealous I am! You lucky son of a gun! I did not inherit even one. . . . In you one can see the spirit of a frustrated slave-owner. (Carrillo 1992: 31)

Misinformation and racist opinions are also presented in universities and schools. The university text *La patria del criollo* speaks of Indian culture, in particular native languages, as "less developed" (Martínez Peláez 1970: 600), explaining that "the language of a society reflects the degree of development of which it is a product. A more advanced technology always supposes a more developed language, in vocabulary and expressive possibilities. Indigenous languages, as spoken today, are known to be plagued by proper words that have no translation" (Martínez Peláez 1970: 768).[3]

Martínez Peláez abuses the Sapir-Whorf hypothesis: lexicons do not define languages. Languages borrow and phoneticize terms constantly (Spanish speakers say or write, for example, *naif* [knife], *picop* [pick-up], *apartied* [apartheid], *disket* [diskette], *mol* [mall], *wisky* [whiskey], and *nais* [nice]). With respect to "expressive possibilities," Spanish discourse lacks the complementary dialectic of Maya discourse; in morphological terms, Spanish lacks the inclusive/exclusive pronouns that some Mayan languages have; in syntactic terms, Spanish apparently does not have intransitive clauses with a degraded object (antipassives) as do Mayan languages, French, Choctaw, and others. Does this mean that Spanish is less developed? No, it is simply a different language. Martínez Peláez proposes learning Spanish as a means of decolonizing the Maya, but, if his theory is correct, it would be better still to learn Japanese or German since these languages are "more developed" than Spanish.

Martínez Peláez adopts the theory of ladinization advanced by North American and Mexican anthropologists in the middle of this century. He states: "It is well understood that an Indian dressed in jeans and wearing boots is no longer Indian. And even less so if he speaks other modern languages besides Spanish. And less still if the *cofradía* has been changed for the labor union, and the sweat bath for antibiotics" (Martínez Peláez 1970: 611). In this same spirit, the aforementioned university vice chancellor, echoing a prevalent line of thought, writes that Rigoberta Menchú Tum is no longer an "authentic" Maya, she is mestiza (Juárez-Paz 1992).

Estudios sociales, a text for secondary students, under the title "Encounter of Two Cultures" states that while Anglo-Saxons proposed the elimination or reduction of the slavery of "aborigines," the Spaniards and Portuguese "said that the most suitable thing was to levelize the Indian to Spanish and Portuguese culture, but to achieve this it was indispensable to unify them juridically" (Castañeda 1962: 173). The text continues by affirming (and contradicting itself) that the unification held fast when "the natives organized their communities in the form to which they were accustomed" (Castañeda 1962: 173). Regarding the religious aspect of European expansion, the text assures the student that "a new religion lull of love and peace" came to substitute the sanguine rites that the natives practiced to please their multiple gods" (Castañeda 1962: 141–142). The students, however, are not informed that this new religion, forged in an epoch of torture, burned men alive and hung them while friars prayed around them. This textbook repeatedly refers to Maya culture with depreciatory terms such as "folklore," "popular culture," "artisans," and "superstitions."[4] Likewise, in the prologue to *Crónicas indígenas de Guatemala,* Francis Polo Sifontes, a member of the Guatemalan Academy of Geography and History, refers to Maya literature as a "peculiar literature" that has been translated into all the "civilized languages" of the world (in Recinos 1984).

In primary school texts, we are misinformed that Tz'utujil is a dialect of Kaqchikel, that Awakateko is a dialect of Mam, that Q'eqchi' is a dialect of Poqomam (Ruiz Recinos 1972). Another text, *Guatemala historia gráfica* (Gordillo Barrios 1987), teaches students that the pre- Columbian Maya "worshiped nature . . . [and] some animals such as the coyote, the raccoon, and the tapir"; that there was a god the Maya "could hardly define but considered the most powerful of all" (86); that Kaqchikel means "fire thieves" (99); that the Indians considered the Spanish "gods'" because of their color"; and that during the first years of the colony the Indians received the priests with "special attention given as a result in grand part because of the little culture that they already had" (167),

Conclusion

1 B'aqtun, 5 K'atuns, and 7 Tuns (500 solar years) after the beginning of European expansion on this continent, colonialism continues in force. It is part of the dominant ideology: "We are the conquistadors. They were our parents and grandparents that came to these beaches and gave us our names and the language we speak," acknowledges Mario Vargas Llosa (1990). "We continue colonizing the Indian," says Cardoza y Aragón (1990), adding, "In Guatemala Pedro de Alvarado is long-lasting" (1989).

In this colonialism, the Other is interpreted, imagined, and represented, and his future is prescribed. With few exceptions, the contemporary Maya and all things Maya are associated with the "past" and "backwardness," and so it is decided that they must renounce their culture and languages and integrate themselves into the "national culture" and speak the official language. The fixation that the Indians should resemble the Ladinos (culturally and linguistically) is so great that the former are interpreted as an inverse image of the latter. It is affirmed that if the Ladino is racist or discriminatory in action, the Maya is the same in reaction. In this configuration it is thought that as Spain expelled the Muslims after eight hundred years of occupation, the Maya are going to expel the Ladinos today. Thus, for some, the very fact that the Maya try to exercise their human rights is equivalent to hating Spain and the Spanish language and signifies a return to "primitive states."

In this dominant ideology, pluralism and peaceful coexistence seem to commit outrage against the evolution of the state, but a "national unity" cannot be constructed while denying an existent plurality. To do so is to construct a future while walking toward the past. The Maya, in contrast, do not base their future on the past; they add their future to their history and to the history of humanity. After 12 October 1992 come 13 October, which in the Maya Long Count is 12 B'aqtuns, 18 K'atuns, 19 Tuns, 9 Winäqs, 6 Q'ij (1 Kame, 9 Yax in the Calendar Round).

Notes

Parts of this article have been published in Sam Colop (1991). This article was translated from the Spanish by Edward F. Fischer and R. McKenna Brown.

1. For greater detail, see Clendinnen (1988), especially pages 32–37.
2. In teaching the Latin alphabet, the friars had an evangelizing aim, but the Maya writers discerned an instrumental function. Tedlock (1985) says that as Christian symbols served in the massacre of ancient deities, the Latin alphabet served to massacre the ancient texts.
3. David Vela says that the Mayan languages had remained stagnant until the middle of the sixteenth century and were relatively "very poor for expressing current contexts and values" (1990: 3).

4. This belittling of that which is of the Other is masterfully captured by Galeano in "Los Nadies":

    Que no son, aunque scan.
    Que no hablan idiomas, sino dialectos.
    Que no profesan religiones, sino supersticiones.
    Que no hacer arte, sino artesanía.
    Que no practican cultura, sino folklore.
    [They do not exist, even if they exist.
    They do not speak languages, but rather dialects.
    They do not profess religions, but rather superstitions.
    They do not make art, but rather crafts.
    They do not practice culture, but rather folklore.] (1991: 59)

The article titled "Social Structure and Civil Society" by J. Booth also explores the concept of a homogeneous national subject. Focusing on modern Costa Rica, his text explores what he calls Costa Rica's national myth, which purports that there is a Costa Rican modern national subject that exists in a context of democracy, minimal class divisions and a lack of cultural and ethnic diversity. However, reality speaks to the contrary. Booth's article explores a variety of issues that have generated divisions within that idea of a cohesive modern national subject in Costa Rica. On the one hand, he discusses the inequalities of wealth produced by Costa Rica's economy, particularly through the production of coffee and bananas, which enriched a small, aristocratic class and that was possible through the labor of Costa Rican peasants who continue to live in poverty and who are particularly hurt today by neoliberal policies. On the other hand, Booth's article explains how the myth of national homogeneity often leads Costa Ricans to overlook and discriminate against diverse cultural and ethnic populations such as Blacks and Indigenous peoples.

Social Structure and Civil Society

J. BOOTH

Costa Rica's great national myth holds,in part that its democracy has roots in a social structure with minimal class divisions and a homogeneous population and culture. As the Biesanzes have noted, this argument sometimes assumes amusing dimensions: "Despite the great value that Costa Ricans place upon democracy, equality, and tolerance, their society manifests inequalities of many types. Although many Ticos begin any commentary about social stratification by denying that there are classes in their country, they [then] immediately insist that all Costa Ricans are of the middle class."[1]

Costa Rica is considerably less homogeneous and egalitarian than its myth suggests. This has had important implications for the nation's organizational life, especially during the severe recession of the 1980s. This chapter explores Costa Rica's social and economic divisions and some of the nation's main institutions, interest sectors, and groups.

Social Structure and Cleavages

Driven by powerful modernizing forces, Costa Rican social structure has changed at an ever accelerating pace since independence. With the advent of coffee exporting in the mid-nineteenth century, the predominantly rural, agrarian society began to evolve quickly. The population boomed from only 60,000 in 1821 to an estimated 3.7 million projected for 1998.[2] Coffee's expansion spread people throughout most of the cultivable national territory by the mid-twentieth century. Coffee also spurred railroad construction, which led to the banana industry, new racial and ethnic groups, and new economic classes and organizations. Cities grew rapidly. Public education expanded and eventually became virtually universal. Middle-class political forces captured the state in the 1948 civil war and for several decades employed their power to promote economic development and redistribute wealth and income to the middle classes. Employment in industry and in the service sector burgeoned.

Social Classes

These social forces have driven powerful alterations in the class structure. In the early nineteenth century, most Costa Ricans were peasants, and there were also a small, urban, middle sector of artisans and government and commercial employees and a tiny aristocracy of larger landowners descended from the conquerors. A century and a half later, the Biesanzes described Costa Rica's 1970s class structure in the following useful terms:

- An upper class (2 percent of the population) made up half of aristocratic families and half of the nouveaux riches, who together earned about 20 percent of national income from larger landholdings, industries, and commercial firms.
- An upper middle class (5 percent of the populace) of prosperous businesspeople, professionals, and agriculturalists who earned another 10 percent of national income.
- A lower middle class (15 percent of the people) of small business owners, public and private white-collar employees, lower-status professionals such as teachers, and prosperous small farmers (earning perhaps 18 percent of national income).
- A working class of better-paid factory workers, lower-level white-collar and blue-collar public employees, service workers, manual laborers, and peasant smallholders (50 percent of the population), earning some 45 percent of income.
- A lower class of landless and land-poor peasants, domestic servants, unskilled urban laborers, and urban informal workers (roughly one-fourth of the populace), earning only 7 percent of national income.[3]

This description of the class structure remained largely valid in the 1990s, although the economic crisis of the 1980s and resultant public policy changes may have begun to alter the class system somewhat.

Income Distribution

Another way to examine Costa Rica's economic divisions is in terms of income distribution. Table 1 presents data on the total share of national income earned by different strata of Tico households from 1961 through 1992. The households are separated into fifths (quintiles) from richest to poorest, plus an extra category of the poorest and richest 10 percent of households.

The data reveal, first, that income distribution in Costa Rica is very unequal. The wealthiest 10 percent of Costa Ricans earned about one-third of all income in 1992. Meanwhile, the poorest quintile earned less than 5 percent of all income. Second, despite Costa Rica's social democratic policies and development efforts, the poorest fifth of Tico families actually lost income share (from 6.2 percent in 1961 to 4.9 percent in 1992). Third, the wealthiest quintile of Tico households also lost income share— though from a much more comfortable position—from 59.7 percent in 1961 down to 49.1 percent by 1992.

Finally, and in sharp contrast to the rich and poor, Costa Rica's middle three income quintiles (roughly the Biesanzes' working and lower middle classes) did well during these three decades. Their combined share of national income rose from 34.1 percent in 1961 to 46.0 percent in 1992. Median family income in constant terms (Table 1) rose roughly 44 percent from 1961 through 1992. Thus middle-income Costa Ricans prospered relatively and absolutely, and did so by capturing income share from both the

TABLE 1 **Estimated Income Distribution Among Costa Rican Households, 1961–1992**

	1961	1971	1983	1986	1988	1992
Poorest 10%	2.8	2.1	1.6	1.3	1.6	1.6
Poorest 20%	6.2	5.4	4.7	4.3	4.8	4.9
Next 20%	7.6	9.3	9.4	9.5	9.9	9.4
Next 20%	9.5	13.7	14.0	14.4	14.8	14.5
Next 20%	17.0	21.0	20.6	21.9	22.1	22.1
Richest 20%	59.7	50.6	51.3	50.1	48.4	49.1
Richest 10%	45.5	34.41	36.1	33.7	31.7	32.2
Gini coefficient*	.50	.43	.45	.44	.43	.42
Median monthly income, constant 1992 colones	48,989	52,455	59,572	67,125	61,024	69,554
GDP per capita, constant 1990 U.S. dollars	1,081	1,474	1,706	1,775	1,807	1,943

*The Gini coefficient measures inequality in distribution, ranging from greatest possible inequality at 1.0 to perfect equality at 0.0.

Sources: Mitchell A. Seligson, Juliana Martínez F., and Juan Diego Trejos S., "Reducción de la pobreza en Costa Rica: El impacto de las políticas públicas," draft manuscript, United Nations Development Program, San José, Costa Rica, November 11, 1995. GDP per capita estimated from Inter-American Development Bank (IADB), *Economic and Social Progress in Latin America: Agricultural Development, 1986* (Washington, D.C.: IADB, 1986), table 3, and IADB, *Economic and Social Progress in Latin America: Overcoming Volatility; 1995 Report* (Baltimore: Johns Hopkins University Press, 1985).

nation's wealthiest and poorest families.[4] Even though not all Ticos are "middle class," then, the income and standard of living of these middle strata markedly improved after the 1960s.

Although Costa Rica's middle sectors did well, the plight of the nation's very poorest citizens worsened relatively and absolutely from the early 1960s through the late 1980s. One measure suggests that the average real disposable income of the poorest fifth of Costa Rican families fell at least 5 percent between 1961 and 1986.[5]

The overall impact of the economic crisis of the 1980s upon this social structure has not fully played out, but by the mid-1990s some effects had become apparent. In the short term, there was some pain for everyone. The crisis hurt wealthier Costa Ricans as their businesses deteriorated and incomes shrank. Many middle-, working-class, and poor Ticos lost their jobs. The incomes of all classes eroded simultaneously, and the ranks of the poor grew rapidly. Real wages in both the public and private sectors dropped as much as 40 percent, and open unemployment rose from below 6 to over 9 percent between 1979 and 1993.[6]

The hardship continued for several years. Table 1 reveals that the median income of Costa Rican households fell more than 9 percent between 1986 and 1988. The most dramatic evidence of this general decline in incomes in the 1980s was a veritable explosion of the informal economic sector. The newly unemployed and newly poor scrambled to sustain themselves in any way possible—as ambulatory vendors, unregulated taxi drivers, and the like.

Conservative elements among the upper and upper middle classes seized the opportunity presented by the 1980s crisis to press the state for neoliberal economic reforms. They sought to lower their taxes and increase their income and wealth by privatizing state enterprises and trimming public employment, regulation, and public services. Costa Rica enacted many such policies during the late 1980s and early 1990s.[7] Less affluent Ticos also mobilized politically to defend themselves as their incomes fell and service costs rose. Government redressed some grievances of the poor and the middle classes by raising wages and providing public assistance with housing and welfare.[8]

These class-based struggles raise a critical question: What actually happened to the relative distribution of income during the 1980s? Did the economic crunch and the resultant new policies shift income back toward the rich? Toward the middle class? Toward the poor? One might suspect that the upper class, with its superior resources with which to influence public policy, would have bested the less-advantaged groups in this struggle.

Table 1 shows no dramatic, short-run redistribution of income away from the middle classes. The recession's general impact on incomes was fairly evenly distributed in the early years. There did occur, however, some subtle deviations from this pattern that portended greater change in the future: The poorest 20 percent of Ticos lost income share between 1983 and 1986 but more than recovered the lost ground by 1988. The income share of the richest 20 percent of Costa Ricans continued its long erosion through 1988 but recovered somewhat by 1992. In contrast, the second poorest and middle quintiles of families each lost some income between 1988 and 1992. Their combined income share fell from 25.7 to 24.9 percent. This reversed a three-decade trend of increasing income for the middle sectors. These income shifts reflect the first measurable income redistributive effects of neoliberal policies and could foretell future growth of income inequality. Over the long term, cuts in national spending and investment in education and health will erode the well-being of poorer Ticos. The Figueres Olsen administration (1994–1998) continued to cut government jobs and curtail public services.[9]

These incipient trends notwithstanding, Costa Rican income distribution remained remarkably stable during the turbulent 1980s given the severity of the recession. All classes lost real income, and all classes recovered significantly by the early 1990s. Despite the nation's constitutional social guarantees, social welfare programs, and redistributive policies, the poorest Costa Ricans became relatively poorer from the 1960s through the early 1990s. Prior to the late 1980s, the real and rather consistent winners were the working and middle classes, whose real incomes and income shares rose markedly. One may reasonably surmise that such improving circumstances for the middle majority of the population would contribute greatly to political stability. One may find in the real and relative income declines of the late 1980s and early 1990s cause for the political mobilization observed among both rich and poor.

Minorities

Compared to much of Latin America, Costa Rica is relatively racially and culturally homogeneous because its original indigenous and black populations were largely assimilated into the predominantly mestizo, culturally Hispanic population. However, the myth of racial and ethnic homogeneity often leads Costa Ricans to overlook their minorities and the discrimination against them.

Blacks. About 3 percent of Costa Ricans are blacks of Jamaican origin, most Protestants and many of them English speaking. Most are descendants of railroad and banana workers brought in during the nineteenth century, and most live in the Atlantic lowlands. African Costa Ricans today make up about one-third of the population of the Atlantic zone.

Costa Ricans of African origin have historically experienced pronounced racial discrimination. After United Fruit moved its operations to the Pacific coast in the 1930s, taking with it most of the Atlantic region's employment, blacks were prohibited from migrating to follow the jobs. Although the revolutionary junta of 1948—1949 lifted the ban on blacks' mobility and placed an antidiscrimination clause in the 1949 constitution, African Ticos—still concentrated heavily in the Atlantic zone—have suffered economically ever since the banana company pull-out. Poverty is widespread, as is racism. Many still speak English and resent the Hispanicization of education. Limón, the major city of the Atlantic zone, experienced major outbreaks of rioting over hard times in 1979 and again in 1996.[10]

Indigenous People. Costa Rica has a small contingent of indigenous people, perhaps 1 percent of the national population, concentrated mainly in "indigenous reserves" in the southern parts of the country. Divided among several distinct language and ethnic groups, Indians suffer from very low public-service levels and much poverty and disease. More than twenty reserves legally incorporate over 6 percent of the national territory, but their populations have use of only an estimated 60 percent of that. Historically, the government, private sector, and other Costa Ricans have exploited the Indians and their lands. Persistent difficulties have included encroachment upon their (nominally) legally protected reserves by the ever spreading mestizo populace, illegal logging, and mineral concessions by the government.

The Legislative Assembly formed the National Commission for Indian Affairs (Comisión Nacional de Asuntos Indígenas, or CONAI) in 1973 to protect Indian interests. Despite CONAI, Indians continue to complain of abuse and discrimination. They have mobilized politically and protested their plight since the 1970s, with the rate of protest increasing into the 1990s. One powerful irritant and source of recent mobilization was that the law treated Indians as foreigners in Costa Rica rather than as citizens. They finally received full political rights by a constitutional amendment in the early 1990s.[11]

Other Minorities. Other minorities include small populations of foreign origin. Among the older groups are Italians, French, Germans, and Chinese. Germans became important participants in the coffee industry. Many German-origin Ticos were interned in the United States during World War II for security reasons. Italian, French, and German Costa Ricans have significantly integrated themselves into the population and national cultural, political, and economic life.

A small Jewish community developed prior to World War II. Many early Jewish immigrants began life in Costa Rica as itinerant peddlers and eventually established commercial enterprises in the larger cities. Despite a period of official anti-Semitism during the government of León Cortés and despite widespread cultural anti-Semitism, Jews have achieved business, professional, and political influence.

The Chinese first came to Costa Rica as contract workers for railroad construction. Chinese Costa Ricans, also targets of discrimination, have found their own entrepreneurial niche. They reside especially in smaller towns and act as commercial intermediaries or operate small hotels, stores, and restaurants.

Foreigners. Since the mid-twentieth century, an important immigrant community has been foreign retirees (*pensionados*), especially from the United States. Beneficial tax laws, the excellent climate, and the modest cost of living in Costa Rica have attracted tens of thousands of foreigners, many from the United States. Because these expatriates normally retain their citizenship of origin, the *pensionado* community remains on the margin of national politics. However, a weekly English-language newspaper, the *Tico Times,* serves this community and from time to time breaks a story that affects domestic politics.

The largest foreign populations in Costa Rica are other Latin Americans. Nicaraguans have long crossed into Costa Rica as migrant laborers for the northern provinces' coffee harvests or simply to live and work in Costa Rica's better economy. During Nicaragua's civil wars and revolution of the late 1970s and 1980s, hundreds of thousands of Nicaraguans came as political and economic refugees. During the 1980s Costa Rica detained thousands of Nicaraguans in crowded camps under extremely trying conditions. Refugee camp residents complained of being taken advantage of by local farmers as nearly captive labor for the coffee harvest (mainly by farmers who refused to pay promised wages to Nicaraguans fearful of complaining to authorities).

Opponents of the Nicaraguan dictator Anastasio Somoza Debayle in 1978 and 1979 located their revolutionary shadow government in San José and openly recruited and trained guerrilla forces on Costa Rican soil. When the Sandinista revolutionaries won in Nicaragua in July 1979, conservative and Somocista exiles flooded into Costa Rica. Aided by the United States and other rightist forces, Nicaraguan counterrevolutionary (*contra*) elements fought for eleven years to oust the Sandinistas.[12] The resultant anticommunist political violence and terrorism within Costa Rica by both exiles and Ticos significantly threatened the nation's stability. This violence led president Oscar Arias Sánchez (1986–1990) aggressively to promote the regional Central American peace accord of August 1987 in hopes of stabilizing regional politics and thus diminishing political turbulence in Costa Rica. Despite the end of the Sandinista revolution in Nicaragua in 1990, many Nicaraguans remained and new illegal immigrants traveled to Costa Rica seeking work. The Nicaraguan government and immigrants in Costa Rica alike have protested mistreatment by Costa Rican officials.[13]

Religion

Roman Catholicism. The Costa Rican Catholic Church played a limited political role during much of the nineteenth century because of its weak institutional presence.[14] Later, under the leadership of the dynamic archbishop Bernardo Thiel, the church hierarchy sought to influence the 1889 election and formed the short-lived Catholic Union (Unión Católica) political party. Motivated both by rising Liberal anticlericalism in Costa Rica and by new social Christian theological currents within Catholicism, the clergy and Catholic Union challenged the *cafetaleros'* traditional dominance of the government. The Liberals quickly suppressed this first burst of Catholic political activism. The government eventually reached an understanding with the church hierarchy by which the latter quietly supported the regime.

From time to time, however, resurgent social Christianity—typically pushed by a few influentials within the hierarchy or clergy—would pull the church back into politics to promote social reform. Former priest Jorge Volio and leftist unions founded the Reformist Party in 1923, but the party disbanded after failing to win the presidency. Archbishop Victor Sanabria Martínez allied with President Calderón Guardia and the communist labor unions in 1943 to rescue Calderón's social and labor legislation.

Father Benjamín Núñez formed Catholic labor unions during the 1940s, fought with the National Liberation movement in 1948, and became labor minister in the 1948— 1949 revolutionary government.

Influenced by the reformism of the Second Vatican Council and the Medellín Latin American Bishops Conference of 1968, bishop of Alajuela Román Arrieta became another progressive voice. In the 1970s he endorsed a government agrarian reform scheme, which aroused fierce criticism from conservatives and large-holding agricultural interests. Liberation theology influenced elements founded the Central American Theological Institute (Instituto Teológico de America Central, or ITAC), which briefly merged with the archdiocese's traditionally conservative Central Seminary. There also appeared a left-leaning weekly newspaper, *Pueblo,* in 1972, and some religious elements embraced pastoral strategies of political mobilization in their ministry to the poor.

Much more typical of Costa Rican Catholicism since the civil war has been the church hierarchy's fairly consistent conservatism: support of the government and its development model, constant anticommunism, anti-Protestantism, and encouragement of *solidarismo* (an antiunion, probusiness substitute for organized labor). Under the conservative tutelage of Archbishop Carlos Humberto Rodríguez Quirós, most social activism was squashed. John Paul II has reinforced these conservative tendencies of the Costa Rican hierarchy, producing what Miguel Picado has characterized as "Costa Rican Catholic neoconservatism." According to Picado, "What is novel . . . is that church organs . . . and the orientation imposed upon religious information by the major media of mass communication offer a sampler of the propositions of the social doctrine of the church that reinforce neoliberal ideas and the institutions that best represent the interests of neoconservative sectors."15

Protestantism.[16] During the nineteenth century, the government tolerated early Protestantism because of Roman Catholic institutional weakness, Liberal anti-clericalism, and because Protestant sects largely confined their efforts to groups considered outsiders (Jamaicans in the Atlantic zone, foreigners in the capital city). But in the late nineteenth century, evangelical Protestant sects entered Costa Rica intent upon "saving" Catholic Ticos. Thus ensued several decades of interdenominational conflict: The *evangélicos* labored to convert the Catholics that some missionaries considered heathen. Catholic clergy responded with strident anti-Protestant propaganda. After the Second Vatican Council, however, Catholic institutional hostility toward the *evangélicos* diminished notably and interdenominational relations improved.

At first Protestantism spread very slowly, but more missionaries arrived, mainly from the United States, and Costa Rica became a center for training evangelical missionaries. In the 1960s Protestant Ticos still were less than 2 percent of the population, but by the 1990s that figure had risen fivefold. Protestant missionaries followed proselytizing tactics that proved very successful. They tended to form small congregations in poor and marginal communities. External financial support, especially from U.S. churches, enabled

Protestant pastors to work with and serve their congregations much more easily than the understaffed Catholic clergy.

Among the Protestants, the number of Pentecostal missions and churches began to increase sharply in the 1970s. The Pentecostals seemed to gain adherents in direct proportion to the deterioration of the economy in the 1970s and again in the 1980s and thus enjoyed explosive growth among the poor in many areas. Critics accuse the Pentecostals and other fundamentalist Protestants of having a profoundly conservative political effect by diverting their poor congregants from mobilizing politically to struggle with the real social problems that confront them.17 Whatever its political implications, Protestantism had gained a strong beachhead in Costa Rica by the 1990s.

Communications Media

In the nineteenth century, both the Liberals and the Catholic Church used the press to persuade and educate.18 This eventually helped "generate a society in which negotiation and consensus gained an advantage over repression."19 As an instrument of powerful politicoeconomic and social forces, the press developed with relatively little censorship or state interference. This freedom permitted the print media, and later radio and television, to make important contributions to political discourse, discussion, and democratization.

A gradually shifting array of daily and weekly newspapers, most with a partisan slant, has been published in San José for over a century. Radio, especially news programming, became a powerful medium during the 1950s. Radio was particularly influential in rural Costa Rica, much less penetrated than the cities by the capital's newspapers. Television developed rapidly during the 1970s and 1980s, supplanting newspapers as the principal source of news for a majority of the population by the end of the 1980s. Cable television systems developed and expanded rapidly in the 1990s. During the Oduber and Carazo administrations (1974–1982), the government established publicly funded cultural and educational television, Radio Nacional, and then the state-supported National System of Radio and Television (Sistema Nacional de Radio y Televisión, or SINART).

Costa Rica has also become a center for book publishing. The government partly subsidizes some publishing through the Ministry of Culture, Youth, and Sport (Editorial Costa Rica) and through the presses of several public universities (e.g., Editorial Universidad de Costa Rica, Editorial Universidad Estatal a Distancia). Several think tanks and intergovernmental entities operate editorial houses as well.[20] There are several smaller, private presses of various ideological perspectives, and individuals, unions, interest groups, and political parties also publish many books. Much of this flood of book publication draws upon a boom of Costa Rican scholarship driven by the rapid growth of higher education, numerous *licenciatura* (roughly equivalent to a master's degree) theses, and the proliferation of research scholars and university faculty with foreign doctorates.

The mass media mostly function without censorship. Indeed, a tradition of investigative journalism has developed, periodically embarrassing the government of the moment. The constitution's article 29 guarantees freedom of expression and press without prior censorship but also establishes civil responsibility for any harm that might be committed in their exercise.[21] In 1989 the Supreme Court of Justice ruled that citizens affected by inaccurate or contentious published information had a "right to rectification or reply" in the offending medium.[22] General press freedom notwithstanding, official censorship of pornographic and violent materials in the press, movies, and broadcast media prevailed for many decades. The censorship of prurient materials, once common, largely broke down by the 1980s.

A press law dating from the early twentieth century has aroused debate, legislative scrutiny, and legal challenge over the decades but has also withstood most efforts to revise or eliminate it. There have been certain encroachments upon press freedom by the courts and the executive branch in recent years. A court in 1994 sentenced *La Nación* columnist Bosco Valverde to a fine and suspended one-year prison term for "offending the honor and decorum of a public official"—specifically, several judges. Also in 1994 the Supreme Court of Justice issued guidelines restricting the press from naming persons or companies under investigation by the police. Stung by an arms purchase scandal and other problems, President Figueres Olsen issued a 1996 decree permitting the government not to disclose information concerning security-related "state secrets," and he has withheld information from the press on a variety of issues.[23]

The government partially regulates access to the practice of journalism through the state-sanctioned College of Journalists (Colegio de Periodistas), one of many quasi-statal professional associations. Only Costa Ricans may own mass communications media, but this law has been evaded on occasion when convenient for political reasons.[24] Debate and discussion in the printed press are vigorous, and Costa Ricans enjoy basically unrestricted access to publications from a wide array of ideological perspectives.

Despite the virtual absence of formal censorship and the general accessibility of diverse ideological materials in print, the media have pronounced and fairly systematic biases. Ownership is highly concentrated, politically conservative, and tied to major business sectors. Major mass media (television, most radio, and major newspapers) tend to be overtly anticommunist and in recent decades fairly critical of the prevailing social democratic development model.

During the 1980s Costa Rica's media generally embraced neoliberal proposals to reduce the state's economic role. Major newspapers' editorials have generally denounced Catholic Church social activism.[25] Criticism of Nicaragua's Sandinista government was consistently strident during the 1980s. *La Nación*—the daily with the largest circulation—cooperated with the CIA in the publication of a Nicaraguan exile newspaper called *Nicaragua Hoy* (Nicaragua today). According to Martha Honey, this insert in *La Nación* was linked to Costa Rican–based anti-Sandinista groups and had CIA financing. Honey also reports that numerous print and broadcast journalists were on the CIA payroll or received payments from a Nicaraguan *contra* organization to promote anti-Sandinista news items during this period. Other journalists were fired or reassigned for insufficient cooperation with the anti-Sandinista line of their media. During the 1980s Costa Rica also permitted various *contra* radio stations to broadcast into Nicaragua, including one operated by the U.S.-funded Voice of America.[26]

Despite the biases of media owners, Costa Ricans still employ the newspapers to communicate an enormous range of political views to each other. Paid newspaper advertisements known as *campos pagados* constitute a major form of social and political discourse in Costa Rica. Ticos regularly congratulate, console, or castigate each other about all manner of social events and public issues. Individuals and interest groups also employ *campos pagados* to argue with the government, the media, and each other or to announce political preferences. During election campaigns the newspapers bulge with these spaces in which groups and individuals endorse particular candidates.

Education

At independence Costa Rica had only a handful of schools and very few literate citizens?[27] But education quickly became a central value of Liberals, and national elites embraced it as a key to modernization and development. The first higher education institution was the Universidad de Santo Tomás, founded in 1821 to provide secondary and some professional education.

An 1825 law charged municipalities with forming primary schools. The constitution of 1844 mentioned education as a right of citizens and the responsibility of the national government. The 1847 constitution more firmly committed the state to education and provided for equal instruction for both sexes.[28] The government established its first national education ministry (Public Instruction) in 1847.

During the 1850s and 1860s, the government took further steps forward in education. Public school construction expanded. Catholic religious orders also began to establish parochial schools. In 1869 alone, for instance, three public and private high schools were founded. Most important, the 1869 constitution established the full constitutional character of education that prevails largely unchanged today: "The primary education of both sexes shall be obligatory, free and supported by the Nation. Its immediate supervision corresponds to the Municipalities, and its supreme inspection to the Government."[29] Subsequent laws created an overall organizational plan for public education and built many more schools. An 1881 decree established full national authority to regulate all aspects of education, including parochial schools.

A national economic and fiscal crisis in the early 1880s forced Costa Rica to review its commitment to education. The near collapse of the public budget at first shut down many schools. The national government in 1888 even closed the Universidad de Santo Tomás, perennially strapped for funding and students.[30]

Costa Rica, however, refused to retreat from its commitment to basic education and fought back with major reforms. The government of President Mauro Fernandéz reformed the entire school curriculum and reorganized the whole education system. The government sharply increased spending on public schools beginning in 1886:

Education budgets rose from an average of only 6 percent of the national budget for 1869–1885 to around 18 percent for 1886–1900.[31] Local school boards were established for every municipality, which helped democratize and deepen local citizens' commitment to education. (The Liberal government's reformers also temporarily expelled the Jesuits from the country and closed several parochial schools to curb church influence on education.)

From then on Costa Rica's public education system gradually expanded its services throughout the national territory and to more grade levels. This eventually gave Costa Rica one of Latin America's highest literacy levels. Visitors trekking in rural Costa Rica were often astonished to find rural primary schools and their intrepid teachers in places of great isolation and privation. From 1900 to 1950, public education absorbed around 16 percent of the national budget and reached nearly 30 percent by the 1970s.

Arguably the most important effects of this love affair with education have been socialization of citizens, democratization, and social mobility. The rapid spread of literacy brought many Ticos into the electorate prior to 1913, when literacy was dropped as a requisite for voting.[32] The schools inculcated several generations with the norms of consensus, conflict avoidance, and patriotism and with the patriotic myths of homogeneity and equality. For much of the twentieth century, the education system enabled innumerable Ticos from working-class backgrounds to move up the social and economic ladder, especially into expanding public and private employment.

Education became a virtual civil religion, embraced by rulers and citizens alike. "The preoccupation with education and the response of different governments to the demand for more education, above all between 1948 and 1980, produced a real expansion of the opportunities of access to education for Costa Ricans and also a hope of social mobility."[33] As more Ticos took advantage of education and the doors it opened, they demanded more education and it became more accessible. Some 98 percent of primary-age children and perhaps one-third of secondary-age children attended school in 1980—both large increases over 1950.[34]

Higher education was the last frontier, expanding dramatically beginning in the 1970s. Founded in 1940 after the country had gone fifty years without a university, the Universidad de Costa Rica would serve as the only national source of higher education other than a seminary for almost three decades. But in the 1970s the government founded several new universities to broaden access and supply a burgeoning demand. By the late 1980s, Costa Rica had four public universities, and five private universities had also appeared. In 1989 there were almost 69,000 university students in tiny Costa Rica, with one-sixth of them enrolled in the private institutions. Overall, university enrollment had risen fivefold since 1970.[35]

Such great national investments in education and the national myths about its value have created powerful vested interests and expectations. Citizens demand education services from the government. Rural communities want neighborhood schools even though tiny rural schools may deliver inferior education. A growing proportion of the national education budget has been dedicated to national-level administration. Unions such as the National Association of Teachers (Asociación National de Educadores, or ANDE) and the National High School Teachers Association (Asociación de Profesores de Segunda Enseñanza, or APSE) represent most of the public school faculty. Teachers have struck several times to defend their wages and benefits.

Virtually free access to public higher education has placed a great and growing burden on the state and created a vast and easily mobilized constituency of university students and faculty. Universities have mobilized faculty and students into massive demonstrations to defend the higher education budget from government pressures to economize and raise tuition and fees.

The economic crisis of the 1980s shocked Costa Rica's education system in several ways. First, education spending fell drastically from a peak of 29.1 percent of the national budget in 1982 to 19.1 percent.[36] Funding cuts contributed to the deterioration of school facilities, the doubling up of schedules, reduction of the length of the school day and year, more unqualified teachers, and increased failure and dropout rates. Such calamitous material and instructional changes aggravated an already notable tendency toward stratification of education quality. There had long been a pronounced quality gap between the public schools and the private and parochial schools used by more prosperous Ticos. The fiscal crisis widened this breach so much that critics worried that it might soon sharpen class inequalities of all sorts.[37]

The financially strapped governments of the 1980s–1990s found themselves unable to rebuild education budgets as governments had a century before after similar difficulties. Under intense neoliberal pressures from international lending and development agencies, the government had to curtail—not increase—public spending by cutting services and promoting privatization. Indeed, there is evidence that the World Bank and other lenders considered Costa Rica's educational development *excessive* for a Third World nation and that it might have to "give up some of what it had achieved."[38]

The choices facing the deteriorated education system seemed so serious in the early 1990s that some observers believed that the nation's democracy and distributive justice hung in the balance. Jorge Rovira feared that both the deterioration of public schools and the proliferation of private universities would deepen and entrench inequalities in the society rather than reduce them as the education system had done for so long.[39] For Yolanda Rojas, the grave challenges of public education required Costa Rica to "consider the rights of all Costa Ricans without distinction of any sort so that we may deepen our democracy rather than destroy it."[40]

Organizations and Political Mobilization

High levels of formal organization characterize Costa Rica. The country has long provided its citizens with a human rights climate that facilitates and welcomes association and organization. Ticos tend to belong to groups of many sorts and through them to mobilize and press demands upon the government.

Following a corporatist tendency common in Latin America, Costa Rica's government helps establish and legitimize some organizations and even gives them certain public functions. Unlike some of its Central American neighbors, the Costa Rican government tends to respond favorably to and accept as legitimate a wide array of groups, even those outside this favored corporatist interest arena. A 1973 nationwide survey of organizations and their projects in over 100 communities found that a large majority had received some form of outside assistance, usually from the national or municipal governments.[41]

The government has long encouraged the growth of organizations. It began by establishing guilds of artisans in the 1830s and has subsequently promoted organizations ranging from professional associations to cooperatives; health, nutrition, and community improvement groups; and even labor unions. There is also a rich historical record of independently formed civil society: Professionals guilds and mutual aid societies appeared in the 1850s, early community improvement groups in the 1880s, and modern labor unions in the early twentieth century: Costa Rica thus has an abundant associational life.[42]

In the twentieth century, the state has chartered professional colleges (*colegios,* analogous to bar associations in the United States) for attorneys, physicians, journalists, architects, engineers, pharmacists, and others. The professional colleges have a quasi-statal character: They are government-chartered monopolies, and some them even regulate and license practitioners. Despite this public function, the *colegios* also actively represent and promote the interests of their members before the state. The professional colleges constitute important representatives of middle-sector interests.

Outside the corporatist interest sector exist manifold other interest and pressure groups. Business organizations function more purely as pressure groups than the professional colleges, and they lack regulatory authority. Considerably compensating for this absence of formal authority, however, is their resource wealth. They enjoy all the tools of effective pressure groups that their members' wealth and organization can purchase, including access to policymakers, the capacity to use the press to shape public opinion, and resources for litigation. Among many others, such business organizations as the National Association for the Promotion of Enterprise (Asociación Nacional de Fomento de la Empresa, or ANFE), Costa Rican Association of Business Managers (Asociación Costarricense de Gerentes de Empresa, or ACOGE), the Chamber of Commerce, Chamber of Industry, and the National Union of Chambers of Commerce represent general or particular business-sector interests. Business groups tend to lobby for lower taxes, less government regulation, and the privatization of public enterprises. Some business groups promote ideological education along conservative lines through sponsored newspaper columns. Because they can mold public opinion through the media, contribute heavily to political candidates and parties, and skillfully lobby the executive and legislature, they have considerable political influence. Their members have also often served in government posts.

During the early 1980s, when economic crisis provoked extensive popular protests and the Sandinista revolution in Nicaragua seemed most threatening, business groups spearheaded by the Chamber of Commerce made boldly forceful demands upon the administration of Luis Alberto Monge. Indeed, in July 1984 they seemed almost to threaten a legal and institutional challenge to the regime should President Monge not quickly restrain the unions and popular unrest, drop proposed consumer protections, and assume a more belligerent posture toward Nicaragua.[43] Although these business interests had key links to Monge's administration, the government countered them with other mobilized groups, avoided an institutional crisis, and directed foreign policy toward a less confrontational line.

Organized labor is an important part of civil society; although in the late twentieth century it has badly divided and declined. Overall, only about 19 percent of the workforce was organized in unions in the late 1970s, a period when membership was probably near its peak.[44] Government policies had fragmented and hobbled—but did not suppress—the labor movement after the 1948 defeat of the Calderón-communist governing coalition. After a period of resurgence in membership during the 1970s, several things undermined the organized workforce and political decline of labor: further fragmentation of various confederations, increasing ideological and employer antagonism, the decline of the Communist Party and its external sponsors, and tactical blunders by particular unions. Many private-sector unions vanished during the 1980s, leaving the movement heavily concentrated in the public sector. Some powerful unions remain independent of any central labor organization, especially those of teachers, telephone and electrical workers, and public health workers, bank employees, and public works employees. These public employees unions, like professional colleges, have strongly represented middle-class interests.[45]

The solidarity association (*asociación solidarista*) is another type of labor organization in Costa Rica. This sector is the most dynamic on the labor scene, much to the chagrin of other labor organizers who deeply resent both the success and goals of *solidarismo*. Solidarity associations involve modest profit-sharing contributions to employees by the owners of a business. Private-sector workers use the associations as self-help entities that can provide loans, support for medical care, and even separation pay, which labor law does not guarantee to private-sector workers. Business interests have promoted the solidarity movement as a conservative alternative to labor unions. They appear to have undercut class-conscious worker mobilization, reduced conflictive labor relations, and raised productivity.[46]

There are myriad community-level groups in Costa Rica, some promoted by the government and others that have arisen spontaneously. Since the late 1960s, the National Community Development Directorate (Dirección Nacional de Desarrollo de la Comunidad, or DINADECO) has promoted the formation of local community development associations. Properly constituted by citizens of a town or neighborhood, these groups receive *personería jurídica* (a formal, legal status) from the government, which permits them to receive and spend legislatively appropriated funds for local improvement projects.

Community development associations bring neighbors together to help with local civic projects, collaborate with government agencies, and pressure local and national public officials to fund their projects. Health-related agencies have also encouraged local groups to foment such projects as infant nutrition and health clinics. Schools have parent organizations to promote cooperation with and improvement of local schools.

Demands from such groups contribute heavily to escalating pork barrel spending by the Legislative Assembly.

Costa Rica has many local organizations not sponsored by the government. These civil society groups have sprung up spontaneously in response to the problems of rapid urbanization and economic hard times. In urban areas organizations of housing squatters have invaded land to build homes and then pressed the government for services, utilities, and land titles. Advising and organizing such squatter groups are nongovernmental organizations such as the Democratic Front for Housing (Frente Democrática de Vivienda, or FDV) and the National Patriotic Committee (Comité Patriótico Nacional, or COPAN).

Rural areas, too, have experienced widespread organization and mobilization independent of government. Rural economic deterioration during the 1980s brought a boom in peasant organizations and mobilizations—some spontaneous, some promoted by national union confederations. The Union of Small and Medium Farmers (Unión de Pequeños y Medianos Agricultores, or UPA-Nacional) organized peasants nationwide to demand land reform and other public assistance. Over half of the 142 agrarian groups registered with the labor ministry in 1990 were independent.[47]

There are sorts of organizations in Costa Rica too numerous to list. Their interests range from ideological issues to sports, environmental protection to social and cultural activities. The next chapter provides examples of the activities of and participation driven by such organizations. When civil society interests require action from the government, Costa Rican organizations usually first contact proper authorities through normal channels and enlist influential citizens to endorse their cause. Should such efforts fail, some groups escalate to confrontational tactics such as demonstrations, strikes, boycotts, or acts of civil disobedience. Often true to its national myth of consensus, the government usually responds to confrontation with study and compromise rather than repression.

Conclusions

Costa Ricans are divided into socioeconomic classes with sharp inequalities of income, wealth, and educational access. The rise to power of the National Liberation Party after the 1948 civil war gave middle-class interests unprecedented political clout for several decades. Guided by a social democratic development program and an activist state, they used it to redistribute income toward middle-income groups and away from the wealthy—and even to some extent away from the poor. Powerful economic and institutional interests such as the wealthy, business associations, the Catholic Church, and the media have resented and resisted this program.

The economic crisis of the 1980s provided conservatives an opportunity and powerful external allies with which to challenge and undermine the social democratic development model. They have largely succeeded in promoting a new neo-liberal development model, especially in the policy arena (Chapter 8). The economic traumas of the 1980s hurt most Ticos, and many of them mobilized to protect their interests. This increased political mobilization swelled Costa Rica's already large civil society and generated more conflict among social classes than the nation was accustomed to.

Income distribution and services had clearly shifted away from the middle sectors by the early 1990s, and severe poverty afflicted more Ticos than in several prior decades. A 1994 study used dramatic terms to describe the growing inequality and consequent political mobilization: "The existent differentiation between distinguished residential areas and popular slums is so sharp that it testifies to the disintegration of the social fabric."[48]

Costa Rica's myths of classlessness and homogeneity thus break down before careful scrutiny. Class, race, institutional position, and interests divide Ticos in diverse ways. Some of these differences frequently set them at odds with one another or with the government. The Biesanzes, however, point out that the myth of tolerance "benefits all groups, given that it constitutes a challenge for the 'white' majority to try to live in accord with its established values and to attempt to resolve the problems of minorities."[49] The shared ideals of consensus, peaceful problem solving, and equality of opportunity—no matter how far they are from actual truth—thus encourage Costa Ricans rulers and ruled alike, to treat each other with restrain and respect often absent in several neighboring countries.

This shared culture has helped keep Costa Rica considerably more peaceable than its neighbors, but it has not prevented inequality, social mobilization, conflict, and political turmoil. The following chapters examine political participation and political culture in more detail. They seek to understand how Costa Ricans engage each other and the state in the political arena, as well as the attitudes and values they bring to the process.

NOTES

1. Mavis Hiltunen de Biesanz, Richard Biesanz, and Karen Zubris de Biesanz, *Los costarricenses* (San José, Costa Rica: Editorial Universidad Estatal a Distancia, 1979), pp. 281–282.
2. Estimate based on Inter-American Development Bank (IADB), *Latin America After a Decade of Reform: Economic and Social Progress in Latin America, 1997 Report* (Baltimore: Johns Hopkins University Press, 1997), tables A-1, A-2.
3. Based on Biesanz et al., *Los costarricenses,* pp. 244–251. Income shares for each group are very rough estimates; the Biesanzes did not estimate shares for all classes.
4. The Gini coefficients in Table 1 confirm declining income inequality, but the benefits clearly failed to reach the poor.
5. Estimate derived from income distribution and median income data in Table 1.
6. Carlos Castro Valverde, "Sector público y ajuste estructural en Costa Rica (1983–1992)," in Trevor Burns, ed., *La transformación neoliberal del sector público: Ajuste estructural y sector público en Centroamérica y el Caribe* (Managua: Coordinador Regional de Investigaciones Económicas y Sociales, 1995), pp. 74, 104–105.
7. Castro Valverde (ibid., pp. 63–67) shows that taxes were shifted to the poor and that government sharply reduced spending and investment in education and health.
8. Ibid., pp. 66–67. See also Jorge Rovira Mas, *Costa Rica en los años '80* (San José, Costa Rica: Editorial Porvenir, 1989), pp. 108–135.

9. Larry Rohter, "Costa Rica Chafes at New Austerity," *New York Times,* September 30, 1996, p. A7.
10. Biesanz et al., *Los costarricenses,* pp. 273–277; Carlos Meléndez and Quince Duncan, *El Negro en Costa Rica* (San José: Editorial Costa Rica, 1972); John A. Booth, Alvaro Hernández C., and Miguel Mondol V., *Tipología de comunidades,* vol. 2: *Estudio para una tipología de comunidades* (San José, Costa Rica: Direction Nacional de Desarrollo de la Comunidad-Acción Internacional Técnica, 1973); Rohter, "Costa Rica Chafes," p. A7; "The Black Community in Costa Rica, *Mesoamerica,* March 1994, pp. 11–13.
11. Marcos Guevara Berger and Rubén Chacón Castro, *Territorios indios en Costa Rica: Orígenes, situación actual y perspectivas* (San José, Costa Rica: García Hermanos, 1992); Biesanz et al., *Los costarricenses,* pp. 270–273; *Mesoamerica,* December 1993, p. 10.
12. Biesanz et al., *Los costarricenses,* pp. 277–280; Martha Honey, *Hostile Acts: U.S. Policy in Costa Rica in the 1980s* (Gainesville: University of Florida Press, 1994).
13. *Mesoamerica,* February 1995, p. 4.
14. Costa Rica became a diocese in 1850, having been previously under the Managua diocese. This section draws heavily on Philip Williams, *The Catholic Church and Politics in Nicaragua and Costa Rica* (Pittsburgh: University of Pittsburgh Press, 1989), chs. 5–7; and Biesanz et al., *Los costarricenses,* ch. 9.
15. Miguel Picado, "Cambios dentro del catolicismo costarricense en los últimos años," in Juan Manuel Villasuso, ed., *El nuevo rostro de Costa Rica* (Heredia, Costa Rica: Centro de Estudios Democráticos de América Latina, 1992), p. 46.
16. This section is drawn from Biesanz et al., *Los costarricenses,* pp, 499–506; Picado, "Cambios dentro del catolicismo," pp. 50–51; Jaime Valverde, *Las sectas en Costa Rica: Pentecostalismo y conflicto social* (San José, Costa Rica: Editorial Departamento Ecuménico de Investigaciones-Centro de Coordinación de Evangelización y Realidad Social-Consejo Superior Universitario Centroamericano, 1990).
17. Valverde, *Las sectas en Costa Rica,* pp. 74–80.
18. This section is based on Maria Pérez Y., "Costa Rica: Las comunicaciones al ritmo del mundo," pp. 209–250, and Eduardo Ulibarri, "Los medios de comunicación: Diversidad con desafíos," pp. 251–262, both in Villasuso, *El nuevo rostro.*
19. Pérez Y., "Costa Rica: Las comunicaciones," p. 213.
20. For instance, there are the social democratic movement's Latin American Center for Democratic Studies (Centro de Estudios Democráticos de América Latina, or CEDAL), the Latin American Social Science Faculty (Facultad Latinoamericano de Ciéncias Sociales, or FLACSO), and the Superior University Council of Central America (Consejo Superior Universitario de Centro America, or CSUCA), whose publishing house is known as the Editorial Universitaria Centroamericana (EDUCA).
21. This law functions similarly to the civil law tradition of libel in Britain and the United States, by which one may recover damages for injury caused by the irresponsible publication of falsehoods.
22. Ulibarri, "Los medios," pp. 260–261.
23. *Mesoamerica,* August 1994, pp. 9–10; June 1996, p. 10; and "Press Freedom in the Americas: Breaking the Chains of Censorship," April 1996, pp. 7–8.
24. For instance, a U.S.-financed Voice of America transmitter started in 1985, and Radio Impacto, a CIA operation setup in 1982, broadcast anti-Sandinista propaganda into Nicaragua. See Honey, *Hostile Acts,* pp. 258–259.

25. Picado, "Cambios dentro del catolicismo," p. 46.
26. Honey, *Hostile Acts,* pp. 255–261.
27. This section is based on Astrid Fischel, *Consenso y represión: Una interpretación socio-política de la educación costarricense* (San José: Editorial Costa Rica, 1987); Yolanda M. Rojas, "Transformaciones recientes en la educación costarricense," pp. 97–122, and Jorge Rovira M., "Las universidades en los años ochenta," pp. 123–140, both in Villasuso, *El nuevo rostro;* and Biesanz et al., *Los costarricenses,* ch. 8.
28. Constitution of 1847, in Fischel, *Consenso y represión,* p. 63.
29. Article 6, constitution of 1869, from Fischel, *Consenso y represión,* pp. 64–65.
30. Costa Rica had no university per se until 1940, when the Universidad de Costa Rica opened. Certain schools, such as the law school, remained open as separate entities.
31. Fischel, *Consenso y represión,* tables 1 and 2.
32. Bernhard Thibaut, "Costa Rica," in Dieter Nohlen, ed., *Enciclopedia electoral latinoamericana y del Caribe* (San José, Costa Rica: Instituto Interamericano de Derechos Humanos, 1993), p. 185.
33. Rojas, "Transformaciones recientes," p. 101.
34. Ibid., p. 166.
35. Rovira M.,"Las universidades," pp. 124–127.
36. Rojas, "Transformaciones recientes," p. 107.
37. My conversations with faculty revealed that universities were also hard hit, eroding programs, research efforts, salaries, and faculty quality.
38. Rojas, "Transformaciones recientes," p. 100.
39. Rovira M., "Las universidades," pp. 133–137.
40. Rojas, "Transformaciones recientes," p. 122.
41. Booth et al., *Tipología de comunidades.*
42. Oscar Arias Sánchez has studied interest groups and *colegios* in his *Grupos de presión en Costa Rica* (San José: Editorial Costa Rica, 1971) and political elites in his *Quién gobierna en Costa Rica?* (San José, Costa Rica: Editorial Universitaria Centroamericana, 1976).
43. Carlos Sojo, *Costa Rica: Política exterior y sandinismo* (San José, Costa Rica: Facultad Latinoamericano de Ciencias Sociales, 1991), pp. 119–123.
44. John A. Booth, "Costa Rican Labor Unions," in Gerald W. Greenfield and Sheldon L. Maram, eds., *Latin American Labor Unions* (New York: Greenwood Press, 1987); Manuel Rojas B., "Un sindicalismo del sector público," in Villasuso, *El nuevo rostro,* pp. 181–189; Elisa Donato M. and Manuel Rojas B., *Sindicatos, política y economía: 1972–1986* (San José, Costa Rica: Ediciones Alma Mater, 1987).
45. Four major confederations divided the rest of the unionized workforce in the late 1970s. About half the organized workforce was linked to the communist-dominated General Confederation of Workers (Confederación General de Trabajadores, or CGT) and other leftist unions combined into the Unitary Confederation of Workers (Confederación Unitaria de Trabajadores, or CUT) in 1981. A series of unsuccessful banana strikes during the 1980s split the CGT and caused a loss of members and affiliates. Other union associations were linked to the Social Christian movement or were part of two social democratic coalitions, the Costa Rican Confederation of Democratic Workers (Confederación Costarricense de Trabajadores Democráticos, or CCTD) and the Authentic Confederation of Democratic Workers (Confederación Auténtica de Trabajadores Democráticos, or CATD). The CUT split in the mid-1980s, giving rise to the Confederation of Workers of Costa Rica (Confederación de Trabajadores de Costa Rica, or CCTR). The National Workers Confederation (Confederación Nacional de Trabajadores, or CNT)

broke away from the CCTD also during the mid-1980s. In 1986 another effort was made to form a general federation of independent union confederations, giving rise to the Permanent Council of Workers (Consejo Permanente de los Trabajadores, or CPT). See Rojas, "Un sindicalismo del sector público," pp. 187–188.

46. Gustavo Blanco and Orlando Navarro, *El solidarismo: Pensamiento y dinámica social de un movimiento obrero patronal* (San José: Editorial Costa Rica, 1984); Oscar Bejarano, "El solidarismo costarricense," in Villasuso, *El nuevo rostro,* pp. 203–298; Centro de Estudios Democráticos de América Latina (CEDAL) and Asociación de Servicios de Promoción Laboral (ASEPROLA), *El problema solidarista y la respuesta sindical en Centroamérica* (Heredia, Costa Rica: CEDAL-ASEPROLA, 1959).
47. Jorge Mora A., "Los movimientos sociales agrarios en la Costa Rica de la década de los ochenta," in Villasuso, *El nuevo rostro,* p. 155.
48. Programa de las Naciones Unidad para el Desarrollo (PNUD), *Estado de la nación en desarrollo humano sostenible 1994* (San José, Costa Rica: Programa de las Naciones Unidas para el Desarrollo—La Defensoría de los Habitantes de la República—Consejo Nacional de Rectores, 1994), p. 12.
49. Biesanz et al., *Los costarricenses,* p. 282.

CHAPTER TWO

LITERATURE

Central American literary production predates the conquest by hundreds of years. Oral traditions and written form recorded it. However, the modern discipline that we now know as literature is linked to European traditions and European ideas about the value of the written word over the oral one, as well as about the formal understanding of what we would consider literature. As a result, Central American literature today is often studied exclusively as the written artistic production in the Spanish language of a variety of texts that fit the modern understanding of what is literature. Therefore, Indigenous literary production, ancient and contemporary, is often excluded from anthologies and the national literary cannons. It is significant to keep this in mind as we sample the literary production in Central America.

Familiarizing ourselves with some examples of ancient Indigenous texts might allow us to form a sense of the artistic and literary complexity of these texts. Furthermore, as readers, it is important to approach the artistic and literary production that emerges outside the modern understanding of art and culture from other perspectives besides the modern understanding of aesthetics and the modern definition of fine arts, particularly because of the spiritual dimensions linked to the cultural and historical context in which these texts emerged.

On the other hand, within an area studies program, we can approach the literary production that emerged as part of the colonial and modern experiences of the Central American region from different points of view. One option is to look at the way each one of the different movements and perspectives defines literature and art and challenges alternative ideas of what literature and art should be. Another option is to pay attention to the ways in which this artistic production contributes to the formation of an idea of what the national subject in each of the Central American nations should be about, its affiliation to Europe and its exclusion of Indigenous experiences on art, literature, culture and daily life.

In light of this, one suggested reading for students interested in further exploring the exclusion of Indigenous peoples from the realm of formally recognized culture, and particularly the understanding of literature from the Spanish perspective, is "Literacy and Colonization: The New World Experience" by Walter Mignolo, published in a volume titled *1492–1992: Re/Discovering Colonial Writing.* This article is critical of the ways Spanish colonial thought imposed the idea of the superiority of written texts over oral ones as part of their justification of the conquest.

As Mignolo explains, the arguments used by Spaniards to justify the conquest were "parternalistic." In addition, they argued that the conquest and colonization were efforts with a "liberating character which aspires to eliminate barbarism and introduce civilization" (75). According to Mignolo, their arguments also convey that "[t]he conquest and colonization have a commercial character which aspires to increase and promote exchange among different countries" (75). As we discussed in our previous chapter, this exchange between different cultures was presented as an event that happened under equal conditions, not as what it was, an exchange that required the enslavement of Indigenous peoples and their forced conversion to Catholicism and European ways.

As we explore ancient Indigenous texts that survive, be it through the transcription of oral texts or through the transcription of ancient codices, we will find that ancient and colonial Indigenous literary production was of great artistic and cultural complexity, and at the same time that it presents spiritual and cultural dimensions that do not relate to the European colonial or modern experience. The fragments that we have included in this chapter of the Ancient Maya Quiché text, *The Popol Vuh*, and of the ancient Maya Cakchiquel text *The Annals of the Cakchiquels*, are examples of these texts.

One of the most significant aspects about *The Popol Vuh* is that it contains the story of creation and an explanation for worldviews, elements of the world, traditions, religion and culture of the Maya Quiché. Because it is not an effort to write history, its narration takes place in mythical time, that is, it lacks dates, locations and names. The narration takes place at a nameless time, with mythical characters, in undefined places such as the underworld and the surface of the earth.

As is the case with several stories of creation that exist around the world, *The Popol Vuh* includes motifs that we are able to relate to those of other cultures, such as the story of creation, the destruction of the first human beings through a flood, the story of a virgin mother that gives birth to saviors of the culture (in this case it is the twins *Hunanhpú* and *Ixbalanqué*), the multiplication of a meal and the existence of a forbidden tree, among several others. As readers we might relate these stories to other narratives of creation, such as the story of the virgin mother Ixquic that some readers might relate to the story of Danae in Greek mythology or the story of Mary in the Bible. However, even though these stories share a narrative structure, the figure of a virgin mother and the key role of the children in a culture, there are no certain explanations about how these diverse stories of creation emerged around the world or why they have some visible similarities. What is important for our purposes is to pay attention to the cultural specificities that each of these stories presents.

These specificities are important because we might find in them the cultural idiosyncrasies that explain the particular worldview of an ethnic or cultural group. For instance, in the case of the forbidden tree, in the biblical tradition this narrative might assign blame for sin and for misfortune to Eve, the first woman who ate the forbidden fruit. On the contrary, in *The Popol Vuh,* Ixquic is presented as a courageous and intelligent woman who is able to carry her pregnancy to term through her victorious escape from the Lords of Xibalbá, who had ordered her death.

Other elements found in ancient Indigenous literary texts are the teachings that they contain about the values of a culture, the appropriate behavior within a community. As a result, in these texts we might find information about the importance of venerating the creators, about honor, about the need to be intelligent and avoid being tricked by others, about sharing food and belongings with the community and about the mandate to stay clear of arrogant behavior. Furthermore, Indigenous literature contains an explanation for the existence of numerous elements of the world. In it we might find an alternative perspective on the existence of animals, plants, planets and stars. For instance, in these texts we might find culturally specific explanations to questions such as: Where do monkeys come from? Why do they look the way they do? Why are mice privileged? Why do insects eat crops? And so forth.

Finally, another aspect that is important to understand about ancient oral traditions is that they inform and make an impact on contemporary Indigenous literary texts produced in the Central American region.

In the following fragment of *The Popol Vuh* we will read about the creation of the world from the perspective of the ancient Maya Quiché.

Popol Vuh: The Mayan Book of the Dawn of Life

TRANSLATION BY DENNIS TEDLOCK

This is the beginning of the Ancient World, here on the place called Quiché. Here we shall inscribe, we shall unplant the Ancient Word, the potential and source for everything done in the citadel of Quiché, in the nation of Quiché people.

And here we shall take up the demonstration, revelation, and account of how things were put in shadow and brought to light

by the Maker, Modeler, named Bearer, Begetter,
Hunahpu Possum, Hunahpu Coyote,
Great White Peccary, Tapir,
Sovereign Plumed Serpent,
Heart of the Lake, Heart of the Sea,
Maker of the Blue-Green Plate,
Maker of the Blue-Green Bowl,

as they are called, also named, also described as

the midwife, matchmaker
named Xpiyacoe, Xmucane,
defender, protector,
twice a midwife, twice a matchmaker,

as is said in the words of Quiché. They accounted for everything—and did it, too—as enlightened beings, in enlightened words. We shall write about this now amid the preaching of God, in Christendom now. We shall bring it out because there is no longer a place to see it, a council Book,

a place to see "The Light That Came from Across the Sea,"
the account of "Our place in the Shadows,"
a place to see "The Dawn of life,"

as it is called. There is the original book and ancient writing, but he who reads and ponders it hides his face. It takes a long performance and account to complete the emergence of all the sky-earth:

the fourfold siding, fourfold cornering,
measuring, fourfold staking,
halving the cord, stretching the cord
in the sky, on the earth,
the four sides, the four corners,

as it is said,

by the Maker, Modeler,
mother-father of life, of humankind,
giver of breath, giver of heart,
bearer, upbringer in the light that lasts
of those born in the light, begotten in the light;
worrier, knower of everything, whatever there is:
sky-earth, lake-sea.

This is the account, here it is:

Now it still ripples, now it still murmurs, ripples, it still sighs, still hums, and it is empty under the sky.

Here follow the first words, the first eloquence:

There is not yet one person, one animal, bird, fish, crab, tree, rock, hollow, canyon, meadow, forest. Only the sky alone is there: the face of the earth is not clear. Only the sea alone is pooled under all the sky; there is nothing whatever gathered together. It is at rest; not a single thing stirs. It is held back, kept at rest under the sky.

Whatever there is that might be is simply not there: only the pooled water, only the calm sea, only it alone is pooled.

Whatever might be is simply not there: only murmurs, ripples, in the dark, in the night. Only the Maker, Modeler alone, Sovereign Plumed Serpent, the Bearers, Begetters are in the water, a glittering light. They are there, they are enclosed in quetzal feathers, in blue-green.

Thus the name, "Plumed Serpent." They are great knowers, great thinkers in their very being.

And of course there is the sky, and there is also the heart of Sky. This is the name of the god, as it is spoken.

And then came his word, he came here to the Sovereign Plumed Serpent, here in the blackness, in the early dawn. He spoke with the Sovereign Plumed Serpent, and they talked, then they thought, then they worried. They agreed with each other, they joined their words, their thoughts. Then it was clear, then they reached accord in the light, and then humanity was clear, when they conceived the growth, the generation of trees, of bushes, and the growth of life, of humankind, in the blackness, in the early dawn, all because of the Heart of Sky, named Hurricane. Thunderbolt Hurricane comes first, the second is Newborn Thunderbolt, and the third is Raw Thunderbolt.

So there were three of them, as Heart of Sky, who came to the Sovereign Plumed Serpent, when the dawn of life was conceived:

"How should it be sown, how should it dawn? Who is to be the provider, nurturer?"

"Let it be this way, think about it: this water should be removed, emptied out for the formation of the earth's own plate and platform, then comes the sowing, the dawning of the sky-earth. But there will be no high days and no bright praise for our work, our design, until the rise of the human work, the human design," they said.

And then the earth arose because of them, it was simply their word that brought it forth. For the forming of the earth they said "Earth." It arose suddenly, just like a cloud, like a mist, now forming, unfolding. Then the mountains were separated from the water, all at once the great mountains came forth. By their genius alone, by their cutting edge alone they carried out the conception of the mountain-plain, whose face grew instant groves of cypress and pine.

And the Plumed Serpent was pleased with this:

"It was good that you came. Heart of Sky, Hurricane, and Newborn Thunderbolt, Raw Thunderbolt. Our work, our design will turn out well," they said.

And the earth was formed first, the mountain-plain. The channels of water were separated; their branches wound their ways among the mountains. The waters were divided when the great mountains appeared.

Such was the formation of the earth, when it was brought forth by the heart of Sky, Heart of Earth, as they are called, since they were the first to think of it. The sky was set apart, and the earth was set apart in the midst of the waters.

Such was their plan when they thought, when they worried about the completion of their work.

Now they planned the animals of the mountains, all the guardians of the forests, creatures of the mountains: the deer, birds, pumas, jaguars, serpents, rattlesnakes, yellowbites, guardians of the bushes.

A Bearer, Begetter speaks:

"Why this pointless humming? Why should there merely be rustling beneath the trees and bushes?"

"Indeed—they had better have guardians," the others replied. As soon as they thought it and said it, deer and birds came forth.

And then they gave out homes to the deer and birds:

"You, the deer: sleep along the rivers, in the canyons. Be here in the meadows, in the thickets, in the forests, multiply yourselves. You will stand and walk on all fours," they were told.

So then they established the nests of the birds, small and great:

"You, precious birds: your nests, your houses are in the trees, in the bushes. Multiply there, scatter there, in the branches of trees, the branches of bushes," the deer and birds were told.

When this deed had been done, all of them had received a place to sleep and a place to stay. So it is that the nests of the animals are on the earth, given by the Bearer, Begetter. Now the arrangement of the deer and birds was complete.

And then the deer and birds were told by the Maker, Modeler, Bearer, Begetter: "Talk, speak out. Don't moan, don't cry out. Please talk, each to each, within each kind, within each group," they were told—the deer, birds, puma, jaguar, serpent.

"Name now our names, praise us. We are your mother, we are your father. Speak now:

'Hurricane,
Newborn Thunderbolt, Raw Thunderbolt,
Heart of Sky, Heart of Earth,
Maker, Modeler,
Bearer, Begetter,'

speak, pray to us, keep our days," they were told. But it didn't turn out that they spoke like people: they just squawked, they just chattered, they just howled. It wasn't apparent what language they spoke: each one gave a different cry. When the Maker, Modeler heard this:

"It hasn't turned out well, they haven't spoken," they said among themselves. "It hasn't turned out that our names have been named. Since we are their mason and sculptor, this will not do," the Bearers and Begetters said among themselves. So they told them:

"You will simply have to be transformed. Since it hasn't turned out well and you haven't spoken, we have changed our word:

"What you feed on, what you eat, the places where you sleep, the places where you stay, whatever is yours will remain in the canyons, the forests. Although it turned out that our days were not kept, nor did you pray to us, there may yet be strength in the keeper of days, the giver of praise whom we have yet to make. Just accept your service, just let your flesh be eaten.

"So be it, this must be your service," they were told when they were instructed—the animals, small and great, on the face of the earth.

And then they wanted to test their timing again, they wanted to experiment again, and they wanted to prepare for the keeping of days again. They had not heard their speech among the animals; it did not come to fruition and it was not complete.

And so their flesh was brought low: they served, they were eaten, they were killed—the animals on the face of the earth.

Again there comes an experiment with the human work, the human design, by the Maker, Modeler, Bearer, Begetter:

"It must simply be tried again. The time for the planting and dawning is nearing. For this we must make a provider and nurturer. How else can we be invoked and remembered on the face of the earth? We have already made our first try at our work and design, but it turned out that they didn't keep our days, nor did they glorify us.

"So now let's try to make a giver of praise, giver of respect, provider, nurturer," they said.

So then comes the building and working with earth and mud. They made a body, but it didn't look good to them. It was just separating, just crumbling, just loosening, just softening, just disintegrating, and just dissolving. Its head wouldn't turn, either. Its face was just lopsided, its face was just twisted. It couldn't look around. It talked at first, but senselessly. It was quickly dissolving in the water.

"It won't last," the mason and sculptor said then. "It seems to be dwindling away, so let it just dwindle. It can't walk and it can't multiply, so let it be merely a thought," they said.

So then they dismantled, again they brought down their work and design. Again they talked:

"What is there for us to make that would turn out well, that would succeed in keeping our days and praying to us?" they said. Then they planned again:

"We'll just tell Xpiyacoe, Xmucane, Hunahpu Possum, Hunahpu Coyote to try a counting of days, a counting of lots," the mason and sculptor said to themselves. Then they invoked Xpiyacoe, Xmucane.

Then comes the naming of those who are the midmost seers: the "Grandmother of Day, Grandmother of Light," as the Maker, Modeler called them. "These are names of Xpiyacoe and Xmucane.

When Hurricane had spoken with the Sovereign Plumed Serpent, they invoked the daykeepers, diviners, the midmost seers:

"There is yet to find, yet to discover how we are to model a person, construct a person again, a provider, nurturer, so that we are called upon and we are recognized: our recompense is in words.

> Midwife, matchmaker,
> our grandmother, our grandfather,
> Xpiyacoe, Xmucane,
> let there be planting, let there be the dawning
> of our invocation, our sustenance, our recognition
> by the human work, the human design,
> the human figure, the human mass.

So be it, fulfill your names:

> Hunahpu Possum, Hunahpu Coyote,
> Bearer twice over, Begetter twice over,

Great Peccary, Great Tapir,
lapidary, jeweler,
sawyer, carpenter,
Maker of the Blue-Green Plate.
Maker of the Blue-Green Bowl.
incense maker, master craftsman
Grandmother of Day, Grandmother of Light.

You have been called upon because of our work, our design. Run your hands over the kernels of corn, over the seeds of the coral tree, just get it done, just let it come out whether we should carve and gouge a mouth, a face in wood," they told the daykeepers.

And then comes the borrowing, the counting of days: the hand is moved over the corn kernels, over the coral seeds, the days, the lots.

Then they spoke to them, one of them a grandmother, the other a grandfather. This is the grandfather, this is the master of the coral seeds: Xpiyacoe is his name. And this is the grandmother, the daykeeper, diviner who stands behind others: Xmucane is her name.

And they said, as they set out the days:

"Just let it be found, just let it be discovered,
say it, our ear is listening,
may you talk, may you speak,
just find the wood for the carving and sculpting
by the builder, sculptor.
Is this to be the provider, the nurturer
when it comes to the planting, the dawning?
You corn kernels, you coral seeds,
you days, you lots:
may you succeed, may you be accurate,"

they said to the corn kernels, coral seeds, days, lots. "Have shame, you up there, Heart of Sky: attempt no deception before the mouth and face of Sovereign Plumed Serpent," they said. Then they spoke straight to the point:

"It is well that there be your manikins, woodcarvings, talking, speaking, there on the face of the earth."

"So be it," they replied. The moment they spoke it was done: the manikins, woodcarvings, human in looks and human in speech.

This was the peopling of the face of the earth:

They came into being, they multiplied, they had daughters, they had sons, these manikins, woodcarvings. But there was nothing in their hearts and nothing in their minds, no memory of their mason and builder. They just went and walked wherever they wanted. Now they did not remember the Heart of Sky.

And so they fell, just an experiment and just a cutout for humankind. They were talking at first but their faces were dry. They were not yet developed in the legs and arms.

They had no blood, no lymph. They had no sweat, no fat. Their complexions were dry, their faces were crusty. They flailed their legs and arms, their bodies were deformed.

And so they accomplished nothing before the Maker, Modeler who gave them birth, gave them heart. They became the first numerous people here on the face of the earth.

Again there comes a humiliation, destruction, and demolition. The manikins, woodcarvings were killed when the Heart of Sky devised a flood for them. A great flood was made; it came down on the heads of the manikins, woodcarvings.

The man's body was carved from the wood of the coral tree by the Maker, Modeler. And as for the woman, the Maker, Modeler needed the pith of reeds for the woman's body. They were not competent, nor did they speak before the builder and sculptor who made them and brought them forth, and so they were killed, done in by a flood:

There came a rain of resin from the sky.

There came the one named Gouger of Faces: he gouged out their eyeballs.

There came Sudden Bloodletter: he snapped off their heads.

There came Crunching Jaguar: he ate their flesh.

There came Tearing Jaguar: he tore them open.

They were pounded down to the bones and tendons, smashed and pulverized even to the bones. Their faces were smashed because they were incompetent before their mother and their father, the Heart of Sky, named Hurricane. The earth was blackened because of this; the black rainstorm began, rain all day and rain all night. Into their houses came the animals, small and great. Their faces were crushed by things of wood and stone. Everything spoke: their water jars, their tortilla griddles, their plates, their cooking pots, their dogs, their grinding stones, each and every thing crushed their faces. Their dogs and turkeys told them:

"You caused us pain, you ate us, but now it is you whom we shall eat." And this is the grinding stone:

"We were undone because of you.

Every day, every day,
in the dark, in the dawn, forever,
r-r-rip, r-r-rip,
r-r-rub, r-r-rub,
right in our faces, because of you.

This was the service we gave you at first, when you were still people, but today you will learn of our power. We shall pound and we shall grind your flesh," their grinding stones told them.

And this is what their dogs said, when they spoke in their turn:

"Why is it you can't seem to give us our food? We just watch and you just keep us down, and you throw us around. You keep a stick ready when you eat, just so you can hit us. We don't talk, so we've received nothing from you, How could you not have known? You *did* know that we were wasting away there, behind you.

"So, this very day you will taste the teeth in our mouths. We shall eat you," their dogs told them, and their faces were crushed.

And then their tortilla griddles and cooking pots spoke to them in turn:

"Pain! That's all you've done for us. Our mouths are sooty, our faces are sooty. By setting us on the fire all the time, you burn us. Since *we* felt no pain, *you* try it. We shall burn you," all their cooking pots said, crushing their faces.

The stones, their hearthstones were shooting out, coming right out of the fire, going for their heads, causing them pain. Now they run for it, helter-skelter.

They want to climb up on the houses, but they fall as the houses collapse. They want to climb the trees: they're thrown off by the trees.

They want to get inside caves, but the caves slam shut in their faces.

Such was the scattering of the human work, the human design. The people were ground down, overthrown. The mouths and faces of all of them were destroyed and crushed. And it used to be said that the monkeys in the forests today are a sign of this. They were left as a sign because wood alone was used for their flesh by the builder and sculptor.

So this is why monkeys look like people: they are a sign of a previous human work, human design—mere manikins, mere woodcarvings.

This was when there was just a trace of early dawn on the face of the earth, there was no sun. But there was one who magnified himself; Seven Macaw is his name. The sky-earth was already there, but the face of the sun-moon was clouded over. Even so, it is said that his light provided a sign for the people who were flooded. He was like a person of genius in his being.

"I am great. My place is now higher than that of the human work, the human design. I am their sun and I am their light, and I am also their months.

"So be it: my light is great. I am the walkway and I am the foothold of the people, because my eyes are of metal. My teeth just glitter with jewels, and turquoise as well; they stand out blue with stones like the face of the sky.

"And this nose of mine shines white into the distance like the moon. Since my nest is metal, it lights up the face of the earth. When I come forth before my nest, I am like the sun and moon for those who are born in the light, begotten in the light. It must be so, because my face reaches into the distance," says Seven Macaw.

It is not true that he is the sun, this Seven Macaw, yet he magnifies himself, his wings, his metal. But the scope of his face lies right around his own perch; his face does not reach everywhere beneath the sky. The faces of the sun, moon, and stars are not yet visible, it has not yet dawned.

And so Seven Macaw pulls himself up as the days and the months, though the light of the sun and moon has not yet clarified. He only wished for surpassing greatness. This was when the flood was worked upon the manikins, woodcarvings.

And now we shall explain how Seven Macaw died, when the people were vanquished, done in by the mason and sculptor.

The Cakchiquel people were living in their ceremonial centers in what is now the Guatemalan highlands when the Spaniards arrived in the early 1500s. The text that we have included here is the story of the emergence of the Cakchiquel people as it was told in ancient times orally. It was later written down in this version. Their story begins with four brothers who left their city of origin, the legendary Toltec city of Tula, and distributed among them the land of what is now southern Mexico and Central America, all the way to what is now the modern nation of Nicaragua. This is how the mythical four ancient nations emerged: the Quichés (Tecpán Utlatlán), the Tzutuhils (Tecpán Atitlán), the Akahals (Tecpán Tezolotlán), and the Cakchiquels (Tecpan Quauhtemallan). This section tells the story of the arrival of two ancestors that gave origin to the elders of the cakchiquel people. In the place called Kaqjay they presented offerings to honor the Gods and their ancestors. Their offerings included nets to caught birds, maguey fiber, and deer leather and then they were accepted and recognized by the Gods.

Excerpt from the Annals of the Cakchiquels

By A Member of the Xahila Family

27. Then they encountered the two, Loch and Xet by name; they encountered them there at the foot of the mountains Cucu and Tzunun. These said when they were encountered, "Do not kill us, O thou our lord; we will be the servants of your throne, of your power." So they said, and entered at once as vassals, each one carrying the bows and drums. Going on, a return was made, and they were hindered by some calabash vines, and were ensnared and scattered. Therefore, that place was called Tzaktzuy, and the Ahquehay took it as their sign, that is, those first fathers and ancestors who brought forth the Ahquehay. This is why they took it, it is said, and such is the name of the place. They chose a portion of the tribe, oh you my children, and truly thus it was that our first fathers and ancestors brought us forth and gave us existence—us, the Cakchiquel people.

28. Then they went forth to meet those at the place Oronic Cakhay, and all the warriors of the seven villages arrived. Then spoke Gagavitz and Zactecauh to the Quiché men: "Let us all go to the place. Let us conquer the glory of all the seven villages of Tecpan, let us weaken their hearts; do thou count their faces, do thou stand here at the place Cakhay; I shall enter the place Cakhay; I shall conquer them; their heart shall be weakened; there, in the place, they shall be conquered, where they never before were conquered." Thus they spoke when they ordered the slaughter, when they were in Cakhay; then it began with all of them in the place, and their hearts were weakened. But on account of the defence with water, and the defence with cinders, they could not enter the place, and

From *The Annals of the Cakchiquels*. Translation by Daniel G. Brinton.

their hearts were weakened. Then it was said: "O thou lord, I will give thee the venison and the honey. I am the lord of the venison, the lord of the honey; but I have not passed because of the cinders," it was said. Thus the venison and the honey were protected by means of the cinders. They went from there to Tunacotzih, "the sounding stone." There Loch and Xet made trial of the bows and drums, and they beat their drums; therefore the name of that spot is Tunacotzih, "the Drum-beating."

29. At this time they met the Cavek under the great pines, at the place called Ximbalxug. They heard the plaint of the doves beneath the great pines; the enchantment of the Cavek. Gagavitz and Zactecauh said: "Who art thou? What is that we hear?" Then said Loch and Xet: "They are our vassals, oh our lord, they obey us." They began to show their burdens; bird nets, maguey, tools for making shoes, were their burdens—no other burdens, for their houses were of deer skins and hides; hence they were called Ahquehay. Then they carried the nets to the woods; they caught doves in them beneath the great pines, and they brought many of these doves caught in the nets, and said: "Oh our lord, do not slay us." "Who art thou?" was asked. They answered: "We have been ruined by the Quiché men, we your brother, your kinsman, we the Cavek; they have diminished their regal dignity." So spoke they, and gave many gifts, they the fathers and ancestors of the Cavek. There were two heroes, Totunay the name of one, Xurcah of the other, the vassals of Cavek Paoh; they were addressed by Gagavitz: "Thou art the fourth of our tribes, Gekaquch, Baqahol, Cavek, and Cibakihay." Thus he addressed them: "Truly thou art my brother, my kinsman." Thus he spoke to those of Ahquehay: "Thou art counted in my tribe, thy vassalage shows that thou art of our ancient home, no longer art thou a vassal nor carriest the net. The Caveks are received, and form part of our tribe." So spoke of yore our fathers and ancestors, oh my children, and we must not forget the words of these rulers.

Nicaraguan born Rubén Darío is known as "the father of *Modernismo*" because as a result of his travels through the Americas he played an important role in the establishment of the network of writers and artists that shaped this literary movement and shared a similar understanding of literature. This literary movement emerged after the independence of the Latin American nations from Spanish colonial rule, and while it is not linked to the colonial traditions, it is heavily affiliated to European culture. We should not confuse it with the English literary movement known as "Modernism," since they are quite different and opposite movements.

Modernismo was a movement that in terms of its content we can view as quite a conservative movement linked to Eurocentric views of art, beauty and culture. However, in terms of its formal elements, *Modernismo* was a revolutionary movement that has had a great impact on literary production in Latin America up until today.

In terms of its content, one could define *Modernismo* as a movement that focused on the search for beauty defined from a Western perspective, with influence from Greek and Western European traditions, and with Paris as the central location of culture. This movement also promoted the idea of art for art's sake, that is, the idea that artists should create art for the pleasure of creating art and not for the purpose of conveying a political or social message. Of course, this is a political position in itself, one promoted by the economic elite in Latin America and later on viewed as an option for indifference in relation to the local situation of political and social turmoil that Latin American nations were experiencing at the time. As a result, this movement also avoided the exploration of local reality, context and politics. On the contrary, in terms of its contents, its art was alienating.

Furthermore, *Modernismo* was a literary movement of cosmopolitan dimensions that presented non-Western subjects and cultures as exotic elements and even possessions of the economic elite affiliated to Eurocentric cultural production. As a result, *Modernismo* was quite elitist in terms of its content. However, in terms of its formal elements, its use of the language, its experimentation with the musicality of poetry and its use of color, it was a revolutionary movement. These poets experimented with the mood that poetry transmitted through its musicality, the impact that the extension of each verse had on the poetry and the way in which the use of color transmitted concepts. Yet at the same time they experimented with poetic structure in ways that liberated literary creation from the rigid poetic form that had been part of poetic production up until then. In other words, musicality and the use of language in *Modernismo* generated a revolution for Latin American literature and impacted literary production in Europe as well.

However, *Modernismo* was also a movement that underwent several transformations, as we can view through the samples of Rubén Darío's poetry included in this chapter. "About Winter" ("*De invierno*") is an example of a poem from the early period of *Modernismo.* "To Roosevelt" ("*A Roosevelt*") is a poem that shows a transformation in Darío's views on literature because once the intervention of the United States in his native Nicaragua became a real

threat, he no longer wanted to avoid relating his work to the local political situation. "Return" ("*Retorno*") shows a later moment in Darío's life when, upon his return to Leon, Nicaragua, he compares his homeland to Rome or Paris in an effort to place them at the center of his cultural map.

Selected Writings

Rubén Darío

A Roosevelt

¡Es con voz de la Biblia, o verso de Walt Whitman,
que habría que llegar hasta ti, Cazador!
Primitivo y moderno, sencillo y complicado,
con un algo de Washington y cuatro de Nemrod!

Eres los Estados Unidos,
eres el futuro invasor
de la América ingenua que tiene sangre indígena,
que aún reza a Jesucristo y aún habla en español.

Eres soberbio y fuerte ejemplar de tu raza;
eres culto, eres hábil; te opones a Tolstoy.
Y domando caballos, o asesinando tigres,
eres un Alejandro-Nabucodonosor.
(Eres un profesor de energía,
como dicen los locos de hoy.)

Crees que la vida es incendio,
que el progreso es erupción;
en donde pones la bala
el porvenir pones.
No.

Los Estados Unidos son potentes y grandes.
Cuando ellos se estremecen hay un hondo temblor
que pasa por las vértebras enormes de los Andes.
Si clamáis, se oye como el rugir del león.

Ya Hugo a Grant le dijo: "Las estrellas son vuestras".
(Apenas brilla, alzándose, el argentino sol
y la estrella chilena se levanta . . .). Sois ricos.

To Roosevelt

The voice of the Bible, or a stanza by Walt Whitman—
isn't that what it would take to reach your ears, Great Hunter?
You're primitive and modern, simple and complicated,
made of one part Washington and perhaps four parts Nimrod!

You yourself are the United States.
You will be a future invader
of naïve America, the one with Indian blood,
that still prays to Jesus Christ and still speaks in the Spanish tongue.

You're arrogant and you're strong, exemplary of your race;
you're cultivated, you're skilled, you stand opposed to Tolstoy.
You're a tamer of horses, you're a killer of tigers,
you're like some Alexander mixed with Nebuchadnezzar.
(You must be the Energy Professor
as the crazies today might put it)

You think that life is one big fire,
that progress is just eruption,
that wherever you put bullets,
you put the future, too.
No.

The U.S. is a country that is powerful and strong.
When the giant yawns and stretches, the earth feels a tremor
rippling through the enormous vertebrae of the Andes.
If you shout, the sound you make is a lion's roar.
Hugo once said this to Grant: "You possess the stars."
(The Argentine sun at dawn gives off hardly any light;
and the Chilean star is rising higher . . .). You're so rich.

- U.S. invason on Panama
- compare them to Washington, Imperialist, Expansionist

Retorno (Fragmento)

A través de las páginas fatales de la historia,
nuestra tierra está hecha de vigor y de gloria,
nuestra tierra está hecha para la Humanidad.

Pueblo vibrante, fuerte, apasionado, altivo;
pueblo que tiene la conciencia de ser vivo,
y que, reuniendo sus energías en haz
portentoso, a la Patria vigoroso demuestra
que puede bravamente presentar en su diestra
el acero de guerra o el olivo de paz.

Si pequeña es la Patria, uno grande la sueña.
Mis ilusiones, y mis deseos, y mis
esperanzas, me dicen que no hay patria pequeña.
Y León es hoy a mí como Roma o París.

[1907]

Return (Fragment)

. . . on every fatal page of its history,
our land has been forged from passion and glory,
our land has been created for Humanity.

Its people are vibrant, passionate, proud, honest—
a people aware of what it means to exist,
who cut down and gather their energies in sheaves
of promise, and demonstrate well for their country
how they're able to raise their right hands and bravely
hold the steel of war or the olive branch of peace.

If one's country is small, it grows bigger in dreams.
My illusions, desires, my hopes of home
convince me no country is as small as it seems.
Today, for me, Leon is my Paris, my Rome.

De Invierno

En invernales horas, mirad a Carolina.
Medio apelotonada, descansa en el sillón,
envuelta con su abrigo de marta cibelina
y no lejos del fuego que brilla en el salón.

El fino angora blanco junto a ella se reclina,
rozando con su hocico la falda de Aleçón,
no lejos de las jarras de porcelana china
que medio oculta un biombo de seda del Japón.

Con sus sutiles filtros la invade un dulce sueño:
entro, sin hacer ruido: dejo mi abrigo gris;
voy a besar su rostro, rosado y halagüeño

como una rosa roja que fuera flor de lis.
Abre los ojos; mírame con su mirar risueño,
y en tanto cae la nieve del cielo de París.

[1889]

About Winter

Here's Carolina on a winter's day,s
languorous, slumped in a comfortable chair,
wrapped in a coat of fur like Cybele
next to the fireplace that shines over there.

The white Angora cat found the right place—
the snug Alençon she wears inside—
not far from the Chinese porcelain vase
that her folding Japanese silk screens hide.

A sweet dream occupies her with its spell:
I come in, take off my gray coat, softly
kiss the alluring face I know so well

like a rose that might be a fleur-de-lis.
She stirs, looks at me with her sunny eyes,
and, meanwhile, snow falls from Parisian skies.

Augusto Monterroso, Guatemalan author, was born in Honduras and lived in Mexico since the 1950s until his death in 2003. He obtained the Mexican Xavier Villaurrutia Prize in 1975 and the Premio Literario Juan Rulfo in 1996, as well as the Guatemalan National Prize in Literature in 1997. His work shows serious criticism of Eurocentric views.

Monterroso was a master of minimalism, as we can see from this piece, in which we are able to find his critical stance on the arrogant views of the Spanish colonizers and their ignorance in relation to the knowledge and scientific advances of Indigenous people in the Americas. In this case, the life of fictional character Brother Bartolomé Arrazola depends on his ability to recognize the knowledge of Indigenous people around him and to respect them and their power in the same way that he respects and fears the power of nature and the rainforest that traps him.

The Eclipse

AUGUSTO MONTERROSO

When Brother Bartolomé Arrazola felt that he was lost, he accepted the fact that now nothing could save him. The powerful jungle of Guatemala, implacable and final, had overwhelmed him. In the face of his topographical ignorance he sat down calmly to wait for death. He wanted to die there, without hope, alone, his thoughts fixed on distant Spain, particularly on the Convent of Los Abrojos, where Charles V had once condescended to come down from his eminence to tell him that he trusted in the religious zeal of his work of redemption.

When he awoke he found himself surrounded by a group of Indians with impassive faces who were preparing to sacrifice him before an altar, an altar that seemed to Bartolomé the bed on which he would finally rest from his fears, from his destiny, from himself.

Three years in the country had given him a passing knowledge of the native languages. He tried something. He spoke a few words that were understood.

Then there blossomed in him an idea which he considered worthy of his talent and his broad education and his profound knowledge of Aristotle. He remembered that a total eclipse of the sun was to take place that day. And he decided, in the deepest part of his being, to use that knowledge to deceive his oppressors and save his life.

"If you kill me," he said, "I can make the sun darken on high."

The Indians stared at him and Bartolomé caught the disbelief in their eyes. He saw them consult with one another and he waited confidently, not without a certain contempt.

Two hours later the heart of Brother Bartolomé Arrazola spurted out its passionate blood on the sacrificing stone (brilliant in the opaque light of the eclipsed sun) while one of the Indians recited tonelessly, slowly, one by one, the infinite list of dates when solar and lunar eclipses would take place, which the astronomers of the Mayan community had predicted and registered in their codices without the estimable help of Aristotle.

Salvadoran author Roque Dalton has been transformed into a legend, a revolutionary hero. However, he was often criticized for questioning the institutionalization of the revolutionary process and the vertical hierarchy of power within the revolutionary organizations in El Salvador. In part as a result of this and in part as a result of an internal power struggle, members of his own revolutionary group, Ejército Revolucionario del Pueblo (ERP) in El Salvador, murdered Dalton in 1975.

During his life, and also after his death, Roque Dalton's work has often been read in partial ways as a "revolutionary" corpus of poems based on the revolutionary principles that it promoted, while its avant-garde artistic dimension was often rejected or overlooked. Two of the most important aspects of his work have been pushed to the background by the emphasis placed on this devotion to the revolution and his tragic death: his artistic commitment with his literary production and his critical vision of the revolutionary project. Of course, these dimensions often clashed with a revolution that had limited interest in an artistic production that it did not always understand. For this chapter, we have selected three of his poems. The poem "Terrible Thing" explores what the poetic voice considers unavoidable reasons for the armed struggle. In his poem "In Case of Doubt," the poetic voice speaks of the enormous distance that separates the idea of the revolution and revolutionary practice. The poem "Saudade" constructs the poetic subject as a revolutionary outsider while he emphasizes the seriousness of his revolutionary commitment.

In sum, through his literary work, Dalton questions the aesthetics of the revolution and its lack of attention to art, humor, the experience of the living as opposed to the dead and the future that was ahead, but he poses these questions from within the revolution, with an unquestioned commitment to the armed struggle.

Selected Poems

ROQUE DALTON

Terrible Thing

My tears, even my tears
have hardened.

I who believed in everything.
In everyone.

Dalton, Roque. "Terrible Thing," from *Small Hours of the Night: Selected Poems of Roque Dalton*, Ed. Hardie St. Martin. Trans. Jonathon Cohen, et al. Willimantic: Curbstone Press, 1996. Published by Curbstone Press.

I who asked only for a little tenderness
which costs nothing
but heart.

It's late now
and tenderness is no longer enough.

I've had a taste of gunpowder.
[JG]

In Case of Doubt

Karl Marx
awe-struck before a butterfly.

Is that
some kind of confession?

The Secretary General of the Central Committee
sticks his thumb up his nose.

Is this,
on the other hand,
chock-full of human beauty?

This nice-looking kid
(recently kicked out of our ranks, but
still nice-looking)
gets a bullet in the eye
and vultures the world over
ask permission to enter the city.

Oh butterflies to strike one dumb!
Ah the offices of the Revolution!

As for me I'll get me a gun.
[RN]

Saudade

Things life has given me
rain-proof horses
often laughing
at my frequent colds

Also a way of being a communist
that the day it becomes the fashion
either one of two things—
but I'd better bite my tongue

Also a heart that goes a little too far.

And a girl who no doubt
must have given it a second thought

On the other hand life took all my poems
written on a kite almost like a meteor
and it also carried off my old clown's outfit
my dumb-friend smell
my smile that makes people feel like crying
and even a little hungry

So
you'd all better get out of my way
[HSM]

Dalton, Roque. "Saudade," from *Small Hours of the Night: Selected Poems of Roque Dalton*, Ed. Hardie St. Martin. Trans. Jonathon Cohen, et al. Willimantic: Curbstone Press, 1996.

This text is a chapter from the autobiographical memoir *The Country Under My Skin* by Nicaraguan author Gioconda Belli. In this section she tells the story about how she found poetry, the revolution, and eventually, love, in the early 1970s in Nicaragua.

Of How Poetry and Revolution Surged into My Life

GIOCONDA BELLI
MANGUA, 1970–1971

I don't remember what came first—poetry or conspiracy. All my memories from that period are luminous, close-up images. Poetry was the result of that exuberant, life-giving spirit. Once I could assert my power and strength as a woman I felt able to shake the impotence our dictatorship made me feel, with all the misery it had sown. I could no longer believe that change was impossible. I had reached a boiling point, and my body celebrated this wonderful affirmation. The simple act of breathing was a thrill. I drank the world in, and I was possessed by such a feeling of plenitude that I wondered how my skin could contain me. Any day now, happiness, like an ectoplasm, was going to spill out of my pores, and I would float off, naked, dancing through the streets of Managua.

One day I walked into the Poet's office, and saw him with a lanky, wiry young man with a face like Don Quixote. He had teeny eyes hidden behind giant eyeglasses, and a long, thin mustache.

"Camilo Ortega," the Poet said to me. "Sit. Camilo just told me that they almost took him away yesterday."

"So," Camilo said, continuing his story as I sat down. "They were about to throw me in the back of their jeep, so I shouted as loud as I could. 'I'm Camilo Ortega and they're taking me away!' You know—the worst thing is for them to get you without anyone else knowing about it. So I yelled and yelled. People came out of their houses. The soldiers got nervous. They hadn't counted on my screaming like that. One of them walked over to me, kicked me from behind and then pushed me around—not to force me into the jeep, just to kick me out of the way and get rid of his urge to beat me up. Then they got in the jeep and drove off."

"And your brother? How is he?"

"It's hopeless. They're not letting him go. In December we'll stage a protest. We'll do graffiti, take over a church, the usual. 'Christmas without political prisoners.'"

"Daniel is Camilo's brother. He's one of the Sandinistas in jail," the Poet explained to me.

I wondered if Camilo was a Sandinista too. He seemed different from the artists and dilettantes I knew. He was quiet but intense, as if he were concentrating hard on something, and he had an air of responsibility that made him seem far older than his years. He spoke softly, almost in a whisper. But what I noticed right away was the intangible power he held over the Poet, who now seemed placated and serious—something highly unusual for him. He gave Camilo a copy of *Praxis*, the magazine he edited, which served as a forum for the group of artists, writers, and painters who worked together under the same name. We discussed the magazine: the essay by Ricardo Morales Avilés about the responsibility of the intellectual, the recently debuted Praxis gallery, which held recitals and art exhibitions. We talked about the widespread anger at the recent price increases—transportation, milk, and bread had all just gone up. Before he left Camilo asked us if we had seen the movie *Woodstock*. The music was great, he said. Joe Cocker did a fantastic rendition of the Beatles song "With a Little Help from My Friends." And then there was Jimi Hendrix and his guitar. We had to see it.

Camilo came back to the office a few more times. We would go across the street to a juice stand where you could look out toward the Gran Hotel, the tropical hotel par excellence in those days, with a green awning and an entrance hall filled with palm trees and birdcages with parrots and macaws. The sidewalks, littered with potholes and loose bricks, bristled with activity—throngs of people bustling about, traffic jams in the streets, taxis honking like mad, as well as a few horse-driven carriages. Modernization had hit Managua like a steamroller, transforming the city into a crazy hybrid of tradition and progress.

Camilo asked me to join the Sandinistas. By then, I was pretty familiar with all the signs and symbols of the underground movement. In the artsy circles, the Sandinistas were regarded with admiration and respect. I had now read all the books I needed to convince me that armed struggle and revolution were Nicaragua's only chance. George Politzer's book, *The Fundamental Principles of Philosophy*, turned me into a philosophical materialist; Frantz Fanon, in *The Wretched of the Earth*, gave me a crash course in colonialism, neocolonialism, and the realities of the Third World. Eduardo Galeano, in *Open Veins of Latin America*, revealed to me the sad, bloody history of my part of the world, and taught me about Big Stick politics, the Alliance for Progress, and the loathsome consequences of the Monroe Doctrine, which declared that "America was for the Americans"—meaning that the American continent had to be considered the exclusive backyard of the United States. I had also read Marcuse, Chomsky, Ernst Fisher, and Che. Socialism had won me over. But joining the Sandinistas was a risky proposition. It meant putting my life in the line of fire. I had my doubts too: the theory known as the "guerrilla focus" had only worked in Cuba. And what kind of system were they proposing, exactly? The Soviet model, from my point of view, placed far too many restrictions on personal freedoms. And how would we foment a revolution without a proletariat? Camilo, who didn't have a car, would often ask me to drop him off at the university on my way home. During the ride, he'd lecture me on subjects ranging from the failed military tactics of the guerrilla focus, to the ideology sponsored by Sandinismo. The revolution would not be communist, he'd say, but

Sandinista, which meant that it would incorporate various theories, including Marxism, but adapting them to our specific reality. He had an answer for everything, and boundless reserves of patience to respond to my many doubts. When he asked me whether I was ready to join the Sandinistas, to give him a straight yes or no answer, I confessed that fear prevented me from committing myself.

"All of us are afraid. That's normal."

"But I have a daughter . . ."

He didn't ask me to go underground. I could do little things. Nothing risky, but enough to make my own small contribution.

"Your daughter is precisely the reason you *should* do it," he said. "You should do it for her, so that she won't have to do the job you are not willing to do."

He was right. I couldn't choose to be a coward.

"All right," I said quickly, without flinching, thinking of the way one slips under a cold shower.

"Don't tell anyone," he said. "Not a word. Not even to the Poet. This has to be between you and me. It's a question of compartmentalizing, of minimizing the risks."

It was night by the time we reached the university, a series of simple, prefab structures connected by hallways and staircases, protected from the elements by corrugated tin roofs. I dropped him off at the parking lot, and watched him disappear into the corridors. My stomach churned as I drove toward my house. I passed through slums, I saw the dilapidated buses slow down to pick up the passengers who piled in, hanging off the doors even as the bus heaved onward. Somewhere within my anguish, a sudden sense of relief—maybe it was joy—washed over me. It was as if the guilt of privilege had suddenly been lifted from my shoulders. I was no longer another transient observer, contemplating the misery from the comfort of my car. I was now one of the people fighting it. I cared about how the people of Managua were suffering, day in and day out, and I would prove it by doing something to effect a change. And that made me feel less alone, for a reassuring voice inside me lifted my spirits and calmed my fears. I was so relieved to leave behind that paternalistic Christian-style charity that always brought me back to the convent school nuns who, each Christmas, asked us to bring gifts for the girls of lesser means who attended our school in a separate annex next door. According to the rules, all gifts had to be the same: a piece of fabric, candy, and a toy. When it was time to give them out, the nuns would line us up in pairs, one rich girl and one poor girl. One by one, in front of the Mother Superior, the gifts would be handed over. As I waited my turn in line, the heavy, shapeless present, wrapped by my mother in simple, plain paper, felt like such an obvious welfare package. I always felt so terrible for the other girl—for her, the ceremony must have seemed like a well-intentioned form of humiliation. Troubled by the role I was forced to play, I could barely look at her as I handed over the gift. Then, we would kiss each other on the cheek and go to the end of our respective lines. That was the only time of year we ever laid eyes on each other, and that was what charity meant to me.

But this was different. I was on the other side now.

At home, everything was the same. Caught up in his work and his depression, my husband barely noticed me. We did some things together, but of our daily life the things I remember most are his apathy, his lethargic gestures, and the television screen, like the glow of a life he could look at but never really touch or feel. I fulfilled my role as wife and mother, and played with Maryam in the garden amid the abundant foliage. Thoughts and verses would spring up in my mind like kernels of popcorn frying in the hot oil of my secret life. It occurred to me that the words were banging down my door, begging to be written down, vet: I resisted committing them to paper. Somehow I felt as if the act of writing would ruin the charm and the emotion of the images I conjured up in my head. I was better off staying where I was, standing motionless by my daughter's swing, watching her romp around while words and phrases rolled before my eyes as if written on banners floating in the sky.

I described all this to the Poet.

"Write," he said. "Write about what you feel. You have a responsibility—a historic one." His eyes were intense, serious.

The next day I arrived at the office with six poems. Shyly, I placed them on his desk.

"I wrote them last night," I said. "They just came out, like rabbits."

He took the sheaf of papers. He lit a cigarette. He sat back in his chair. He propped his feet up on his desk. The Poet had a potbelly from all the rum and beer he loved to drink. He wore long-sleeved shirts. As he read the poems, he exhaled long curls of cigarette smoke.

"Very good," he said, as he went from one page to the next. His voice, deep and clear, sounded surprised. Years later he would confess how astonished he had been by what I, a relative novice, had written—he had been half joking when he made that "historical responsibility" comment. He finished reading, stood up, and walked around the desk to sit down next to me. I can't remember his exact words, but something in his voice told me that he meant what he said. That was when Carlitos Alemán Ocampo arrived. The Poet gave him my poems to read, and Carlos seconded his opinion.

"They need a Little work," said the Poet. "Once you get to be like us"—he allowed himself a devilish grin at that—"all your writing will be grand, but in the beginning, you have to polish, edit. A poem should be like a tamale, closed up and tightly bound. Nothing extraneous, but nothing missing either. Take a look at this one, for example. Study it. Think about the words it doesn't need."

"I'm sure you can get Pablo to publish them," Carlitos said. "He'll love them."

I worked hard as I weighed each word, removing myself so that I could look at the poem objectively, without me in the middle. It was so hard. That lovely metaphor, for example, was unnecessary. I marked it. I was never able to be a very merciless surgeon, because I was so infatuated with words. Only with time has it become easier.

We went in to see Pablo Antonio, Cuadra, the editor of *La Prensa's* literary supplement. He had a proud bearing, like a Nahuatl prince. His dark skin was the color of cinnamon and his thicket of hair, pure white. He was a tall man, with an elongated body that could have walked right out of an El Greco painting. I felt as if I were in the presence of a living monument, for this was Nicaragua's most renowned poet. His office was packed with books, folders, papers. Just outside sat his chubby, longhaired, moon-faced secretary who pecked away frantically at her typewriter. Rosario Murillo. I would get to know her later on.

"I'd like to publish these poems. With a portrait of you next to them," said Pablo Antonio. "When would you be free for a sitting?"

Not long after, Róger Pérez de la Rocha arrived at my house to paint my portrait, which he did in black printer's ink. We ended up having a lot of fun. Even my husband laughed, watching us like someone studying exotic animals in an encyclopedia. Róger was another character from Managua's bohemian scene—a jovial young artist like all of us. He cursed nonstop and hummed ranchera music as he worked. He was a barrio kid, proudly so, but extremely well read, able to recite from memory entire poems by Carlos Martínez Rivas.

Barely fifteen days after I had written my first poems, *La Prensa Literaria* published them, devoting almost an entire page to me. "A new voice in Nicaraguan poetry," read the headline next to the portrait Róger had painted. I looked dark and mysterious.

"Your poor husband," one of my aunts commented the day after the poems appeared. "How could you write—and publish—those poems? What on earth would make you write about menstruation? How awful. How embarrassing."

"Embarrassing?" I retorted. "Why should I be embarrassed?"

My aunt looked at me, horrified. And with an *ay! bijita!,* she got up and left.

The publication of my poems was nothing less than a scandal which rocked the upper echelons of Managuan society.

"Vaginal poetry," declared the matrons. "Shameless pornography."

"It's a good thing you published them under your maiden name," remarked my mother-in-law. Men leered at me with hungry, knowing looks.

"You must be quite a passionate woman," they would say with glazed eyes.

It was 1970. I wasn't saying anything that had not been said before by men, but I was a woman. It was not done. Women were objects, not subjects of their own sex drive. I wrote joyfully about my body, my passion, my pleasure. The poems were not explicit—they weren't even remotely pornographic. They were simply a female celebration of her senses, the wonder of her body. But they created an uproar.

My husband then announced to me that he didn't want me publishing any more poems unless he read and edited them first. Absolutely not, I told him. Over my dead body. I would give up writing first. Fortunately the High Priests of Nicaraguan literature rallied to my defense. The great poets José Coronel, Pablo Antonio Cuadra, and Carlos Martínez Rivas championed my cause. And in Nicaragua, poets are venerated, celebrated figures. Our national hero, the most acclaimed Nicaraguan, is Rubén Darío, a poet who is considered the Father of Modernism in the Spanish language. To be known as a poet in my country is to enjoy one of the highest, most cherished status symbols in society My husband and family, finally, were forced to surrender to the blessings of prestige.

The controversy didn't deter me—it inspired me. To upset the most conservative circles of Nicaraguan society made me realize there were more ways than one to subvert the establishment.

The Poet, meanwhile, was busy building fabulous castles in the air, fantasies in which he and I would live happily ever after, writing poems to each other on our naked bodies until the end of time. My love for him, though, was more like that of a playmate, a partner in crime. The Poet would have been a nightmare as a husband. I could never picture him sharing responsibilities—he would have dumped them all on me as he went on proclaiming his "wild exuberance."

It wasn't long before I realized that when you break certain societal rules there is always a price to pay. The rumors grew louder and louder, until they eventually reached my father's ears. Blissfully ignorant in the happy little bubble we had created for ourselves, the Poet and I acted as though we were invisible. Instead of treating one another as furtive lovers, we walked through the city streets smelling of sex, our hair tousled and our eves aflame. Anyone could see that we were euphoric, possessed by both the passion and defiance we liked to think only a chosen few ever knew. Unfettered in our arrogant sense of freedom, we made love on mattresses surrounded by canvases and smelling of turpentine in the tiny, ramshackle studios of our artist friends or in borrowed apartments. We even made love on top of our desks at work, giggling as papers went flying in every direction, gasping for breath to muffle the sounds of our lovemaking as typewriters hummed and coworkers bustled about outside our office door. Our cheeky disregard for discretion made us the hot topic of local gossip. Even my absent, distracted husband began to sit up and take notice. Sooner or later someone was going to say something to him. There was no way on earth I could escape the obvious: I had to make a decision: stay with the Poet—and assume the corresponding risks—or return to the familiarity of my marriage. No matter what I chose, I knew that nothing would ever be the same. I had grown wings. I felt ready to take flight. But the Poet was like a hurricane, too turbulent for me to handle, and I was terrified at the prospect of making the wrong decision and dragging my daughter with me. When I saw how my father was suffering, I made up my mind.

I'll never forget the look on the Poet's face on the other side of the desk when I told him. I feel as though I can still see the landscape behind the window, hear the rumble of the air conditioner. We couldn't go on like this, I said. I couldn't go with him. He had figured as much, he said. He knew it would have been too hard on me, having to confront my entire family about it. The conversation was sad, but not tragic—I think we both understood that we had pushed things as far as they could go. At least we still had our friendship, our mutual affection. More than anything I felt relieved—I was worn out by the tension of the weeks that had led up to this, and all the subterfuge that went with it. And while the Poet may have sparked the revolution that now raged inside me, I knew that what felt went far beyond him or any partner I would ever have.

"I would have made you happy," he said, wrapping his hands around mine.

"You *did* make me happy," I replied.

He smiled. He was never one for melodrama. He got what he could out of life but he also knew when to give in.

Not long afterward, I changed jobs, sometime in the middle of 1972, I think. I was really making an effort to extricate myself from that love affair, like a snake shedding a layer of skin. I returned to the regular, married life that I had been sleepwalking through during my affair. It was a shock to see my husband again as the man who shared my life, my bed, the morning bathroom rituals, when for many months I had dismissed him from my life.

The payoff was slim: sure, I didn't have to worry about accusations—"I know you have a lover"—and I suppose I felt honorable again. In spite of myself, I was mortified by the malicious smiles of my mother's friends, as they elbowed one another whenever I walked by, and the men who would cluster around me murmuring all sorts of double entendres as if I were wearing some kind of sign inviting them to try their luck with me. Much later on I would stop caring about what they said, and even relish disturbing their hypocritical sense of decency. But I hadn't quite reached that point yet. At the time, my fear of ostracism, of being left out in the cold, won over the need I felt to get away, to leave that environment altogether.

Camilo Ortega was the person who helped me realize it was important to keep up the pretense of my bourgeois life. The more time I spent undercover, without raising any suspicion, the more useful I could be to the Sandinista movement. By maintaining a facade of innocence and continuing to do my rounds in the traditional social circles, I could keep my finger on the pulse of the bourgeoisie, and report their feelings and thoughts regarding the dictatorship. Being an upper-class woman was an ideal alibi for my subversive endeavors. I knew that I had to keep my position in that world in order to eventually blow it up from the inside.

Not long afterward, Camilo told me he was going away for a long while. Someone else would call me, he said, and through that person we would resume contact. We said goodbye on a street corner.

That was the last time I saw him.

Rodrigo Rey Rosa was born in Guatemala. His work was first published in an English translation by the renowned American author Paul Bowles by City Lights in San Francisco. Nowadays, Rey Rosa is one of the most widely distributed, read and recognized Central American authors. His works have been published in the Spanish original, both in Spain and in Central America, as well as in English, French and German, among others.

"Dust on Her Tongue" is an example of Rey Rosa's early works. The main character is a woman who might or might not be in a hotel, who might or might not be trapped, and who might or might not be hurt. As with many of his works, the reader is immersed in a story of violence, fear, paranoia and isolation that Central American readers might share and recognize as some of their own daily experiences. However, in the end, Rey Rosa's work holds much space for interpretation, and, as a result, the reader is not always presented with all the answers.

Dust on Her Tongue

RODRIGO REY ROSA

Another one, she said to herself smiling. She was alone in what she took to be a sordid hotel room. The brick wall did not reach the ceiling, and a gray light came from the next room. She sat up in the sagging bed in which she was unable to sleep. The green pill which she put into her mouth had a bitter flavor, and she made a face as she swallowed it. She had no idea of where she was or of how she had got there. She was lost. But surely this was a hotel. A rooster crowed, and there was the diminishing sound of an automobiles engine in the distance. The bed seemed to move beneath her. Another pill.

In the morning she felt empty, without memory, and with an unpleasant sensation of having consumed too much alcohol. Her feet stuck out at the foot of the bed and her back ached. My god, my god, my god, she murmured, her voice low, ironic and desperate. The floor was of concrete but it was not cold.

She pushed the door, which did not open entirely, and looked at the low gray sky. She was in the patio of a hotel she did not remember having entered. The doors to the rooms bore no numbers. She crossed the courtyard and went out into the street.

She remembered this street, paved with cobblestones. She had seen it the day before, but yesterday was very remote. It seemed to her she remembered the white walls, the tiled roofs. Had there been people in the street? It was a quiet town—too quiet. The silence was not natural, and she knew it boded no good. She did not recall the name of the town.

Why did she see nobody? What day of the week was it? She counted on her fingers. Monday? Sunday? Monday, probably. For a town to be this silent on a Sunday would have upset her too much. The place was dead. She remembered that in the night a rooster had crowed, and that was some consolation, at least. Now she could hear the sound of her own footsteps on the stones. She came to the main square. At the end of the street she saw the side of a church. Something warned her not to go any nearer. She stood still and looked up and down the street. Then she turned and ran back leaving the plaza behind. A cry had come feebly from somewhere. The cry of a child? It had issued from inside the church, or had she imagined it? She ceased running, but continued to walk quickly, and stopped only when she had got inside the hotel. She shut the door, then reopened it to thrust her head out. The street was deserted.

She wanted to ask someone the name of this town. Where was the manager of the hotel?

Ave Maria, she said softly, not daring to call out. She had one hand on her bosom, and walked step by step across the vestibule, looking from side to side.

She remembered a bus filled with people. That was how she had come here. She stopped moving when she got to the gallery. Silence. This was a fourth-class establishment. Why had she spent the night here? She went across the patio to her room and sat down on the bed. She had no watch. Where was the sun? She looked at her hands. What had she done the night before?

A ditty, the words of a song. Yes. A room full of people, pine needles on the floor. A dance? Something she had wanted to forget. A man, the one who had given her the pills. If must be because of him that she was here. She studied the lines in her hand, as though something had been written there. She recalled a dirt road and a river that ran between mountains. It had been getting dark. She remembered that the little bus had jolted and made sudden turnings. But she could not remember getting into it, or what was supposed to be its destination. She did not know whether she had gone towards the north or the south. The memory of the road was rapidly growing dim; she did not want it to disappear, for fear of not finding it again.

She went out into the patio. With this dark sky the sun was invisible, and on the stone floor no object cast a shadow. It seemed as though all the rooms were empty. She heard footsteps from the direction of the street. Frightened, she ran into her room. As she shut the door it occurred to her that whatever was happening out there was something she preferred not to know about. Then she had a flash of recall which could have been the memory of a dream. With a stone in her hand, a heavy stone shaped like an egg, she had pounded the back of a man's head. She had given no warning. The man was her husband.

The sounds coming from the vestibule were men's voices, one of them highpitched and shrill. They came across the gallery. There was knocking on the door of the adjoining room on the right. A moment later there came three sharp raps on her own door. She held her breath. The door opened.

Under the bed the air was foul. The sheet hung down from the edge of the bed to the floor, so that she could not see the feet of the person who had come in. She had left the bottle of pills on the bed, and she felt that the man had leaned over and picked it up. She heard him turn on his heels, and the door was shut. Now he knocked on the door of the room on the left.

She looked at the rolls of dust and the ancient spiderwebs which trembled with her breathing. She could not stay under there any longer. As the sound of the feet died away, she felt her fear becoming a sensation of discomfort and shame. Slowly she crawled out from under the bed. She wanted to find the reception clerk and pay her bill. She would go to the main square and get something to eat. Then she would find out when the next bus left for the city. She tried to open the door, but it would not move. She pushed against it with her shoulder; she was locked in.

She did not want to kick the door or call out. She stood on the bed and looked over the top of the dividing wall: the space was too narrow for her body. She sat down. She was hungry and her mouth tasted like paper. She stared fixedly at the floor because she had remembered that before taking the bus she and her husband had been traveling in a plane. The size of the metal wing beneath her window had struck her as absurd. She felt that she had come so far on this trip that she would find it impossible to go back. She stood up and tried the door once more, pushing it with all her strength and kicking it. It was stronger than it looked. She shouted, and had the terrifying conviction that the shout remained in the room. She cried out again.

It was ridiculous! She was sure that it would be useless to complain to the proprietor. She hammered on the door with her fists. Someone had to come.

Overcome by fatigue, she suddenly stretched out on the bed. The wall was damp and smelled musty. Why was she so certain that she was in a hotel? The ceiling was too low. She shut her eyes, wishing that she had someone to massage her neck, which ached. She folded her hands over her abdomen and began to rub her stomach, in order to feel less hungry. She must be calm. It was not easy to lie still, feeling nervous. She had clear memories, but they came from so long ago that she was unable to situate them in time. How old had she been the first time she saw her own face? She recalled the mirror's fancy frame.

Her mother had led her to the room which a few years later was to be hers. The curtains were drawn. Her dead grandmother seemed to be asleep in the bed. Her mother had carried her to the bed, and she had stretched out her hand and touched the nose, already cold. No, said her mother. Give her a kiss. She wondered whether dead people could hear. Now she ceased remembering, and listened for a sound. The light had grown weaker. The frozen face of her grandmother was telling her: You have died, too. You are dead.

Since she had become aware that the door was locked from the outside, since she had screamed and felt that her voice could not be heard, that idea had begun to work in her brain. Now it flashed through her and left her paralyzed. She tried to raise her hand, was unable to, and this gave her a feeling of cold in her breast. The cold descended through her legs to her feet, and returned, as if it were something in her blood. Were her eyes open or shut? She blinked. Now there was no light.

How long had she been there? She could not believe it had been one day. The bed began to rock, and she sprang out of it. Beside herself, she rolled on the floor. She had heard a sound which had now become a roar. The floor also was rocking. She had hit her head. The legs of the bed squeaked.

I have to be dreaming, she told herself. I'm dead and I'm continuing to dream. The idea intrigued her. She imagined that somehow she would be able to follow, step by step, the process of her own decomposition. The flesh would turn into worms; the body would not feel, yet would be conscious. She would be composed of worms. It was the most humble form of transmigration imaginable, but it that moment it was enough. There was a sudden terrible racket. She jumped and fell backwards. She could not possibly be dead, she thought. Bits of earth fell from the ceiling. Were they burying her? I'm alive! she cried. And she repeated under her breath: I'm alive. There was dust on her tongue. She wanted to spit.

A few moments of calm. She did not want to open her eyes, but neither did she want to keep them shut. She began to feel sleepy, knowing that she should not fall asleep. It seemed to her that if she slept she would forget who she was, and that when she awoke she would have been changed into someone else: the tutelary goddess of a colony of worms. Madness. Finally she was overcome by sleep.

She came to. Two men were dragging her across the patio in a not too uncomfortable posture. She realized that she was not afraid of them. The warmth of their arms was reassuring: she was cold.

They went out into the street. The sky was red. She felt that she did not need the two men in order to walk, but she allowed them to go on supporting her. From time to time the earth trembled and there was that muffled roar that she had heard earlier. They went through a low door into a circular enclosure. The cloth walls moved in the wind. The men were young. One of them set to rubbing her arms and legs. Then he made her open her mouth so he could look inside.

Does your head ache?

Where am I? she said. What happened?

You may have a fractured skull, señora, although I don't think so. Try to be calm. I'll do what I can.

But I don't remember anything, she protested. Don't you understand?

Yes, I understand, he said. You'll remember.

From the center of the ceiling hung a wire basket. There, among other objects which she recognized as hers, she saw the bottle of pills: it was the proof of an infraction she did not remember having committed. The owner of the hotel arrived to present her bill.

In the afternoon they told her that she would leave for the city, where her husband expected her. A rented car arrived to pick her up. They crossed the partially destroyed town. Men wearing green uniforms were beginning to clear away the rubble. The cornfields were ruined and the earth was the color of ashes. Beside the road, on a treeless hill, a kneeling Indian was burning incense. He swung the burner and the smoke dissolved in the gray air.

Claudia Hernandez is one of the youngest, darkest and more widely read Salvadoran authors. She was born in El Salvador in 1975 and began publishing her work in newspapers in the late 1990s. She is the author of five short story collections, and important anthologies in El Salvador, Nicaragua, Spain and Germany have included her work. In 2004 she received the prestigious "Juan Rulfo" award from Radio France International for the short story category and also the prestigious "Anna Seghers" award in Germany for her published works.

Her short story "Sewer Fauna" presents characters with sub-human value. This text explores the culture of a middle-class neighborhood in which domestic dogs and cats are disappearing; a family that lives in the sewer is eating them. As you will notice, the narrator of this story is affiliated to the worldviews of the middle-class neighborhood where the pets are disappearing. From there s/he defines the scaled beings that live in the sewer. In the narration, two things become evident about these beings: They are human and they have an inferior value to the narrator than the domestic animals that they devour. They are described in animal terms, as feline, scaly beings that might belong at the zoo. And yet, these beings are human, since the narrator also points out that the zoo rejects them for being human. It seems to be the case that in this society there are human beings that are worth less than domestic animals and less than the wild animals at the zoo; they are the beings that live at the margins of society, in this case, in the symbolic space of the sewer that holds underground the wastes of the world built on the surface. It is a metaphor for life in contemporary Central America.

Sewer Fauna

CLAUDIA HERNANDEZ

Three times a day you would hear the sounds of four jaws grinding animal bones. Dogs were disappearing from houses and cats were no longer seen on roofs.

It wasn't a hallucination. A naked man with scales on his skin was creeping up out of the sewer. Coming to hunt. Cats and dogs. To eat.

The scene didn't last but a moment. Then the man disappeared. The sewers swallowed him up. He wouldn't come out again until hunger howled once more.

He wasn't alone. He had come with his wife and his two children. But they never came up, they were nothing but six bright eyes, canine eyes, that peered out from the darkness below the streets. He was the one who took all the risks. He was the man. He hunted for all of them. And he was good at it. Precise. His prey never eluded him. They weren't even aware of their moment of death. He came out of the silence and put them to sleep at once, sinking his nails into their consciousness. Then they would eat them, before their flesh had cooled for lack of breathing.

Three times a day you would hear the sound of four jaws grinding animal bones. Dogs were disappearing from houses and cats were no longer seen on roofs.

Distressed, the neighbors begged the local officer to arrest the creature from the sewers who was devouring their pets. And he managed to snare him. He lay in wait behind a shadow and, when the scaly man came out in pursuit of an orange dog, the officer grabbed him and didn't let him escape no matter how much he kicked and bit. It wasn't hard. He controlled him like an animal. Then he gave him up to the neighbors so they could do with him as they saw fit. The police department—as they well knew—had no jurisdiction over this kind of case. But the man got away from them. In a flash. In a moment of distraction he slipped from their hands and went back to the sewer. They all heard the family's jubilation at his return, amplified by the echoing sewers. Then they were terrified. They felt invaded, surrounded by the plague. Astonished, the officer suggested they contact the zoo; they would be better equipped to handle the situation.

The neighbors found that to be a terrific idea. They called right away, but the supervisors refused to take in the scaly specimen. They weren't interested. They only kept animals there, not men, and certainly not men with families. No matter what they ate. No matter whether they had scales or not. It was animals they wanted. They had once taken in a man and he had been a problem; he made the animals uncomfortable, he was too demanding . . .

The neighbors had to solve this thing on their own.

They sealed off the sewers. So they couldn't get out. So the pets would stop disappearing. To get rid of the problem. To suffocate them.

It worked.

A week later, the moaning ceased, and the smell of lifeless, scaly creatures filled the neighborhood. To counteract the stench, they reopened the drains and covered the bodies with lime.

Weeks later it occurred to them that it might have been easier to convince them to go back where they had come from, or to trap them in a net and throw them into a bog, which is where they had probably come from. But it was much too late: their bones were already turning to dust.

They'd have to keep that in mind for another time.

CHAPTER THREE

HUMAN RIGHTS

Since the time of the Spanish conquest and the colonization of the region that we call Central America today, there have been numerous abuses committed against entire ethnic groups in the name of a better and civilized world. In the late nineteenth century and during most of the twentieth century this violence continued in order to justify the process of modernization of the young Central American republics. These violations to human rights in Central America have been based particularly on the profound inequalities that characterized the colonial societies in the region. The chronicles of the conquest and Bartolomé de las Casas' *Brief Destruction of the Indies* document at length the abuses towards Indigenous peoples, as well as the arguments and religious motivations that Spanish colonizers used to consider this a "just war," as they destroyed Indigenous homes, social structure, religion and cultures. William L. Sherman, in *Forced Native Labor in Sixteenth-Century Central America* documents the enslavement of the surviving Indigenous populations in the region during the colonial period. In this work, Sherman discusses at length the slave trade that took place in the area. This included the claim of the local population as slaves assigned to conquerors and the traffic of slaves from Africa once the local Indigenous population had been decimated. Sherman documents the reaction of Indigenous populations who rebelled against the abuses they were subjected to. This often resulted in increased violence against them, including the murder of small children, the chaining of slaves, burning a number of them alive, the destruction of whole villages and working Indigenous populations to death.

After the colonial period ended and the new modern nations formed, the global exports of bananas and coffee made the existence of a new system of slavery in disguise possible in the region. This system of unequal distribution of wealth and labor has continued in different shapes and forms through the current globalized service economic model of contemporary Central America. However, human rights violations continue to take place not only because of class inequalities, but also because of the imposition of traditional gendered identities, the lack of protection of children's rights and the lack of recognition of the rights of Indigenous and Afro-Caribbean peoples in the region. Furthermore, an ever growing number of immigrants take the tortuous trip to the nations north of Central America on foot under sub-human conditions and then live a marginal existence as undocumented immigrants in these nations searching for a means to survive and provide for the subsistence of their families left back home.

However, the violation of human rights during the recent civil wars in Central America by far exceeded all official reports and, in most cases, the human imagination. As a result, this chapter concentrates on the violation of human rights and the documentation of such violations in relation to this period of armed conflict, particularly in Guatemala and El Salvador. Although modern forms of violating human rights were based on the legacy of a strong patriarchal society and racist views on ethnic diversity, it was the institutionalization of violence through the imposition of military dictatorships that determined the pace of such violations during the past century. This normalization of violence in the everyday life of Central Americans took different paths but had the same objective: the perpetuation of privileges via socio-political and economic control.

Under these political conditions, the groups in power consolidated their economic advantages and created societies with profound material inequalities, but they also provoked dissent and protests. Despite their promises, those in political power did not provide access to education, health care and basic human needs, and those social deficiencies impacted traditionally excluded members of the society. Physical brutality was the most visible form of violence against those who protested the anti-democratic socio-political and economic measures by the dictatorial military regimes of Guatemala, El Salvador, Honduras and Nicaragua.

The demands and writing by human rights activists, academic research and publication and the opening of U.S. government classified archives have brought to light knowledge about the cruel methods utilized against entire communities and the level of military and civilian involvement in these violations, as well as the number of lives lost during this dark period of modern Central America. Today we can identify the violent forms most often utilized that allowed these dictatorial regimes to maintain power for almost sixty years. The military governed this period by enforcing military *coup d'états,* massacres, disappearances, torture, martial law, and suspension of civil rights. The overthrowing of the democratically elected government of Jacobo Arbenz in Guatemala in 1954, the Indigenous massacre of 1932 in El Salvador and the systematic destruction of more than 400 Indigenous villages in Guatemala in the period of 1982–1984 exemplify the repressive methods used by these dictatorial governments.

This social and political violence generated armed responses from those who were the object of governmental repression, culminating in years of conflict more commonly known as the Central American civil wars of the 1980s. After twelve years of armed struggle in El Salvador and thirty-six years of officially recognized civil war in Guatemala, the governments and the opposition carried out dialogues and negotiations under the auspices of the United Nations that aimed at ending the regional conflict through a process that culminated in the signing of peace agreements. The signing of the Peace Accords on January 16, 1992 put an end to the armed conflict in El Salvador, as did the signing of the Peace Accords on December 18, 1996 in the case of Guatemala. The publication of testimonies by people who witnessed or experienced the violent forms of solving political, social and economic problems in the Central American region during the 1980s and 1990s helped the world to understand the seriousness of such human rights violations.

One of the most important components of these peace agreements was meant to address the issue of the violations of human rights through the unveiling of the truth—a paramount task. The uncovering of the truth required the exposure of the facts, the naming of those who committed the crimes and the documentation of the testimonials by the victims. The United Nations, human rights organizations, local churches and international organizations interested in human rights established commissions that had the task of investigating and reporting on their findings while some of the victims made their testimonials available to the international community. A look at the following fragments illustrates the history of human rights violations in Central America.

Furthermore, after the end of the civil wars in Central America, human rights violations have continued with the support of neoliberal policies, as well as class based and racist views that do not protect the interests of the poor, Indigenous, and other excluded communities. The last reading, titled "The Garifuna Fight Back," explores the mechanisms of resistance of the Garifuna people in Trujillo, Honduras, in face of the continued neoliberal encroachment and marginalization.

Historic memory aims at bringing human dignity to the forefront in the struggle for social and economic justice. The publication of the *Truth Commission Report on El Salvador, From Madness to Hope: The 12-Year War in El Salvador* emphasized in its title the conviction that the postwar would arrive filled with hope, particularly based on the possibility that this report would remove from public office those responsible for the gravest violations of human rights during the recent civil war in El Salvador. However, that was not to be. As the paperback edition indicates, this report openly states the names of the military officers responsible for human rights violations and recommends their removal from the Salvadoran Army. However, less than a week after the publication of this report by the commission on Human Rights in El Salvador appointed by the United Nations, the Salvadoran Supreme Court approved an amnesty law that pardoned *a priori* all violations of human rights committed during the recently ended civil war in El Salvador. The hope that came with this report and that marked its title quickly evaporated with the same impunity that characterized these acts throughout the civil war in this country.

The current fragment of the report tells the story of the illustrative case of the Massacre of El Mozote, which took place in December 1980. The Atlacatl Battalion of the Salvadoran Army eradicated a whole village; the majority of those murdered were children, women and elders.

Illustrative Case: El Mozote

Summary of the Case

On 10 December 1981, in the village of El Mozote in the Department of Morazán, units of the Atlacatl Battalion detained, without resistance, all the men, women and children who were in the place. The following day, 11 December, after spending the night locked in their homes, they were deliberately and systematically executed in groups. First, the men were tortured and executed, then the women were executed and, lastly, the children, in the place where they had been locked up. The number of victims identified was over 200. The figure is higher if other unidentified victims are taken into account.

These events occurred in the course of an anti-guerrilla action known as "Operación Rescate" in which, in addition to the Atlacatl Battalion, units from the Third Infantry Brigade and the San Francisco Gotera Commando Training Centre took part.

"Illustrative Case: El Mozote," From *Madness to Hope: The 12-Year War in El Salvador: Report of the Commission on the Truth for El Salvador,* S/25500, 1993, 1140126. The United Nations is the author of the original material.

In the course of "Operación Rescate," massacres of civilians also occurred in the following places: 11 December, more than 20 people in La Joya canton; 12 December, some 30 people in the village of La Ranchería; the same day, by units of the Atlacatl Battalion, the inhabitants of the village of Los Toriles; and 13 December, the inhabitants of the village of Jocote Amarillo and Cerro Pando canton. More than 500 identified victims perished at El Mozote and in the other villages. Many other victims have not been identified.

We have accounts of these massacres provided by eyewitnesses and by other witnesses who later saw the bodies, which were left unburied. In the case of El Mozote, the accounts were fully corroborated by the results of the 1992 exhumation of the remains.

Despite the public complaints of a massacre and the ease with which they could have been verified, the Salvadorian authorities did not order an investigation and consistently denied that the massacre had taken place.

The Minister of Defence and the Chief of the Armed Forces Joint Staff have denied to the Commission on the Truth that they have any information that would make it possible to identify the units and officers who participated in 'Operación Rescate.' They say that there are no records for the period.

The President of the Supreme Court has interfered in a biased and political way in the judicial proceedings on the massacre instituted in 1990.

Description of the Facts

Village of El Mozote

On the afternoon of 10 December 1981, units of the Atlacatl Rapid Deployment Infantry Battalion (BIRI) arrived in the village of El Mozote, Department of Morazán, after a clash with guerrillas in the vicinity.

The village consisted of about 20 houses situated on open ground around a square. Facing onto the square was a church and behind it a small building known as "the convent," used by the priest to change into his vestments when he came to the village to celebrate mass. Not far from the village was a school, the Grupo Escolar.

When the soldiers arrived in the village they found, in addition to the residents, other peasants who were refugees from the surrounding areas. They ordered everyone out of the houses and into the square; they made them lie face down, searched them and asked them about the guerrillas. They then ordered them to lock themselves in their houses until the next day, warning that anyone coming out would be shot. The soldiers remained in the village during the night.

Early next morning, 11 December, the soldiers reassembled the entire population in the square. They separated the men from the women and children and locked everyone up in different groups in the church, the convent and various houses.

During the morning, they proceeded to interrogate, torture and execute the men in various locations. Around noon, they began taking out the women in groups, separating them from their children and machine gunning them. Finally, they killed the children.

A group of children who had been locked in the convent were machine-gunned through the windows. After exterminating the entire population, the soldiers set fire to the buildings.

The soldiers remained in El Mozote that night. The next day, they went through the village of Los Toriles, situated 2 kilometres away. Some of the inhabitants managed to escape. The others, men, women and children, were taken from their homes, lined up and machine-gunned.

The victims at El Mozote were left unburied. During the weeks that followed the bodies were seen by many people who passed by there. In Los Toriles, the survivors subsequently buried the bodies.

Background

The Atlacatl Battalion arrived at El Mozote in the course of a military action known as "Operación Rescate," which had begun two days earlier on 6 December and also involved units from the Third Brigade and the San Francisco Gotera Commando Training Centre.

The Atlacatl Battalion was a "Rapid Deployment Infantry Battalion" or "BIRI," that is, a unit specially trained for "counter-insurgency" warfare. It was the first unit of its kind in the armed forces and had completed its training, under the supervision of United States military advisers, at the beginning of that year, 1981.

Nine months before "Operación Rescate" took place, a company of the Atlacatl Battalion, under the command of Captain Juan Ernesto Méndez, had taken part in an anti-guerrilla operation in the same northern zone of Morazán. On that occasion, it had come under heavy attack from guerrillas and had had to withdraw with heavy casualties without achieving its military objective. This setback for the brand new "Rapid Deployment Infantry Battalion" made it the butt of criticism and jokes by officers of other units, who nicknamed it the "Rapid Retreat Infantry Battalion".

The goal of "Operación Rescate" was to eliminate the guerrilla presence in a small sector in northern Morazán, where the guerrillas had a camp and a training centre at a place called La Guacamaya.

Colonel Jaime Flores Grijalva, Commander of the Third Brigade, was responsible for overseeing the operation. Lieutenant Colonel Domingo Monterrosa Barrios, Commander of the Atlacatl BIRI, was in command of the units taking part.

On 9 December, clashes took place between Government troops and the guerrillas. That same day, a company of the Atlacatl BIRI entered the town of Arambala. They rounded up the population in the town square and separated the men from the women and children. They locked the women and children in the church and ordered the men to lie face down in the square. A number of men were accused of being guerrilla collaborators. They were tied up, blindfolded and tortured. Residents later found the bodies of three of them, stabbed to death.

In Cumaro canton as well, residents were rounded up in the main square by Atlacatl units on the morning of 10 December. There, however, no one was killed.

There is sufficient evidence that units of the Atlacatl BIRI participated in all these actions. In the course of "Operación Rescate," however, other mass executions were carried out by units which it has not been possible to identify with certainty.

In all instances, troops acted in the same way: they killed anyone they came across, men, women and children, and then set fire to the houses. This is what happened in La Joya canton on 11 December, in the village of La Ranchería on 12 December, and in the village of Jocote Amarillo and Cerro Pando canton on 13 December.

Subsequent Events

The El Mozote massacre became public knowledge on 27 January 1982, when *The New York Times* and *The Washington Post* published articles by Raymond Bonner and Alma Guillermoprieto, respectively, reporting the massacre. In January, they had visited the scene of the massacre and had seen the bodies and the ruined houses.

In the course of the year, a number of human rights organizations denounced the massacre. The Salvadorian authorities categorically denied that a massacre had taken place. No judicial investigation was launched and there was no word of any investigation by the Government or the armed forces.

On 26 October 1990, on a criminal complaint brought by Pedro Chicas Romero, criminal proceedings were instituted in the San Francisco Gotera Court of the First Instance. During the trial, which is still going on, statements were taken from witnesses for the prosecution; eventually, the remains were ordered exhumed, and this provided irrefutable evidence of the El Mozote massacre. The judge asked the Government repeatedly for a list of the officers who took part in the military operation. He received the reply that the Government did not have such information.

The Results of the Exhumation

The exhumation of the remains in the ruins of the little building known as the convent, adjacent to the El Mozote church, took place between 13 and 17 November 1992.

The material found in the convent was analysed by expert anthropologists and then studied in minute detail in the laboratories of the Santa Tecla Institute of Forensic Medicine and of the Commission for the Investigation of Criminal Acts by Dr. Clyde Snow (forensic anthropologist), Dr. Robert H. Kirschner (forensic pathologist), Dr. Douglas Scott (archaeologist and ballistics analyst), and Dr. John Fitzpatrick (radiologist), in collaboration with the Argentine Team of Forensic Anthropologists made up of Patricia Bernardi, Mercedes Doretti and Luis Fondebrider.

The study made by the experts led to the following conclusions:

1. "All the skeletons recovered from the site and the associated evidence were deposited during the same temporal event . . ."[1] The physical evidence recovered in the site excludes the possibility that the site could have been used as a clandestine cemetery in which the dead were placed at different times.
2. "The events under investigation are unlikely to have occurred later than 1981."[2] Coins and bullet cartridges bearing their date of manufacture were found in the convent. In no case was this date later than 1981.
3. In the convent, bone remains of at least 143 people were found.[3] However, the laboratory analysis indicates that "there may, in fact, have been a greater number of deaths. This uncertainty regarding the number of skeletons is a reflection of the extensive perimortem skeletal injuries, postmortem skeletal damage and associated commingling. Many young infants may have been entirely cremated; other children may not have been counted because of extensive fragmentation of body parts."[4]
4. The bone remains and other evidence found in the convent show numerous signs of damage caused by crushing and by fire.
5. Most of the victims were minors.

   The experts determined, initially, after the exhumation, that "approximately 85 per cent of the 117 victims were children under 12 years of age,"[5] and indicated that a more precise estimate of the victims' ages would be made in the laboratory.[6]

   In the laboratory, the skeletal remains of 143 bodies were identified, including 131 children under the age of 12, 5 adolescents and 7 adults The experts noted, in addition, that "the average age of the children was approximately 6 years."[7]
6. One of the victims was a pregnant woman.[8]
7. Although it could not be determined with certainty that all the victims were alive when they were brought into the convent, "it can be concluded that at least some of the victims were struck by bullets, with an effect that may well have been lethal, inside the building."[9]

This conclusion is based on various factors:

1. A "large quantity of bullet fragments [were] found inside the building . . ."[10] "Virtually all the ballistic evidence was found at level 3, in direct contact with or imbedded in the bone remains, clothing, household goods and floor of the building."[11] Moreover, "the spatial distribution of most of the bullet fragments coincides with the area of greatest concentration of skeletons and with concentrations of

bone remains."[12] Also, the second and third areas of concentration of bullet fragments coincide with the second and third areas of concentration of skeletons, respectively.

2. "Of 117 skeletons identified in the field, 67 were associated with bullet fragments. In 43 out of this subtotal of 67, the fragments were found in the areas of the skull and/or the thorax, i.e., parts of the body where they could have been the cause of death."[13]

3. "In at least nine cases, the victims were shot inside the building while lying in a horizontal position on the floor. The shots were fired downwards. In at least six of the nine cases mentioned, these shots could have caused the victims' deaths."[14]

4. "Direct skeletal examination showed intact gunshot wounds of entrance in only a few skulls because of the extensive fracturing that is characteristically associated with such high-velocity injuries. Skull reconstruction identified many more entrance wounds, but relatively few exit wounds. This is consistent with the ballistic evidence that the ammunition involved in the shootings was of a type likely to fragment upon impact, becoming essentially frangible bullets. Radiologic examination of skull bones demonstrated small metallic densities consistent with bullet fragments in 45.2 per cent (51/115).

   In long bones, vertebrae, pelvis and ribs there were defects characteristic of high velocity gunshot wounds."[15]

5. The weapons used to fire at the victims were M-16 rifles.

   As the ballistics analyst described, two hundred forty-five cartridge cases recovered from the El Mozote site were studied. Of these, 184 had discernible headstamps, identifying the ammunition as having been manufactured for the United States Government at Lake City, Missouri. Thirty-four cartridges were sufficiently well preserved to analyze for individual as well as class characteristics. All of the projectiles except one appear to have been fired from United States-manufactured M-16 rifles."[16]

6. At least 24 people participated in the shooting.[17] They fired "from within the house, from the doorway, and probably through a window to the right of the door."[18]

   An important point that emerges from the results of the observations is that "no bullet fragments were found in the outside west façade of the stone wall."[19]

   The evidence presented above is full proof that the victims were summarily executed, as the witnesses have testified.

   The experts who carried out the exhumation reached the following conclusion: "All these facts tend to indicate the perpetration of a massive crime, there being no evidence to support the theory of a confrontation between two groups."[20]

For their part, the experts who conducted the laboratory analysis said that the physical evidence from the exhumation of the convent house at El Mozote confirms the allegations of a mass murder."[21] They went on to say, on the same point: "There is no evidence to support the contention that these victims, almost all young children, were involved in combat or were caught in the crossfire of combat forces. Rather the evidence strongly supports the conclusion that they were the intentional victims of a mass extra-judicial execution."[22]

Action by the Commission

Before the Commission on the Truth began its work, the Director of the Human Rights Division of the United Nations Observer Mission in El Salvador (ONUSAL) brought a motion before the judge hearing the case to have qualified foreign experts appointed.

The Commission on the Truth, from the moment it was set up, took a special interest in having the exhumation conducted under conditions that guaranteed the necessary scientific rigour and impartiality.

The Commission also reviewed the available publications, documentation and court records. It took testimony directly from eyewitnesses and was present at the exhumation site.

The Commission wrote three times to the Minister of Defence and once to the Chief of the Armed Forces Joint Staff requesting information about the units and officers who took part in "Operación Rescate," and about any orders, reports or other documents relating to that operation that might be in the archives. The only response it received was that there were no records for that period.

Special mention must be made of the interference in the case by the President of the Supreme Court of El Salvador, Mr. Mauricio Gutiérrez Castro. When on 17 July 1991 representatives of the Legal Protection Office asked the trial judge to appoint qualified foreign experts to conduct the exhumations, he told them that this would require the approval of Mr. Gutiérrez Castro. It was not until nine months later, on 29 April 1992. after ONUSAL stepped in, that he proceeded to appoint them.

On 16 July 1992, when the members of the Commission on the Truth went to see him, Mr. Gutiérrez Castro said that the exhumation ordered by the trial judge would prove that "only dead guerrillas are buried" at El Mozote.

A few days later, the court hearing the case ruled that its appointment of foreign experts was not valid without a complicated procedure of consultation with foreign Governments through the Supreme Court of Justice, with the result that the exhumation was on the point of going ahead without the presence of such experts.

On 21 October, Mr. Mauricio Gutiérrez Castro came to the exhumation site and, in giving his opinion on how future excavations in the zone should be carried out, said that care should be taken not to "favour one of the parties" (presumably the Government and FMLN) "because of the political implications of this process, which override legal considerations."

Findings

There is full proof that on 11 December 1981, in the village of El Mozote, units of the Atlacatl Battalion deliberately and systematically killed a group of more than 200 men, women and children, constituting the entire civilian population that they had found there the previous day and had since been holding prisoner.

The officers in command of the Atlacatl Battalion at the time of the operation whom the Commission has managed to identify are the following: Battalion Commander: Lieutenant Colonel Domingo Monterrosa Barrios (deceased); Commanding Officer: Major Natividad de Jesús Caceres Cabrera (now Colonel); Chief of Operations: Major José Armando Azmitia Melara (deceased); Company Commanders: Juan Ernesto Méndez Rodriguez (now Colonel); Roberto Alfonso Mendoza Portillo (deceased); Jose Antonio Rodriguez Molina (now Lieutenant Colonel), Captain Walter Oswaldo Salazar (now Lieutenant Colonel) and José Alfredo Jiménez (currently a fugitive from justice).

There is sufficient evidence that in the days preceding and following the El Mozote massacre, troops participating in "Operación Rescate" massacred the non-combatant civilian population in La Joya canton, in the villages of La Ranchería, Jocote Amarillo y Los Toriles, and in Cerro Pando canton.

Participating in this operation, in addition to the Atlacatl Battalion, were units of the Third Infantry Brigade, commanded by Colonel Jaime Flores Grijalba (now retired) who was also responsible for supervising the operation, and units from the San Francisco Gotera Commando Training Centre commanded by Colonel Alejandro Cisneros (now retired).

Although it received news of the massacre, which would have been easy to corroborate because of the profusion of unburied bodies, the Armed Forces High Command did not conduct or did not give any word of an investigation and repeatedly denied that the massacre had occurred. There is full evidence that General José Guillermo García, then Minister of Defence, initiated no investigations that might have enabled the facts to be established. There is sufficient evidence that General Rafael Flores Lima, Chief of the Armed Forces Joint Staff at the time, was aware that the massacre had occurred and also failed to undertake any investigation.

The High Command also took no steps whatsoever to prevent the repetition of such acts, with the result that the same units were used in other operations and followed the same procedures.

The El Mozote massacre was a serious violation of international humanitarian law and international human rights law.

The President of the Supreme Court of Justice of El Salvador, Mr. Mauricio Gutiérrez Castro, has interfered unduly and prejudicially, for biased political reasons, in the ongoing judicial proceedings on the case.

The Commission recommends that the competent authorities implement the recommendations made in the experts' reports (see annex 1).

NOTES

1. The convent was—in the words of the experts—a *"primary synchronous common* grave." Patricia Bernardi, Mercedes Doretti and Luis Fondebrider, *Archaeological Report,* p. 15.
2. *Archaeological Report,* p. 18.
3. When the exhumed bone remains were analysed, the expert anthropologists were able to identify 117 anatomically articulated skeletons, as indicated in their report. After the laboratory analysis was done, it was possible to identify at least 143 skeletons. See Clyde Snow, John Fitzpatrick, Robert H. Kirschner and Douglas Scott, *Report of Forensic Investigation.*
4. *Report of Forensic Investigation,* p. 1.
5. The basis for this assertion is "the simultaneous presence of both deciduous and permanent teeth" and "the fact that their primary and/or secondary centres of ossification had not fused" (*Archaeological Report.* pp. 17–18; cf. ibid., p. 8).
6. Ibid., p. 18.
7. *Report of Forensic Investigation,* p. 1.
8. ". . . The remains of a foetus were wedged in the pelvic region, with the head between the two coxal bones and on the sacrum" (*Archaeological Report,* p. 8). As indicated in the laboratory report, it was determined that the mother "was in the third trimester of pregnancy" (*Report of Forensic Investigation,* p. 1).
9. *Archaeological Report,* p. 16.
10. Ibid.. p. 16.
11. Ibid., p. 11.
12. Ibid., p. 11. The report went on to say: "We are referring to grid squares B2, B3, C3 and the south-west corner of C2, where 82 bodies—almost 70 per cent of the skeletons—and 18 of the 24 concentrations of bone remains—almost 80 per cent—were found. In these grid squares, 159 bullet fragments were found: 102 fragments in B3; 13 fragments in B2; 30 fragments in C3; and 14 fragments in C2. In these grid squares, all these bullet fragments were in direct contact with bone remains. In other words, 159 bullet fragments had struck a large proportion of the 82 skeletons and 18 concentrations discovered in this zone."
13. Ibid., p. 17.
14. Ibid., p. 16. The report supported this assertion as follows:
    "(1) Observation of peri-mortem lesions, together with bullet fragments and holes in the floor underneath such fragments. This observation applies to skeletons 2, 5, 9, 10, 26, 57, 92, 110 and 113, located in grid squares C1, C2, C1, D2, B4, C3, B2, B3-C3 and 83 respectively . . .;
    "(2) The only way such shots could have produced holes in the floor is by shoaling downwards, either straight down or diagonally;
    "(3) In the case of skeletons 2, 10, 92, 110 and 57, the bullets which made the holes in the floor were found in the area of the skull; in the case of skeleton 26, in the cervical vertebrae (very close to the skull)."
15. *Report of Forensic Investigation,* p. 2.
16. *Report of Forensic Investigation,* p. 3.
17. "24 separate weapons were identified, consistent with at least 24 individual shooters" (*Report of Forensic investigation,* p. 3).
18. Ibid., p. 3. The experts who exhumed the bone remains reached the same conclusion. Cf. *Archaeological Report,* p. 17.

19. *Archaeological Report,* p. 17.
20. *Archaeological Report,* p. 18.
21. *Report of Forensic Investigation,* p. 1.
22. They also stated that all their conclusions "are stated with a reasonable degree of medical and scientific certainty" and that they were willing to testify in a court of law regarding these conclusions. See *Report of Forensic Investigation,* p. 3.

In Guatemala, *The Official Report of the Human Rights Office* of the Archdiocese of Guatemala, also known as REMHI, was published in April 1998. During the presentation ceremony, Bishop Juan Gerardi expressed a reserved idea of hope, yet he pointed out that "when we carried out this labor we were interested in learning the truth in order to share it, to reconstruct the history of pain and death, understanding the motives, the reasons, the means. We wanted to show the human drama, to share the pain, and anguish of the thousands of dead, disappeared and tortured; to see the root of injustice and the absence of value" (our translation of Bishop Gerardi's speech, April 24, 1998). As a result, REMHI would not become part of the process of victim reparation, but rather it would be an effort to show collective responsibility to face the truth. This cycle of hope was finalized only two days later when on Sunday, April 26, 1998 Bishop Juan Gerardi was murdered in his home next to the Church of Saint Sebastian in Guatemala City.

By the time REMHI was published an agreement had been reached in Guatemala that made the publication of the names of those responsible for the crimes no longer possible. As a result, the memory that we are allowed to have of the human rights abuses that took place during the recent civil war in Guatemala is relative, and as long as it is published under the label *Guatemala Never Again!* it is also ambivalent. It helps give visibility to the human rights violations, which in their majority were directed against Indigenous peoples in Guatemala during the recently ended thirty-six years of civil war. At the same time it contributes to the invisibility of the violence that continues to be reproduced and perpetuated against Indigenous peoples in Guatemala today in spite of the affirmation that it would not ever happen again.

The following are three fragments of testimonials given by Indigenous people in diverse regions of Guatemala to volunteer catechists working for the Archdiocese of Guatemala's Human Rights Office.

Guatemala Never Again!

REMHI
RECOVERY OF HISTORICAL MEMORY PROJECT
THE OFFICIAL REPORT OF THE HUMAN RIGHTS OFFICE,
ARCHDIOCESE OF GUATEMALA

From "Case 8673, Sibinal, San Marcos, 1982," "Case 9014 (massacre), San José Xix, Chajul, Quiché, 1982" and "Case 3031 (abduction in Salamá and murder in Cuilapa), Cuilapa, Santa Rosa, 1981," *Guatemala Never Again!, REMHI: Recovery of Historical Memory Project: The Official Report of the Human Rights Office*, Archdiocese of Guatemala, New York: Orbis Books, 1999. Reprinted by permission of Orbis Books.

Forced Disappearances

The inability to hold a wake makes it more difficult to face the loss and bring closure to the grieving process, although some people find ways to symbolize the presence of the disappeared person or find a memento to remember them by.

> For three days I cried, crying that I wanted to see him. I sat there below that piece of ground. Just a little bit of earth to be able to say there he is. There is the little cross, he is there, everything is there. There is our little bit of dust and we will go to show our respect, leave a candle . . . but when are we going to light the candle? and where are we going to . . . ? There isn't any place. I feel so much pain. Each night I get up to pray, every night. Where can we go? *Case 8673, Sibinal, San Marcos, 1982.*

Sociopolitical Violence and Altered Grief

The Magnitude and Brutality of the Violence

Since massacres were usually public spectacles, the impact of death was magnified by having witnessed the atrocities. Many of those who gave their testimony were eyewitnesses to the aftermath of the massacres. Others lived with critically wounded victims who didn't die immediately, and they experienced their agony firsthand.

When the army returned, [the soldiers] came out of that house. And they went by to tell my uncle, who is the military commissioner: "Look, you, go and bury those people, we finished off a whole family. They are bad folks, we finished them off and now go and bury them. Some are not quite dead yet, they're still twitching; wait until they die, so they're not jumping, and then bury them." When we got there, oh, but it was horrible. I can't forget it. Even though some say you have to put the past behind you, I can't. I remember . . . we went to the kitchen and there was the whole family, my aunt, my daughter-in-law, her sons and daughters; there were two little children hacked to pieces with machetes. They were still alive. The boy, Romualdo, lived for a few more days. The one who couldn't last any longer was Santa, the one with her guts hanging out. She only lasted half a day and then she died. *Case 9014 (massacre), San José Xix, Chajul, Quiché, 1982.*

Exemplary Terror (Terror as a Warning to Others)

The strategy of terror in Guatemala degenerated into the most extreme displays of disregard for human life with public torture sessions, public display of corpses, and the appearance of mutilated bodies bearing signs of torture.

They had cut out his tongue. His eyes were blindfolded with a wide bandage or wide tape and there were punctures everywhere on his rib cage, and it seemed that one of his arms was broken. They left him unrecognizable. And I could tell that it was him only because I had lived with him for many years and I knew about certain scars. I also took a recent photo that showed his whole body and I told the forensic doctor that he was my husband. Then "yes," he told me, "he was your husband. Yes, you may take him."
Case 3031 (abduction in Salamá and murder in Cuilapa), Cuilapa, Santa Rosa, 1981.

Community organizing by the Garifuna people in Santa Rosa Aguán, Northern Honduras, shows the resilience and pioneering work of the members of this community in defense of their rights. The text illustrates how the devastating forces of Hurricane Mitch impacted their community, as well as their fight to restore basic services within the bureaucratic machinery of the Honduran state. It also displays the legal obstacles developed by the state to marginalize these communities. In sum, this article presents the innovative community proposals and actions that help them to fight back against unlawful state practices.

The Garifuna Fight Back

HELEN DRUSINE

Trujillo, Honduras: Maylor Florentina Palacios is frustrated, angry, and worried. She worries about malaria and about dengue fever, about contaminated water, about the theft of her community's ancestral lands. She also worries about the loss of traditions and culture.

Palacios is one of the 250,000 Garifuna, an Afro-Honduran people living on the North Coast, who are marginalised and ignored by the government of this predominantly non-black, Latino country. She is angry now because the people of her community cannot get the fuel they need to power road-building machinery. The road would make it possible for them to build new homes further inland so they will be safe from the huge waves that accompany hurricanes.

Palacios, vice-president of the committee for reconstruction of roads and housing in Santa Rosa de Aguan, describes how her town was the coastal town hardest hit during Hurricane Mitch seven years ago and how it has still not recovered. At the time, more than forty people died, more than two hundred houses were washed out to sea, the town lost its kindergarten, its primary, its high school, and its health centre. Not even cement buildings were spared the hurricane's fury. During the tropical storms Michelle and Katrina in subsequent years the town was again cut off, areas flooded, and two houses fell into the waves after the sea cut away the coastline.

I am writing a book called 'Mitch and the Destruction of the World', Palacios tells a visitor, trying to fight back tears. 'The first chapter will be "The Land and Big Landowners". The second chapter will be "Mitch, The Road and Housing". Because I am living what is happening, because we lived all of this.'

Aguan, perched on a sandbar at the mouth of the river, was hit by both high seas and the flooding river. Floodwaters killed hundreds in the broad, flat Rio Aguan Valley and put entire towns under water. An estimated 30 acres of land where houses, schools, and churches once stood became rivers and lagoons. More than half of their cultivated fields were washed away.

Broken palm trees, rutted roads, and rivers still without proper bridges are visible reminders that another hurricane could strike at any time. A school bus, half-submerged in a river that was once the main road into town, is a silent witness to all that was lost. The inhabitants of this Caribbean coastal village know it can happen again. That is why they are so anxious to rebuild their homes away from the low-lying part of the coast.

'Here we have a small community trying to do all the right things – take care of the environment, stop deforestation, protect its water supplies', says Suzanne Shende, a Trinidadian American human and civil rights lawyer who has been working with the Garifuna for nine years. 'Every international conference and all the aid agencies say they want to mitigate the consequences of natural disasters and here is a community trying to do just that. And yet when a community needs such a small thing as fuel, the international donors aren't there.'

After both Mitch and Michelle, the government's reconstruction efforts focused mainly on the central parts of the country and left the Garifuna to fend for themselves. So the Garifuna women came together to try to save their communities on their own. *The Comite de Emergencia Garifuna de Honduras*, based in Trujillo, the Garifuna capital, was formed. And despite Palacios's concerns and the problems the Garifuna still face, the *Comite* has been able to transform the lives of many of the people whose lives it touches. In the past seven years, it has raised money and built houses for single mothers, supported artisans, farmers, and fishermen, and set up kitchens to feed children and the elderly, begun training projects, supported micro businesses, and defended human rights.

The *Comite* built houses for people without resources who had lost their homes, sent materials to help repair more than forty schools, provided equipment and medicines for hospitals and health centres, repaired cultural centres, houses, schools, and small businesses, and delivered donations to the needy. These had to be transported by whatever means available – by boat, canoe, horse, mule, horse cart, pickup truck, or on foot. Because of the bad roads, many of which are impassable during the rainy season, there is no established method of transporting medicines and supplies. Some of these same obstacles are keeping donations from reaching the neediest people after the tsunamis in Asia.

After the hurricane, even stems and seeds utilised by Garifuna farmers were not available (although international agencies and the government provided the seeds used by the Latino population, says Ana Lucy Bengochea, *Comite* secretary) so the *Comite* looked further away for seeds they could donate to the villages most in need. Its work includes collecting seedlings from one town that has a surplus and taking them to other towns that have none, often by pickup truck across rutted and sometimes flooded roads and then by boat across a river to a still isolated town. Three towns are accessible only by boat. People who receive the seeds are committed to providing future seeds to other farmers, making the project sustainable. They also direct a small portion of their harvest to needy community members.

The *Comite* works on communal projects such as planting a coconut tree nursery or transplanting tree seedlings. It bought 2000 hybrid or resistant coconut trees for 16 towns after disease killed a majority of the region's coconut trees. Now people are awarded a coconut plant after completing work on a community project – repair of a bridge, reforesting the beach with coconuts, cleaning up the piers and waterways, or cutting the grass around the kindergarten and health centre. It also brings agronomists to teach communities about the cultivation and diversification of crops so they can combine this knowledge with their traditional knowledge. 'We have these young academics talking with 70-year-old women who are planting according to the cycles of the moon', says Shende.

The *Comite* is also planting yucca, mahogany, and hardwood trees with the aim of reforesting Barranco, whose productive capacity was destroyed by Mitch. The homes in this area, a small peninsula jutting out from Trujillo, were all destroyed so its residents now live in Trujillo and are transported there once a week by the *Comite* to work in the newly planted fields. The *Comite* is looking for funding to rebuild those houses so the people can move back and tend their crops more regularly.

'The *Comite* gives us so much', says Sotera Martinez, who at 69 still leaves before dawn to walk two hours each way to tend her crops in an area near Trujillo and then carry home firewood on her head in the afternoon. She lost her house and all her fields in Barranco. 'It transports us to the fields, it provides us with seeds, it helps us establish nurseries. It brought in an agronomist to talk to us about diversification and sterilising the seeds. Now we are also planting ginger for diversification in addition to our more traditional crops such as yucca.'

The *Comite*, which reaches 9000 people, also teaches community members to write proposals, evaluations, and reports, and basic typing and computer skills. And it was the *Comite* that bought the land so the people of Aguan could rebuild their houses. But the land just sits there. The only access is by boat. The heavy road-building machinery they finally got the government to provide stands idle. The building materials necessary to construct their homes cannot be effectively transported without a road. The town does not have the notice change $50,000 needed to buy the gasoline to power the trucks, and build a bridge to make the road complete. Few have responded to their requests for funds. A student volunteer from the University of Massachusetts Medical School, on a recent visit here, felt so sorry for the inhabitants that she donated $100 so they could buy one barrel of fuel at least to begin construction.

The present struggle for the people of Santa Rosa de Aguan is the road. But the Garifuna in this country have long struggled against injustice and discrimination. More than 300 years ago, according to one theory, they escaped from slave ships that were shipwrecked off the coast of Saint Vincent. On that island they mixed with the Carib and Arawak Indians. In 1797, after the British defeated the French, they were deported to the Bay Islands in the Caribbean and then made their way to the mainland coast of Honduras. Most live in seaside villages of huts with steep thatched roofs and cultivate traditional root crops such as manioc or yucca, yams and taro. (After Mitch, it was reported that nearly 90% of the crops supporting Garifuna villages were wiped out). Many are boat-builders and fisherman. One dozen villages are without electricity and telephones. Few have hot water and healthcare is minimal.

The Garifuna have retained their African roots through their unique language (a mixture of Arawak, Carib, and Bantu with a sprinkling of French, Spanish, and English), dances, music, stories, drumming, and religious beliefs that somewhat resemble other African-based religions like Santeria and Haitian Voodoo. They also have traditional foods, medicinal herbs, farming and fishing methods, handmade instruments, and cooking utensils. Many of the smaller towns still try to be self-sufficient. They have asked the government for bilingual, bicultural education to protect their culture. 'Masterpiece of the oral and intangible heritage of humanity' UNESCO had declared entire culture a masterpiece of the Oral and intangible heritage of humanity Patrimony to Humanity.

Their poverty and suffering provide a stark contrast to the beauty that surrounds them – the sparkling blue waters of the Caribbean on one side and the lush tropical forests of the soaring mountains peaks on the other. Mares with their colts graze outside quaint thatched roof houses, pigs with their young, chickens, and goats roam everywhere. Although horses seem to be plentiful, in some towns most people still prefer to carry firewood and other material back from the fields on their heads with other heavy bundles suspended from their foreheads.

They believe that this way of life is now being threatened by what they call 'invaders' – large, wealthy landowners, many of whom are armed, and cattle ranchers. In addition, they say the government is attempting to sell their land along the coast to tourism developers. Tourist development, they fear, would leave them waiters and maids on their ancestral lands.

The *Comite* also works on human rights issues in sixteen communities. One of these issues is the construction of an illegal highway through mountainous communal land. Four years ago, the wealthy cattle ranchers of the town of Sico built without permission this road that passes through the mountains from the coastal town of Iriona Viejo to the inland town of Sico. The road builders bulldozed numerous fields, felling cocoa, mango, and plantain trees and destroying yucca, bananas, corn, taro, and arrowroot crops, cultivated by the subsistence farmers of the area. The road cut a swath through old-growth tropical forest passing above the protected forest watershed of three reservoirs that serve eleven towns. Their formerly pristine water supply is no longer potable. The erosion caused by the massive deforestation led to soil entering the water supply. The oil from cars is also washing into it. When it rains, the water looks like chocolate, say the region's inhabitants who have been reporting a lot more illnesses, especially among the children.

On a visit to the area to inaugurate the opening of another, legal road, the Honduran president, Ricardo Maduro, said the water looked like 'tamarind juice'. However, according to Shende, the government has done nothing to close the road, although it admits its illegality and the harm it is causing. Meanwhile, the only option is for residents to try to catch rainwater, but rains have been infrequent and many have no money to buy the buckets and barrels to store adequate amounts.

A permit to build the road was denied by the Iriona Viejo mayor's office and no authorisation was given by the national highway authority. No environmental impact study was done, nor was the required environmental permit extended. Road-building machinery ran over some fifteen to twenty acres of crops, but nearly one hundred acres are now unusable because armed ranchers keep the villagers out, according to residents. Vegetation was destroyed, streams blockaded and rerouted, flooding nearby cornfields, and existing bridges were destroyed. The mayor, as well as the president of the local community group, has received death threats.

'More than 10,000 Garifuna are now without potable water. A fifteen kilometre road was opened … in order to exploit natural resources that for decades had been protected', according to the local paper Costa Norte. 'The situation is so lamentable. The water which comes [from these reservoirs] is so dirty that it is not fit for human consumption.'

Victoria Suazo, an Iriona Viejo resident, wants the government (which took office earlier this year) to get rid of the road. 'We want to bring the old government to court and insist the new government close the road down', she says. 'We want to be reimbursed for all our lost land and crops.' In addition to the contamination of the water supply by humans and machinery, residents fear that by creating soil erosion and deforestation, this project may contribute to the water supply's ultimate disappearance. The community had proposed that an old route once used by the Standard Fruit Company that does not go into the mountains and would not cause ecological damage be upgraded and used instead. The ranchers refused.

'This illegal highway affects our water. When it rains it is pure mud', says Pastor Suazo. 'There has been so much illness since it was built – diarrhoea, vomiting, fevers, parasites, fungal infections. We are also finding human faeces from construction workers and the houses built by the invaders who came because of the road. There were no houses before. We are all afraid the kids will die.'

Iriona Viejo is not the only town where the *Comite* faces severe human rights abuses. In another Garifuna town, Vallecito, a Garifuna leader was assassinated in January 2004, their land has been invaded, their crops bulldozed, two people have been shot at, a thatched-roof house was set on fire with children inside, and two months ago a training centre where community residents were learning about the mechanisation of agriculture was burnt down. They believe that one of the country's richest and biggest landowners, an uncle to the former president and owner of most of the palm oil plantations in the country, is paying people to attack them. They feel they are under siege. The rice and corn they used to grow now have to be bought, a difficult task since there is almost no employment. They used to go alone to tend their crops, now they can only go in groups.

In Punta Piedra, a cooperative of thirty-nine women was formed to cultivate and fight for the land. These women have marched on the capital twice, but they said no one would listen to their grievances during the four days they protested in front of the Chamber of Deputies. The second time, in April, they slept on the street by the Chamber on pieces of cardboard and beat drums so the government would notice them. They said they were told that the government would release money to the National Agrarian Institute so that the invaders could be reimbursed for the houses they had built and leave the Garifuna lands. The money was never released, they say. Formal complaints have been made to the ministry of the environment and other government institutions and both civil and criminal lawsuits have been filed by many of the communities affected.

Other work of the *Comite* involves projects with young people. They meet with them to determine what kinds of programmes they themselves want. Young women have received a sewing course and started a micro business. Other support for small businesses includes collaboration with collectives which are raising chickens, fish, and making tortillas. Still other young people on sports teams have received equipment and support and now work together to maintain their faculties and the surrounding area. One group is trying to form a musical ensemble, which the *Comite* hopes will keep them from joining gangs or getting involved with drugs. They have the drums but are trying to raise funds for a piano, guitar, electric drums, and a violin. Another group wants to build the first basketball court in their town.

The Garifuna are afraid that the art of making utensils needed to make casave, a bread made from yucca, will die out with the old people, so in one town the *Comite* provided tools, materials, and two months of training to a group of young people so they can learn to make wood crafts and other saleable items. They want to be able to replicate this in all the villages.

The *Comite* provides tools for the towns it works with. Each town elects representatives (at least half are women) to run the local tool bank and lend out the tools to the farmers who need them. The delivery of seedlings is done in much the same way. Ginger and plantain seeds, for example, are collected by members of the *Comite* who take them by truck and boat to the villages. There they are distributed to the farmers by representatives of the tool bank, with the agreement that after the harvest they will give back a certain portion of it to other farmers and to those community members who can no longer work because they are either too old or disabled. What is not donated to the sick or elderly can be used in a children's breakfast programme.

A free breakfast for 125 kindergarten children in Punta Piedra is another initiative launched by the *Comite* – the only free, complete daily meal programme in the country. In this town without electricity, telephones, or sources of employment, many children suffered from poor nutrition. Some were not going to school because they had nothing to eat.

The Garifuna have many traditional and medicinal plants, and Balaire, which the *Comite* is now trying to save, is one that has become increasingly scarce. A thorny, wild vine, closely resembling bamboo, it has been used for centuries to make everything from cooking utensils to furniture. However, with deforestation, the areas where these plants were growing wild have been lost.

The *Comite* is pioneering a reforestation programme for this vine. Growing it against tall trees in the partial shade of the tropical forest will also help promote an entire ecosystem that the people will then want to preserve, Shende says. She believes that the cultivation of this vine is an example of sustainable use of the land and an attempt to keep the traditional culture alive. The pilot project will be carried out in eight villages with everyone, including the teenagers, pitching in to help. According to agronomists, the Garifuna will be among the first communities in the world to plant and cultivate this vine. For this groundbreaking work, the Comite was recognized by the UN's development program (UNDP) as one of the twenty-six worldwide finalists for the 2004 equator initiative prize for outstanding work in promoting bio diversity and combating poverty.

'The Garifuna, in some towns, were given the title to their lands in 1901, but their rights continue to be ignored', says Shende. 'A just solution needs to be sought or it could be a powder keg. Everyday there are new threats. In January 2004, A leader was killed, and in January 2005 a law was passed changing constitutional protections and allowing sale of ancestral coastal lands to foreigners. The Garifuna have a right to decide what is in their best interest, to determine how they want to develop their land. They have a right to self-determination and to continue their practice of sustainable development. One of their chief demands – access to clean water – is a human right.'

CHAPTER FOUR

GENDER

Central American societies have implemented a very traditional construction of gender reflected in the social practices, labor distribution, laws, and the limited participation of women in public office. While this understanding of gender is often naturalized, the fact is that there is nothing *natural* about it; it is a cultural construction greatly influenced by the Spanish colonial legacy that continues to permeate Central American societies.

The physical sex of persons and their sexual preferences do not dictate who they are or how society perceives them. It is the cultural understanding or the interpretation of someone's sexuality that brings with it a whole cultural baggage in terms of the way society perceives or "reads" that person, as well as how socialization brings understanding of his or her role in the world and the appropriate behavior that comes with it. As a result, contemporary theories on gender discuss at length the performative dimensions of gender, that is, the way gender is not only read but also performed, often unconsciously, by all of us.

Culturally speaking, the traditional definition of gender in Central America has been a binary construction of male/female where society has perceived the male as powerful, independent, strong, intellectual and capable of leadership positions in public space. The construction of the female, on the other hand, has been traditionally linked to private space, to subservient and complementary roles associated with physical beauty and greatly excluded from public space. Beyond stating that such a construction is largely removed from realities and daily practices in Central America, it is important to recognize from the start that gender is a cultural construction, that it is fluid and that it is not binary because there are a number of other positions beyond the male/female paradigm, and that the traditional understanding of gender has greatly relegated gays, lesbians, women and all those who do not conform to that paradigm to a place as outsiders in society.

However, cultural practices in Central America have brought to life alternative understandings of gender. Organizations providing visibility and fighting for the rights of gay, lesbian, bisexual and transgender persons have emerged in all Central American nations. Some of these organizations are: United Belize Advocacy Movement (Belize), Coordinadora Ciudadana para la Diversidad Sexual (Guatemala), Asociación Entre Amigos (El Salvador), Asociación de Mujeres para la Dignidad y la Vida—Las Dignas (El Salvador), Asociación de Homosexuales Hondureños contra el Sida—AHHCOS (Honduras), Colectivo Violeta (Honduras), Prisma (Honduras), Puntos de Encuentro (Nicaragua), Asociación Gay Lésbica Trans Intermunicipal de Nicaragua (Nicaragua), Red LAC/Trans (Nicaragua), Asociación Triángulo Rosa (Costa Rica) and Asociación Hombres y Mujeres Nuevos (Panama). Furthermore, gender has become an increasingly important topic of academic studies in Central America, as the emergence of academic programs specializing in gender can testify. These include the Programa Interdisciplinario de Estudios de Género at the University of Costa Rica, or the Gender Section that meets bi-annually as part of the Central American History Congress.

In spite of the visibility that these organizations have obtained through their work in recent decades, the fact is that extremely violent reactions have resisted the challenge to the binary construction of gender that they pose in public space, particularly in societies with militarized backgrounds such as Honduras, Guatemala and El Salvador. To illustrate this situation, we would like to mention the case of El Salvador, where attacks on gays, lesbians, transvestites and activists have been numerous since the end of the civil war. A widely documented case relates to the attacks on the Asociación Entre Amigos (Between Friends), particularly as it presented the case in the National Assembly (Congress) for the right of gays and lesbians to marry. As the Amnesty International report (2006) states: The "Christian Democratic Party (Partido Demócrata Cristiano, PDC) and the Catholic Church in El Salvador are campaigning for an amendment to the constitution that would make it illegal for same-sex couples to marry and adopt children. The amendment was approved by the Legislative Assembly in 2005." At the time of the increased attacks on the organization, the legislative assembly was debating the amendment. On August 7, 2006 Amnesty International reported that the non-governmental organization Entre Amigos, which works with lesbian, gay, bisexual and transgender people and provides educational programs to the general public, had received death threats and was under surveillance after its members had lobbied in the Legislative Assembly against this amendment.

At the time of the Amnesty International reports, the Entre Amigos office had been raided at least seven times within a period of five years. A police report documented one of the death threats, made at gun point to William Hernández, the Association's Executive Director. The report quoted the unidentified armed man as saying that Mr. Hernández would be killed before he is able to marry. The National Civilian Police largely ignored the reports. As a result, the International Gay and Lesbian Human Rights Commission denounced the incidents and requested that letters be sent from human rights organizations and the international community.

In the case of women, the State's regulation of their role in Central American societies has changed throughout the modern history of Central America. However, what has remained intact is the idea that women's lives, bodies and roles in society should be regulated, controlled, normalized and policed for the benefit of the *status quo*. During colonial times the Catholic Church and its institutions, among them the Inquisition, largely controlled the roles of women. Within Catholic social circles, the opportunities that women had to participate in public life were often limited to the space of the convent.

After the formation of Central American modern nations, women were used as prostitute labor in banana plantations. Those interested in exploring this topic further would benefit from reading Lara Putnam's *The Company They Kept. Migrants and the Politics of Gender in Caribbean Costa Rica, 1870–1960*. This book-length study explores, among other things, the role of prostitution in maintaining the labor force for agricultural production during Costa Rica's first century as a nation state. Furthermore, since policies for economic dependency were implemented for coffee, banana, cotton and sugar plantations in the different Central American nations, labor opportunities have often been sporadic in different regions, forcing men and sometimes women to migrate internally in order to find agricultural jobs. This dynamic as well as the experience of the armed conflict in Nicaragua, El Salvador and Guatemala has generated a population composed of increasing numbers of single women as heads of households and of families with single women as the sole parent to their children.

In addition, with the advent of the revolutionary struggles, women were forced to abandon their seclusion in private space and to take an active part in the popular organizations. In spite of this, they have not had an easy time obtaining recognition for their contributions by their male counterparts. A famous quote by FMLN Comandante Facundo Guardado in El Salvador states that, "War is men's business and as hard as women try, they will never play the same role" (quoted by Illa A. Luciak in *After the Revolution. Gender and Democracy in El Salvador, Nicaragua, and Guatemala*). Women's contributions were often downplayed and overlooked, and their positions of power often questioned. In spite of this, women held leadership positions in the Sandinista government in Nicaragua, and some women held leadership positions in the Central American revolutions in Nicaragua, El Salvador and Guatemala, while others were armed combatants, radio operators and members of logistic teams. Women also carried out important work as part of human rights organizations, such as the Coordinadora Nacional de Viudas de Guatemala, CONAVIGUA (The National Coordinatorship of Guatemalan Widows) and the Comité de Madres y Familiares de Presos, Desaparecidos y Asesinados de El Salvador, COMADRES (Committee of Mothers of the Disappeared, Imprisoned, and Murdered of El Salvador). They also play important roles as leaders of Indigenous organizations, labor unions, teachers' unions and so forth. However, women's role in the revolution and the emergence of feminist movements within revolutionary culture in Central America was linked to the struggle for national liberation, and it was only conceived as an independent struggle after the end of the armed conflicts in the region.

After the end of the revolution, a woman won the presidential elections for the first time in Central America. Nicaraguan President Violeta Barrios de Chamorro served in the highest office from 1990 until 1997. In Panama, President Mireya Moscoso served as president from 1999 to 2004. In Costa Rica, Laura Chinchilla served as president from 2010 to 2014.

Immigration has also impacted the role of women in the home and has separated mothers from their children. Women represent a large percentage of Central American immigrants. In the Salvadoran case it is estimated that women represent close to 48.5 percent of all Salvadoran immigrants residing in the United States. As a result, issues of abandonment have divided numerous families and greatly impacted children as their mothers have been forced to migrate to the North in order to find the means for their children's livelihood.

The following readings illustrate some of the struggles that women and members of the LGBT community have faced in contemporary times in Central America.

In this testimonial narrative, Honduran peasant rights activist Elvia Alvarado shares her experience growing up uninformed about sexual health and education. Her story not only reflects her struggles to raise her children on her own but also the difficulties that she experienced in her relationships with her children's fathers. Her narrative also reflects the violence against women exemplified by her own life story. This violence came from members of her own family, society in general and the government, particularly given the lack of social services for women. Elvia Alvarado talks about her experiences with domestic violence, both as a child growing up with an alcoholic and violent father, and in her own relationships with men. She also talks about the way her own brother reacted when she became pregnant and the fear that led her to leave her home for the capital city of Tegucigalpa, Honduras. In the following fragment, she discusses the lack of rights that pregnant domestic workers have and the difficulties she encountered as she struggled to keep her children close to her and to make sure that they were able to eat. In her book-length testimony, Elvia Alvarado discusses the role of women and the importance of gender considerations in social movements in Central America today.

Childhood to Motherhood

Elvia Alvarado

My father was a campesino. He didn't have any land of his own, so he worked for the big landowners as a day worker. My mother raised chickens and pigs, and baked bread to sell at the market. They had seven children—five girls and two boys.

By the time I was six years old, I knew that my parents didn't get along. One of the problems was that there wasn't much work for my father. He'd go looking for work every day, but most of the time he didn't find anything. So he'd go out and get drunk instead. Then he'd come home and pick fights with my mother and hit her with his machete.

My mother would keep quiet when my father hit her. She knew that if she opened her mouth, if she dared to argue with him, he'd hit her more. But we kids would cry and scream and beg him to stop.

My mother finally decided that she couldn't take such abuse any longer, and she left him when I was seven.

After we left, my father moved to the coast. We never saw him again. Years later, after I had my first child, we got a telegram saying he had died. He was buried out there on the coast.

My mother worked like a mule to take care of us, and we all helped out. We'd get up at three in the morning, in the dark, to help bake bread, make tortillas, feed the pigs, and clean the house. All my brothers and sisters worked hard—the boys in the fields of the big landowners, the girls in our house. At the age of seven, we were all working.

My father never let my older sisters go to school. He couldn't see why girls needed an education, since they'd only go live with a man and have babies. But my mother wanted us to learn, and since I was still young enough she decided to send me to school.

I was in school from the time I was seven until I was 12, but I only finished second grade. That's because the school in the town where I grew up only went to second grade. But I really wanted to learn, so I kept repeating second grade over and over again—five times—since there was nowhere else for me to go.

I can't say I had a happy childhood. We didn't have any toys; we didn't have time for games. We were too busy for that, since we were always working.

The only happy moments I recall were the dances on Saturdays, when my mother let me go dancing with my girlfriends. There'd be guitar players in the village square, and on special occasions they'd bring in a marimba band.

The other thing I liked was going to church. On Sundays we'd go to catechism class; we'd sing religious songs and learn the prayers. Sometimes the priest would make *piñatas* for us in the square. All the kids in the catechism class would get candy, bananas, and sodas. That was a big treat for us.

I never really had much of a childhood at all. By the time I was 13, I was already on my own. My mother went to live with a man in town. He' didn't want to take care of her children, so she left us behind in the village. I wouldn't say she abandoned us; it's just one of those things that happens in life. She kept coming around to see how we were. To this day my mother always comes by my house to see how we're doing.

But it was hard when she first left us. I went to live with my older brother, who was married and had his own family.

My brother no longer talks to me because of the work I do. He works for one of the big landowners, and he calls me a communist because I try to organize the campesinos that don't have any land. But when I first went to live with his family, he treated me well.

After I'd been living with my brother for about two years, I started going out with a boy named Samuel. We were both 15 years old and didn't know what we were doing. When we fooled around, I had no idea I'd get pregnant—but I did. In those days, no one ever taught us the facts of life. The adults said that children weren't supposed to learn about such things. So we were left to figure it out on our own.

I remember that the first time I got my period I was terrified. I saw that my vagina was bleeding from the inside. I ran into the woods to take off my panties and look at the blood. I went back home, got a pail from the kitchen, and went to bathe myself. I thought that maybe taking a bath would stop the bleeding. But I just kept bleeding and bleeding.

I was so scared that I stuck some rags in my panties and laid down in the bed. I wrapped the blanket around me, covering myself from head to foot.

My mother came in and asked what was wrong, but I was too ashamed to tell her. I said I had a headache, but she knew I was lying. After I'd been in bed for a few hours, she finally said, "OK. You better tell me what's wrong, or else get out of bed and get back to work."

So I told her I was bleeding between my legs. "Don't be scared," she said. "All women get the same thing. It'll last about three days and then go away." When I got the same thing the next month, I wasn't so scared because at least I knew what it was.

Nowadays, the kids learn these things in school. But when I was young nobody told us anything.

Anyway, when my brother found out I was pregnant, he was furious. He said he was going to kill me. I hid in my older sister's house and he went there looking for me. When she told him I wasn't there, he said, "OK. Tell that little slut that I'll be back, and that I'm going to get her with the six bullets I have left in my gun. Because I don't like what she's done to me. I've taken care of her for two years, and look how she's repaid me."

My sister came back crying. She'd never seen my brother so mad. "You better get out of here quick," she said. "The best thing you can do is go to the capital where he won't be able to find you."

I didn't know what to do. I was only 15, and I'd never been to the capital before. I'd never even been to Comayagua, which is just a short bus ride away. What on earth would I do in the capital all by myself?

I wrapped my two dresses in a piece of cloth—that was my suitcase. I was barefoot because I didn't even own a pair of shoes at that time. My sister gave me the money for the bus fare, and I took off for the capital.

When I got off the bus, I didn't know where to go and I didn't have any money. I asked someone where the nearest park was, and I went and sat down on the park bench. I was three months pregnant, and my stomach was just beginning to show.

I sat on the bench for hours, crying and crying. I kept thinking, "What in the world will become of me? Where can I go? How am I going to eat? Where am I going to sleep?" It was getting dark. People kept walking by and staring at me.

At about 11 P.M., the caretaker of the park came and asked me why I was sitting there so long. I told him I was just relaxing, but he said, "You've been here for hours. I saw you when I came on at 6 o'clock and it's now 11. What's wrong?" He looked at my bundle. "You're not from here, are you?"

I told him I was from Lejamani, and that I was sitting in the park because I'd never been to the city before and I didn't know where else to go. I said I was exhausted and asked if I could spend the night in the park.

He said, yes, I could sleep in the park, and that he would watch me and make sure nothing happened to me. I put my bundle under my head as a pillow and fell asleep.

Early in the morning I woke up to the sounds of the women setting up their stalls in the market nearby. They were lighting fires to warm up coffee and milk for breakfast. I sat on the bench watching them. I was starving but I didn't have a cent.

The caretaker saw me and came over. "You don't have any money, do you?" he said. "Here, take this and buy yourself some bread and a cup of coffee." He gave me 50 cents (one *lempira*).

When the caretaker's shift was over, he warned me, "Look, muchacha, another man will be coming on now. He's not like me, and he might not let you stay here."

So I left. I put my bundle under my arm and started ringing doorbells, asking for work. But I was dirty and dressed in rags, so no one wanted to give me work. I walked up and down the streets, day and night, but couldn't find anything.

In the evening I went back to the park after the same caretaker returned for the night shift. I slept in the park again and began knocking on doors the next day. At the end of the second day, I found work.

I was hired as a cook in someone's house. It was a husband and wife with two children. The woman hired me because she realized I was pregnant and felt sorry for me. She said she'd pay me $10 a month, and I could stay there until I had my baby. But after that I'd have to leave, because she didn't want a baby in the house.

I worked there for six months. The woman was good to me, and every month I'd save the $10 I earned so I'd have money to buy things for my baby.

Some women have all kinds of problems when they get pregnant—they get nauseous and lose their appetite, or they have headaches and get real tired. Not me. The only way I ever know I'm pregnant is because I don't get my period. Otherwise I have no other signs.

I worked right up to the last day. When I started getting bad pains, I told the woman I worked for and she took me to the hospital.

I didn't know anything, because it was my first child. But when I felt the labor pains, I just gritted my teeth and clenched my fists until it passed. I didn't cry or anything.

The nurse said, "When you get a really strong pain that doesn't go away fast, push so the baby comes out."

She showed me this cement board they strap you on with your legs wide open— with everything sticking out. She said I should use it when the baby was ready to come out.

I had these pains, and they'd come and go, come and go. Then they started coming faster and faster, until I got this big pain that wouldn't go away. I said to myself, "Ah-ha. This must be what the nurse was talking about."

So I ran over to the board, stuck my legs in the stirrups, and pushed hard. I felt something wet coming out first. And then I felt the baby zooming out, like water rushing out of a bottle when you take the top off. The baby started crying, and one of the other pregnant women ran to tell the nurse.

The nurse came running over, furious. "Why didn't you call me?" she yelled. "You're not supposed to do this on your own." She grabbed the baby, cut his cord, and stuck him in a tub of water.

I don't know why she was so mad. She never told me to call for help, so how was I supposed to know? I just did it by myself. The next day I left the hospital.

After I had my baby, I went back to Lejamani and lived with one of my sisters. Two years later I got pregnant again.

It's very recent that women have started taking pills and things to keep from getting pregnant. When I was young there was nothing like that. We just got pregnant and had our children.

We were taught that women should have as many children as they can. And we were also taught that when a woman gets pregnant it's her responsibility, not the man's, because she let him touch her. If the man didn't want to marry the woman or help support the child, there wasn't anything the woman could do about it.

When I got pregnant the second time, I didn't bother going to a hospital. I just had the baby at home. I suppose I'm lucky that all my births have been easy; I never had any problems. I've heard the doctors say that when you're pregnant it's good to get exercise so that the child doesn't stick to your stomach. I think that's true, because with all my children I worked and worked until the last minute—washing clothes, ironing, baking bread, grinding corn, making cheese. My stomach would be tremendous. But when it came time to give birth, one big push and whoosh—they'd come out.

The father of my second child didn't have a job, and he wasn't faithful to me either. On top of that he tried to boss me around. So I decided to raise the child by myself.

The father of my third child was no better. As soon as he found out I was pregnant, he left. So many men in Honduras are like that. They stay with a woman just long enough to have a child, then they disappear and don't do anything to help support the children. They usually don't even admit that the children are theirs.

After my third child, I went to work in the capital as a maid so I could support my children. They stayed behind with my mother. By that time my mother was living on her own, and she wanted the children to keep her company. I earned $15 a month and I sent all the money home.

This time the people I worked for didn't treat me very well. They were always yelling at me for something—that I didn't cook the food right, that I burned a pot, that I broke a dish. If I broke something, they'd take it out of my salary. I'd get so nervous whenever mealtime came around, because I knew they'd yell at me for one thing or another.

Part of my job was feeding their big dog. You should've seen the food that dog got! Sometimes he got the leftovers, but sometimes I'd make a special meal for him. My boss would give me meat, tomatoes, and oil and tell me to cook it up for the dog.

And every time I fed that dog, I'd think of my own children. My children never got to eat meat. The $15 a month I sent them was hardly enough to buy beans and corn. But that dog got meat almost every day.

I wasn't allowed to eat the same food the family ate. I'd get beans, tortillas, and rice. The family would eat in a beautiful, big dining room, and I'd eat in the kitchen with the dog. So sometimes I'd steal the dog's food. I knew he wasn't about to say anything, so I'd swap dishes with him. But I always wished I could wrap the food up and somehow get it to my children.

I only got time off to visit my children every three months. I'd leave early on Saturday and return Sunday night so I could be back at work on Monday. Aside from that one weekend every three months, the rest of the time I never had a fixed day off— only when they felt like giving it to me.

I stayed there for two years. Then I returned home to Lejamani.

It was there that I met Alberto and we started living together. I left my children with my mother because she wanted to keep them. But a few months after Alberto and I started living together, the children told me they wanted to come live with us.

I was delighted. But a few days after they arrived, Alberto started fighting with them. He wouldn't give them food. "Let them go back to your mother's house," he told me, "because I'm not about to feed another man's children." What could I do? I had to send them back.

Even while they were living with my mother, they'd come to see me during the day when Alberto wasn't around. I'd give them whatever I had—a tortilla, a piece of bread. I remember one day the oldest boy was sitting at the table eating a tortilla when he heard Alberto come in. He grabbed the tortilla, stuffed it in his shirt, and ran out of the house. I felt awful.

"Look what you've done," I yelled at Alberto. "I can't even give my own children a scrap of food. They're terrified of you. I work my ass off trying to make a few pennies to support my children, and you have no right to stop me from feeding them."

That was when I started having my doubts about living with Alberto. But I was pregnant again, and had nowhere to go.

Alberto and I had three children together. While he worked out in the fields, I stayed in the house taking care of the children, cleaning, making bread to sell, collecting milk from the landowners to make cheese—anything to earn a few pennies.

Part of the time we were happy together, but Alberto had the same problem my father did—he liked to drink. So while I scraped and saved to buy food for the children, he would spend his money on booze. But at least he didn't hit me like my father hit my mother, and he was good to his own children. That's why I stayed with him.

This article argues for the recognition of the important role that women played as bridges between the popular and revolutionary movements during El Salvador's civil war (1979–1992) and the unorganized civilian population. The study analyzes the factors that led to the increased incorporation of women in the armed struggles and their participation in labor unions as well as in such important organizations as the 21 de Junio Asociación Nacional de Educadores Salvadoreños, ANDES (June 21st National Association of Salvadoran Educators) and human rights organizations, such as COMADRES. Women members of these organizations and of labor unions were greatly exposed since they were unarmed and working in the open. This article also discusses women's participation in the guerrilla movement and the lack of recognition they received for their contributions to the armed struggle.

Gendered Revolutionary Bridges

Women in the Salvadoran Resistance Movement (1979–1992)

JULIA DENISE SHAYNE

> *If women as a sector of the population . . . 52.9 percent of the population . . . achieve a level of development and capabilities and join the process in a dynamic and active way, all of the processes of social development, the winner is society.*
>
> —MARÍA MORALES, 1993

Is a "liberated nation" an inherently male concept? What happens if women insurgents do not map out a site for gendered demands within the revolutionary movement? If women had been fully encouraged revolutionary actors, could there have been a military triumph for the guerrillas in El Salvador? In other words, are women a strategic sector with the potential to alter revolutionary outcomes? The answers to these questions may expand the current boundaries of sociological theories of revolution and the literature on gender and revolution. By focusing on the case of women revolutionaries in El Salvador, we can move toward unpacking the significance of these issues. I argue that women revolutionaries served the unconscious yet highly strategic role of *gendered revolutionary bridges.* In short, armed and unarmed women revolutionaries were able to bridge gaps between the guerrillas and unincorporated Salvadoran civilians, thus expanding the revolutionary base and movement. Salvadoran women demonstrated a revolutionary capacity that proved eminently effective but was consistently belittled, and this has had both practical and theoretical consequences. This article aims at addressing the latter.

Theories of Revolution and Gender

Revolution is as difficult a terrain to theorize as it is to negotiate. Theda Skocpol's (1979) groundbreaking *States and Social Revolutions* offers a theory of revolution that has been much contested. One fundamental component of Timothy WickhamCrowley's multifaceted approach is a presumably male "cross-class revolutionary alliance led militarily by rural-based guerrilla organizations" (1991: 89). John Foran departs from a purely structural argument with the concept of "political cultures of opposition" (1992: 9–10), and his analysis implicitly includes women as potential agents of such cultures. Revolutionary theory tends to be structural, thus minimizing contributions of specific actors (see also Goldfrank, 1979; Goldstone, 1991; Walton, 1984). Although these theories move us closer to understanding the complex dynamics of revolution, this article attempts to understand the strategic role of women as a revolutionary entity. To what extent do women participate in revolutionary movements? What specific contributions do women revolutionaries offer? These questions are central for students of gender-and-revolution theory (see, e.g., Randall, 1992; Kruks, Rapp, and Young, 1989; Afshar, 1996; Lobao, 1990; Moghadam, 1997).

Lobao analyzes the structural and social barriers to and factors that encourage the incorporation of women into Latin American guerrilla movements. The major barriers for women lie in "the structural constraint of women's roles in reproductive activities and traditional ideological constraints . . . that define women's roles" (1990: 183). The factors encouraging the incorporation of women include the adoption of a strategy such as prolonged war and the spread of feminism (1990: 185). Middle-class women tend to face fewer barriers to entering political struggle, and they are less vulnerable to the imprisonment and job loss that tend to inhibit activism for working-class or poor women (1990: 188–189).

Moghadam argues that there are two types of revolutions, "the 'woman-in-thefamily' or patriarchal model of revolution, and the 'women's emancipation' or modernizing model" (1997: 142). The woman-in-the-family model "excludes or marginalizes women from definitions and constructions of independence, liberation, and liberty. It frequently constructs an ideological linkage between patriarchal values, nationalism, and the religious order" (1997: 143). Among the goals of the revolutionary movement there is no explicit call for the eradication of a male-dominated family unit; this model extols the role of woman as wife and mother both in the revolutionary process and in postrevolutionary society. During the revolution, for example, women would be expected to reproduce and raise children who would eventually become revolutionaries. Child rearing thus becomes compatible with female revolutionary tasks. According to the women's emancipation model, in contrast, "the emancipation of women is an essential part of the revolution or project of social transformation. It constructs Woman as part of the productive forces and citizenry, to be mobilized for economic and political purposes" (1997: 152).

In developing the strategic role of women revolutionaries as gendered revolutionary bridges, revolutionary theory that departs from the structuralist tradition by highlighting human/cultural agency is highly relevant. Similarly, Wickham-Crowley's (1991) discussion of a multiclass coalition lays the foundation for the conceptualization of the roles of women within that coalition, and a feminist critique significantly enhances these theoretical axes. How do women complement political cultures of opposition? How can women strengthen cross-class coalitions? What do women do to build the alliances between the guerrillas and the masses? Gender-and-revolution theories stop short of fully answering these questions. In both Lobao's (1990) and Moghadam's (1997) analyses, there is a certain reification of the gendered division of labor as justified by the revolutionary project. My hope is to move beyond this.

The roles women played in the Salvadoran resistance movement were strategically significant in their unique ability to foster needed connections with the civilian base. Salvadoran women reduced the anxiety and discomfort of the unincorporated (or uninvolved) bases, broadening the support from the masses and working toward multiclass coalitions. They consciously acted as revolutionaries; rather than allowing the sexist discourse of this counterculture to restrict their positions in the revolutionary movement to that of "support," they challenged it through their strategic actions. They could serve as liaisons with the base communities because they seemed to the newer and unincorporated members of the populace less alien than their male counterparts. The roles that they played individually and together could not be replicated by men. This theory will take on flesh as we look at the organizational work of the 21 de Junio Asociación Nacional de Educadores Salvadoreñas (June 21st National Association of Salvadoran Educators—ANDES), the Comité de Madres y Familiares de Presos, Desaparecidos y Asesinados de El Salvador "Monseñor Romero" (Msgr. Romero Committee of Mothers of the Disappeared—CO-MADRES), the women of the Frente Farabundo Martí para la Liberación Nacional (Farabundo Martí National Liberation Front—FMLN), and the women's movement during the revolutionary war.

My research is based predominantly on in-depth interviews conducted in El Salvador and the United States. I returned to EL Salvador for the fourth time in March 1994 as part of a group of 10 women hosted by the Movimiento de Mujeres "Mélida Anaya Montes" (Mélida Anaya Montes Women's Movement, MAM) and organized by the Committee in Solidarity with the People of El Salvador (CISPES) that in turn was part of a larger delegation of 150 hosted by the Fuerzas Populares de Liberación-Farabundo Martí (Popular Forces of Liberation, FPL).[1]

Gendered Revolutionary Bridges

The Labor Movement: ANDES

ANDES was founded by Mélida Anaya Montes in 1965. The name 21 de Junio refers to the association's first demonstration, when 20,000 teachers and other workers marched through the streets of San Salvador, surrounded the Presidential Palace, and forced the government to pay attention to their demands for legal status as a union. Women currently make up approximately 70 percent of the membership of ANDES (Esperanza Ramos, personal communication, February 1995). María Alicia Rivera, a former organizer with ANDES, describes the strikes of 1968 and 1971 (New America Press [NAP], 1989: 50):

> In 1968, we held a strike that paralyzed the educational system. Participation by the teachers in the strike was almost 100 percent. We occupied the central offices of the Ministry of Education and demonstrated in front of other government buildings and public places. This strike and occupation lasted fifty-eight days; two of our supporters were killed and many others were wounded. Thousands of us were jailed and subjected to physical and psychological torture. In July and August of 1971, we held a second strike to demand raises and educational reforms. Again the government responded with violence.

The strikes of 1967, 1968, and 1971 were led by women. The 1971 event was one of the most massive national strikes ever held against the government (Golden, 1991: 166). These strikes were historically significant to the revolution for the political support they fostered. Women played crucial roles as leaders, organizers, and supporters of militant resistance that predated the declaration of war. Thus, from *before* the beginning, women were building political cultures of opposition that inevitably became foundations for the revolutionary movement.

In a sense, popular organizing was more dangerous than guerrilla warfare because members of the popular movement were unarmed and unable to take immediate defensive action. According to Ramos, however, some members of ANDES were members of the FMLN, concealing their double identity. (She made it clear that she could discuss these issues now but during the war such frankness had not been an option.) Part of the psychological war waged against the women of ANDES was the ever-present threat of losing one's job. This risk was significant since in 1978, twenty-six percent of women were reported as heads of households. By 1989, the figure had almost doubled to fifty-one percent" (Stephen, 1994: 197). In addition, more than half of the women in El Salvador are single mothers: "The fathers have either abandoned their children or they have been killed in the war" (1994: 178). These realities required that the women's marginal incomes remain as reliable as possible.

Many of ANDES's organizers experienced severe repression. Both Esperanza Ramos and Alicia de Astorga (the current secretary general) were captured and tortured. Ramos explained that detention, abuse, and exile served to deepen their commitment to the struggle (personal communication, 1995):

> In 1982 we were a team of collaborators and at this time the executive council was [coordinating] support for our work . . . in secretive ways because in that year there was intensive repression against the teachers. They had already assassinated 300 or 400 teachers. . . . People were disappeared or forced into exile. By the 14th of August we already had

> three unions, and on that day they captured us. First men came in civilian clothes, heavily armed, but when they realized our numbers . . . [there] were uniformed soldiers as well. They took us in a huge truck and they stepped on us, and pinned us down, they tied our hands and then they took us to the Hacienda Police. They took pictures of us in all sorts of positions, they interrogated us . . . and they separated us, the men in one room the women in another. And then four of them they took to another place, and Alicia was one of them, On the four they used the *capucha,*[2] etc. They tortured us . . . in all sorts of ways. . . . They gave us electric shocks, they put us in rooms with bright reflective lights, they wouldn't give us water or any food, they kept us standing up. . . . In total we spent nineteen days. But after seventeen days they stopped torturing and interrogating us because they said they couldn't rip out our tongues and we wouldn't talk.

Ramos and Astorga lived to recall these horrific injustices. They were eventually escorted by the International Red Cross to Mexico, where they remained in exile for 11 months. Then they returned to El Salvador, vindicated and with a renewed commitment to militancy, and joined the FPL.

As is evidenced by the above testimonies, women did not opt for union organizing because it was safe. Women workers are not expected to resist so forcefully, and in doing so en masse the women of ANDES not only shattered stereotypes but acted as gendered revolutionary bridges by providing a. model for other disenchanted sectors of society. Their activities dated back 15 years; they were one of the first and most revolutionary unions in Salvadoran history. According to Rivera (NAP, 1989: 50),

> When ANDES was first organized, teachers joined because of the union's stand on labor issues, such as pensions and raises. But within a couple of years, we began to realize that injustice was a reality for everyone—not just teachers. We began to redefine ourselves, and we came to understand that ANDES faced two struggles: one for our immediate goals as teachers, and one to achieve peace and self-determination for our country in the long run. . . . So in 1975 . . . we joined the Popular Revolutionary Bloc [Bloque Popular Revolucionario—BPR].

Rivera highlights the tendency for people to organize within their own sectors but at the same time reach out to others through such organizations as the BPR. This emphasizes the interdependency of the resistance movement and the fluidity of popular organizing. Similarly, she points to the inability to sequester one sector's struggle (teachers) from the revolutionary movement as a whole. Thus we can see the women of ANDES working through the BPR to build what eventually became multiclass coalitions in support of the revolution. In this respect, women acted as gendered revolutionary bridges between organizations.

The impact of militant women on one another was very significant. In effect, ANDES women demonstrated to their counterparts in other sectors, both organized and unorganized, that there was both a need and a place for them in the resistance movement. Working with one's sector in coalition with other sectors strengthened the popular movement.

The Salvadoran government, military, and death squads abducted, tortured, and killed those they perceived as subversive. Because of this there was a fear of getting involved or even showing sympathy with any dissenting group. Practice was perhaps the only way for organizers to perfect their tactics and remain out of jail or alive. Given the constant threats that the resistance movement faced, people outside it had to overcome their fears and trust the work of the organized sectors. The development of this trust was greatly due to the work of the women members of ANDES; women were able to build the needed bridges. What I am suggesting is that women demonstrating in the city streets put human faces on what the media and government termed "Cubanbacked terrorists." It was important for men and women to see that some members of the opposition were not only unarmed but in fact women.

The Human Rights Movement: CO-MADRES

The human rights sector, also dominated by women, had a strong effect on the masses. The war produced 8,000 disappearances and 80,000 mostly civilian casualties (Stephen, 1994: 196), and CO-MADRES confronted the tortured, raped, and maimed bodies of their own and others' loved ones found on train tracks and in clandestine cemeteries. Its work was fundamental to the resistance movement because it was confronting the Salvadoran and U.S. governments regarding heinous human rights violations that were supposedly not happening.

Both as a unit and individually, the members of CO-MADRES, with the support of the Archdiocese of the Catholic Church, were moved to action because of their own pain. María Teresa Tula initially became involved after her husband, a union activist, was detained and tortured by the National Guard (Stephen, 1994: 97, 51). During 1978–1979, the sites of CO-MADRES actions ranged from the United Nations (UN) to the Red Cross to Catholic churches, depending on the goal. To receive international attention and put pressure on the Salvadoran government, CO-MADRES conducted a peaceful occupation of the office of the UN in El Salvador. They insisted that their demands for the release of the disappeared and political prisoners be forwarded to Geneva and refused to leave until this had been done. This and similar confrontations drew international attention to human rights violations in El Salvador and forced those at various levels of leadership to acknowledge that women were aware of and resisting the atrocities, This inevitably brought attention and thus risk to themselves and their families. As with ANDES, all of this took place before the declaration of war.

María Teresa Tula explained that in 1979 the government felt threatened by the truth that CO-MADRES exposed regarding the disappeared because it contradicted the fabricated image of democracy and respect for human rights (Stephen, 1994: 83–84):

> Every day we would dig up about 25–30 bodies that would be sent in plastic bags to the central cemetery. We found a lot of clandestine cemeteries that became famous as body dumps. . . . We did this all over El Salvador. . . . Many people found their disappeared relatives this way. Sometimes they identified them because of their belt buckle . . . or

> something they were wearing. Often, the bodies were decapitated or mutilated so badly that you couldn't tell who it was. . . . The media was paying a lot more attention to us. . . . When the government saw that we were turning up lots of bodies, they tried to stop us by increasing the repression against us. They started to watch us and we had to be more careful.

In 1980 the CO-MADRES office was bombed (Stephen, 1994: 103). In the same year Archbishop Romero was assassinated. As María Teresa Tula put it, "They took his life because he was telling the truth. Telling the truth was his death sentence" (1994: 87). The members of CO-MADRES knew who their enemies were, but they refused to stop organizing.

The work that CO-MADRES did as gendered revolutionary bridges was somewhat different from that of ANDES. As a human rights organization, it did not carry the same stigma as a labor union, and in addition, it worked through and with the support of the church. Clearly, this did not reduce government hostility toward its members. Human rights organizations are often positioned as apolitical; when one thinks of a revolutionary organization, CO-MADRES is not generally the first group to come to mind. This is not to imply that the work that it did was not itself revolutionary. It peacefully called on the state to end the war with justice—a demand that was operationalized without weapons but resulted in severe repression. Because of its members' innocent demeanor as a group of mothers, grandmothers, sisters, and wives, CO-MADRES not only served as a bridge to legitimate the popular movement in the eyes of the unorganized but also provided a small amount of security (Stephen, 1994: 106):

> We participated in celebrations for international workers' day. . . . We were always invited to participate in the marches on this day. We would dress up in black and mingle with the workers and students in the march. The authorities usually respected us a little more than the young people and our presence could help keep them from being harassed. Often the police would grab people participating in the march and we would intervene. Also, whenever we saw someone taking pictures of the demonstrators, and we recognized that person as being from the police, we would take away their camera, remove the film, and destroy it.

As the war escalated and CO-MADRES continued to carry out confrontational actions, the repression increased. In 1982 the first member of CO-MADRES was abducted and jailed (Stephen, 1994: 111):

> She was left on the railroad tracks with her hands tied behind her back and a gag in her mouth so that she couldn't scream for help. . . . Her face was completely swollen and her teeth were broken where they had smashed her mouth in with the butt of a rifle. . . . They had burned her body with cigarette butts. . . . They rammed their rifle butts into her breasts and burned her. They took off all of her clothes and she was raped by seven men.

In the mid-1980s CO-MADRES reconfirmed their indispensability to the popular movement by revitalizing it. Public protests had become less frequent during 1983 and 1984, but in 1984 CO-MADRES went to the U.S. Embassy to demand an end to U.S. military aid and intervention. The bold action of these women again mobilized other sectors to march in solidarity with them. "This was how the silence of public protest from a wide range of sectors was broken. No one had been in the streets for years [—just] tanks and the military" (Stephen, 1994: 119).

Both the leadership that CO-MADRES provided and the pain they endured were clearly effective and even necessary to the national resistance movement in El Salvador. The government and military would not have followed, abducted, and brutalized a relatively small group of "mothers" had they been of no threat to their hold on power. The arena of CO-MADRES' struggle was human rights, a vision of social justice that explicitly included women. The urgency and brutality of the war led it to join the broader struggle. Consciously or not, the women of CO-MADRES strategically projected their femininity as mothers and wives; the less threatening they appeared, the more inviting they were to unincorporated masses. As trustworthy mothers, they bridged gaps between the bases, the popular movement, and the guerrillas as no other group of women could.

The Women of the FMLN

Perhaps the clearest example of women working as gendered revolutionary bridges was within the guerrilla movement. Living amid poverty and injustice drew some women to the FMLN for its political stands. As Elsy, one excombatant with the FPL, put it, "We realized that the Frente was there to protect us, so for many of us, our aspiration was to join the Frente" (personal communication, 1994). Salvadoran women drew strength and inspiration from each other to overcome internal and social battles against those who claimed that the inclusion of women was inappropriate. A handful of revered women revolutionaries, including Mélida Anaya Montes (Comandante "Ana María"), Nidia Díaz, Eugenia, and Ana Guadalupe Martínez, had been active members of the FMLN since its inception, and they served as role models, challenging the stereotype of women as unfit for military tasks. In this sense, women guerrillas served as gendered revolutionary bridges through their mere existence.

Ana Guadalupe Martínez gained her initial consciousness through a Christian family upbringing. She went on to the University of El Salvador and became active in student politics regarding the university budget and its restrictions on working-class students who could not afford tuition. Eventually, she joined the Ejército Revolucionarío del Pueblo (People's Revolutionary Army—ERP) and attained one of the highest positions in the FMLN held by a woman. She explained in an interview in 1986 how the participation of women in the FMLN affected other women (NAP, 1989: 158):

> The women saw me and talked with me and realized that we weren't exceptional people, we were just like them, with the same fears and hopes and faith. Well, in a little

> while they were so identified with us and with their husbands and their brothers that the ideological barriers between women and men diminished. . . . The women are immediately more *confident when they see a compañera* [emphasis added].

Many of these women eventually supported the FMLN by hiding weapons, cooking, or obtaining cloth for flags. The trust that Martínez refers to is another result of women's work as gendered revolutionary bridges in the Salvadoran revolution.

Women played many different roles within the FMLN: logistics, radio and communication, food distribution, health and first-aid services, the rear guard, the frontlines, and political-diplomatic work. Guerrilla organizing is a highly interdependent project. An area of work such as "logistics" may sound insignificant, but if the woman in charge of transporting weapons failed to make a connection, the military action would not happen, causing a chain reaction of failed guerrilla encounters. Female ex-combatants repeatedly said that they knew they had contributed significantly to the struggle even if their work has since been ignored by their male compañeros. Some are now struggling to call attention to their contributions. Other women ex-combatants felt that because they did the same tasks as men they were clearly as competent and needed no "official" recognition from men.

María Morales joined the revolutionary struggle when she was 11 years old, and by the time she was 15 she was the head of a platoon composed of older men. She had this to say about the role of women in the FPL (personal communication, 1993):

> During the military actions, women for the most part took "secondary" roles, for example, taking care of the rear guard, communication, logistics, health—work that was very important and put their lives in danger but was not [recognized]. And when a woman would go to the front lines into battle, that would be a very new kind of thing that had a great impact upon the populace as well as the men in the fighting force.

The participation that Morales describes helped to pave the way for a reconceptualization of the role and status of women in Salvadoran society. This recalls Lobao's (1990) suggestion that feminism encouraged the incorporation of women into guerrilla movements, but Morales indicates that it was the result of women's demonstrating their capabilities as opposed to engaging with male comrades about the virtues of feminism.

Nidia Díaz became active in the political struggle in El Salvador in 1971, and by 1975 she was part of the leadership of the revolutionary movement. During this time she completed four years of advanced study in psychology. She is a member of the Partido Revolucionario de Trabajadores Centroamericanos (Revolutionary Party of Central American Workers—PRTC), and her work with the PRTC and the FMLN eventually placed her at the UN-sponsored negotiation table in Geneva in 1991. She was captured by a U.S. military adviser in April 1985 and held for seven months in jail, eventually to be released in a prisoner exchange with Inés Duarte, the then president's daughter (Díaz, 1992). This was an extremely risky operation, given that it occurred in the capital of San Salvador, which had about 25,000 soldiers in readiness for its defense, and its implementation underlines the importance of Nidia Díaz to the FMLN's leadership.

At the same time, it is important to hear how differently some other women of the FMLN felt about their placement, treatment, and roles. There is a certain anonymity and even loss of gender (Gladis Sibrián, personal communication, October 1994) that is characteristic of guerrilla organizing, but this does not, however, account for the skewed ratio of women in high positions. The general command of the FMLN has been all-male since its inception. Leaders such as Mélida Anaya Montes, Ana Guadalupe Martínez, and Nidia Díaz were exceptions, and many women felt a lack of encouragement and support for their efforts. Camila, an ex-combatant with the Resistencia Nacional (National Resistance—RN) who participated in the 1989 final offensive, observes (Ueltzen, 1993: 104):

> The combatant's life has been similar for men and women. . . . Women have participated in all aspects of the war, but in a very limited way in the area of decision making. Women were incorporated into the areas of communications, service, health, etc. This is a reflection of the culture and society, where machismo has always existed—in that sense there is a differentiation between what it means to be a male combatant and a female combatant. During combat you didn't notice differences.

María Morales and Gladis Sibrián expressed similar sentiments in reflecting on the roles of women in the FMLN. Both women felt that not only did women have to work two or three times as hard to prove themselves but because of their domestic and child-rearing tasks they often failed to receive the training to rise above levels of support combat (María Morales, personal communication, 1993):

> At the opportunity of receiving military or any sort of training, those who would go were the men because they had the space and the time and so women had to take care of the house, and if you were young, you had to take care of your brothers and sisters, So the logical result was that men keep having more opportunities to advance . . . and because of these capabilities they are in commanding posts; they decide how a strategy is going to be defined and we are not there. . . . They don't take us into account.

Gladis Sibrián has a double perspective regarding the position of women within the FMLN and FPL because in addition to fighting in El Salvador she was one of three women to represent the FMLN in the United States (personal communication, October 1995). She told me that she had felt a lack of encouragement for her work abroad, and this was significant because she had agreed to serve as representative even though she wanted to return home to join the struggle there.

Ileana, a combatant with the guerrilla army of the Partido Comunista Salvadoreño (Salvadoran Communist party—PC) who became commander of an all-woman platoon and was killed in combat in 1984, reported (NAP, 1989: 162–163):

> At first I performed a variety of tasks, but I eventually was given greater responsibilities as I developed and acquired skill. Eventually I became the commander of a squadron with seven women under my command. My leadership experience plus valid

> complaints that the women were being stationed only to cover and hold our combat positions led to the command's decision to form an all-woman platoon.

Ana Matilde Rodar, who fought in San Salvador with the FPL and is now very active with the Mélida Anaya Montes Women's Movement, recalls her own and other women's roles within the FMLN (personal communication, 1994):

> Women had the role of cooks, as radio operators, working hospitals, doing a lot of work with the population, and doing a lot of running from one place to another. . . . I fought here in the metropolitan area [San Salvador], and my job was as a nurse. I passed as a student of medicine, so when the compañeros, the combatants, would come down from the mountains wounded, I would also arrange for them to be entered into the hospital. I also had the job of hiding arms in houses, also to arrange the arms so that they were hidden in cars so that they could be carried up to the mountains. It was logistical work, as they say.

Again we see that women were working with the population, serving as bridges. Without their political work with the civilian population, the military struggle would have been impossible, There was a clear need for civilians to understand, support, and not feel frightened by the struggle of the FMLN. Their support was essential if they were to be willing to risk their own lives protecting the lives of FMLN combatants. This organizational link is the result of predominantly women's working with the population—serving as bridges.

María (Serrano) Chichilco, an elected member of the FPL's Political Commission, joined the struggle in 1974 as a member of a popular peasant organization. Throughout the war, she too worked with base communities including peasants and internal refugees and also served as a combatant. She believes that participating in the war was an opportunity to prove by action that women have the same ability to perform revolutionary tasks as do men. She acknowledged that only 30 percent of all revolutionary contingents were women but believes that the reason for this is that "women are not incorporated into society itself. We women, since birth, have unfortunately a 'disadvantage,' that is the 'disadvantage' of being a woman" (Ueltzen, 1993: 231).

This sentiment is one echoed by many women. The analysis is implicitly feminist, as it faults societal conditioning rather than men, suggesting that social change is possible and will remedy the situation. Complaints from female ex-combatants regarding machismo, however, are common. Women often confronted machismo directly, again indicating a hope for change. For example, there were male guerrillas who thought it inappropriate for their wives to join. In February 1975 Compañera Eugenia joined the FPL after a long history of work in Christian base comtunities, concluding that the only road to true social change was through revolutionary armed struggle (NAP, 1989: 139):

> Eugenia's assignment to train cadre took her all over the countryside of El Salvador. When speaking to male recruits, she stressed the importance of abolishing *machismo;* she encouraged these men to take on domestic responsibilities and to treat women as

> equals. She also organized groups of women and energetically promoted the participation of women in all aspects of political work. The fact that women in rural areas were so successfully integrated into the movement in spite of deeply ingrained *machismo* can be attributed to two factors: organizational principles which explicitly promoted equality, and the determined efforts of *compañeras* like Eugenia.

In this case, Eugenia's commitment both to the revolution and to just treatment for women served as a bridge, helping to reduce the impact of machismo and providing access to the movement to other women.

Lorena Peña (Rebeca Palacios) has been a member of the Political Commission of the FPL and the Political-Diplomatic Commission of the FMLN and now represents the FMLN in the current Legislative Assembly. In 1991, she assessed the role of women in the FPL as follows (Golden, 1991: 173):

> The statutes of the organization prohibit discrimination against women. The fact is that the whole culture is sexist, and there is not a single comrade who is not affected by this. If its true that our organization provides the opportunities for women to develop themselves in daily concrete work, it is also true that the woman herself has to overcome a thousand and one obstacles—with her *compañero,* with her children, with her co-workers, with the organization itself, And above all, she has to overcome the idea that being a party militant requires her to be less of a woman.

Every female FMLN ex-combatant has her own account of sexism in the party and the reasons for it. To some women, it was not an obstacle, while others worked three times as hard and still others were prevented by their compañeros from joining. Many of the women who felt "equal" within the FMLN are also now part of the growing movement expressing the urgent need to come together as women, as feminists, and as (predominantly) ex-combatants to expand the revolution of the nation to include the feminist revolution.

From the above testimonies we can see that there were two mechanisms placing women guerrillas in the position of bridges. First, they served as role models for one another; male guerrillas could not be role models for women who were feeling alienated from military politics because of personal or party experiences with machismo. Second, within the context of the larger guerrilla project, women worked with the population, thus fostering the necessary trust between the guerrillas and the masses that facilitated the transport of weapons, the care of the wounded, and the other logistical tasks of guerrilla warfare.

The Women's Movement

The final example of women's role as bridges occurred, quite ironically, under the auspices of a women's movement. Gloria Guzmán, the coordinator of the Women's Program of the Archdiocese of San Salvador and a self-described "woman of the left" (personal communication, 1994), said that the women's movement that was born during the war was a result of the war—that the resistance movement saw a strategic need to incorporate women into the struggle and found that an effective way of accomplishing this was establishing woman-focused organizations. In other words, the parties of the FMLN identified women as potential guerrillas and undertook the creation of women's organizations to recruit them. Each of the parties of the FMLN eventually formed its own women's organization, and these organizations have become something much more dynamic than women's commissions for these parties. According to Dilcia Maroquín of Mujeres por La Dignidad y La Vida (Women for Dignity and Life—Las Dignas), "All of the women's groups came into being for convenience's sake because the men wanted them to, because they could get resources; they weren't formed by women because of their needs" (personal communication, 1994). Again, what we are hearing regarding women's organizing during the war is that the FMLN virtually used women as a sector to recruit new women. Again, we see women serving as bridges. I would suspect, however, that no one in the FMLN expected that women's organizing would not only continue but eventually demand autonomy from leftist parties. Women's organizing during the war, especially that which was initiated by men of the FMLN, is another example of women's receiving training and creative tools while simultaneously being used and treated with disrespect. This all too prevalent theme helps to fuel the Salvadoran contemporary women's movement.

Conclusion

What would have happened in El Salvador if women had been fully acknowledged actors in the revolutionary process? Clearly, we will never know, but let us speculate for a moment. Wickham-Crowley (1991) identifies cross-class revolutionary alliances led by guerrilla movements as a central factor in successful revolutions. Coupled with Lobao's (1990) analysis that middle-class women are often more likely to join guerrilla movements as a result of fewer economic restrictions, this indicates that had the task of developing cross-class alliances been assigned to women, the Salvadoran revolution could have expanded beyond the working and peasant classes. Similarly, Foran's (1992; 1997a; 1997b) political cultures of opposition, if crafted by rather than simply given the support of women, could have expanded the popular movement. If the revolutionary significance of women had been acknowledged by their male comrades, the popular movement would certainly have been strengthened: women were marginalized at the very least as women, regardless of class position, and often several times over as shanty-town dwellers, students, peasants, and so forth. Thus, a coupling of Moghadam's (1997) emancipation model with Foran's (1992) political cultures of opposition could have greatly expanded the revolutionary project. Similarly, I am confident that the guerrilla movement in El Salvador would have been strengthened had women revolutionaries been explicitly recognized for their crucial work with the masses.

We can only speculate about what the U.S. response to a strengthened opposition movement in El Salvador might have been. Similarly, we do not know whether the ruling regime would have responded to this opposition by replacing the democratic facade with an individual dictator—which, according to Foran's (1992) theory of revolution, is another necessary component of a successful revolution. We do know that women did indeed strengthen the revolutionary movement through their action as gendered revolutionary bridges, and it is probable that the outcome would have been different had this role been recognized and extended to other sectors of the population.

ANDES served as a gendered revolutionary bridge in the strictest sense. The women of ANDES worked predominantly in urban areas, using city streets and protests to provide female faces to the so-called guerrilla terrorists of the countryside. Their demonstrations and militancy long predated the declaration of war. Despite their militancy, they were able to reduce obstacles to joining the opposition for newer political actors. ANDES eventually joined the BPR, while individual members simultaneously took up arms with the FMLN. This process of incorporation resulted in previously apolitical individuals becoming at least members of the popular movement if not full members of the FMLN.

The work of CO-MADRES as a gendered revolutionary bridge was very different from but equally as important as that of ANDES. Despite its militancy, it maintained a relatively apolitical demeanor. Superficially, it was a small group of mothers and widows looking for their loved ones, sanctioned by the church. It could be argued that CO-MADRES reinforced the patriarchal (thus counterrevolutionary) divisions of gender by projecting its members' femininity, but this assessment belittles the strategic agency of a nominally nonrevolutionary organization. CO-MADRES capitalized on its normative social positioning and appearance to serve as a bridge for angry and frightened women but also for the greater popular movement.

Women in the FMLN also served as gendered revolutionary bridges. Women guerrillas were responsible for the crucial work with the population; the women fostered the trust of the masses that was eventually transformed into support. Similarly, women guerrillas were often the most important reason that women opted to join the guerrillas; women served as bridges to one another in a context in which female role models were few. The men of the FMLN used women to incorporate other women into the wartime women's movement as potential FMLN combatants, but this strategy had the unexpected consequence of providing the contemporary women's movement with more skills and bitter memories. I have spoken of the sense of betrayal and frustration that many women revolutionaries are currently confronting. In conclusion, it is worth asking: Had the demands, abilities, and revolutionary significance of women been addressed and the revolution been successful, where would El Salvador and its women be today?

NOTES

1. I mention the hosts and coordinators here because this prearranged dynamic had a tremendous impact on my research. First, it gave me access to many meetings and interviews that I would not have otherwise been privy to. It is not at all uncommon when doing fieldwork and interviews in particular to be confronted by a seemingly impenetrable barrier. Our hosts in El Salvador were very familiar with the Committee in Solidarity with the People of El Salvador (CISPES) and its long history of solidarity work in the United States, and this relationship created trust before any interactions with the subjects of the research ever occurred. No one turned down my request for an interview except because of time constraints. While in

El Salvador I conducted six semistructured interviews and was a participant observer of ten group discussions with audiences from 10 to 150 persons, always followed by questions and answers. Three interviews were conducted during the International Women's Day March in San Salvador, when I approached strangers who could only assume that my presence was an act of solidarity. Five more semistructured interviews were conducted in El Salvador for me with questions I had written and left with my colleagues Victoría Polanco and Leslie Schuld. I also conducted five semistructured interviews with Salvadoran women and men who were in California for political reasons. In the Bay area I was a participant observer at six public presentations, two addressed to large mixed audiences and four to a small group of women who were familiar with the situation in El Salvador.

2. The *capucha* is a form of torture in which the prisoner's head is covered with a hood (usually the inside of the hood is coated with toxic chemicals). As the prisoner breathes, the hood sticks to his or her face, resulting in suffocation (Stephen, 1994: 237).

References

Afshar, Haleh. 1996. *Women and Politics in the Third World.* London: Routledge.

Díaz, Nidia. 1992. *I Was Never Alone: A Prison Diary from El Salvador.* New York: Ocean Press.

Foran, John (ed.). 1992. "A theory of Third World social revolutions: Iran, Nicaragua, and El Salvador compared." *Critical Sociology* 19(2): 3–27.

———. 1997a. "The comparative-historical sociology of Third World social revolutions: why a few succeed, why most fail," in John Foran (ed.), *Theorizing Revolutions.* London: Routledge.

———. 1997b. *Theorizing Revolutions.* London: Routledge.

Golden, Renny. 1991. *The Hour of the Poor, the Hour of Women: Salvadoran Women Speak.* New York: Crossroad.

Goldfrank, Walter (ed.). 1979. *The World-System of Capitalism: Past and Present.* Beverly Hills, CA, Sage.

Goldstone, Jack A. 1991. *Revolution and Rebellion in the Early Modern World.* Berkeley: University of California Press.

Kruks, Sonia, Rayna Rapp, and Marilyn Young (eds.). 1989. *Promissory Notes: Women in the Transition to Socialism.* New York; Monthly Review Press.

Lobao, Linda. 1990. "Women in revolutionary movements: changing patterns of Latin American guerrilla struggle," in Guida West and Rhoda Lois Blumberg (eds.), *Women and Social Protest.* New York: Oxford University Press.

Moghadam, Valentine M. 1997. "Gender and revolutions," in John Foran (ed.), *Theorizing Revolutions.* London: Routledge.

New Americas Press (NAP) (ed.). 1989. *A Dream Compels Us: Voices of Salvadoran Women.* Boston: South End Press.

Randall, Margaret. 1992. *Gathering Rage; The Failure of 20th Century Revolutions to Develop a Feminist Agenda.* New York: Monthly Review Press.

Skocpol, Theda. 1979. *Stares and Social Revolutions.* Cambridge, U.K.: Cambridge University Press.

Stephen, Lynn (ed. and trans.). 1994. *Hear My Testimony: María Teresa Tula, Human Rights Activist of El Salvador.* Boston: South End Press.

Ueltzen, Stefan. 1993. *Canto salvadoreña que soy: Entrevistas con mujeres en la lucha.* San Salvador: Editorial Sombrero Azul.

Walton, John. 1984. *Reluctant Rebels.* New York: Columbia University Press.

Wickham-Crowley, Timothy. 1991. "A qualitative comparative approach to Latin American revolutions." *International Journal of Comparative Sociology* 32(1–2): 82–109.

Below is a section of The Shadow Report on Guatemala, which was presented in March 2012 during the 104th Session of the Human Rights Committee to the United Nations in New York. It was submitted by the following organizations: Organización Trans Reinas de la Noche (OTRANS), Red Latinoamericana y del Caribe de Personas Trans (RED LACTRANS), The International Gay and Lesbian Human Rights Commission (IGLHRC), The Heartland Alliance for Human Needs & Human Rights, and The George Washington University Law School of International Human Rights. Their purpose was to document human rights violations to the LGBT community in Guatemala.

Excerpts from

Human Rights Violations of Lesbian, Gay, Bisexual, and Transgender (LGBT) People in Guatemala: A Shadow Report

Submitted for consideration at the 104th Session of the Human Rights Committee

March 2012, New York

Submitted to the United Nations Human Rights Committee by:

* Organizacion Trans Reinas de la Noche Organizacion (OTRANS)
* Red Latinoamericana y del Caribe de Personas Trans (RED LACTRANS)
* The International Gay and Lesbian Human Rights Commission (IGLHRC)
* The Heartland Alliance for Human Needs & Human Rights
* The George Washington University Law School International Human Rights Clinic

Introduction

This shadow report on the human rights situation of LGBT people in Guatemala was written and submitted through the collaborative efforts of Organizacion Trans Reinas de la Noche (OTRANS), Red Latinoamericana y del Caribe de Personas Trans (RED LACTRANS), the International Gay and Lesbian Human Rights Commission (IGLHRC), the Heartland Alliance for Human Needs & Human Rights, and The George Washington University Law School International Human Rights Clinic.

Guatemala became party to the International Covenant on Civil and Political Rights on May 5, 1992.[1] Guatemala submitted its third report under Article 40 of the ICCPR on March 31, 2010.[2]

This shadow report discusses the human rights situation of LGBT people in Guatemala. The ICCPR guarantees protections to individuals that are guaranteed by the state and must be ensured in the form of positive and negative binding legal obligations. These rights are guaranteed to all people within the state territory or subject to the state's jurisdiction, regardless of that person's status under domestic law.[3]

Various UN bodies have recently called for States parties to ensure that their laws prohibit discrimination on the basis of sex, sexual orientation, and gender identity.[4] These calls to action represent an important step for the augmentation of human rights for LGBT individuals, which the UN Human Rights Council identified as a key concern when it passed Resolution 17/19, *Human rights, sexual orientation, and gender identity*, in June 2011.[5] Guatemala, then a member of the Human Rights Council, voted in support of this resolution.[6] In practice, however, the Guatemalan State has done little to protect the human rights of sexual minorities.

The Human Rights Committee has demonstrated serious concern for the rights of sexual minorities in several other countries. This should be taken as guidance by the government of Guatemala. In its recent Concluding Observations following its review of Jamaica, the Committee encouraged Jamaica to take steps to protect individuals from discrimination on the basis of sexual orientation and gender identity. It stated that Jamaica "should send a clear message that it does not tolerate any form of harassment, discrimination or violence against persons for their sexual orientation."[7] While the specifics of those concluding observations focused on the situation of individuals who identify as homosexual, or, on rights associated with sexual orientation, the HRC also demonstrated concern about rights associated with gender identity, as will be discussed below.[8]

Furthermore, during the course of the 2008 Universal Periodic Review Process at the Human Rights Council, Switzerland, Slovenia, and the Czech Republic made recommendations to Guatemala calling attention to the lack of compliance with human rights standards regarding LGBT individuals. These three countries recommended that Guatemala implement measures to combat discrimination against human rights defenders and others on the basis of sexual orientation and gender identity, and to end impunity for such attacks, including "specific education and awareness programmes for law enforcement, judicial and other authorities, with focus, *inter alia*, on protection of enjoyment of human rights by persons of minority sexual orientation and gender identity."[9] Despite these calls to action, the Government has taken no steps to implement these much-needed changes in the intervening years.[10]

Despite the importance of observing and protecting LGBT rights, the State of Guatemala makes no mention of issues faced by the LGBT community in its report to the HRC.[11] The State's failure to protect these rights results in egregious human rights violations, including violations of the right to protection from nondiscrimination, the right to equal treatment of men and women, the right to life, the right to freedom from torture, cruel, inhuman, and degrading treatment, the right to liberty, the right to security of person, the right to a fair trial, the right to legal personhood, the right to privacy, the right to freedom of expression, the right to freedom of association, the right to a family life, and the rights of children.

LGBT abuse in Guatemala is all the more surprising as, according to the recent *National Plan of Human Rights: 2007–2017* (published by the Presidential Commission of Human Rights Guatemala, 2007) there is a recognition of the "importance of developing a social culture of tolerance, of respect of difference…to create and promote public policies that allow the integration and acceptance of people of diverse sexual orientation in society."

Background

A. Sexual Orientation and Gender Identity

Sexual orientation refers to "each person's capacity for profound emotional, affectional and sexual attraction to, and intimate and sexual relations with, individuals of a different gender or the same gender or more than one gender."[12] This term includes lesbian, gay, bisexual, or heterosexual (straight) orientations.[13]

Gender identity refers to

> [E]ach person's deeply felt internal and individual experience of gender, which may or may not correspond with the sex assigned at birth, including the personal sense of the body (which may involve, if freely chosen, modification of bodily appearance or function by medical, surgical or other means) and other expressions of gender, including dress, speech and mannerisms.[14]

The external manifestation of a person's gender identity is called gender expression.[15] Gender expression usually involves "masculine," "feminine," or gender-variant behavior.[16] Transgender people generally seek to make their gender expression match their gender identity, rather than their sex at birth.[17] In other words, a person whose sex at birth is determined to be male, but who has an internal sense of being a female, is a transgender woman.

Transgender is a term for people whose gender identity and/or gender expression and their sex at birth do not match.[18] This term may include transsexuals, cross-dressers, and other gender-variant people.[19] Altering one's birth sex is not a simple or short process, but rather a process that occurs over a long period of time known as "transition."[20] Steps that may be, but are not always, included in transition are: telling one's family and friends, changing ones name and/or sex on legal documents, hormone therapy, and medical treatment including surgery.[21]

B. Strong Pattern of Generalized Violence and Human Rights Offenses in Guatemala

Guatemala experienced an armed conflict from 1962 to 1996. Even now, years after conflict has ended, the country still suffers from extremely high rates of violence. Recorded killings in Guatemala routinely exceed 5,000 per year.[22] In fact, in 2010, 4,925 violent deaths were recorded, including 41 lynchings, as well as 6,132 reports injury as a result of violent attacks.[23] This general societal violence is intrinsic to the documented, widespread patterns of social cleansing and lynching.[24] Though much of this violence occurs at the hands of private individuals, the UN Special Rapporteur on extrajudicial, summary or arbitrary executions recommends that the State must take responsibility and take steps to reduce these occurrences.[25] Within Guatemalan society, minority groups, including LGBT individuals, are subject to particularly high levels of violence.

C. Lack of Reporting and Recording

Justice systems in Guatemala are ineffective largely due to a lack of infrastructure for recording and reporting crimes, discrimination, and violations of human rights. As described by Phillip Alston, the U.N. Special Rapporteur on extrajudicial, summary or arbitrary executions:

> Structural changes in security and justice have not been put forward, neither to diminish the causes of crime nor to address the social, cultural and economic risk factors of violence. Insecurity and impunity affect daily life and generate mistrust and social dissatisfaction. All this is exacerbated by the lack of adequate attention to victims.[26]

As the systems stand, even where statistics exist, their accuracy is questionable. Statistics that may actually reflect hate crimes or discrimination may instead be characterized as reflecting drug trafficking or gang violence, thereby allowing the government to overlook important societal issues pertaining to the LGBT community.[27] In addition to a lack of clarity around the causes of violence, in Guatemala the security and justice sectors also lack appropriate methods to disaggregate statistics, which results in unclear statistics that may not accurately portray the impact of violence in various communities. Furthermore, these statistics, whether accurate or not, may be misused by the police. Thus, in any individual crime that is documented by the police, a record of the crime itself may exist, but numerous important details relevant to the appropriate classification and understanding of what actually transpired, may be missing.

Another area in which reporting and recording of statistics fails the LGBT community in Guatemala is in the area of HIV/AIDS infection rates. These statistics reflect infection rates for men who have sex with men (MSM) and for female sex workers, but may or may not accurately reflect numbers among the population of transgender women sex workers (who are regarded under Guatemalan law as male).[28] The lack of accurate statistics makes it difficult to fully call attention to the problems faced by the transgender community in Guatemala.

Prohibition of Torture and Cruel, Inhuman or Degrading Treatment or Punishment; Right to Liberty and Security of Persons; and Treatment of Persons Deprived of Liberty (Art 7, 9, and 10)

Articles 7, 9 and 10(1), recognize the right of every individual to be free from torture; arbitrary arrest; and cruel, inhuman or degrading treatment or punishment. In its General Comments on Article 7, the Committee has noted that States have a positive obligation to provide specific training for law enforcement officers and must hold responsible all those who violate the prohibition on torture.[29] The time and place of all interrogations must be recorded, together with the names of all those present, and this information should be available for purposes of judicial or administrative proceedings. By its General Comments on Article 10, the Committee has stated "treating all persons deprived of their liberty with humanity and with respect for their dignity is a fundamental and universally applicable rule...[which] must be applied without distinction of any kind, such as race, colour, sex, language, religion, political or other opinion, national or social origin, property, birth or other status."[30] In recent Concluding Observations, the HRC has called for an end to "enforced disappearance," "arbitrary detention,"[31] "torture" and "forced displacement."[32] It has reaffirmed that a judge should not admit evidence obtained under torture,[33] and where allegations of mistreatment in detention have been made, the State must put in place the appropriate structures to ensure that all claims are robustly and transparently investigated.[34]

1. Prohibition of Torture and Cruel, Inhuman or Degrading Treatment or Punishment. The prohibition of torture relates not only to physical abuse but also to "acts that cause mental suffering to the victim," including intimidation.[35] In Guatemala, the transgender community lives under threat of physical attack. In 2010, for instance, a transgender woman and human rights defender named Johana Ramirez was the victim of an attempt on her life. While in a public place, she realized that she was being followed by a group of four men. When Johana recognized that one of them had a gun and was preparing to shoot her, she narrowly escaped the attack by running away and hiding in a nearby store.[36]

Forced or involuntary disappearances also qualify as torture under the terms of the Covenant as well as other international human rights law.[37] Transgender individuals in Guatemala may be subject to forced disappearances that amount to torture. On February 23, 2010, for instance, a witness observed a young man in a blue jeep abduct a transgender woman named Catherine Mishel Barrios from the Central Historic district of Guatemala City.[38] She has never reappeared. According to local activists and media reports, the State has taken no steps to locate Catherine or identify what happened to her.[39]

Rape within Guatemalan detention centers is widespread,[40] and rape in detention is an act, which the Committee has interpreted as torture.[41] Because the Government of Guatemala routinely houses transgender women in men's prisons and jails, they are at high risk of sexual violence including rape.[42] One transgender woman, for instance, reported that she was raped in a Guatemalan prison more that eighty times in a single year.[43] Furthermore, the act of housing transgender women with men disregards their identities and can produce substantial mental distress that amounts to torture. Because incarcerated gay men may be stereotyped as physically weak, may be assumed to consent to all male-on-male sexual contact, and/or may be isolated from other prisoners and networks of support, they are at high risk of sexual violence.[44] Lesbians who are incarcerated, like all incarcerated women, are at risk of sexual violence. The perpetrators may be prison officials themselves or other incarcerated individuals. However, because the State controls all activities within detention centers, the State is also responsible for all sexual violence by individuals acting in their official capacity, outside their official capacity, and by individual private actors against incarcerated LGBT individuals.

2. Right to Liberty and Security of Person. Documented incidents of arbitrary arrest in Guatemala–including of LGBT individuals—constitute violations of article 9(1).[45] Police threaten "persons engaged in prostitution and other commercial sexual activities with false drug charges to extort money or sexual favors."[46] LGBT sex workers are subjected to particular harassment, despite the fact that prostitution is legal in Guatemala.[47] By threatening and in some cases illegally detaining women engaged in prostitution, the police are acting in violation of both the Guatemalan penal code, and in violation of the prohibition on arbitrary arrests under Article 9.[48]

Detained individuals find themselves in jail and prison conditions in Guatemala that are "harsh and dangerous," in violation of Article 10(1).[49] In 2009, for instance, the General Prison System Directorate reported to the HRC that twenty people in their custody were killed.[50] Despite the State's responsibility to diligently protect the safety of those in custody under Article 10, prison officials breach the minimum standard of care required when they permit inherently dangerous situations to develop.[51] As indicated above, LGBT individuals in detention are frequently subjected to emotional, physical and sexual abuse by fellow inmates, treatment that prison officials fail to prevent and/or adequately punish.[52]

Prisoners in Guatemala have been subject to medical testing without their consent. One transgender woman reported that, while in prison, she was given an HIV test without her consent.[53] This is illegal under Guatemalan law, which requires that obligatory testing be limited to specific circumstances and that the written, informed consent of the test subject be obtained.[54] In addition to carrying out non-consensual testing, authorities in Guatemalan prisons also fail to provide appropriate medical care. The same transgender woman who reported being subject to the HIV test also stated that officials did not provide her with medical assistance when they learned that she was HIV-positive.[55]

Recommendations

The State of Guatemala must adopt legislative, administrative, and judicial measures to ensure respect, protection, and promotion of, and minimize violation of, human rights without any distinction based on an individual's sexual orientation or gender identity. To that end, the Human Rights Committee should recommend:

A. Guatemala should take action to end all violence committed against individuals on the basis of their sexual orientation and gender identity. In particular, the State party should introduce a comprehensive system of laws which protect LGBT persons from discrimination and violence.

B. Guatemala should take appropriate measures to ensure that all persons have the enjoyment of their rights and are entitled to access basic services, such as healthcare and education, regardless of their sexual orientation and gender identity. In this regard, particular attention should be paid to the vulnerability of transgender persons.

C. Guatemala should adopt appropriate laws which permit transgender persons to legally transition, and to receive identity documents which reflect an individual's identified gender.

D. Guatemala should end impunity for individuals who violate the human rights of LGBT persons and those who defend the rights of LGBT persons. The State party should put in place measures to fully investigate alleged crimes on the basis of sexual orientation and gender identity, and where appropriate, should ensure that such crimes are properly prosecuted and punished. If and when a person is forcibly disappeared, Guatemala must take all steps necessary to locate the individual, and to ensure his or her immediate return to safety.

Notes

1. Status of Ratifications, International Covenant on Civil and Political Rights, available at http://treaties.un.org/Pages/ViewDetails.aspx?src=TREATY&mtdsg_no=IV-4&chapter=4&lang=en
2. Third Periodic Report of Guatemala, U.N. Doc. No. CCPR/C/GTM/3 (March 31, 2010).

3. General Comment 31 of the Human Rights Committee, CCPR/C/21/Rev.1/Add.13, at 4¶ 10, May 26, 2004.
4. Concluding Observations of the Human Rights Committee: Jamaica, 103rd Session, 17 October-4 November 2011, Advance Unedited Version, available at http://www2.ohchr.org/english/bodies/hrc/hrcs103.htm
5. U.N. Human Rights Council, Resolution 17/19, Human rights, sexual orientation and gender identity, U.N. Doc. A/HRC/17/L.9/Rev.1 (June 17, 2011).
6. U.N. Human Rights Council, Resolution 17/19, Human rights, sexual orientation and gender identity, U.N. Doc. A/HRC/17/L.9/Rev.1 (June 17, 2011).
7. U.N. Human Rights Committee (HRC), Concluding Observations: Jamaica, 103rd Session, 17 October-4 November 2011, Advance Unedited Version, available at http://www2.ohchr.org/english/bodies/hrc/hrcs103.htm.
8. Concluding Observations: Jamaica, *supra* at ¶ 8. ("The state should amend its laws with a view to prohibiting discrimination on the basis of sex, sexual orientation, and gender identity").
9. U.N. Human Rights Council, *Report of the Working Group on the Universal Periodic Review: Guatemala*, pp. 17, 19, U.N. Doc. No. A/HRC/8/38 (May 29, 2008).
10. Interview with Anonymous Sources, in Washington, D.C. (October 28, 2011). On file with George Washington University Law School International Human Rights Clinic.
11. Third Periodic Report of Guatemala, *supra* note 4.
12. *The Yogyakarta Principles: The Application of International Human Rights Law in relation to Sexual Orientation and Gender Identity* at 6 FN 1 (March 2007) available at http://www.yogyakartaprinciples.org/principles_en.htm
13. *Ibid.*
14. The Gay & Lesbian Alliance against Defamation (GLAAD), Media Reference Guide 7 (8th Edition, May 2010).
15. GLAAD Media Guide, *supra* note 16 at 9.
16. GLAAD Media Guide, *supra* note 16 at 8.
17. GLAAD Media Guide, *supra* note 16 at 8.
18. GLAAD Media Guide, *supra* note 16 at 8.
19. GLAAD Media Guide, *supra* note 16 at 8.
20. GLAAD Media Guide, *supra* note 16 at 9.
21. GLAAD Media Guide, *supra* note 16 at 9.
22. U.N. Special Rapporteur on extrajudicial, summary or arbitrary executions, Philip Alston, Addendum Report on Mission to Guatemala of 21–25 August 2006, U.N. Doc. No. A/HRC/4/20/Add.2 ¶ 7 (19 February 2007).
23. U.N. Office of the High Commissioner on Human Rights, *Report of the High Commissioner on Human Rights on the activities of her office in Guatemala, Addendum*, p. 6, U.N. Doc. No. A/HRC/16/20/Add.1 (Jan. 26, 2011).
24. See generally Alston, *supra* note 24.
25. Alston, *supra* note 24 at ¶¶ 7–8.
26. High Commissioner Addendum, *supra* note 25 at p. 6.
27. Anonymous Sources, *supra* note 12.
28. Telephone Interview with Dr. Tamara Adrian, Partner, Adrian & Adrian, Caracas, Venezuela (November 9, 2011).
29. Human Rights Committee, General Comment No. 20, 10 March, (1992).
30. Human Rights Committee, General Comment No. 21, ¶ 4, 10 April, (1992).

31. Human Rights Committee, Concluding Observations, Togo, ¶ 17, UN Doc CCPR /C/TGO/CO/4, 18 April 2011.
32. Human Rights Committee, Concluding Observations, Ethiopia, ¶ 16 UN Doc CCPR/C/ETH/CO/1, 25 July 2011.
33. Human Rights Committee, Concluding Observations, Kazakhstan, ¶ 22, UN Doc CCPR/C/KAZ/CO/1, 21 July 2011.
34. *Ibid* at 14.
35. Report of the Special Rapporteur on the question of torture and other cruel, inhuman or degrading treatment or punishment, ¶ 3, U.N. Doc. No. A/56/156, (July 3, 2001).
36. International HIV/AIDS Alliance, "Special report: Transphobia and hate crimes in Guatemala," (Apr. 6, 2010) available at http://www.aidsalliance.org/Newsdetails.aspx?Id = 543
37. In its recent Concluding Observations on El Salvador, the Committee considered past instances of 'enforced disappearances' under the heading of Article 7 (CCPR/C/SLV/CO/6) at para 5. Similarly, in its Concluding Observations on Ethiopia, the Committee also considered "enforced disappearance" in the Somali Regional State of Ethiopia as a violation of Article 7 (CCPR/C/ETH/CO/1) at para 16. Likewise, see the report of the Special Rapporteur on the question of torture and other cruel, inhuman or degrading treatment or punishment, ¶¶ 9–10, U.N. Doc. No. A/56/156, (July 3, 2001).
38. "A un Año …," supra note 39.
39. Anonymous Sources, supra 12.
40. Bureau of Democracy, Human Rights, and Labor, Department of State, 2008 Human Rights Report: Guatemala, 2008 Country Reports on Human Rights Practices (March 11, 2008), available at http://www.state.gov/g/drl/rls/hrrpt/2007/100641.htm [hereinafter 2008 DRL Guatemala Report]; Comisión Específica Para el Abordaje del Femicidio [Special Commission to Address Femicide], Estrategia para el Abordaje del Femicidio Una Visión desde el Estado [Strategy for Addressing Femicide: A Vision from the State] at 18 (2006), cited in Karen Musalo, Elisabeth Pellegrin, S. Shawn Roberts, Crimes Without Punishment: Violence Against Women in Guatemala, Hastings Women's Law Journal, p. 181.
41. CCPR/C/JAM/CO/3 (Advance Edited Version) Geneva, 17 October–4 November 2011. Accessed at http://www2.ohchr.org/english/bodies/hrc/hrcs103.htm.
42. "In this context, the Special Rapporteur wishes to stress the plight and extreme vulnerability of transgender maleto-female persons who, in most circumstances, will be imprisoned in male detention facilities, even though they identify with the female gender, and recommends that States consider taking appropriate measures to avert further victimization of transgender persons in detention, as well as lesbian and gay prisoners." Note by the Secretary-General transmitting the interim report of the Special Rapporteur on the independence of judges and lawyers. A/66/289 at para 81.
43. Anonymous Sources, *supra* note 12.
44. Just Detention International, "LGBTQ Detainees Chief Targets for Sexual Abuse in Detention", February 2009. Accessed January 31, 2012 at http://www.spr.org/en/fact_sheets.aspx.
45. 2008 DRL Guatemala Report, *supra* 97.
46. *Ibid.*
47. *Ibid.*
48. Cogdigo Penal de Guatemala. Accessed February 1, 2012 at http://www.google.com/url?sa=t&rct=j&q=&esrc=s&source=web&cd=2&ved=0CDYQFjAB&url=http%3A%2F%2Fwww.oas.org%2Fdil%2Fesp%2FCodigo_Penal_Guatemala.pdf&ei=814pT434AuPL0QHk4_mmAg&usg=AFQj CNHBZnJ86Pdcyq_DbfZ_t1kU-I2qBw

49. 2008 DRL Guatemala Report, *supra* 98.
50. High Commissioner, *supra* note 6, ¶ 43.
51. Alston, *supra* note 24.
52. Anonymous Sources, *supra* note 12.
53. Anonymous Sources, *supra* note 12.
54. Decree 27-2000, Article 19: The conduct of any test for the diagnosis of HIV infection and their results must respect the confidentiality of persons should be conducted with due respect for the applicant, with advice and guidance before and after the test, unless otherwise provided in this Act. Article 20—Prohibits the authorization of the tests for the diagnosis of infection a compulsory HIV. Except in the following cases: a) When a judgment of the physician, which consist in the clinical record, there is need for test purposes exclusively for the care of patient's health, in order to count with a better criterion of treatment. b) In the case of donation of blood and blood products, breast milk, semen, organs and tissues. c) When necessary for purposes of criminal procedure and with previous order of the competent judicial authority.
55. Anonymous Sources, *supra* note 12.

Nicaragua and Costa Rica have very similar and different histories and contexts. Costa Rica has become an example of liberal democratic practices in the political and social spheres in the Central American region. The concern for human rights such as access to education and healthcare are symbols of a democratic society. Moreover, the Costa Rican experience in political participation contrasts sharply with those of the Central American region that are plagued with political rigidity and strong measures. Costa Rica's idea of democracy is understood within civil society that looks for dialogue and consensus rather than confrontation. Nicaragua, on the other hand, has a history of an unequal distribution of wealth despite its recent revolutionary experience. However, its promotion for political participation has touched every Nicaraguan citizen since 1979. Nicaragua's concern for the poor has shaped the political organization of the emerging social movements. The decisive political views against those that are better positioned socially and economically, make the emerging social movement more confrontational. These contrasting realities have greatly impacted their LGBT social movements.

Identity, Revolution, and Democracy: Lesbian Movements in Central America*

Millie Thayer

Through case studies of lesbian movements in Costa Rica and Nicaragua, this paper examines the phenomenon of identity-based movements, finding that it embraces significant differences in the content and forms of collective identities. New social movement theory calls attention to the role of identity in contemporary movements, but overlooks variation in the nature of identities. Resource mobilization and political process theories, on the other hand, offer tools for explaining differences, but have not generally been applied to cross-national comparisons of movements around identity. Drawing on interviews with lesbian activists in Costa Rica and Nicaragua, on participant observation, and on archival research, I argue that three factors account for the differences in the way movements in distinctive national contexts construct collective identities: 1) economic structure/model of development; 2) state-civil society relations; and 3) the broader field of social movements.

In the 1970s and 1980s, revolutionary guerrilla movements fought poverty and dictatorship throughout much of the Central American isthmus. In the late 1980s, a new kind of social movement was born in the region. In the space of five years, fledgling lesbian movements surfaced in

"Identity, Revolution, and Democracy: Lesbian Movements in Central America" by Millie Thayer, in *Social Problems*, 44(3), August 1997, pp. 386–407. Published by University of California Press.

+Honduras & El Salvador

four Central American countries: Costa Rica (1987), Honduras (1987), Nicaragua (1991), and El Salvador (1992). These movements were a product, in part, of the political and social upheaval of preceding decades; in part they were related to underlying structural changes, to the onset of AIDS in the region, and to the influence of gay and lesbian movements elsewhere.

Despite some common roots, however, there were striking differences among the movements that developed in different countries. In Costa Rica, the movement turned inward to construct its collective identity. The lesbian feminist group, *Las Entendidas,* combined therapeutic support for its members with efforts to create a larger lesbian community, and used an idiom of spirituality and woman-centered culture that might be familiar to students of the 1970s lesbian movement in the United States.[1]

In contrast, Nicaraguan lesbians took an assertive public stance, insisting on their right to membership in society and on the rights of all people to a "sexuality free of prejudice." *Fundación Xochiquetzal,* a non-profit organization founded by lesbians and gays, sought to remake social mores in the sexual realm. The *Nosotras* collective provided emotional support and education about sexuality and feminism to its members, but many of them also joined in a coalition effort to fight a repressive anti-gay law passed by the country's legislative assembly.[2]

Lesbian movements in Nicaragua and Costa Rica represent two points on opposite ends of a continuum of social movements from a more internal to a more external orientation. At one end, there is a stress on the self-esteem and personal identity of group members that, in the case of Costa Rica, extends to efforts to construct a broader lesbian community out of existing social networks. At the most "extroverted" end, lesbians in Nicaragua sought to revolutionize how society conceives of sexuality, while simultaneously claiming a place in that society. Though both orientations were founded on a concern with identity, lesbian movements in these two Central American countries defined that identity and their goals and arenas of action in sharply divergent ways.

In the following paper, I examine these contrasting approaches to lesbian organizing and explain the differences in the nature of the two movements' collective identities and the ways they were manifested in the social origins of members, organizational structure, ideology, goals, and inward versus outward orientation of practice.[3]

Theorizing Variation in Social Movement Identities

New social movement (NSM) theorists have situated lesbian movements among a new genre of social movements which they see as a product of global shifts from societies based on production to post-material, infortnation societies, in which states and complex systems have come to intrude on the individual's very core. According to these scholars, the peace, feminist, ecological, community, and gay and lesbian movements of the 1970s and 1980s represented means of resisting these growing threats to personal autonomy (Escobar 1992; Habermas 1984; Melucci 1980, 1985, 1994; Offe 1985; Slater 1985; Touraine 1985, 1988).

The protagonists of these movements, according to NSM theorists, were both those sensitized to the negative effects of modernity—the new middle class—and those suffering from it; the proletariat was no longer the epic actor on the stage. Unlike traditionaL class-based movements, NSM modes of action tended toward direct democracy, horizontal organization, and a rejection of hierarchical forms of representation and institutionalization. Furthermore, resistance to domination of everyday life occurred on cultural, not political ground. Rather than contesting for political power, or pressing demands on the state, these movements struggled for the right to difference. Construction and defense of identity were central concerns.[4]

Some recent analyses support the idea that certain elements shared by many contemporary movements, such as the politicization of the private and the assertion of identity as a primary goal, represent a significant departure from the past (Buechler 1995; Johnston, Laraña and Gusfield 1994). But others criticize the reification of a category that does not take into account differences among collective identities (Gamson, J. 1989; Gamson, W. 1992).[5] In privileging identity-based movements, NSM theory offers important insights into movements such as those analyzed here. However, its sweeping structural explanations obscure distinctions among these movements and overlook the historical specificities that might enable us to explain why, for example, Nicaraguan lesbians constructed their movement differently than their Costa Rican counterparts.

Theorists in the resource mobilization and political process traditions, on the other hand, have been more concerned with explaining variation. By situating social movements in their political and historical environments, they provide a number of useful tools for comparative analysis of the forces which shape different movements (Jenkins 1983; McAdam 1982; McCarthy and Zald 1977; Oberschall1973; Tarrow 1988, 1994; Tilly 1978). However, much of this work rests on a definition of social movements that unduly narrows the field of inquiry to what Tarrow (1994:3–4) describes as "collective challenges by people with common purposes and solidarity in sustained interaction with elites, opponents, and authorities." Although social networks, symbols, and collective identities sometimes are given a place in movement formation, these are usually viewed as means to an end—the moment of overt engagement with political institutions. This exclusive focus on a certain kind of social movement eliminates, as objects of study, movements for whom construction of identity is an end, rather than a means, and whose field of engagement does not (or does not primarily) include the state.

There is a growing body of scholarly literature from this perspective that compares social movements that have been considered "new" across different national contexts (della Porta and Rucht 1995; Kitschelt 1986; Kriesi 1995, 1996; Rucht 1996). But, because of their bounded view of what constitutes a social movement, these theorists tend to take the conceptualization of goals and orientation of action as given,[6] directing their attention instead to explaining mobilization, structure, degree of militancy, or political outcomes. Although it offers useful insights into variation among "political" movements, most work in the resource mobilization and political process traditions is less helpful in explaining why movements concerned with constructing identities outside the institutional political arena take fundamentally different forms in divergent national contexts.

A number of recent works, however, have begun to integrate NSM-inspired concerns with collective identity and the sociopolitical factors often cited by resource mobilization and political process theorists (Taylor 1989; Taylor and Rupp 1993; Taylor and Whittier 1992; Whittier 1995). Much of this analysis focuses on changes over time within one movement, the shift from Melucci's (1985) visible moment, when movements emerge to confront a political authority, to what he calls "latency," during which subterranean movement networks construct new "cultural models", (what Taylor [1989] calls "abeyance"). While they offer an important corrective to studies that recognize only the overt, political aspects of organizing, there is a tendency among these authors to identify a "cultural" orientation with low points in the life of a social movement, a characterization that does not apply to movements, such as that of Costa Rican lesbians, which are inwardly focused during their most active moments. Nevertheless, these temporal analyses suggest the possibility of applying political factors to explanations of differences among identity-based movements. In the following pages, I will continue in this spirit, seeking to extend the tools of resource mobilization and political process theories in order to explain the varying orientations of movements that assert identities beyond the space of formal politics. Rather than comparing single movements over time, I will analyze cross-national differences in the ways movements express their identities.

In Costa Rica, the lesbian movement looked inward toward definition of personal identity, creation of community, and assertion of autonomy as a sexual minority. The Nicaraguan movement took a different path, choosing instead to defend the right of lesbians (and gays) to full social integration. and to project to the society at large its vision of a free sexuality for all. I argue that these contrasts can best be understood by attention to the way three factors are expressed in a given society: 1) the impact of the particular economic structure and development model on social actors, 2) the relationship between state and civil society, and 3) the nature of the broader sea of social movements—including political parties—within which any given movement must navigate.

Economic Structure

In their efforts to dichotomize old and new movements and declare an end to the dominion of material concerns, NSM theorists usually eschew consideration of the limits and opportunities presented by the economy in specific national contexts, preferring to remain at the level of epochal transformations.[7] Resource mobilization theory generally goes to the opposite extreme, focusing its analytic eye on the micro level of resources available to particular movements. In contrast, I argue that the class structure in a given country, while in no way determining the nature of social movements, plays a role in providing or denying a potential social base for different kinds of movements.[8] Costa Rica's more diversified economy and sizable middle class, and Nicaragua's agroexport orientation and polarized class structure, offered distinct possibilities and limitations for social movements.

State-Civil Society Relations

NSM theory sees the growing penetration of the state into private life as key to the contemporary creation of movements which assert the right to define identities, but pays less attention to the ways distinctive state-civil society configurations influence the nature of these identities. Political process theorists have introduced the concept of "political opportunity structures," the complex of interrelations among state and party institutions, elite and oppositional strategies, as an important variable in the mobilization of social movements (della Porta and Rucht 1995; Kitschelt 1986; Kriesi 1995, 1996; Meyer and Staggenborg 1996; Rucht 1996; Tarrow 1994). However, while such an approach helps analyze the behavior of movements within the formal political sphere, it does little to explain the formation of collective identity among movements not primarily concerned with making demands on the state (cf. Rucht 1996).[9] If NSM theorists have a lens set at too wide an angle to take in variations among identity-based movements, the political process literature tends to locate movements too narrowly within the context of political institutions.

I argue that it is not only these political institutions, but also their relationship with civil society, the "'private' apparatus of 'hegemony'" which plays a key role, not only in shaping class-based movements as Gramsci argued, but in the fundamental nature of all kinds of movements (1971:261). The state-civil society relationship is particularly important for movements around issues, such as sexuality, that are constructed and struggled over in a variety of arenas—the family, the community, the church, popular culture, the economy, and others, as well as the state.

In Costa Rica, where the state exercised a stable form of hegemony through civil society, interest groups competed within a status quo that was rarely challenged, and the possibility of a unifying identity seemed either utopian or authoritarian. In Nicaragua, on the other hand, a state-civil society relationship that had seesawed over the previous two decades, along with the heritage of a vanquished revolutionary regime, left a fragile conservative state hegemony and a cadre of activists with the memory of an inclusive form of social integration as a model.

Social Movement Field

In NSM theory, identity-based movements tend to spring fully-formed from the fissures produced by structural transformation. There is little concern with conjunctural mediating influences in the environment, and, more specifically, with other movements which have left their mark on both participants and their interlocutors. Political process scholars, on the other hand, theorize the importance of previously existing organizational resources in the development of new movements (McAdam 1982), the role of "early risers" in a social movement cycle in expanding opportunities for later-emerging movements (Tarrow 1988), and the mechanisms of "spillover" from one movement to another (Meyer and Whittier 1994). From a symbolic interactionist perspective, "frame" theorists elaborate the process by which social movement "master frames" established early in a given cycle constrain and influence later conceptions of organizing (Snow and Benford 1992; see also Snow and Benford 1988; Hunt, Benford and Snow 1994). While all of these theories offer intriguing insights about the processes by which one social movement affects others, they tend to treat inter-movement relationships in isolation from a broader political and social context, failing to link the influence of particular movements to the kind of state-civil society relationship and structural environment in which they are located.

In this paper I emphasize the relationship of new movements to a broader "social movement family" with similar fundamental values (della Porta and Rucht 1995), while at the same time locating these movements in an expanded historical framework. In Costa Rica, lesbian organizing grew out of a feminist movement with a long history and strong liberal and academic feminist components; whatever small left had once existed, had long since been silenced. In Nicaragua, the feminist and lesbian movements were born simultaneously, led by women whose worldview and sense of politics was shaped by a once-strong, class-based movement.

While class structure both restricts and creates possibilities, it is an expanded political realm that shapes social movement orientations and fundamental conceptions of goals and strategy. In the sections that follow, I describe the Nicaraguan and Costa Rican lesbian movements, and then show how economic structure and political context work together to construct the profound differences between them.

Costa Rica: Circling the Wagons

Costa Rica's first lesbian organization, founded in March 1987, appeared in some ways to be the quintessential "new social movement" described by theorists. A small group, whose activists never reached more than twenty, *Las Entendidas* never tried to recruit on a mass scale and actually limited membership by criteria such as knowledge and acceptance of feminism. Until 1990, when its first coordinator was elected, the group had a loose structure made up of ad hoc commissions. All but one of its active members were professionals, members of the "new middle-class" evoked by NSM adherents.

Theorists describe new social movements as growing out of a reaction to the failures of so-called old social movements, rather than being inspired by and allied with them. Whether the formation of a lesbian organization responded to shortcomings of the small Costa Rican left is difficult to say; what is certain is that there were no ties between the two movements. None of the group's members came out of left party activism and, according to its coordinator, *Las Entendidas* had no ongoing relationship to left organizations.

Most importantly, the group's goals reflected the inward turn noted by analysts of many contemporary movements. In an article summarizing their first five years of work, members of *Las Entendidas* expressed their ongoing commitment: "We continue giving soul and body to [our] lesbian identity. . ." (*Las Entendidas* 1992:8).[10] From the beginning, a primary objective was to build internal strength by promoting self-esteem, combating internalized guilt and "lesbophobia," and developing a new lesbian (and later lesbian feminist) identity. *Las Entendidas* functioned as a support and social group for its members; time was set aside at the meetings for sharing personal feelings and experiences, and members went on recreational outings together. The group sought personal liberation via intellectual practice, engaging in discussions of feminist literature and the collective elaboration of new theories.

As the organization evolved, the concept of identity came to embrace not only individuals, but a wider community. By the end of 1987, *Las Entendidas* had begun to define its ideology as feminist and set itself a second goal: to create a lesbian feminist community through outreach and consciousness-raising among Costa Rican lesbians. With this in mind, the group founded a monthly "women's night" at a San José gay bar, where they offered speakers and workshops on topics such as sexuality, feminism, self-esteem, and alcoholism, as well as theater, poetry readings, and other cultural events. One historian of the movement comments: "It was an activity. . . which may have made [women] feel part of a community, of a larger group with the capacity to be involved in activities outside of the ordinary, and the possibility of learning new things" (Serrano n.d.:8).

The group also conducted a survey of lesbian life, organized a therapy group for survivors of incest and published a newsletter bearing the slogan, "For a Lesbian Solidarity". In part with the hope of involving and educating new local members, *Las Entendidas* hosted the Second Latin American and Caribbean Lesbian Feminist Encounter in 1990. Despite an extremely hostile atmosphere, the event was attended by 150 women from Costa Rica and all over the continent (see Carstensen 1992; Jiménez 1990; Madden Arias 1994; No author 1990).

A third goal articulated by members of *Las Entendidas* was to win space and acceptance in the broader feminist movement. But this objective was never fully realized. For reasons discussed below, most members of *Las Entendidas* were reluctant to go public about their sexual orientation, even within women's organizations.

The final set of goals claimed by *Las Entendidas* was "to conquer invisibility" *vis a vis* the rest of the popular movement and society at large, and to demand rights in a patriarchal society (No author 1990:1). But, while these objectives were occasionally stated, it is difficult to find their expression in the group's practices. Apart from their appearance at a women's march against violence, *Las Entendidas* seems to have entered the public eye only reluctantly. The international Lesbian Feminist Encounter, for example, was intended more as an opportunity to strengthen the different participating groups internally and establish networks between them, than as an effort to confront homophobia in Costa Rican society. The conference was not locally advertised outside of feminist circles, and it was only when the press got wind of the event, and opposition began to escalate, that members of *Las Entendidas* agreed to meet with reporters.[11] One activist commented: *"Las Entendidas'* goal is collective visibility of lesbians, but we continue to work internally and fear coming out."

There are at least four possible arenas of struggle for lesbian movements such as *Las Entendidas,* ranging from the most intimate to the most public. Groups may focus 1) on strengthening and developing a sense of identity among their *own members;* 2) on reaching and involving a wider *lesbian community;* 3) on educating those active in the *women's movement;* or 4) on addressing *society as a whole.* In the case of the Costa Rican movement, the emphasis was clearly on the first two arenas. Participation in the women's movement was sporadic and limited to only some members; efforts to have an impact on society at large were rare.[12]

In an editorial on the fifth anniversary of *Las Entendidas'* founding. Lila Silvestre wrote: "Today, although discrimination against lesbians continues to affect us, we have more strength to create our own spaces and new relationships because we have a support group in which we recognize and nurture each other. . ." (Silvestre 1992:1). In many ways, *Las Entendidas* presented the ideal-typical profile of a new social movement. Its educated, middleclass membership, loose structure, personal identity focus and lack of involvement with traditional politics of left or right, as well as its efforts to create an autonomous space for difference, seemed to confirm NSM theorists' predictions about the kinds of movements that would arise in this period. Within this conception, *Las Entendidas,* even at its apogee, fell at the latent, defensive end of Melucci's continuum. That this form of development was not inevitable, however, becomes clear when we examine the lesbian movement just across the border to the north in Nicaragua.

Nicaragua: Publicizing the Private

The lesbian movement in Nicaragua in the late 1980s and early 1990s consisted of two organizations which worked directly with lesbians, and a number of other individuals and non-governmental organizations (NGOs), which played an important role in promoting and supporting the movement. Here analysis will concentrate on *Nosotras* and *Xochiquetzal,* the two entities which brought lesbians together to work on issues of sexuality and sexual preference. Though each had a different structure and functions, their memberships and goals overlapped—in fact *Xochiquetzal* served for three years as a kind of umbrella for *Nosotras,* as well as the gay collective, *SHomos*—and, during this period, they can be considered complementary parts of one movement.[13]

In contrast to *Las Entendidas* in Costa Rica, the lesbian movement in Nicaragua was not an archetypal new social movement. Instead, it was a kind of hybrid, combining features of both "new" and "old," in the context of the construction and defense of identity. While the coordinators of *Xochiquetzal* were middle class, the membership of the *Nosotras* collective, some 30 altogether, was a mixture of urban working class and professional women. Unlike the Costa Rican movement, Nicaraguan lesbians had close ties to the left. Despite the sometimes conflictive history of FSLN-gay and lesbian relations, all the members were (or had been) Sandinista supporters and continued to identify with the party's revolutionary goals. Several activists were party members and at least one had important political and administrative responsibilities during the decade of Sandinista state power. Although *Nosotras* had a loose structure, with a rotating coordinator and no formal legal status, *Xochiquetzal,* which provided resources and support to the collective, was a staff-based institution with legal status and funding sources abroad.

Through their movement, lesbians in Nicaragua addressed a broader and somewhat different set of goals than did their sisters in Costa Rica, with *Nosotras* focusing more on internal identity and *Xochiquetzal* more on outreach beyond the lesbian community, although neither confined itself entirely to one end of the spectrum. Within the collective, members of *Nosotras* sought to build self-esteem, to strengthen their identity as women and as lesbians, and to "learn about our gender condition," as one woman put it. The group held monthly meetings dedicated to study and recreational activities. One of their main endeavors was a nine-month course coordinated by *Xochiquetzal* on feminism, sexuality, and women's health issues.

A second goal, this one articulated by *Xochiquetzal* staff, was outreach in the lesbian community and support for the formation of new collectives. Besides the training and logistical support it offered initially for lesbian and gay groups, the foundation organized a series of fiestas in an effort to reach the broader lesbian community. However, these were soon abandoned for lack of funds and because they did not succeed in drawing in new activists, and plans for *Nosotras* to do outreach at the few, newly founded lesbian social clubs were slow to get off the ground.

A third goal for the lesbian movement was to support and influence the growing feminist movement. To this end, representatives of both *Xochiquetzal* and *Nosotras* participated in meetings and activities of the National Feminist Committee (CNF), a coalition of some 25 women's groups who conducted feminist education and organizing projects. The two lesbian organizations successfully insisted that the groups in the CNF support the right to sexual preference as a principle of their educational work and that the committee as a whole incorporate this as a plank in its platform (No author 1992a; Blandón 1993). *Xochiquetzal* offered workshops on sexuality to women's organizations, and staff members aggressively challenged homophobia in feminist meetings.

A final cluster of goals addressed the broader social arena. In their literature, leaders of *Xochiquetzal* linked personal and social change, defining their mission as: "Promoting the integral development of people on the terrain of sexuality, through a knowledge of human sexuality free of prejudices, and the creation of social conditions which favor [such development]" (*Fundadón Xochiquetzal* n.d.:2).

Organized lesbians in Nicaragua went beyond defending their existence as individual members of a sexual minority. *Xochiquetzal* made demands for rights based on lesbian membership in and identification with a range of other marginalized groups, including: "equal rights to participate. . .without any kind of political, economic, or social or cultural discrimination. . ." and "the right to peace and security" (No author 1993b:15). These were demands not just for space in society, but for a thorough transformation of the society in which lesbians wanted to be included.

These objectives required moving beyond the lesbian and feminist communities. As the *Xochiquetzal* sub-director explained:

> . . .[We] realized that if we wanted to influence the population and promote respect and tolerance for sexual preference, we couldn't do it by staying in the ghetto. [Also], gays and lesbians are not only those who are organized, but they are in all sectors; the majority are in the closet. So we broadened the groups that we worked with.

The foundation conducted workshops and produced radio programs, articles and educational materials aimed at society at large, but in particular at students, women's groups, and medical personnel. In these forums, besides advocating lesbian and gay rights, the foundation sought to demystify the arena of sexuality and preached a doctrine of self-acceptance, liberation from the tyranny of norms, and the right of all people—gay or straight—to sexual pleasure. This social orientation was shared by members of *Nosotras* as well. Along with the foundation, *Nosotras* joined coalitions to plan Gay Pride and AIDS awareness events designed to reach heterosexual society, as well as gays and lesbians. At the first public gay and lesbian celebration in 1991, organizers were explicit about this aim, choosing to invite well-known straight intellectuals to make presentations, alongside gays and lesbians. Perhaps most visibly, in 1992 the lesbian movement participated in a "Campaign for a Sexuality Free of Prejudice" to oppose a newly enacted anti-sodomy law and educate the Nicaraguan public about the issue (see Andersson 1993; Bolt González 1995; No author 1993a; *Fundadón Xochiquetzal* 1992). More than 25 organizations were involved in the campaign. When their requests to speak with President Violeta Chamorro were ignored, they held public forums and debates, presented their case in the media, gathered over 4,000 signatures against the law, and challenged its constitutionality in court.

The goals and activities of the Nicaraguan lesbian movement extended across the spectrum of strategic arenas, from an inward focus on its own members to an outward focus on the rest of society, with much of its energy going in the latter direction. While *Nosotras* worked to build lesbian identity among its members, *Xochiquetzal* took on the task of coordinating educational and political activities directed toward civil society and, in self-defense, toward the state. Until 1994, the two groups worked together to promote awareness in the women's movement and, to a lesser extent, to reach the unorganized sectors of the lesbian community.

In contrast to the Costa Rican experience, the Nicaraguan lesbian movement combined the concern with subjectivity stressed by NSM analysts with other features often associated with older, class-based movements. It was a movement with both a loosely structured and an institutionalized expression; with both middle-class and working-class members, and With a concern for personal identity, as well as a commitment to recreating society in an inclusive image.

If anything, this movement leaned toward the visible, political end of the continuum theorists have described. Unlike some other identity-based movements including *Las Entendidas, Xochiquetzal* and *Nosotras* chose to enter the political sphere, not seeking to win power as "old" movements had, but to defend rights and further educational goals. They sought, not just to gain tolerance, but to reshape society's thinking about sexuality. The goal was not primarily autonomous space, but social integration. As one Nicaraguan activist told Margaret Randall: ". . .not creating ghettos really is important. We need to defend our place in society as a whole and make society respect us for what we are, for what we do, for our work" (Randall 1992:75).

Costa Rica: Sex and Democracy

The Costa Rican and Nicaraguan lesbian movements offered a stark contrast not easily explained by current social movement theory. While one consisted primarily of middle class professionals, the other had a strong working class representation; while one functioned in a fairly ad hoc manner, the other had both informal and institutionalized components; while one adhered to a radical feminist ideology, focusing its attention on personal growth and building community, the other embodied revolutionary feminism, building alliances within civil society around a totalizing, liberatory vision. Three factors, one economic/structural and the other two rooted in the political domain, seem to account for these differences.

For a series of historical reasons, Costa Rica developed a significantly different class structure than Nicaragua. A relatively wealthy country with a more diversified economy, its 1992 GNP per inhabitant was more than three times that of Nicaragua. Whereas 68.7 percent of Nicaraguans lived in poverty in 1985, only 28.1 percent of Costa Ricans did. Though Costa Rica was no more urbanized than its northern neighbor, it had a larger middle class and more educated population. In 1990, higher education accounted for 11.6 percent of all Costa Rican students enrolled in school; in Nicaragua the figure was 2.6 percent. In 1980, professionals, technicians, administrators, and managers made up more than one-fifth of the economically active population in Costa Rica; these sectors in Nicaragua were less than one-tenth of those employed (FLACSO 1995:36, 104, 113, 139, 140).

These structural conditions had important implications for lesbians and gays, particularly in the context of urbanization, which began in the 1950s and reached its peak in the 1970s. For both gays and lesbians, life in the city offered greater opportunities to interact, and a degree of anonymity, economic independence and freedom from the constraints of the extended family.[14] While there was no real homosexual "ghetto," the number of gays in the growing middle class made possible a small gay male culture organized around bars and private parties. Though lesbian culture was much less visible and lesbians as a group were certainly much less economically independent than gay men, it is likely that urban life had some of the same effects on them, bringing them together and offering those with the means the option of a somewhat less clandestine lifestyle. From the 1950s onward, educational opportunities for women expanded, and so, to some extent, did the possibilities for financial independence for the educated middle-class woman. (Although in Nicaragua women made up a slightly greater percentage of the working population than in Costa Rica, the percentage of women in professional and technical occupations was nearly twice as high in Costa Rica [FLASCO 1995: 117, 119].) All of these factors laid the groundwork for the growth of an urban lesbian community.

This parallel culture and the availability of individual solutions meant that it was possible for some lesbians to avoid direct confrontation with the dominant society, and there was less sense of urgency around economic and social issues that might have linked lesbians more closely to other groups than there was in Nicaragua. Participation in a semi-autonomous community was a viable possibility for a certain group of women. Furthermore, there was a significant academic community which could support a more intellectually-oriented movement than developed in Nicaragua.

But class structure does not determine, and cannot by itself explain, the shape social movements take in a given society. It is to the political realm—more specifically to the kind of state and its relationship to civil society—that we must turn to further understand the variation in movements.

Since 1948, Costa Rica has had a stable, constitutional democracy with a pervasive discourse of individual rights and justice. Despite moves toward neoliberal retrenchment in the 1980s, Costa Rica's was a modified welfare state that offered significant social protection to at least some sectors, and actively promoted the institutionalization of interests.

This state rested firmly on a hegemony based in civil society (Gramsci 1971). While occasionally resorting to coercion, the state relied primarily on eliciting the consent of the governed through cooptation and the legitimacy of its representative political institutions (see Vilas 1995; Palma 1989). Clearly delineated and institutionalized interest groups competed within the framework of the status quo. At the same time, an internally-differentiated elite maintained control of the reins of state through a long-established system of rotation of power. The overall effect, according to activists, was a political culture dominated by apathy, individualism, and a fear of conflict that went beyond the boundaries of the hegemonic consensus.

Costa Rica enjoys a reputation as a leader in the area of women's rights. In 1949, in response to local feminist demands as well as to international pressure, the country became the first in the region to guarantee political rights for women, and since then the state has continually intervened in gender politics as a champion—at least rhetorically—of women's equality (see Escalante Herrera 1990; García and Gomariz 1989; Saint-Germain 1993; Saint-Germain and Morgan 1991). In a country with a sizable group of educated women and "femocrats"—female bureaucrats—as well as an active grassroots women's movement, political leaders were quick to try to tum gender issues to their advantage.[15]

On gender, as with other themes, challengers faced the sense of exceptionalism fostered by the state and shared by many Costa Ricans. As one feminist put it: "In Costa Rica you can't question the venerated and mythical 'equality' of all Costa Ricans without running the risk of being called a traitor to the country" (Facio 1988:9). But the permeability of the state to women's concerns masked continuing social and economic inequalities, such as discrimination in land ownership and employment, as well as rape, domestic abuse, and paternal irresponsibility (Facio 1988).

For lesbians in particular, oppression was rooted in civil society rather than within the confines of law. The first line of defense of the dominant sexual order was what participants in the lesbian movement called "invisibilization." As one journalist noted, the topic of lesbianism did not appear in either university or public library catalogs, and only entered the media in relationship to the 1990 Lesbian Feminist Encounter (Mandell 1991:9). One longtime member of *Las Entendidas* explained one aspect of social control: "Here, repression isn't carried out by the police or the army, but by your neighbor. . . .It's a democratic country, but all the aggression takes place in the family." Related, but even more insidious, was what Mandell called "self-censorship." Another activist commented: "They don't have any army, because they don't need one. . . .Lesbophobia is internalized; people are afraid and don't even try to come out."

In Costa Rica, the relationship between state and civil society had been stable over a long period of time. The state promoted a particular set of moral values which only became visible when sexual hegemony was under threat. Minister of Government Alvarez Desanti, reacting to holding the international lesbian conference in Costa Rica, made this quite clear:

> This is a democratic country, where the laws guarantee us the right to meet freely; nevertheless, there are ethical and moral values which the national authorities should defend. For this reason, we believe that a congress such as the one which has been announced affects our lifestyle and threatens the education and moral principles which we wish to inculcate in our youth." (No author 1990)

An earlier challenge to conventional mores, in the mid-1980s, when AIDS began making inroads among gays, had also produced a vigorous governmental response. On the one hand, the disease's appearance drew people together and sparked initial organizing efforts; on the other, it made gays visible to the straight community and aroused irrational fears. The government made no efforts to respond to the medical emergency provoked by the epidemic, and instead moved to shut down gay and lesbian bars and harass their clientele. In March 1987, police raided a bar called *La Torre,* frequented by middle class gay men, and arrested 253 people. Meanwhile, the government began requiring public employees to take AIDS tests, a move criticized by gays as blatantly discriminatory and without international precedent. These actions were the spark which led to the birth of a movement among both lesbians and gay men.[16] By the end of 1987, four gay and lesbian organizations had formed, among them *Las Entendidas.*

But these moments of overt state repression were rare, and, for the most part, the illusion of a value-free democracy was preserved. The Costa Rican state, with its largely invisible moral foundation and stable integration with civil society, offered a slippery target for transformatory challenges and discouraged a focus on politics, per se. The proliferation of interest groups also left little room for inclusive identities. Together, these conditions help account for the development of a lesbian movement that withdrew into a semi-autonomous community founded on conceptions of women's essential difference, rather than pursuing a crusade to change broader social values, as the movement did in Nicaragua. In the end, retreat may have seemed more attractive than participation in a rejecting society that offered meager sources of common identity.

The third factor shaping any given social movement is also political: the field of other movements within which it moves, particularly those that share underlying values. In Costa Rica, the virtual absence of the left in the 1980s was a product, in part, of the mediating effects of the country's civilian welfare state, representative political institutions, and dominant liberal discourse (Solís 1989). The resulting lack of widespread experience with cross-class relations around a common political project, left *Las Entendidas,* despite its attempts to reach working class lesbians, with a professional and intellectual constituency. The unifying left ideology and identity that shaped those who founded the lesbian movement in Nicaragua was absent in Costa Rica, opening the way for a movement that stressed difference, demanded autonomy, and retreated into self-healing and self-protection, rather than seeking to reshape society. In the end, lesbians became another interest group of sorts, struggling to carve out a niche for yet another particularized identity.

Whereas, in Nicaragua, a class-based movement established a "master frame" with which other movements had to contend (Snow and Benford 1992), in Costa Rica, gender-based organizing set the stage. Perhaps in part inspired by the state's liberal democratic discourse, in the mid to late 1970s, during the UN Decade for Women, an active women's movement emerged (see Berrón 1995; Candelaria Navas 1985; García and Gomariz 1989; Saint-Germain and Morgan 1991). By the end of the 1980s, Costa Rica had over 150 women's groups, more than any other country in Central America (García and Gomariz 1989:212). Many of the women later involved in *Las Entendidas* participated in women's organizations of one kind or another, and all were shaped by the political climate this movement helped create.

The feminist movement in Costa Rica had three main strands in the 1980s: liberal (Saint-Germain 1993), academic feminist (González Suárez 1988), popular feminist (*Colectivo Pancha Carrasco* 1994). The first—and dominant—sector consisted of mainstream institutions, political party members, government functionaries, and independent, professional women, and set its scope on legislative change, an arena where there was little room for addressing lesbian concerns. Academic feminists centered around a gender and a women's studies program in each of the two principal universities. Popular feminism was the focus of several small, nongovernmental organizations, staffed by middle-class women, who sought to build a movement among women of the working class. *Las Entendidas* was primarily influenced by university-based feminists, a fact that is reflected in its intellectual discourse. Some members' experience with popular feminism may have been expressed in its efforts—albeit unsuccessful—to reach working class lesbians in the bars.

Although homophobia and fear of being identified as lesbians may have been more widespread among mainstream feminists, it was expressed in all sectors of the women's movement, reflecting the kind of internalized repression in the wider society. For the most part, *Las Entendidas'* initiatives to the feminist movement met with rejection, despite group members' long history of activism in women's organizations. Feminists not only failed to openly defend organizers of the 1990 Lesbian Feminist Encounter when the state, the church and the media launched vicious attacks, but one group withdrew its sponsorship of the lesbians' request for a meeting space at the university.

The Encounter did force feminist recognition of lesbian existence and, subsequently, *Las Entendidas* was invited to participate in several women's events, but the reception remained chilly. After their presentation at one conference, the published version of the proceedings changed *Las Entendidas'* name to disguise the group's nature. Feminist homophobia functioned as another force pushing *Las Entendidas* back into the collective closet. If lesbians could not be confident of allies even in the feminist movement, how could they make links to broader issues of sexuality and take on the task of outreach to the larger society?

In Costa Rica, a diversified class structure, stable and hegemonic state-civil society relations, and the dominance of a particular kind of feminism with particular attitudes toward lesbianism combined to generate a lesbian movement which resisted the imposition of dominant values by reinforcing its own boundaries, rather than by seeking allies with whom to reinvent society's sexual practices.

Nicaragua: Sex and Revolution

Compared with Costa Rica, Nicaragua had a much more underdeveloped agroexport economy, with a class structure polarized between a very small, educated upper class and a large, impoverished majority. Though urbanization was no less significant in Nicaragua than in Costa Rica, the middle class was too small to provide an economic base for the kind of gay and lesbian community built around consumption that developed in San José. Most lesbians continued to live with, and depend on, their families, and there was little chance of individual autonomy for the majority who were working class. A movement based on the creation of an enclave community could have little appeal (Ferguson 1991). The structural constraints also meant that it would have been difficult to create a viable lesbian movement limited to the middle class and isolated from the broader social issues that affected the poor majority.

Turning to the political sphere, both the nature of the state and its relationship to civil society had undergone drastic shifts, passing through three distinct phases in the 15 years prior to the movement's founding: from dictatorship, to revolutionary government, to conservative, neoliberal state.

Perched for more than 40 years atop a vastly unequal distribution of wealth in an agricultural export economy, the Somoza dictatorship destroyed or coopted all organized identities independent of its own interests. In this way, the Somozas stunted the growth of civil society and polarized the populace, managing to unify a heterogeneous opposition and ultimately spelling the end of their long reign in 1979. As the regime grew more repressive, it invaded the sphere of personal life in dramatic ways, killing, torturing and disappearing suspected opponents. In the process, new sectors, including housewives and young women, mobilized into the opposition and took on unaccustomed roles as soldiers, weaponsmakers, and logistical support for revolutionary forces.

After the dictatorship's defeat, the FSLN came to power in a country without a civil society or history of democratic practice and set about creating these from the top down (Vilas 1995). Throughout the eighties, the Sandinistas built popular organizations and sought to draw society's castoffs into the political process.[17]

Both before and after the taking of power, the Sandinista movement had a profound impact on the personal lives of its followers. In effect, the revolution too invaded the personal realm, turning traditional gender and generational arrangements upside down. Young people who joined the movement exchanged the structure of patriarchal authority within the family for a newfound personal and sexual freedom. Mobilized to fight in the army, teach literacy in remote areas, pick coffee and cotton, and work far from home, Nicaragua's youth, particularly its young women, took on new roles and formed new kinds of relationships. Much like the World War II period in the United States (D'Emilio

1983), Nicaraguan lesbians, as well as gays, found, if not social acceptance, at least greater room for maneuver amidst the social turmoil. Though there was no real gay "community" to speak of and the Sandinista regime had closed down the few gay clubs that had existed during the Somoza period, gays and lesbians did begin to find one another.[18]

The regime which came to power in Nicaragua in 1979, sought to bring together a broad spectrum of social sectors around an interventionist political project to benefit the poor and the previously powerless, including women (see Chinchilla 1990,1994; Criquillion 1995; Murguialday 1990; Thayer 1994). The Sandinista government spoke of women's rights to equal participation in society and made concrete advances which alleviated some of women's burdens and allowed them more independence from oppressive family structures.[19] Beyond their new freedoms, women also won legitimation for their claims to be treated as integral, equal members of society, a lesson not lost on the lesbians among them.

But, while there seemed to be consensus within the revolutionary government on the subject of women's rights, at least at a rhetorical level, the same was not true of lesbian and gay issues. At the end of 1986, a semi-clandestine gay and lesbian organization, the Nicaraguan Gay Movement, formed to offer emotional support, internal education about sexuality and AIDS, and discussion of sexual identity, as well as opportunities for social contact (see No author 1992b; Merrett 1992; Zúñiga 1995). These activities came to an abrupt halt three months later when the group was infiltrated by Sandinista State Security. Members were taken to Security headquarters, questioned about their personal lives and collective activities, and told in no uncertain terms that such gatherings were considered counterrevolutionary, despite most of the participants having long histories of revolutionary activism.[20]

Meanwhile, other parts of the state and revolutionary leadership took an entirely different position. As in Costa Rica, AIDS served as both catalyst to and cover for gay and lesbian organization. After their organization was disbanded, Nicaraguan gay and lesbian activists formed the Popular AIDS Education Collective (CEPSIDA), which eventually grew to some 200 people, including both men and women. The group conducted AIDS prevention workshops in a Managua park that served as the gay cruising ground and among the prostitutes at a local shopping mall (see No author 1992b; Merrett 1992; Nicaragua Information Center 1988; Otis 1991). Health Minister Dora María Téllez offered support for CEPSIDA and intervened with the revolutionary leadership to prevent harassment of group members.

Despite contradictions within the state on the issue of sexual orientation, for the most part during the Sandinista period, society was organized around an explicit moral and political consensus under the hegemony of the FSLN. The new institutions and identities were fluid and there was an ideology of makeover—the "new man" was under construction. While many lesbians questioned the absence of the "new woman," and at least some experienced rejection from party functionaries, the revolutionary process as a whole offered the basis for a social integration that had not earlier seemed possible. It also legitimated the conception of a society founded on an explicit set of values which could be articulated to reflect a broad array of interests. It is fitting that, once the Sandinistas lost state power and commitments to the FSLN began to fade, lesbians who had come of age in the 1980s should develop a movement that stressed continuities as well as differences and should pursue inclusion in a reconstructed society organized around transformed values.

With the FSLN loss at the polls in 1990, an internally divided state with a neoliberal economic plan and a conservative gender agenda came to power, and the fledgling civil society was on its own without tutelage for the first time. The new government revamped education to reflect traditional conceptions of morality: sex education was banned and new textbooks called *Morality and Civics* were distributed. An anti-abortion campaign was launched and efforts to criminalize domestic violence were defeated (Kampwirth 1992).

The incoming mayor of Managua, Amoldo Alemán, launched a campaign to "clean up" the city and eliminate homosexual activity from public spaces (Merrett 1992). One month after he assumed office the doors to the ruined cathedral that had served as a gay socializing and cruising area were barred and police harassment of gays in the nearby park escalated. In June 1992, as part of its "family values" campaign, the new legislature passed what has been called the most repressive anti-sodomy law in the hemisphere. According to the law, anyone who "induces, promotes, propagandizes or practices cohabitation among people of the same sex in a scandalous manner" is guilty of the crime of sodomy, punishable by up to three years in prison (*Asamblea Nacional* 1992).[21]

Given the history of mobilization and popular education about rights in Nicaragua, these moves generated a sense of outrage and generalized opposition to the regime among lesbian as well as other activists and reinforced ties among different groups within civil society. In fact, legal attacks on gay rights only provoked a more militant opposition which sought allies and defined the issues in ways that drew support from many sectors of the population. In general, the dramatic shift in the values being promoted by those in power seemed only to serve to make clearer the constructed nature of gender and to invite a movement dedicated to reconstructing it along different lines.

Before the elections, gays and lesbians had already made their first public appearance when a group of some 50 Nicaraguans and 30 internationalists, wearing T-shirts emblazoned with pink triangles, marched and danced together at the celebration of the tenth anniversary of the revolution (Matthews 1989). But the effect of the election results accelerated organizational efforts, and gays and lesbians increasingly claimed visibility, with a public presence at International Women's Day celebrations in 1990 and 1991, and the first open Gay Pride celebration in June 1991 (Merrett 1992; Quirós 1991). It was during these years that the lesbian collective, *Nosotras*, and the gay and lesbian non-governmental organization, *Xochiquetzal*, were founded.[22]

A third factor shaping the identity of the lesbian movement and linked to these different relations between state and society, was the panorama of social movements. In Nicaragua, a class-based, rather than a gender-based, movement defined the terrain. There, a revolutionary party, which held power for ten years, created a totalizing identity and culture and left behind a legacy of popular activism. This historical experience shaped the identity, the ideology, and the sense of goals and strategy of those who ultimately became lesbian activists. The drive to integrate society, and the common project around which the Sandinistas sought to organize it, were based on a revolutionary framework influenced by Marxism and liberation theology. The commitment to social justice for the majority and to collective, rather than individual, solutions left their mark on the lesbian movement which surfaced after the 1990 elections. Although the Sandinista defeat discredited use of the state as a vehicle for change, the lesbian and gay movement continued to work within the arena of civil society, and addressed the state when necessary to defend its room to maneuver.

The presence of a mass movement of the left also created networks of people with similar ideologies and history. While in the 1980s many of these people—including those who would later become active in the gay and lesbian movement—channeled their energies through the state, in the 1990s they moved into the institutions of civil society. Whether or not the FSLN as a party continued to claim their allegiance, their shared world view facilitated building alliances. In the concrete case of gays and lesbians, it led to a model of cross-gender collaboration which began with the formation of the first collectives and AIDS education efforts, and continued into the 1990s.

The FSLN's strategy of cross-class alliances under middle-class leadership was also reflected in the lesbian movement. In an environment where working class people were mobilized and active, and where there was a commitment to eliminating the exclusions of class, it was not only natural for middle-class activists to look beyond their own social class for participants, but also for working class lesbians to respond or even take leadership.

Finally, the strong—indeed dominant—left presence in Nicaragua in the 1980s attracted politicized gay and lesbian fellow travelers from around the world who helped spark organizing efforts and reinforced the social orientation of the budding movement in Nicaragua.[23] It also attracted support from social democratic governments and progressive foundations who, after the 1990 elections, shifted their support to non-governmental organizations, including those, like *Xochiquetzal,* working on issues of gender and sexuality. The requirements for aid recipients in tum had consequences visible in the kind of formal structure—so unlike that of *Las Entendidas*—that *Xochiquetzal* adopted.

By the end of the 1980s, as the unifying revolutionary identity that had prevailed earlier in the decade began to disintegrate in the face of wartime hardships and an increasingly undemocratic style of party leadership, a small but significant autonomous feminist movement had developed. Its growth was due, in large pan, to the contradictions between FSLN rhetoric and action on women's issues (see Chinchilla 1990,1994; *Colectivo Las Malinches* 1993; *Comité Nacional Feminista* 1993; Criquillion 1995; Murguialday 1990; Quandt 1993; Thayer 1994).[24] This growing women's movement provided a space where lesbians could meet and interact. Participating in a movement that questioned traditional sex roles opened the possibility of challenging traditional models of sexuality as well. However, while this movement fought for women's concerns, for the most part in the 1980s, lesbians' concerns were left unspoken. For the time being, even here, lesbians remained invisible.

Ironically, the FSLN's defeat at the polls gave a further impetus to both the feminist, and the lesbian and gay movements, as Sandinista activists were freed from commitments to suppress what had been seen as particularistic needs in favor of defending an embattled revolutionary project. The party leadership was exposed as fallible and newly legitimized critiques began to proliferate, including those of women, gays, and lesbians.

While in Costa Rica the feminist movement was firmly established by the time lesbians began to organize, in Nicaragua the two movements came into their own simultaneously, after a period of semi-clandestine gestation under the revolutionary government. This created a situation of mutual influence, in which it was possible to put lesbian demands on the feminist agenda. Some women's organizations actively promoted public attention to gay and lesbian issues, through Gay Pride celebrations and other means, and there were fewer complaints of feminist homophobia among Nicaraguan, than among Costa Rican, activists. Overall, feminist support made it possible to forge links between concerns about the right to choose sexual partners and fundamental issues about the nature of sexuality, as well as a kind of collective "corning out" around these issues to the wider society.

In contrast with the Costa Rican experience, in building their movement, Nicaraguan lesbians encountered a polarized class structure, a history of wild swings in state-civil society relationships, culminating, in the 1990s, with an unstable and only partial hegemony, and the persistent hold of revolutionary ideology on the popular psyche. Together, these produced a lesbian movement with broad ambitions to reconstruct society in a new image.

Conclusion

In recent decades, a new collective phenomenon—the identity-based movement—has made its appearance on the analytical stage. An examination of lesbian movements in Central America, however, makes clear that the category of new social movements is not as monolithic as it is often made to seem. NSMs manifest a wide variety of expressions, from more outwardly oriented to more internally focused. This raises questions about not only why identity comes to be a concern, but what that identity consists of in each case, and why the movements inspired by these identities take the forms that they do.

While activist lesbians in both Nicaragua and Costa Rica shared a commitment to defining and defending identity, identity itself, as well as what it took to defend it, meant something different in each country. In Costa Rica, lesbian identity was a relatively private affair, embodied in the individual and a solidary community of peers that shared a culture and world view. *Las Entendidas* sought to fortify individuals and the group against a hostile world and, when necessary, to defend their space against incursions. In Nicaragua, lesbians involved in *Nosotras* and *Xochiquetzal* defined themselves as members of a larger polity and as messengers for a new way of thinking about sexuality. Their goals included social, as well as personal, transformation, and their arenas of action extended to include the whole society.

In explaining these differences, I have suggested that economic-structural factors created possibilities and/or foreclosed options for the movements in each country, but that the influences most crucial in defining how members conceived of both their own and movement identity were to be found in a broadly defined political space.

Organizing lesbian movements anywhere in Central America, and many other places, requires the will to defy deeply rooted notions of sexuality and personhood, and the courage to imagine different kinds of relationships. But social movements are built, and collective identities constructed, by particular people in particular locations at particular moments in history. These movements are, as Snow and Benford argue, "signifying agents" (1992:136). What they signify and why, what they struggle for and how, these are questions which can only be answered by looking beyond global structural shifts and the confines of formal political institutions to the sociopolitical relationships that shape the lives of the human beings who make them.

Notes

* Thanks to Michael Burawoy, Laura Enriquez, and Raka Ray for repeated and thorough readings of this paper; to Amy Bank, Lissa Bell, Bill Bigelow, Norma Chinchilla, Ana Criquillion, Norm Diamond, Ana Quirós, and the anonymous reviewers for their thoughtful comments on earlier drafts; and to the many colleagues and friends with whom I discussed the ideas presented here along the way. Thanks also to the International Gay and Lesbian Human Rights Commission for the use of their archives, to Maxine Downs and Judy Haier for invaluable logistical support, and, most of all, to the Central American lesbian activists who shared their struggles and their stories.

My work was supported under a National Science Foundation Graduate Research Fellowship and a fellowship from the Andrew W. Mellon Foundation. Any opinions, findings, conclusions or recommendations expressed in this publication are those of the author and do not necessarily reflect the views of either foundation. Versions of this paper were presented at the XIX International Congress of the Latin American Studies Association in Washington D.C., Sept. 1995, and at the Conference on Feminism(s) in Latin America and the Caribbean, at the University of California at Berkeley, April 1996. Correspondence: Dept. of Sociology, 410 Barrows Hall, University of California, Berkeley CA 94720.

1. On the Costa Rican lesbian movement, see Carstensen (1992); Cruz (1995); *Las Entendidas* (1992); Madden Arias (1994); Mandell (1991); No author (1990); and Serrano (n.d.). *Las Entendidas* roughly translates as "those in the know" and is a term often used by lesbians in Latin America to refer to themselves.
2. On the Nicaraguan movement, see Bolt Gonzalez (1995); No author (1992b); No author (1993b); *Fundación Xochiquetzal* (n.d., 1992); and Merrett (1992). *Nosotras* is the feminine form of "we" in Spanish; *Xochiquetzal* (pronounced so-chee-ketsahl) was the Aztec goddess of flowers and patron of domestic labors, as well as the guardian of counesans.
3. This paper is based on interviews with lesbian and feminist activists from Costa Rica and Nicaragua, as well as participant observation and an analysis of newsletters and other documents from the organizations described here. The research was conducted during two trips, the first to El Salvador to the VI Latin American and Caribbean Feminist Encounter in October and November, 1993, and the second to Costa Rica and Nicaragua in June and July, 1995.
4. Melucci was among the first to theorize the dynamics of collective identity construction. More recently, others have addressed this issue from various perspectives (Friedman and McAdam 1992; Gamson, W. 1992; Taylor and Whittier 1992).
5. Other critics of NSM theory argue that its supposedly distinct features appeared in earlier movements as well (D'Anieri, Ernst and Kier 1990) and may be no more than the product of a stage in a cycle of development (Tarrow 1988).

6. Ferree (1987) is one of the few who asks why movements—in her case women's movements—in different countries take divergent approaches to similar issues.
7. Some authors, such as Melucci (1985) and Offe (1985), analyze the particular actors attracted to new European movements, but generalize across countries.
8. Rucht (1996) identifies class structure as pan of the social context that influences movement form, but does not link it to movement orientation.
9. Ferree's (1987) explanatory factors go beyond narrowly defined political opportunities to include both historical political configurations and the discourses linked to them. Nevertheless, she continues to give substantial weight to the formal political realm.
10. All translations are my own, unless otherwise noted.
11. In fact, this may have been a wise calculation, given the intensity of the opposition that developed once word was out. Conference organizers faced site cancellations, condemnation from church leaders, and a decision by the Ministry of Government to deny visas to single women seeking to enter the country for the period surrounding the Encounter. The final night of the event, participants were terrorized by a group of drunken would-be assailants outside the secluded estate where Encounter was being held . Nevertheless, the shock apparent in conference organizers' accounts of these events suggests that a particular strategic vision, rather than fear of hostility, no matter how justified, dictated their initial conceptions of the Encounter.
12. A second, fairly short-lived organization, formed by a group of lesbians in their 20's, never really went beyond the first level described here. *Las Humanas* ("the female humans") functioned primarily as a recreation and support group for members. It fell apart in 1992 when discussions were initiated about more public political activity within the lesbian and gay community (Serrano n.d.).
13. Although *Xochiquetzal* worked on behalf of lesbians and gays, I will treat it as part of the lesbian movement. The organization was directed by lesbians and played an important role in the coordinating of lesbian organizing.

    The collaboration between *Xochiquetzal* and *Nosotras* lasted until 1994, when the collective became independent. This recent development, as well as the founding in 1993 of another gay and lesbian group, *Neconi,* remain to be analyzed, but may represent shifts in orientation based on the changing political panorama of post-revolutionary Nicaragua.
14. See Schifter Sikora (1989) for a history of the Costa Rican gay male movement, including the initial formation of a homosexual community. See D'Emilio (1983) for a discussion of how similar factors operated in the U.S.
15. To illustrate, in his successful election campaign in 1986, Oscar Arias promised to bring about a "government with the soul of a woman." Once in office, he launched a widely publicized "feminist offensive" to put women's issues on the agenda. In 1988, the Arias administration proposed a "Law of Real Equality for Women" aimed at increasing women's political participation, as well as their access to social and economic rights (Saint-Germain 1993; Saint-Germain and Morgan 1991).
16. A month after the raid, an open letter to the Ministers of Health and Security criticizing government harassment of gays and calling instead for preventive measures to fight the disease was published in the country's largest newspaper, signed by 150 prominent intellectuals, politicians, and professionals, gay and straight. The letter made full use of the political discourse of Costa Rican exceptionalism noted earlier, ending: "To begin to distinguish among Costa Ricans with slanderous labels is an attack on all our civic and democratic traditions and opens a dangerous door to arbitrariness and State terrorism" (Open letter published in *La Nación,* April 5, 1987, cited in Schifter Sikora 1989: 292). A few days later, a sympathetic editorial echoed the letter.

Despite the entrenched homophobia in Costa Rican society, at this particular political moment the Arias administration was vulnerable to the claims of marginalized groups. In an effort to restore the country's image as a neutral peacemaker and to prevent regional conflicts from spilling across borders, Arias had taken the lead in Central American peace negotiations and been awarded the Nobel peace prize. According to Schlfter Sikora (1989), Arias' role in promoting the peace plan put the focus on Costa Rica as a supposed model of democracy for the region and raised the level of international scrutiny of its human rights record. It was an opportune moment for the fledgling gay and lesbian movement. A week after the open letter was published, the government suspended mandatory AIDS testing.

17. It is important to note that these efforts were often paternalistic and frequently resisted by the groups targeted for integration. For my argument, however, what is important is the way inclusiveness was established as a societal goal.
18. The Sandinistas seem to have taken the same approach to gay institutions as had the Cuban revolution earlier, classifying them as pan of the corruption of the defeated dictatorship, along with casinos and prostitution rings, which the new Nicaraguan government also closed down.
19. In the first few years, the government appointed women to leadership positions in state institutions, banned advertising that exploited women's bodies, instituted the principle of equal pay for equal work, granted maternity leave, and launched the first agrarian reform in the hemisphere to recognize women as potential recipients of land. Women were encouraged to organize and the new women's association, AMNLAE, fought for and won legislative victories, including laws challenging patriarchal relations in the family and mandating sharing domestic work. In addition, women, who made up 60 percent of the country's poor, benefited from increased access to state-funded health services and educational facilities, as well as new job opportunities in the growing state sector.
20. Testimony to the group's commitment to the Sandinista state was its decision not to discuss the interrogations with anyone outside the organization. It was only after the FSLN's 1990 electoral loss that the news spread in the lesbian and gay community.
21. The law went into effect in spring 1994 after a prolonged legal battle over its constitutionality.
22. Earlier, in 1989, a non-governmental organization known as *Nimehuatzin,* which was dedicated to AIDS prevention and treatment, had been established. Although it briefly served as a center for gays and lesbians, this function was later taken on by the groups described In this article.
23. Some of these gay and lesbian internationalists came on delegations or work brigades, such as the all-gay and lesbian Victoria Mercado Brigade, that came to work on a construction project in a low-income Managua neighborhood in 1985, or the San Francisco AIDS workers who came down for an international Health Colloquium in 1987. Others came to stay, integrating themselves into Nicaraguan institutions and neighborhoods. Many Nicaraguan gays and lesbians later involved in organizing efforts came into contact with these visitors and learned from them about gay and lesbian movements around the world (Zúñiga 1995).
24. As the 1980s progressed, Nicaraguan feminists became increasingly critical of Sandinista gender policy. The government's auspicious beginnings in the area of women's rights soon faded under the pressures of war and the machismo of most of the party leadership. Gender-specific concerns took a back seat to national priorities and an ambitious feminist legislative campaign was shelved as potentially divisive. As early as 1983, a few Sandinista feminists, frustrated with the party's foot-dragging, began to launch their own independent projects—women's clinics, research teams, theater groups and legal offices—and to make inroads in the press.

REFERENCES

Andersson, Suzanne

1993 "The fight against penal code article 204: Embracing a sexual right." Barricada Intemacional 365:22–23.

Asamblea Nacional

1992 "Ley 150: Ley de Refonnas al Código Penal." Managua: Comisión Pennanente Mujer-Niñez-Juventud y Familia.

Berrón, Linda

1995 Feminismo en Costa Rica? Testimonios, reflexiones, ensayos. San José: Editorial Mujeres.

Blandón, María Teresa

1993 "Por qué defendemos una sexualidad libre de prejuicios." La Feminista 3:12–13.

Bolt González, María

1995 "Nicaragua." In Unspoken Rules: Sexual Orientation and Women's Human Rights, Rachel Rosenbloom (ed.), 133–137. San Francisco: IGLHRC.

Buechler, Steven M.

1995 "New social movement theories." Sociological Quarterly 36:441–464.

Candelaria Navas, María

1985 "Los movimientos femeninos en Centroamérica: 1970–1983." In Movimientos populares en Centroamérica, eds. Daniel Camacho and Rafael Menjivar, 200–236. San José: EDUCA.

Carstensen, Jeanne

1992 "Fighting fear in Costa Rica." Advocate 595:36–37.

Chinchilla, Norma

1990 "Revolutionary popular feminism in Nicaragua: Articulating class, gender and national sovereignty." Gender and Society 4:370–397.

1994 "Feminism, revolution and democratic transitions in Nicaragua." In The Women's Movement in Latin America: Participation and Democracy, Jane Jaquette (ed.), 177–197. Boulder: Westview.

Colectivo Las Malinches

1993 "La experiencia de Nicaragua." Paper presented at the VI Encuentro Femlnista de Latinoamérica y el Caribe, Costa del Sol, El Salvador, Oct. 3I.

Colectivo Pancha Carrasco

1994 "Del feminismo popular al feminismo como opción vital política." In Lo que siempre quisiste saber sobre feminismo en Centroamérica y no te atreviste a preguntar, Clara Murguialday and Norma Vázquez (eds.). Centro Editorial de la Mujer.

Comité Nactonal Feminista

1993 "Comité Nactonal Feminista: Procesos y desafíos." Paper presented at the VI Encuentro Feminista de Latinoamérica y el Caribe, Costa del Sol, El Salvador, Oct. 31.

Criquillion, Ana

1995 "The Nicaraguan women's movement: Feminist reflections from within." In The New Politics of Survival: Grassroots Movements in Central America, Minor Sinclair (ed.), 209–237. New York: Monthly Review Press.

Cruz, Paquita

1995 "The lesbian feminist group las Entendidas." Paper presented at the XIX International Congress of the Latin American Studies Association, Washington D.C., September 30.

D'Anieri, Paul, Claire Ernst, and Elizabeth Kier
1990 "New social movements in historical perspective." Comparative Politics 22:445–458.
della Porta, Donatella, and Dieter Rucht
1995 "Left-libertarian movements in context: A comparison of Italy and West Germany, 1965–1990." In The Politics of Social Protest: Comparative Perspectives on States and Social Movements, J. Craig Jenkins and Bert Klandermans (eds.), 229–272. Minneapolis: University of Minnesota Press.
D'Emilio, John
1983 "Capitalism and gay identity." In Powers of Desire: The Politics of Sexuality, Ann Snitow, Christine Stansell, and Sharon Thompson (eds.), 100–113. New York: Monthly Review Press.
Escalante Herrera, Ana C.
1990 El subdesarrollo, la paz y la mujer en Costa Rica. San José: Universidad de Costa Rica.
Escobar, Arturo
1992 "Culture, economics and politics in Latin American social movements theory and research." In The Making of Social Movements in Latin America: Identity, Strategy, and Democracy, Arturo Escobar and Sonia E. Alvarez (eds.), 62–85. Boulder: Westview Press.
Facio, Alda
1988 "Igualdad?" Mujer/Fempress 80: 9–10.
Ferguson, Ann
1991 "Lesbianism, feminism and empowerment in Nicaragua." Socialist Review 3-4:75–97.
Ferree, Myra Marx
1987 "Equality and autonomy: Feminist politics in the United States and West Germany." In The Women's Movements of the United States and Western Europe: Consciousness, Political Opponunity, and Public Policy, Mary Fainsod Katzenstein and Carol McClurg Mueller (eds.), 172–195. Philadelphia: Temple University Press.
FLACSO
1995 Centroamérica en cifras, 1980–1992. San José: FLACSO.
Friedman, Debra, and Doug McAdam
1992 "Collective identity and activism : Networks, choices, and the life of a social movement." In Frontiers in Social Movement Theory, eds. Aldon D. Morris and Carol McClurg Mueller, 156–173. New Haven: Yale University Press.
Fundación Xochiquetzal
1992 "Campaña por una sexualidad libre de prejuictos." Pamphlet, Managua, (December). n.d. "Fundación Xochiquetzal." Brochure, Managua.
Gamson, Josh
1989 "Silence, death, and the invisible enemy: AIDS activism and social movement 'newness.'" Social Problems 36:351–367.
Gamson, William A.
1992 "The social psychology of collective action." In Frontiers in Social Movement Theory, Aldon D. Morris and Carol McClurg Mueller (eds.), 53–76. New Haven: Yale University Press.
García, Ana Isabel, and Enrique Gomariz
1989 Mujeres centroamericanas: Efectos del conflicto: 2. San José: FLACSO.
González Suárez, Mirta
1988 Estudios de Ia mujer: Conocimiento y cambio. San José: EDUCA.

Gramsci, Antonio
1971 Selections from the Prison Notebooks, eds., translated by Quintin Hoare and Geoffrey Nowell Smith. New York: International Publishers.
Habermas, Jurgen
1984 The Theory of Communicative Action, Volume 1. Translated by Thomas McCarthy. Boston: Beacon Press.
Hunt, Scott A., Robert D. Benford, and David A. Snow
1994 "Identity fields: Framing processes and the social construction of movement identities." In New Social Movements: From Ideology to Identity, Enrique Laraña, Hank Johnston and Joseph R. Gusfield (eds.), 185–208. Philadelphia: Temple University Press.
Jenkins, J. Craig
1983 "Resource mobilization theory and the study of social movements." Annual Review of Sociology 9:527–553.
Jiménez. Amparo
1990 "Despite hostility, Latina lesbians gather in Costa Rica." Outlines June:28.
Johnston, Hank, Enrique Laraña, and Joseph R. Gusfield
1994 "Identities, grievances, and new social movements." In New Social Movements: From Ideology to Identity, Enrique Laraña, Hank Johnston and Joseph R. Gusfield (eds.), 3–35. Philadelphia: Temple University Press.
Kampwirth, Karen
1992 "The revolution continues: Nicaraguan women's organizations under the UNO." Paper presented at the American Political Science Association Meeting. Chicago, September 3–6.
Kitschelt, Herbert P.
1986 "Political opportunity structures and political protest: Anti-nuclear movements in four democracies." British Journal of Political Science 60:57–85.
Kriesi, Hanspeter
1995 "The political opportunity structure of new social movements : Its impact on their mobilization." In The Politics of Social Protest: Comparative Perspectives on States and Social Movements, J. Craig Jenkins and Bert Klandermans (eds.), 167–198. Minneapolis: University of Minnesota Press.
1996 "The organizational structure of new social movements in a political context." In Comparative Perspectives on Social Movements: Political Opportunities, Mobilizing Structures, and Cultural Framings, eds. Doug McAdam, John D. McCarthy and Mayer N. Zald, 152–184. Cambridge: Cambridge University Press.
Las Entendidas
1992 "Han pasado cinco años *y* todavía soñamos." Confidencial March:8.
Madden Arias, Rose Mary
1994 "La experiencia de un grupo lésbico feminista en Costa Rica." In Lo que siempre quisiste saber sobre feminismo en Centroameíca y no te atrevlste a preguntar, Clara Murguialday and Norma Vázquez (eds.). Centro Editorial deal Mujer.
Mandell, Zoe
1991 "La lucha por las mentes de la gente: El conflicto de baja intensidad y Ia liberación lésbica en Costa Rica." Iconoclasta 2:6–15.
Matthews, Tede
1989 "Without the participation of lesbians and gays . . . there is no revolution." NICCA Bulletin Sept.–Oct.

McAdam, Doug

1982 Political Process and the Development of Black Insurgency 1930–1970. Chicago: University of Chicago Press.

McCarthy, John D., and Mayer N. Zald

1977 "Resource mobilization and social movements: A partial theory." American Journal of Sociology 82:1212–1241.

Melucci, Alberto

1980 "The new social movements: A theoretical approach." Social Science Information 19:199–226.

1985 "The symbolic challenge of contemporary movements." Social Research 52:789–816.

1994 "A strange kind of newness: What's 'new' in new social movements?" In New Social Movements: From Ideology to Identity, Enrique Laraña, Hank Johnston and Joseph R. Gusfield (eds.), 101–130. Philadelphia: Temple University Press.

Merrett, Jim

1992 "Nicaraguan gays fight new conservatism." Advocate 601:42–43.

Meyer, David S., and Suzanne Staggenborg

1996 "Movements, countermovements, and the structure of political opportunity." American Journal of Sociology 101:1628–1660.

Meyer, David S., and Nancy Whittier

1994 "Social movement spillover." Social Problems 41:277–298.

Murguialday, Clara

1990 Nicaragua, revolución y feminismo (1977–1989). Madrid: Editorial Revolución.

Nicaragua Information Center

1988 "Nicaragua responds to AIDS." Bulletin of the Nicaragua Information Center Dec.–Jan.:1–4.

No Author

1990 Memoria de un encuentro inolvidable. Costa Rica: II encuentro lésbico feminista de América Latina y el Caribe.

1992a Aunque Ud. no lo crea "La Boletina" 6:25–26.

1992b De Ambiente: "Interviews with members of the Nicaraguan movement of lesbian feminists and gay men." Breakthrough 16:17–23.

1993a "Crónicas de Ia II Jornada por una sexualidad libre de prejuicios." La Feminista 3:6–16.

1993b "Derechos de lesbianas y homosexuales." Fuera del Closet 0:15.

Oberschall, Anthony

1973 Social Conflict and Social Movements. Englewood Cliffs, N.J.: Prentice-Hall.

Offe, Claus

1985 "New social movements: Challenging the boundaries of institutional politics." Social Research 52:817–868.

Otis, John

1991 "Fight against AIDS started Nicaragua's 'gay revolution." *San Francisco Chronicle* (November 15).

Palma, Diego

1989 "The state and social co-optation in Costa Rica." In The Costa Rica Reader, Marc Edelman, and Joanne Kenen (eds.), 132–137. New York: Grove Weidenfeld.

Quandt, Midge

1993 "New directions for Nicaraguan feminists: 'No political daddy needed.'" Against the Current 8:23–25.

Quirós, Ana
1991 "Construyendo una sociedad sin etiquetas." Paper presented at the Gay Pride Day celebration, Managua, June 23.
Randall, Margaret
1992 Gathering Rage: The Failure of Twentieth Century Revolutions to Develop a Feminist Agenda. New York: Monthly Review Press.
Rucht, Dieter
1996 "The impact of national contexts on social movement structures: A cross-movement and cross-national comparison." In Comparative Perspectives on Social Movements: Political Opportunities, Mobilizing Structures, and Cultural Framings, Doug McAdam, John D. McCarthy, and Mayer N. Zald (eds.), 152–184. Cambridge: Cambridge University Press.
Saint-Germain, Michelle A.
1993 "Paths to Power of Women Legislators in Costa Rica and Nicaragua." Women's Studies International Forum 16:119–138.
Saint-Germain, Michelle A., and Martha I. Morgan
1991 "Equality: Costa Rican women demand 'the real thing.'" Women and Politics 2/3:23–75.
Schifter Sikora, Jacobo
1989 La formación de una contracultura: Homosexualismo y SIDA en Costa Rica. San José: Guayacan.
Serrano Madrigal, Ester
n.d. "Breve historia de las organizadones formales de mujeres lesbianas en Costa Rica." Unpublished Manuscript.
Silvestre, Lila
1992 "Editorial." Las Entendidas 14:1.
Slater, David
1985 New Soda! Movements and the State in Latin America. Amsterdam: CEDLA.
Snow, David A., and Robert D. Benford
1988 "Ideology, frame resonance, and participant mobilization." In From Structure to Action: Social Movement Participation Across Cultures, Ben Klandermans, Hanspeter Kriesi, and Sidney Tarrow (eds.), 197–217. Greenwich, Conn.: JAI Press.
1992 "Master frames and cycles of protest." In Frontiers in Social Movement Theory, Aldon D. Morris and Carol McClurg Mueller (eds.), 133–155. New Haven: Yale University Press.
Solís, Manuel
1989 "The fragmentation and disappearance of the Costa Rican left." In The Costa Rica Reader, Marc Edelman and Joanne Kenen (eds.), 309–313. New York: Grove Weidenfeld.
Tarrow, Sidney
1988 "Old Movements in new cycles of protest: The career of an Italian religious community." In From Structure to Action: Social Movement Participation Across Cultures, Bert Klandermans, Hanspeter Kriesi, and Sidney Tarrow (eds.), 281–304. Greenwich, Conn.: JAI Press.
1994 Power in Movement: Social Movements, Collective Action and Politics. Cambridge: Cambridge University Press.
Taylor, Verta
1989 "Social movement continuity: The women's movement in abeyance." American Sociological Review 54:761–775.

Taylor, Verta, and Leila J. Rupp
1993 "Women's culture and lesbian feminist activism: A reconsideration of cultural feminism." Signs 19:32–61.
Taylor, Verta, and Nancy E. Whittier
1992 "Collective identity In social movement communities: Lesbian feminist mobilization." In Frontiers in Social Movement Theory, Aldon D. Morris and Carol McClurg Mueller (eds.), 104–129. New Haven: Yale University Press.
Thayer, Millie
1994 "After the Fall: The Nicaraguan Women's Movement in the 1990s." Paper presented at the XVIII International Congress of the Latin American Studies Association, Atlanta, March 10.
Tilly, Charles
1978 From Mobilization to Revolution. Reading, Mass.: Addison-Wesley.
Touraine, Alain
1985 "An Introduction to the study of social movements." Social Research 52:749–787.
1988 Return of the Actor: Social Theory In Postindustrial Society. Translated by Myrna Godzich. Minneapolis: University of Minnesota Press.
Vilas, Carlos
1995 Between Earthquakes and Volcanoes: Market, State and Revolutions in Central America. Translated by Ted Kuster. New York: Monthly Review Press.
Whittier, Nancy
1995 Feminist Generations: The Persistence of the Radical Women's Movement. Philadelphia: Temple University Press.
Zúñiga, Joel
1995 "La casa cinquenta." Unpublished Manuscript.

CHAPTER FIVE

ENVIRONMENT

Since the conquest, colonial and imperial powers have taken from the Central American isthmus its natural resources obtained through the labor of Central American peoples. When the Spanish conquerors realized that the region lacked precious minerals and stones, agricultural production for commercial ends became the potential wealth for this region. As a result, the Spanish colonial authorities began a process that allowed them to extract the wealth of the region's natural resources through the enslavement of Indigenous labor, as we discussed in Chapter 3.

Throughout the centuries, the economic interests of external powers have modified the Central American environment without carefully measuring the consequences for future generations. Because the concept of the environment includes plants, animals and human beings, the urgency of protecting the environment reflects the numerous ways in which these three main components and their survival interconnect.

After independence, liberal caudillos opened their countries to foreign investment and expanded the production of non-traditional exports such as coffee and bananas and the infrastructure around it: railroads, ports, roads and banking. The most favorable zone for coffee cultivation was the same area where most of the woodlands of the region were found. They cleared woodlands and mountains in order to plant coffee, destroying several natural forests. They also threatened the survival of Indigenous peoples as they eliminated their communal lands and militarized rural space to maintain this system of coffee plantations and cheap labor.

The transformation of the landscape through the emergence of private property in the region also changed the surface of Central American nations into the checkered landscape of private property that it is now. Meanwhile, the emergence of massive monocultures increased the need to use pesticides that have damaged the environment and poisoned those who work on these plantations. To analyze the more contemporary damaging impact on the Central American environment we must look at the developmental policies instituted since the end of World War II. The process of modernization that took place during this period forced the Central American governments to implement developmental policies aimed at increasing and diversifying the mode of production. Likewise, the process of modernization since the middle of the twentieth century refined the agro-export model by including sugar cane, cotton and other agricultural products to supply the demands of the international market.

For most of their working history the owners of large mono-crop plantations such as the United Fruit Company and the manufacturers of pesticides have gone unpunished in spite of their massive use of DDT and other poisonous pesticides in the region. This was the case even at a time when the United States banned the use of these chemicals. It wasn't until 2007 when a U.S. civil court found Dole, one of the lead banana producing companies, and Dow Chemical, one of the manufacturing companies of the pesticides used in Central America, guilty of knowingly exposing their workers to poison in Nicaragua. This lawsuit was possible due to the presence of both the companies and the workers on American soil. It was an unlikely result of the contemporary migratory trends in the hemisphere.

Unfortunately, as Indigenous and peasant communities lost their land, they were forced to cut into parts of the rainforest with slash and burn agricultural practices. Central America experienced a rapid and dramatic process of deforestation as a result of their use of the land to survive, the pollution brought by foreign firms and the destruction of the rainforest by companies such as the United Fruit Company and the Belize Estate & Produce Company.

Furthermore, the Central American governments initiated the process of industrialization by introducing manufacturing plants that transformed thousands of peasants into industrial workers. This massive infusion of workers created an internal and regional migration that profoundly modified the rural and urban landscape of Central America. More tropical rainforest was cleared in order to fulfill the demands of new agricultural products and industries and the need for more housing and infrastructure (highways, bridges, ports and electrical plants) to support this modernizing process. At the end of the 1960s this process also displaced hundreds of thousands of people who lost their land to make room for the modern industries, thus creating a social time bomb that exploded in the following decades.

The unfulfilled promises of a better life under the modern developmental policies that, quite to the contrary, polluted the environment (people and landscape) resulted in politico-military upheavals particularly in Guatemala, Nicaragua and El Salvador. An evolving process of militarization of the entire region confronted this socio-political and economic crisis, adding more stress to the already fragile ecosystem. Military repression accompanied the new developmental policies similar to the early version of land privatization in the nineteenth century. However, the scale was larger and more devastating for the people and for the land. The 1970s and the 1980s saw an unprecedented movement of people in the Central American region and further developmental policies that ultimately continued to impact the environment.

More recently, global political trends, such as neoliberal policies, continue the implementation of neoliberal agreements that directly affect the Central American environment, such as the Central American Free Trade Agreement, CAFTA. Furthermore, there are numerous efforts by companies and foreign governments to privatize the natural resources of the region and to sell them to the local populations for profit or to other populations as exports. As a result, what is left of the immense wealth of the Central American ecosystem is not easily accessible by the general Central American population, and what is accessible to them is greatly contaminated, unhealthy and poisonous. In sum, they live in a damaged environment. As larger and larger numbers of Central Americans migrate to the United States, we are experiencing in our lifetime displacement from areas of limited resources to an area that consumes most of the resources of the planet. The destruction of the Central American environment that we are witnessing is part of the price that is paid so that developed countries can maintain their own lifestyles today.

As the author states, this article offers "an ecological Marxist critique" (17) on the impact of ecological destruction in Nicaragua. One of the main points of emphasis is the role of U.S. imperialism in the creation of the ecological crisis in Central America. As he moves through the history of Central America, Faber names the effects that the different monocrops have had on the environment, including coffee, bananas, sugar and cotton, as well as the use of the land for cattle ranching. Furthermore, Faber argues that "Marxist and socialist theory should place the ecological crisis at the center of any analysis of revolution and imperialism in Central America" (39). Finally, he illustrates his argument for the need of a socialist reconstruction of the environment with the environmental programs of the revolution in Nicaragua as an example of comprehensive socialist ecological policy.

Imperialism, Revolution, and the Ecological Crisis of Central America

DANIEL FABER

The ecological crisis created by capitalist development in Central America has been the subject of considerable research, but most of this work has failed to systematically examine the causes, manifestations, and impacts of ecological destruction from a Marxist or socialist perspective. Instead, most explanations of the crisis have been based on a Malthusian notion of overpopulation (Daugherty, 1969), irrational and inefficient environmental planning (Leonard, 1987), and/or the idea of "excessive demand" in the First World for environmentally destructive commodities (such as beef) from the Third (Nations and Komer, 1983). In contrast, I offer an ecological Marxist critique (see Faber, 1988; O'Connor, 1988). I examine the role of U.S. imperialism in creating the ecological, communal, and human conditions of production for capitalist export agriculture and industry in Central America and argue that social and ecological marginalization of the peasant subsistence sector has been a functional component of this process, providing the necessary supplies of highly exploitable semiproletarian workers for the capitalist export sector. I explore the thesis that the survival strategies adopted by the peasantry in response to its impoverishment have resulted in the widespread degradation and collapse of the ecological conditions necessary for the reproduction of semiproletarian labor-power. I go on to point to the contribution of the ecological crisis, aggravated by U.S. policies of "low-intensity conflict" and "ecocide," to the development of powerful reformist and revolutionary movements for social and ecological justice and conclude

"Imperialism, Revolution, and the Ecological Crisis in Central America" by Daniel Faber, *Latin American Perspectives*, 19(1), pp. 17–44, copyright © 1992 by SAGE Publications, Inc. Reprinted by permission of SAGE Publications, Inc.

that Marxist and socialist theory should place the ecological crisis at the center of any analysis of revolution and imperialism in Central America.

Disarticulated Development and the Capitalization of Nature

The ecological crisis of Central America is grounded in a particular model of capitalist development that has been promoted by the United States for the last four decades. At the end of the Second World War, the nations of Central America remained economically and socially "underdeveloped," highly dependent on the markets of the First World (particularly the United States) for their own prosperity. Just two commodity crops, coffee and bananas, dominated the region's exports, generating nearly 90 percent of Costa Rica's, El Salvador's, and Guatemala's total foreign exchange earnings in 1954. Although the prices for these exports initially improved after the Second World War, they had declined again by the mid-1950s (Webb, 1985: 19), revealing the region's economic vulnerability.

With the rise of the Rockefeller foreign policy camp in the 1950s, the United States assumed a more active role in expanding "dependent" capitalist development in Central America (Szymanski, 1981: 181). This role was enlarged even further with the creation of the Alliance for Progress in 1961. Largely a response to the Cuban Revolution, the Alliance aimed to promote social and economic stability (or the creation of "middle classes") in Central America through the modernization, diversification, and expansion of capitalist export agriculture and industry.

The social and ecological impacts of the Alliance in the various Central American countries proved somewhat similar. In El Salvador, Guatemala, and Nicaragua, the traditional coffee oligarchies and surrogate security forces (along with the Somocista bourgeoisie) used U.S. economic and military assistance to promote the development of large-scale agricultural estates (de Janvry, 1981: 82–107). Pristine forest lands, unique wildlife habitats, and peasant communities alike were cleared to make way for vast *latifundios* devoted to the production of traditional and nontraditional export crops, principally coffee, cotton, sugar, bananas, and cattle, In Honduras and Costa Rica, in contrast, foreign capital was used by small peasant farmers, the urban bourgeoisie, and landed oligarchs to modernize and expand coffee farms and cattle holdings. Large-scale banana plantations also witnessed rapid growth. Because the form of capitalist development took a generally more mixed *minifundio-latifundio* form, state repression of the popular classes assumed much less significance in these two countries (Flora and Torres-Rivas, 1989: 39–55).

One of the first areas to be developed was the Pacific coastal plain, Guarded by the majestic volcanos and steep slopes of the western highlands and extending from Mexico through Panama, these lowlands, with their hot, dry climate and rich volcanic soils, were ideal for the cultivation of two new export commodities—cotton and sugar. Spurred by infusions of financial capital from the U.S. Agency for International Development (USAID), the World Bank, the Inter-American Development Bank (IADB), and other international development agencies, malaria and disease eradication projects, road and port construction, land speculation, and other state programs quickly served to create the appropriate ecological and communal (or infrastructural) conditions of production for capitalist export agriculture (Chapin and Wasserstrom, 1983: 115–117; Williams, 1986: 21).

From 1950 through the 1970s, peasants were evicted from their traditional landholdings, often by brutal military force. For many dispossessed families, the only income-earning opportunities that remained in the Pacific littoral were as wage laborers during the short cotton-picking season (Brockett, 1988: 68–9). Virtually all of the coastal humid hardwood forests were destroyed, including stands of old-growth ebony, cedar, mahogany, and granadilla. Coastal savannas, evergreen forests, and large areas of coastal mangroves were also cleared. With their habitats destroyed, many species of animals, including howler monkeys, anteaters, and white-lipped peccaries, were widely eliminated. Numerous other mammals of the lowland deciduous forest were exterminated or greatly reduced, including the nine-banded armadillo, the aguti, the coyote, the grey fox, the tepescuintle, the puma, and the white-tailed deer, as well as large birds such as the ornate hawk-eagle, the scarlet macaw, the yellow-headed parrot, and the great curassow (Daugherty, 1969: 202; Daugherty, Jeannert-Grosjean, and Fletcher, 1979: 32–34; USAID-Nicaragua I, 1981: 5; USAID-Guatemala I, 1981: 5–19).

Cotton was responsible for most of the damage. Along Nicaragua's Pacific plain, cotton land expanded 400 percent and peasants' land devoted to corn, beans, sorghum, and other food grains dropped over 50 percent from 1952 to 1967 (Darner and Quiros, 1983: 228). By 1970, cotton occupied 80 percent of the Pacific plain's arable land—40 percent of all the cultivated land in Nicaragua (Swezey, Murray, and Daxl, 1986: 8). In Guatemala, some 221,312 acres of the Pacific lowlands were in cotton by 1972, almost completely displacing the area's poor *campesinos.* In fact, the largest 3.7 percent of farms along Guatemala's Pacific coast monopolized 80.3 percent of the land, one of the highest degrees of land concentration in all Latin America (Caltagirone et al., 1972: 13; Brockett, 1988: 70). By the late 1970s, the landed oligarchy and the newly emerging agrarian bourgeoisie had carved over 10,000 farms and some 1,004,796 acres of cotton fields from the ancient tropical forests of the Pacific lowlands and employed half a million workers. By then, Central America was producing over a million bales of cotton annually, which ranked the region third, behind the United States and Egypt, in sales on the world market (Williams, 1986: 13–32; ICAITI, 1977: 177; Thrupp, 1988: 198–203). Only 2 percent of the original coastal forests remained (Whelan, 1987: 16).

Another nontraditional export commodity that transformed the Central American landscape was beef cattle. Cattle ranching was less restricted geographically than production of cotton or coffee. Beef could be raised wherever pasture grass would grow, particularly in the lush lower montane and lowland Caribbean rain forests of the interior. Funded by grants and/or loans from U.S. government agencies and international financial institutions, large-scale cattle ranches quickly expanded toward the rolling mountains and valleys in the interior, displacing peasant farmers from their traditional agricultural lands. In Nicaragua and Guatemala, thousands of peasants resisting eviction by large-scale cattle ranchers were killed in U.S.-supported counterinsurgency operations during the 1960s and 1970s. In fact, military officers and government officials have historically promoted counterinsurgency programs as a means of capitalizing or privatizing nature for their own personal gain (Williams, 1986).

The expansion of cattle ranching quickly proved to be an ecological as well as a social disaster (Nations and Kamer, 1983; Faber, Karliner, and Rice, 1986). During the height of the cattle boom of 1970 to 1980, 15 percent of the region's forests, covering an area larger than Belgium, were destroyed (Leonard, 1987: 7). As a result, deboned frozen beef emerged as the region's most dynamic export commodity, with a 400 percent increase in trade between 1961 and 1974 alone (Nations and Leonard, 1986: 72). During the 1980s, Central America's rain forests, one of the richest reserves of biological and genetic diversity in the world, disappeared at a rate of almost 3,500 to 4,000 square kilometers annually. In fact, over two-thirds of Central America's (broad-leafed) lowland and lower montane rain forests, the largest expanse north of the Amazon Basin, have been destroyed since 1960 (Nations and Leonard, 1986). Today, over 22 percent of the region's landmass, more land than used for all other agricultural commodities combined, is in permanent pasture (Leonard, 1987: 99).

Under the Alliance for Progress, capitalist development had the effect of more fully integrating Central America into the world economy as a supplier of cheap agricultural commodities and raw materials. By the mid-1970s, nontraditional commodities of cotton, beef, and sugar had combined with traditional crops of coffee and bananas to constitute 82 to 85 percent of all extraregional trade and over 60 percent of the region's export earnings (Weeks, 1985: 96–98). In addition, the creation of the Central America Common Market (CACM) facilitated 7 to 9 percent increases in industrial output in every Central American country (except Honduras and Belize) between 1960 and 1976 (Flora and Torres-Rivas, 1989: 37). But rather than bringing greater economic independence, the development of export agriculture and industry merely intensified Central American dependency on U.S. and international capital. In short, capitalist development left the region both sectorally and socially disarticulated (de Janvry, 1981: 32–49).

Central America was sectorally disarticulated in that forward and backward linkages related to the processing of primary commodities produced by the capitalist export sector were underdeveloped (in terms of both employment and percentage of GNP). Despite the creation of the CACM and restricted import-substitution industrialization around some durable consumer goods, industries that manufactured inputs for agricultural or raw material production or processed agricultural products into another commodity form remained extremely limited, particularly in comparison with the rest of Latin America (Gorostiaga and Marchetti, 1988). As a result, the capitalist export sector remained highly dependent on imported capital goods and highly vulnerable to trade and credit fluctuations in the international market (Bulmer-Thomas, 1987: 189). The region was also socially disarticulated in that it had little consumption capacity for commodities produced by the capitalist export sector, especially in those countries pursuing the more repressive *latifundia* path of capitalist development. The peasantry and poor working classes were not the primary sources of aggregate demand. As a result, the region's economy was extremely vulnerable to world market conditions (falling prices for major exports, protectionism, overproduction, etc.), particularly during times of economic recession in the advanced capitalist countries (Weeks, 1985: 55–86). This condition was magnified by the extremely small size and openness of the region's economy. Contraction or expansion in the supply of Central America's leading agricultural exports had little impact on the world prices for these commodities. As a consequence, the volume of these exports became "determined by production costs in Central American countries compared to costs elsewhere and the margin between world prices and production costs" (Weeks, 1985: 59–60).

With the primary market located abroad, both the production and consumption capacities of Central America's capitalist sector were increased by minimizing costs, including expenditures relating to environmental protection. Not being burdened by effective environmental and community health and safety regulations that would impose greater production costs on capital without boosting labor productivity or increasing revenues (and therefore serving as a drain on profits and damaging competitiveness), a host of Central American industries freely damaged the environment. Textile factories, tanneries, slaughterhouses, pesticide formulating plants, coffee processing units, and other industries that grew up under the Alliance were compelled to externalize the social and ecological costs of capitalist production in the form of harmful pollution.

Since the 1960s, Central America's workers, peasants, and larger environment have absorbed these costs or negative externalities in the form of increasingly severe health problems, etc. Except in Costa Rica, enteritis and diarrheal disorders related to polluted water are major causes of death throughout the region. Waterborne disease accounts for 12 percent of all fatalities in Honduras, contributing to the third worst infant mortality rate in all of Latin America and the Caribbean (USAID-Honduras II, 1982: 23–155), and only one in 10 Salvadorans has access to safe drinking water (Blackman and Sharpe, 1988: 111).

Some of the worst offenders are coffee processing plants that often discharge high levels of boron, chloride, and arsenic-laden wastewater into the environment. In Costa Rica, for example, these *beneficios* produce 66 percent of the country's water contaminants. In El Salvador, more than 200 such plants dump contaminated wastewater directly into the country's rivers and streams, According to a USAID report, industrial and agricultural pollution is a "problem that now permeates almost every facet of Salvadoran life: . . . it includes toxic chemicals building up in soil, livestock, human and ecological food chain and urban waste disposal" (USAID-El Salvador I, 1982: 91–92). In Nicaragua, 37 industrial plants located an Lake Managua, the second largest freshwater lake in Central America, were permitted by the Somoza dictatorship to dump toxic wastes. The worst polluter was the U.S. corporation Pennwalt, which escaped environmental regulations in the United States to dump an estimated 40 tons of mercury in the lake between 1968 and 1981. In January 1980, environmental health officials found that 37 percent of the workers at the plant were suffering from chronic mercury poisoning (Michaels, Barrera, and Gacharna, 1985: 12). Contaminated water from Lake Managua has begun to seep toward neighboring Asososca Lagoon, threatening the drinking supply for the capital city of Managua (FRENA, 1983: 170).

The primary means by which Central American capital maximized its competitive position in the world economy was by minimizing the cost (while maximizing the productivity in both relative and absolute terms) of labor in the agricultural export sector. To this end, capital resisted costly procedures designed to protect worker health and safety as well as the environment. Dangerous working and living conditions are particularly evident for seasonal, unskilled laborers involved in the export harvests of cotton, coffee, bananas, and other commodity crops. For example, in the Pacific cotton belt, some 80 percent of the proletariat lives within 100 meters of the fields, often in substandard *champas* (wooden shacks) provided by the growers that offer little protection against pesticide drift. Facilities often lack running water, leaving workers and their families little option but to bathe in pesticide-laden irrigation ditches or streams surrounding the fields (Wolterding, 1981: 64; ICAITI, 1977: 91). As a result, mothers in the cotton-growing regions have been found to have as much as 45 to 185 times more DDT (a carcinogenic organochlorine pesticide) in their breast milk than is deemed "safe" by the World Health Organization (Swezey, Murray, and Daxl, 1986; Gardner, Garb, and Williams, 1990).

To cut labor and fuel costs, the cotton bourgeoisie use aircraft equipped with ultralow-volume spray equipment, which results in greater pesticide drift and danger to workers (ICAITI, 1977: 64–190). Workers also seldom have access to protective devices such as gloves, boots, and masks (Murray, 1984). For example, only 10 to 15 percent of Costa Rican field workers have protective clothing (USAID-Costa Rica I, 1982: 7). Approximately 1,000 Costa Rican banana workers have been rendered infertile through exposure to the nematicide DBCP and another 4,000 to 5,000 exposed workers are considered at risk (Thrupp, 1988: 157–174). As a result of these and many other abuses, Leonard (1987: 148–149) reports some 19,000 pesticide poisonings in the region between 1971 and 1976. In fact, Honduras and Nicaragua were world leaders in per capita illness and deaths from pesticide poisonings during the 1960s and 1970s (ICAITI, 1977; Swezey, Murray, and Daxl, 1986; Swezey and Faber, 1988). Some 73,230 cases of acute pesticide poisoning may well have occurred in Central America, principally in the cotton industry, during the 1970s alone (Faber, 1989: 251–294). Even today, Nicaraguans and Guatemalans have more DDT (as well as other organochlorine pesticides) in their body fat than any population of human beings on earth (ICAITI, 1977: 2). Because 19 of the 25 most commonly used organochlorines prove carcinogenic in laboratory tests, the future may reveal higher cancer rates among Central American workers (Swezey, Murray, and Daxl, 1986: 29–30).

Functional Dualism, Ecological Impoverishment, and the Proletarianization of the Peasantry

Labor costs were of particularly critical importance to the agricultural export sector in that the three-month seasonal harvest period for the region's primary commodity crops required the availability of hundreds of thousands of migratory wage laborers. And because these seasonal workers did not constitute the principal source of aggregate consumer demand for the agricultural export sector, low wage rates were essential for insuring and/or increasing the competitiveness and profitability of Central American capital (Paige, 1984; Enríquez, 1991). To create and maintain this large and super-exploitable labor force during the six to nine months of unemployment between harvests, the capitalist export sector relied on the perpetuation of the peasant subsistence sector. Because part of the subsistence costs of hired wage labor was provided by unpaid family members laboring on small subsistence plots or *minifundios,* the capitalist sector offered wages lower than the cost of maintaining the worker for the whole year. The production of maize, beans, rice, sorghum, wheat, fruits, and other crops on peasant plots lowered the cost of labor-power but was inadequate to insure the freedom of the peasant family from wage slavery. Maintenance of the peasant subsistence sector as a source of semiproletarian wage labor on a seasonal basis became the main "functional" prerequisite for continued accumulation in the capitalist export sector, a relation de Janvry (1981: 80–83) calls *functional dualism.*[1]

The proper "balance" between these two sectors is rather precarious. If the peasantry were to become completely proletarianized, the socially necessary labor time required for the production and reproduction of seasonal wage workers for the export sector (and therefore costs) would be increased, damaging the competiveness of Central American capital in the world market (Deere, 1979: 138). Likewise, if the vast majority of peasant families were provided with sufficient natural resources (or ecological conditions of production in the form of fertile land, water, wildlife, and fuelwood supplies) and sufficient social resources (or means of production in the form of technical and financial assistance, fertilizers and equipment) to appropriate these natural resources to meet their subsistence needs, the capitalist export sector would be denied its supply of exploitable wage labor (see also de Janvey and Garramon, 1977). In effect, functional dualism in Central America involved the overdevelopment of the export sector and underdevelopment of the subsistence sector that is manifest in the social and ecological impoverishment of the peasants, who are forced to work as migratory, semiproletarian laborers to survive.

Development of the Pacific coastal plains during the 1940s initially benefited the peasantry, as families were allowed to migrate into and establish new farms in the area. But by the early 1950s the rate of subsistence agricultural expansion slowed dramatically as the traditional oligarchy and "new" bourgeoisie monopolized the majority of new landholdings and financial resources for cotton, coffee, sugar, banana and cattle production (Bulmer-Thomas, 1987: 115–128). With the increased flow of U.S. military and economic aid under the Alliance for Progress, this process accelerated. Between 1950 and 1968, the export sector grew by almost 700,000 hectares, claiming 73 percent of all newly developed agricultural land. Although the number of farms worked by the peasantry also increased significantly, these farms occupied only 8 percent of the newly developed farm land. As a result, Central America's rapidly growing population of peasants became increasingly land-poor (Dorner and Quiros, 1983: 222–223). By the early 1960s, 6 percent of Central America's largest farms controlled 72 percent of the farm land and employed 28 percent of the rural labor force. Conversely, 78 percent of Central America's farms occupied only 11 percent of the region's farm land. Too small to provide adequate income or full employment for the peasant families living on them, these farms provided 60 percent of the rural labor force for the export sector (Dorner and Quiros, 1983: 221).

Despite such widespread marginalization of the subsistence sector, labor shortages persisted in some areas of Central America, particularly along the Pacific plain (Williams, 1986: 58). By the mid-1960s, however, large-scale cattle ranches had expanded into ecological and geographical zones previously immune to capitalist development, including vast zones of peasant agriculture. By 1975, over 10 million cattle were grazing on 20 million acres of pasture, an area exceeding that of all other agricultural land combined (Williams, 1986: 113). Even though beef exports jumped from approximately $9 million in 1961 to $290 million in 1979, primarily to serve as fast-food hamburgers and pet food in the United States, marginalization of the subsistence sector resulted in declining beef consumption per capita over the same period, as well as falling income and food production (Brackett, 1988: 76–82; Nations and Leonard, 1986: 72). Today, the average Central American consumes less beef than the average North American house cat (Nations and Komer, 1983). In essence, by continually displacing the subsistence sector, serving as a efficient instrument for land speculation and monopolization, and requiring little in the way of a labor force, cattle ranching was the most important mechanism for accelerating the ecological impoverishment of the subsistence sector that the capitalist export sector required.

Today, the vast majority of Central America's minifundios are smaller than the 7 hectares required to provide a family with sustenance (Brockett, 1988: 73; DeWalt, 1985: 43–54). But figures on land tenure only partly convey the magnitude of the peasantry's impoverishment. The expansion of the capitalist export sector also displaced peasant farmers onto infertile lands ecologically unsuitable for slash-and-burn (or swidden) agriculture, particularly the steep hillsides of the Pacific mountains and rugged interior highlands and the nutrient-poor rain forest soils of the Caribbean lowlands. In El Salvador, for example, 40 percent of the land designated as ecologically unsuitable for agriculture was occupied by peasant cultivators during the 1970s (Ewert, 1978: 77). Over 60 percent of the Honduran population lives in the fragile Choluteca Valley and the western hills bordering El Salvador and Nicaragua, even though a mere 14 percent of the land deemed suitable for intensive agriculture is located in these areas (USAID-Honduras El, 1982: 37). Likewise, some 10,000 to 18,000 km, 23 percent, of the terrain considered unsuitable for agriculture or pasture in Panama has been deforested and put to this use (USAID-Panama II, 1980: 61). As a result, peasant families displaced from 5 hectares of fertile land to 7 hectares of degraded hillside improved their landholding position in quantitative terms but experienced deteriorating living standards (Brockett, 1988: 75).

Ecological impoverishment of the subsistence sector was dialectically aggravated by state policies and private practices of social impoverishment that denied it favorable marketing, financial, and technological assistance and services. The capitalist export sector received over half and in some countries nearly three-fourths of the institutional credit allocated through national banking systems, often at usurious rates (Enríquez, 1991: 51; Dorner and Quiros, 1983: 225). As a result of these policies, even where the land was of high quality for agriculture, subsistence-based methods often resulted "in extremely inefficient yields, and a general deterioration of the soil and water quality" (USAID-Nicaragua I, 1981: 56–7).

We can conclude, then, that social and ecological impoverishment of the peasant subsistence sector created the necessary *human conditions of production* for disarticulated capitalist development—a large army of semi-proletarian wage labor. By the late 1970s, the vast majority of Central America's rural peasantry lived on subfamily subsistence plots incapable of satisfying the most minimum needs, forcing family members to engage in superexploitive wage work under a system of functional dualism for survival. Hundreds of thousands of impoverished semiproletarian peasants, over 40 percent of Central America's total work force, migrated each year to the coastal and interior zones to pick export crops during the dry season harvest and then returned to their small minifundios to plant subsistence crops in time for the rains (Michaels, Barrera, and Gacharna, 1985: 96–97). Roughly half a million wage laborers, over 17 percent of Central America's total work force were employed in the weeding and harvesting of one commodity crop alone—cotton—at an average wage of $1.25 to $1.50 a day.

Semiproletarianization and marginalization of the peasantry under conditions of functional dualism were particularly advanced in El Salvador, Guatemala, and, to a lesser extent, Nicaragua, where the rapid expansion of large-scale coffee, cotton, and sugar estates created the greatest demand for seasonal wage workers. Consequently, the state repression necessary to establish and maintain such conditions found its fullest imperative and most brutal expression in these three countries and would eventually give birth to powerful revolutionary movements. In contrast, capitalist development in Honduras and Costa Rica was less dependent on the creation of a large semiproletarian peasantry, and therefore the ruling bourgeoisie had less incentive (as well as less power) to impoverish the subsistence sector.

In summary, class struggles over the capitalization of nature represented efforts to create not only the appropriate communal and ecological conditions of production for the capitalist export sector but also the necessary human conditions of production.

The Ecological Crisis of Disarticulated Capitalist Development

In the context of functional dualism, the peasantry depended for its survival on access to adequate social and natural resources. But with the marginalization of the subsistence sector, conventional methods for both obtaining and maintaining these resources became increasingly disrupted during the 1960s and 1970s. In addition to selling its labor-power to the capitalist export sector for the seasonal harvests, the peasantry responded to its growing impoverishment by overexploiting the limited natural resources to which it had access. The surrounding forests and other sources of fuel, land and agricultural soils, water supplies, fish and wildlife populations, and other critical resources increasingly deteriorated during the 1970s and 1980s, particularly in the highlands.

Often overlooked is the fact that disarticulated capitalist development in Central America not only *produced* severe ecological exploitation but *depended* on it for the subsidized reproduction of semiproletarian labor and generation of a larger mass of surplus value. To appropriate (and therefore exploit) capitalized nature for the purpose of producing use-values (commodities) for sale in the world market, the export sector required adequate supplies of exploitable wage labor. Likewise, to exploit human nature (or labor) for the purpose of producing surplus value and profits in the world market, the export sector required the overexploitation of noncapitalized nature in the peasant subsistence sector to generate and maintain these needed supplies of exploitable wage labor. In effect, exploitation of labor and exploitation of the environment were two different sides of the same coin, namely, functional dualism, and reflected the class privileges and power of Central America's ruling oligarchies and agrarian bourgeoisie.

There is growing evidence that the environmental conditions of subsistence production in many areas are in a state of ecological collapse. Symptoms of this ecological crisis of the peasantry can be found in rampant deforestation, declining fallow cycles and land degradation, severe soil erosion and watershed destruction, critical fish, wildlife, and fuelwood shortages, declining food production and increased poverty, disease, widespread migration, growing problems of drought in the dry season and damaging floods in the rainy season, and other ecological problems.

Overexploitation of agricultural soils is perhaps the most ecologically destructive response to functional dualism. Traditionally, *milpa* or slash-and-burn (swidden) agriculture worked relatively well for the peasantry, making use of an abundant resource (land) and economizing on scarce resources in the form of labor and capital. Peasant families would cut and burn vegetation on a plot of land and plant a mixture of crops (typically maize, beans, sorghum, and other basic grains and/or semiperennial plants) for two to four years. After this period, an idle or fallow period of a few years was critical for regenerating soil fertility. After the fallow period, the area would be cleared once again for planting, If properly practiced, these methods were usually sustainable, minimizing deforestation, habitat destruction, soil erosion, and other problems of land degradation (Browning, 1971). With increased social and ecological impoverishment of the peasantry, sustainable systems of rotating swidden agriculture have evolved into semipermanent or permanent agriculture without the fallow periods necessary for nutrient recovery by successional vegetation (USAID-Honduras II, 1982: 37). This and the abandonment of other soil conservation efforts including contoured or terraced planting, reforestation, protection of vulnerable areas with forest cover, and so on, have resulted in accelerated erosion and fertility loss, watershed degradation, and even desertification (Barlett, 1976; Barlett, 1980; Lustgarden, 1984: 43–46). As a result, land degradation is now reaching crisis proportions in many areas (Leonard, 1987: 128).

For instance, over 17 percent of Costa Rica is severely eroded and another 24 percent moderately eroded. Virtually every major watershed in the country is seriously degraded, particularly in areas of subsistence agriculture and cattle ranching on the Pacific side. Erosion considered severe affects 30 percent of the country's Pacific terrain, with an additional 30 percent of the land suffering erosion classified as moderate. Soil loss, primarily from degraded pasture lands, is estimated at 680 million tons a year (USAID-Costa Rica I, 1982: 6–64). These ecological problems have contributed to a 5.1 percent decline in per capita food production during the 1980s (Leonard, 1987: 82). An estimated 1,810,000 hectares of degraded land currently under agricultural use are in need of immediate reforestation if the processes described above are to be halted (USAID-Costa Rica I, 1982: 3–35).

The ecological situation is somewhat worse in the highlands of Honduras, which have largely been reduced to a degraded patchwork of highly eroded, acidic soils laced with scattered trees and rocky surfaces. In a country where more than 75 percent of the land possesses slopes greater than 25 percent, soil erosion averages 100 to 500 metric tons per hectare over 2,2 million hectares of agricultural land (USAID-Honduras II, 1982: 93). Two-thirds of the peasant families in the southern highlands cannot produce enough food to meet their own subsistence needs (Boyer, 1983: 226–234). In fact, per capita production of beans and other basic grains common to the minifundio has declined 22.2 percent since the mid-1970s (Leonard, 1987: 82). Sorghum, which grows much better on rocky and degraded soils but is much less valued by small farmers as a human food source than corn, now comprises up to one-half of food production in Honduras (Brockett, 1988: 80).

In Guatemala, over 65 percent of the country's original forests have been destroyed in the last 30 years (Gardner, Garb, and Williams, 1990). Traditional Indian systems of the Central and Western Highlands "constructed terraces, planted and cultivated on the contour of the hills, reserved steeply sloped land for forests, and replaced soil nutrients by fallowing" (Gardener, Garb, and Williams, 1990: 2). These are rapidly being replaced with highly destructive practices. As a result, the moderately fertile andosanic surface soils and clayish subsoils are literally being washed down the mountainsides. Soil losses in some areas now average five to 35 tons per hectare a year (USAID-Guatemala I, 1981: 18). In the northern rain forests of the Petén, annual soil losses in zones of cattle ranching and peasant colonization amount to 700 to 1100 metric tons per square kilometer (USAID-Guatemala II, 1984).

Nowhere is the situation more critical than in El Salvador, the most ecologically devastated country in Latin America. According to the United Nations Food and Agriculture Organization, the country is undergoing a process of desertification. More than 95 percent of the original tropical deciduous forests have been destroyed, and less than 7 percent, compared to a regional average of just under 40 percent, of the country is currently forested (Hall and Faber, 1989). Roughly 86.7 percent of all rural families live on 4 hectares of land or less, and of these *microfundios* over 50 percent are less than 1 hectare in size (Weeks, 1985: 112; Brockett, 1988: 74). Aggravated by transitions from shifting to permanent or semipermanent swidden agriculture, overexploitation is resulting in extensive fertility loss, soil erosion, ravine and gully formation, and widespread collapse of the agricultural resource base. Much of the land base is already abandoned due to fertility loss and destruction by abundant gullies, exposure of subsoil, landslips, and large landslides (Leonard, 1987: 128–129). More than 77 percent of the country suffers serious soil erosion, including the severely eroded peasant plots in the central volcanic highlands (OAS, 1974; Daugherty et al., 1979: 40). Much of the fragile Cordillera Norte, home to hundreds of thousands of impoverished semiproletarian peasants, has been irreversibly destroyed by erosion, gully formation, laterization, and "scorched-earth" counterinsurgency programs (USAID-El Salvador I, 1982: 89). With the destruction of watersheds and evaporation of groundwater sources, many campesinos are finding their wells dry and must spend more of their valuable labor-time and energy searching for increasingly scarce supplies of usable water (Hall and Faber, 1989). As one result, per capita basic grain production declined more than 29 percent between 1975 and 1985 (Blachman and Sharpe, 1988: 111).

Deforestation and land degradation are aggravated by the peasantry's dependence on wood as a source of energy. Some 14.5 million people, or nearly three-fourths of all Central Americans, consume more than 22 million cubic meters of wood annually—47 percent of the region's total energy use (Jones, 1984: 6–9). Denied access to alternative energy sources, more efficient stoves, state-sponsored reforestation programs, or woodlands on capitalist private property, peasants experience acute local shortages of firewood, particularly in the more arid highlands of El Salvador, Guatemala, and Honduras (Jones, 1984: 6–7; Leonard, 1987: 62). Urbanization and capitalist agricultural development in the Pacific littoral and interior valleys has also severely degraded fuel sources along the western slopes, as well as fragile watersheds surrounding major cities (Place, 1981: 176). For example, the hillsides surrounding the Honduran capital of Tegucigalpa have been virtually denuded of once rich pine and hardwood forests (USAID-Honduras II, 1982: 61). Members of many urban and rural households who once gathered wood free by walking to nearby lands must now purchase fuels transported from far greater distances, diverting scarce economic resources from the family budget for increasingly expensive commodity fuels (van Buren, 1988: 1–97).

Another symptom of the peasantry's ecological crisis is protein malnutrition, a major health problem in Central America. Many peasants depend quite regularly on fish and game obtained from local forests, fields, and streams (Place, 1981: 173–176; Daugherty et al., 1979: 32), and in the face of declining agricultural production and other resource problems poor rural families are turning increasingly to wildlife for supplemental food and income. But here, as with firewood, the capitalization of nature and the marginalization of the peasantry have reduced the supply while increasing the demand for wildlife. The destruction of localized fish and wildlife populations is especially severe in the highlands of Guatemala, El Salvador, and Honduras. In El Salvador, capitalist destruction of native flora and fauna is "so extensive that there appears to be no hope of meaningful recovery"—almost all economically important wildlife species are now extinct (USAID-El Salvador I, 1982: 89–90). Some 72 percent of the wild game sold in local markets is imported from Honduras, Nicaragua, and Guatemala (Leonard, 1987: 155).

Coastal marine resources (shrimp, fish, sea turtles, etc.) are also suffering heavy exploitation by commercial operators. Of these, sea turtles (especially the green, hawksbill, and Pacific ridley) are the most important (Leonard, 1987: 155–158). In Honduras, some 5,000 families have formed the Committee for the Defense and Development of the Flora and Fauna in the Gulf of Fonseca to oppose the mass destruction of mangrove forests by USAID-sponsored shrimp export projects controlled by local military officers and wealthy leaders of the Honduran Congress. Nearby fishing communities have successfully harvested shrimp for local consumption from the mangroves for years, but with the advent of football-field-sized artificial shrimping pools, local communities are finding "no trespassing" signs and fences sealing off access to the coastal commons (McAlevey, 1990: 1–13).

In Guatemala, the ecological and social crisis of the peasantry has been magnified by the horror of the army's latest program of repression. In direct response to widespread organizing by the country's growing popular movements and emergence of a persistent armed opposition of four guerrilla groups, joined under the banner of Unidad Revolucionaria Nacional Guatemalteca (Guatemalan National Revolutionary Unity—UNRG), the Guatemalan military has systematically murdered civilians, eliminated entire villages, and destroyed vast areas of forests and field (Amnesty International, 1989). In September of 1982, the Dutch Catholic Congress reported on the violence, saying:

> The massacres were also destroying in a systematic manner all that sustains the life of the community; houses, woods, harvests; to the point that the water in the rivers is polluted to drive the people to desperation. The current wave of terror appears to have as a principal object to disarticulate the social life and the cultural inheritance of the Indian people and the peasant, to end the resistance of those that now won't support the weight of centuries of robbery, of maltreatment and of persecution (Handy, 1984: 260).

Since the early 1980s, "low-intensity conflict" has claimed over 45,000 lives, mostly Indian, and caused the displacement of more than a million Guatemalans. Over the last 10 years counterinsurgency operations have relocated some 60,000 people to some 70 so-called model villages (modeled on the "strategic hamlets" of Vietnam) particularly in the northwestern highlands, as means for achieving maximum military surveillance over the civilian population (WOLA, 1985). Another half a million Guatemalans live within the boundaries of existing "development poles," which the army defines as "organized population centers . . . that guarantee the adherence of the population, and their support and participation with the Armed Institution against communist subversion" (Gardner, Garb, and Williams, 1990: 9). Taken together, an interacting system of "model villages," "development poles," and "civil defense patrols" has ensured the army's control over many aspects of rural Guatemalan life and hastened the economic and ecological breakdown of peasant cultural practices (for a discussion, see Gardner, Garb, and Williams, 1990: 8–9).

As in Guatemala, the U.S.-supported war by the Salvadoran oligarchy against the popular classes is deepening the social and ecological crisis to the point that the economic viability of disarticulated capitalist development may never be recovered. As part of its fight against the Frente Farabundo Martí para la Liberación Nacional (Farabundo Martí National Liberation Front—FMLN), the Salvadoran military has unleashed a policy of "scorched earth" or "ecocide" designed to destroy the resource base of peasants suspected of offering support to the revolution. Military analysts liken the civilian population to a "sea" in which the FMLN swims, and, as in Vietnam and Guatemala, the military solution over the last decade has been to "drain the sea" by bombing and burning forest areas and fields with 500-pound bombs, as well as napalm and white phosphorus, razing croplands and villages, and initiating counterinsurgency sweeps (*guindas*) to drive out the population in areas of FMLN control (Pearce, 1986; MacLean, 1987: 11). More than 70,000 people have died in the civil war and from repression at the hands of government forces that continue to commit gross violations of human rights. In one of the most destructive wars in Western Hemisphere history, one of every five Salvadorans has been displaced since 1980, a greater percentage than the number of Vietnamese displaced during the Vietnam war (Hall and Faber, 1989).

Perhaps even more menacing than these direct impacts are the indirect environmental effects of the war. War refugees are causing extensive ecological damage themselves, clearing forested areas or further taxing fragile natural resources in settlements that lack environmental planning or government social programs. According to a USAID report, 13 percent of San Salvador's population is located on "land regarded as unsuitable for ordinary development because of flooding, uneven terrain or proximity to pollution sources" (USAID-El Salvador I, 1982: 23). For example, the Salvadoran government allowed establishment of refugee settlements and neighborhoods at the base of Monte Bello even though it had been deforested by landless peasants and was known to suffer from massive erosion and flash flooding. When in 1982 torrential rains caused the mountain to give way, hundreds of homes were buried under 40 feet of mud. While government estimates claim that 700 people died in the Monte Bello avalanche, it is widely believed that more than 1,000 died (Hall and Faber, 1989: 9).

Marginalization of Central America's peasantry was offset in the past by migration, much of which merely displaced the ecological crisis of the subsistence sector and reproduced it in new forms (Taylor, 1980). Internal migration to urban barrios, the steep slopes of the western mountains, or the tropical rain forests of the agricultural frontier often proved highly functional, however, for disarticulated capitalist development, providing a large army of reserve labor for the expansion of capitalist agriculture and industry along the Pacific coast or serving as an efficient "first wave" in clearing and colonizing lush rain forests free of charge for a second wave of private land speculators, cattle ranchers, and military officers (Nations and Komer, 1983). Today, as exemplified by the Monte Bello tragedy, migration as a survival strategy is becoming increasingly unviable. Peasant colonization of nutrient-poor rain forest soils and marginal agricultural land has proved to be in large part a social and ecological disaster. For instance, more than 22,400 Honduran families have received over 97,000 hectares of national and *ejidal* land since 1978 under the national agrarian reform, but some 40 percent of the original farms have already been abandoned (Brockett, 1988: 133–134). And with the failure of the Central American Common Market to generate a large, highly skilled industrial or agrarian working class, governments (with the exceptions of Costa Rica and Panama) are presented with little incentive to invest significant quantities of social capital in the healthy reproduction of urban-based labor-power (Weeks, 1985; 145–196). As a result, the crisis of urban living conditions for some 40 percent of Central America's mostly unemployed population is every bit as acute as that faced by their rural counterparts (Alonso, 1984: 101). As the economic crisis deepens and the ecological crisis widens, it is likely that immigration to Mexico and the United States will increase.

Growing impoverishment of the peasantry has transformed the household division of labor by gender, in which women typically produced petty commodities and use-values (or means of subsistence) on the minifundio, cheapening the reproduction of semiproletarian male labor power (Deere, 1979: 133–134). The increasingly difficult daily struggle to secure subsistence through the superexploitation of nature is often achieved through the superexploitation of familial labor. This burden falls particularly hard on women (along with children) in a double sense, for they are charged not only with raising the animals, preparing food, gathering firewood and water, going to market, and in many cases cultivating the subsistence plot but also with joining their male partners as seasonal wage laborers (de Janvry, 1981: 88; Fogel, 1985: 221–225; Pearce, 1986: 64–79).[2]

To offset these hardships, peasant households have adopted a number of demographic strategies to insure family survival. One of the more important of these is the bearing of children as production agents for incorporation into the household labor process at an early age. In fact, for extremely poor peasant families, children are often one of the few productive resources available to assist with highly labor-intensive family tasks. As social impoverishment has worsened, it has become necessary to have larger and larger families to generate income, guard against high child and infant mortality rates, and provide protection for parents in case of disability, unemployment, old age, and changing economic conditions (de Janvry, 1981: 89–91). Today Central America's combined population is well over 25 million people, of whom over 44 percent are under 15 years of age. The demographic dynamics associated with functional dualism and disarticulated capitalist development have combined to produce the world's highest population growth rate (2.8 percent), a rate at which the region's population will double in less than 24 years (Leonard, 1987: 37–41). The most rapid growth rates are occurring among resource-poor and semiproletarian peasants, with the poorest women often reproducing at their biological maximum (Malloy and Borzutzky, 1982: 77–98; de Janvry, 1981: 85–93).

The dynamics of human population are historically specific to the mode of production and social formation in which they occur. And in Central America, against the Malthusian current, it is not rapid population growth but the expansion of capitalist export agriculture and the systematic impoverishment of the subsistence sector that are causing hunger and ecological devastation (Durham, 1979: 18–51; Weeks, 1985; 102–115). In the context of functional dualism, the economic conditions which fostered ecological impoverishment have also spawned rapid population growth as a survival strategy, which is contributing to the fragmentation of the minifundio and therefore indirectly exacerbating degradation of the peasant's natural-resource base (Durham, 1979: 18). In the words of de Janvry (1981: 91–93), "under functional dualism, sheer individual economic rationality in reacting to the pressures of poverty leads to quantitative and qualitative demographic contradictions that reinforce ecological contradictions and reproduce conditions of impoverishment and misery in rural areas." However, these demographic strategies may be increasingly unviable in the face of a deepening ecological crisis.

Rather than addressing the systemic sources of poverty and rapid population growth, population control programs and policies have been for the most part coercive and reactionary and therefore highly ineffective (Mass, 1976). Typically, population growth has slowed only when living standards have risen and health, education, and other services have been provided to the majority of workers and peasants (Hartmann, 1987; Murdoch, 1980).

Ironically, the ecological crisis of the subsistence sector is also affecting profit rates in the capitalist export sector. Problems stemming from the ecological deterioration of the peasantry's resource base are damaging the ecological and communal conditions of capitalist production throughout the region. Thousands of lives have been lost, and damage amounting to billions of dollars has occurred to hydroelectric projects, state infrastructure, export crops, industry, etc. (Leonard, 1987). The ecological and economic damage inflicted on these productive conditions has been a significant factor in the advent of state fiscal crises and national debt/balance of payments crises throughout the region and constitute an important barrier to the continuation of disarticulated capitalist development (for a theoretical discussion, see O'Connor, 1988: 11–38; 1987: 53; Faber, 1989: 372–379). For instance, flooding in the Sula Valley (a 370 km area), Aguan River and Atlantic littoral watersheds, Choluteca River valley, and other degraded watersheds in Honduras causes some $40 to $50 million in damage *annually* to the capitalist export sector and state infrastructure (USAID-Honduras II, 1982; 12–95). In Nicaragua, heavy rains in May 1982 led to floods that destroyed almost all of the bridges in the León and Chinandega areas, costing the Nicaraguan government some $20 million (IRENA, 1988; Karliner, 1989).

Revolution and the Ecological Crisis

The continuing marginalization of peasants and the resultant ecological impoverishment that they are forced to endure have spurred popular movements for more equitable access to and democratic management of social and natural resources. The intransigence of the region's oligarchies in the face of demands for reform, combined with the U.S. government's support of these oligarchies, has given birth to popularbased revolutionary movements in El Salvador, Guatemala, and Nicaragua. It is in these countries that functional dualism has reached its ultimate expression, creating a large, intensely exploited agrarian working class as well as a growing industrial working class and a threatened artisanry (Flora and Torres-Rivas, 1989: 48). As semiproletarians, members of this agrarian working class have been exploited both as migratory wage laborers in the capitalist export sector and as socially and ecologically impoverished peasants in the rural subsistence and urban informal sectors. Therefore, the development of popular-based revolutionary movements in Central America has been highly dependent not only on the level of proletarianization but also on the rate of exploitation of semiproletarian labor in terms of both total employment, wages, hours, and working conditions and the quantity and quality of access to land, credit rates, food prices, and so on. Therefore the ecological and social conditions of subsistence production figure prominently in considerations of the development of political movements and revolutionary struggles in Central America.

Since the mid-to-late 1970s, in connection with U.S. foreign policy and a global economic crisis, Central America's growing ecological crisis has contributed to untenable increases in the rate of exploitation and impoverishment of semipraletarian labor, breaking down the political viability of functional dualism and disarticulated capitalist development. On the one hand, the ecological and economic crisis of the subsistence sector has invigorated worker movements for better wages, benefits, working and living conditions, and services (Pearce, 1986: 164–174; Painter, 1987: 16). In other words, as life for poor semiproletarian peasants has became more difficult, struggles against the unusually severe exploitation of wage labor have increased. On the other hand, the economic and ecological crisis of the capitalist export sector has invigorated peasant movements for agrarian and economic reform of the subsistence sector. When agricultural wages in El Salvador fell by 30 percent between 1973 and 1978, for instance, the Popular Revolutionary Bloc and other popular organizations stepped up their efforts for better land and wages by organizing land invasions and strikes (Brackett, 1988: 153). This situation has been magnified by the crisis of cotton production in Central America, which has led to the adoption of less labor-intensive substitutes, eliminating an important source of income for tens of thousands of migrant workers. Also, in Guatemala, cotton declined from 120,000 hectares to only 20,000 hectares between the late 1970s and 1985. Increased labor competition for scarce jobs has resulted in a drop in wages to far below the minimum of $1.20 a day. Overall, real wages for cotton, coffee, sugar, and banana workers dropped 20 percent between 1973 and 1979, pushing many Guatemalan families beyond the margins of survival (Painter, 1987: 2–23). The big drops in employment and wage income are thus ironically increasing family dependence on what is a rapidly deteriorating resource base in the subsistence sector. In other words, as life for migrant wage laborers becomes more difficult, struggles against the exploitation and impoverishment of peasant farmers have increased.

These popularly based movements are pushing for agrarian and economic reforms, democratization of the state and political institutions, and respect for human rights. However, the ruling coffee oligarchies and U.S.-backed militaries of El Salvador and Guatemala (as in prerevolutionary Nicaragua) have combined to block substantive economic reform and political expression and have escalated repression against the popular classes, reinforcing the social inequalities and ecological deterioration that gave birth to the crisis in the first place. As a result, these countries exploded into revolutionary civil war. To defend disarticulated capitalism from revolutionary transformation, the U.S. response has been the militarization of Central America, deepening the ecological crisis (Karliner, 1989; Karliner and Rice, 1986).

In Honduras and Costa Rica, in contrast, despite recent U.S. government attempts to promote militarization, political compromise has proved critical in submerging revolutionary tendencies. The most extensive land reforms (aside from Nicaragua's during the 1980s) have occurred in Honduras. Peasant mobilization by organizations like the National Federation of Honduran Peasants in the 1960s spurred government programs to lessen marginalization and impoverishment: including colonization projects (arid deforestation of tropical rain forests), adjudication of land disputes and land occupations, redistribution of property, and titling of peasant landholdings. Between 1962 and 1980, for instance, about 36,000 rural families benefited from agrarian reform (Brockett, 1988: 130–134).

In Costa Rica, colonization projects, the security of land title, and the strategic location in the export sector of a "rich" segment of the peasantry, as well as a relatively advanced welfare state, have so far defused any strategic alliance between urban labor and the rural working class and peasantry (Flora and Torres-Rivas, 1989: 50). In addition, relatively higher wages for agrarian and industrial workers have also constrained rural income inequality and limited social unrest in Costa Rica, although this situation appears to be changing (Brockett, 1988: 140). Whether such reforms, which diminished considerably during the 1980s, will prove adequate to maintain "social stability" in Costa Rica and Honduras as the economic and ecological crisis grows remains to be seen.

To overcome the root causes of the social and ecological crisis in Central America, disarticulated capitalist development must be transformed. Popular organizations and revolutionary movements in Central America are currently struggling for governmental respect for human rights; democratization of the state; a negotiated settlement to regional conflicts; authentic agrarian and economic reforms, including democratic control of natural resources; a nonaligned foreign policy and an end to U.S. intervention; and other changes necessary for this transformation to occur. Only when the basic obstacles to national liberation and democratic socialism are removed can the ecological conditions of production be reconstructed and protected in such a way as to benefit the vast majority of Central Americans. In this regard, the successes and failures of revolutionary ecology in Nicaragua are informative.

While a sophisticated discussion of the rise and fall of socialist ecology and the Nicaraguan revolution is well beyond the scope of this article, it is clear that in the early 1980s Nicaragua developed some of the most innovative and comprehensive environmental programs of any country in Latin America (Karliner, Faber, and Rice, 1986). With the nationalization of the country's forest, mineral, and aquatic resources and the creation of the Instituto Nicaragüense de Recursos Naturales y del Ambiente (Nicaraguan Institute of Natural Resources and the Environment—IRENA) in 1979, there developed within a limited sector of the Nicaraguan government an ecological socialist political tendency that recognized that not only was comprehensive social and economic reform of the existing development model essential for addressing the country's ecological crisis but also that comprehensive environmental programs and policies were absolutely essential for addressing the country's social and economic crisis. This political tendency toward a revolutionary ecology came to be reflected in IRENA's environmental policies, which included programs in reforestation, erosion and watershed management, pollution control, wildlife conservation, environmental education, and the conservation of genetic diversity. Other governmental agencies began working with IRENA on pesticide control and regulation, national parks, energy conservation, agrarian reform, worker health and safety, and appropriate technology (see Wieberdink and van Ketel, 1988; Karliner, Faber, and Rice, 1986; Hassan et al., 1981; Swezey, Murray, and Daxl, 1986; Swezey and Faber, 1988; Rice, 1989).

The basic aims of the programs were to reverse the social and ecological impoverishment of the subsistence sector; to reconstruct and protect the ecological and communal conditions of the agricultural export sector, including the development of more ecologically and economically appropriate productive forces that would lessen Nicaragua's dependency on expensive oil imports and other inputs; to address the social and ecological costs (or negative externalities) of capitalist production by eliminating work hazards and reducing pollution, and so on; and finally, to preserve and protect nature as means of consumption (such as national parks) for the majority of Nicaraguans, present and future. These environmental programs were unique in that they contributed to a larger process of social transformation and national liberation that had as its goal a new model of economic development devoted to the needs of the "popular classes." For its achievements, the nation received worldwide attention from the international environmental movement, serving as host to the Fourth Biennial Congress on the Fate and Hope of the Earth in June 1988.[3] Many of these programs have since been all but destroyed by the contra war and the economic crisis. It is highly doubtful that those hallmarks of revolutionary environmentalism that remain will be perpetuated by the Unión Nacional Opositora (Nicaraguan Opposition Union— UNO) government of Violeta Chamorro. Nevertheless, the Nicaraguan environmental movement continues to show political strength and could signal the widespread birth of a new Latin American environmental politics oriented to progressive social transformation. The development of revolutionary ecology in Nicaragua may also indicate a growing recognition by some of the Latin American Left that socialist reconstruction of the ecological conditions of production, as opposed to simply the process of socialist construction, is the first and most fundamental step in the transition to a genuine democratic socialism.

Notes

1. Wages for Guatemala's semiproletarian cotton workers in 1979 to 1980 represented only 10.3 percent of total production costs, compared with around one-third for Argentina, Mexico, and Paraguay (Painter, 1987; 40).
2. Women made up to 40 percent of Nicaragua's coffee pickers just prior to the revolution. Women make up 13.7 percent of the wage work force in Guatemala and 10 percent of the total rural labor force in El Salvador.
3. The congress was attended by nearly 1,200 people from 70 different countries and indigenous nations, representing hundreds of grass-roots organizations around the world.

References

Alonso, Marcelo, 1984. *Central America in Crisis: Washington Institute Task Force Report.* Washington, DC: Washington Institute for Values in Public Policy.

Amnesty International, 1989. *Guatemala: Human Rights Violations Under the Civilian Goverment.* New York: Amnesty International Publications.

Barlett, P. F., 1976. "Labor efficiency and the mechanism of agricultural evolution." *Journal of Anthropological Research* 32 (2): 124–140.

______. 1980. "Adaptive strategies in peasant agricultural production." *Annual Review of Anthropology* 9: 545–573.

Blachman, Morris J., and Kenneth E. Sharpe, 1988. "Things fall apart: Trouble ahead in El Salvador." *World Policy Journal* (Winter).

Boyer, Jefferson, 1983. "Agrarian capitalism and peasant praxis in southern Honduras." Ph.D, dissertation, University of North Carolina.

Brockett, Charles D., 1988. *Land, Power, and Poverty: Agrarian Transformation and Political Conflict in Central America.* Boston: Unwin Hyman.

Browning, David, 1971. *El Salvador: Landscape and Society.* Oxford: Clarendon.

Bulmer-Thomas, Victor, 1987. *The Political Economy of Central America since 1920.* Cambridge: Cambridge University Press.

Caltagirone, Leo, Merlin Allen, Walter Kaiser, Jr., and Joseph Orsenigo, 1972. "The crop protection situation in Guatemala, Honduras, Nicaragua, Costa Rica, Panama, and Guyana." Study prepared for the U.S. Agency for International Development, University of California at Berkeley.

Chapin, Georgeanne, and Robert Wasserstrom, 1983. "Pesticide use and malaria resurgence in Central America and India." *The Ecologist* 13 (4): 115–126.

Daugherty, Howard, 1969. "Man-induced ecological change in El Salvador." PhD. dissertation, University of California at Los Angeles.

Daugherty, Howard, Charles A. Jeannert-Grosjean, and H. F. Fletcher, 1979. *Ecodevelopment and International Cooperation: Potential Applications for El Salvador.* Ottawa: CIDA and Advanced Concepts Center of the Environment.

Deere, Carmen Diana, 1979. "Rural women's subsistence production in the capitalist periphery," in Robin Cohen, Peter Gutkind and Phyllis Brazier (eds.), *Peasants and Proletarians: The Struggle of Third World Workers.* New York: Monthly Reveiw Press.

de Janvey, Alain, 1981. *The Agrarian Question and Reformism in Latin America.* Baltimore, MD: John Hopkins Press.

de Janvry, Alain, and C. Garramon, 1977. "The dynamics of rural poverty in Latin America." *Journal of Peasant Studies* 4: 206–216.

DeWalt, Billie R., 1985. "Microcosmic and macrocosmic processes of agrarian change in southern Honduras: the cattle are eating the forest," pp. 165–186 in Billie DeWalt and Pertti J. Pelto (eds.), *Micro and Macro Levels of Analysis in Anthropology: Issues in Theory and Research,* Boulder, CO: Westview.

Dorner, Peter, and Rodolfo Quitos, 1983. "Institutional dualism in Central America's agricultural development," pp. 220–231 in Stanford Central America Action Network (ed.), *Revolution in Central America.* Boulder, CO: West view.

Durham, William H., 1979. *Scarcity and Survival in Central America: The Ecological Origins of the Soccer War.* Stanford, CA: Stanford University Press.

Enriquez, Laura J., 1991. *Harvesting Change: Labor and Agrarian Reform in Nicaragua, 1979–1990.* Chapel Hill: University of North Carolina Press.

Ewert, Monica, 1978. "Human impact on the aquatic ecosystem of the Rio Lempa, El Salvador." M.A. thesis in Environmental Studies, York University, Ottawa.

Faber, Daniel, 1988. "Imperialism and the crisis of nature in Central America." *Capitalism, Nature, Socialism: A Journal of Socialist Ecology* 1 (1): 39–46.

_______. 1989. "Imperialism and the crisis of nature in Central America." Ph.D. dissertation, University of California at Santa Cruz.

Faber, Daniel, with Joshua N. Karliner and Robert Rice, 1986. *Central America: Roots of Environmental Destruction.* Environmental Project on Central America, Green Paper no. 2.

Flora, Jan L., and Edelberto Torres-Rivas, 1989. "Sociology of developing societies: Historical bases of insurgency in Central America," in Jan L. Flora and Edelberto Torres-Rivas (eds.), *Central America: Sociology of Developing Countries.* New York: Monthly Review Press.

Fogel, Daniel, 1985. *Revolution in Central America.* San Francisco: Ism Press.

Gardner, Florence, with Yaakov Garb and Marta Williams, 1990. *Guatemala: A Political Ecology.* Environmental Project on Central America, Green Paper no. 5.

Gorostiaga, Xabier, and Peter Marchetti, 1988. "The Central American economy: conflict and crisis," pp. 119–136 in Nora Hamilton, Jeffrey A. Frieden, Linda Fuller, and Manuel Pastor, Jr. (eds.), *Crisis in Central America: Regional Dynamics and U.S. Policy in the 1980s.* Boulder, CO: Westview.

Hall, Bill, and Daniel Faber, 1989. *El Salvador: Ecology of Conflict.* Environmental Project on Central America, Green Paper no. 4.

Handy, Jim, 1984. *Gift of the Devil: A History of Guatemala.* Boston: South End Press.

Hartmann, Betsy, 1987. *Reproductive Rights and Wrongs.* New York: Harper & Row.

Hassan, Amin, Eliana Velasquez, Robert Belmar, Molly Coye, Ernest Drucker, Phillip J. Landrigan, David Michaels, and Kevin B. Sidel, 1981. "Mercury poisoning in Nicaragua: a case study of the export of environmental and occupational health hazards by a multinational corporation." *International Journal of Health Services* 11 (2).

ICAITI (Instituto Centroamericano de Investigación y Tecnología Industrial), 1977. *An Environmental and Economic Study of the Consequences of Pesticide Use in Central American Cotton Production: Final Report.* Guatemala City.

IRENA (Instituto Nicaragüense de Recursos Naturales y del Ambiente), 1983. *Planificación de cuencas hidrográfices: Plan de ordenamiento y manejo 3, Managua.* 1988. *Proyecto Heroes y Martires de Veracruz Nicaragua, C.A.: Resumen ejecutivo,* Managua.

Jones, Jeffrey R., 1984. "The Central American energy problem: anthropological perspectives on fuelwood supply and production," *Culture and Agriculture* 22: 6–9.

Karliner, Joshua, 1989. "The ecological destabilization of Central America," *World Policy Journal* 7 (Fall): 787–810.

Karliner, Joshua, and Robert Rice, 1986. *Militarization: The Environmental Impact.* Environmental Project on Central America, Green Paper no. 3.

Karliner, Joshua N., and Daniel Faber, with Robert Rice, 1986. Nicaragua: An Environmental Project on Central America, Green Paper no. 1.

Leonard, H. Jeffrey, 1987. *Natural Resources and Economic Development in Central America; A Regional Environmental Profile.* New Brunswick: Transaction Books.

Lustgarden, Steve G., 1984. "El Salvador: The political economy of environmental destruction." Unpublished manuscript.

McAlevey, Jane F., 1990. "Honduras: multi-nationals, military, and ecological crisis." *EPOCA Update* (Spring): 1–13.

MacLean, John, 1987. *Prolonging the Agony: The Human Cost of Low Intensity Conflict.* London: El Salvador Committee for Human Rights.

Malloy, James M., and Silvia Borzutzky, 1982. "Politics, social welfare policy, and the population problem in Latin America." *International Journal of Health Services* 12 (1).

Mass, Bonnie, 1976. *Population Target: The Political Economy of Population Control in Latin America.* Brampton: Charter's Publishing.

Michaels, David, Clara Barrera, and Manuel G. Gacharna, 1985. "Occupational health and the economic development of Latin America," pp. 94–114 in Jane H. Ives (ed.), *The Export of Hazard: Transnational Corporations and Environmental Control Issues.* Boston: Routledge & Kegan Paul.

Murdoch, William W., 1980. *The Poverty of Nations: The Political Economy of Hunger and Population.* Baltimore: John Hopkins University Press.

Murray, Douglas L., 1984. "Pesticides, politics and the Nicaraguan Revolution." *Policy Studies Review* 4 (November): 219–229.

Nations, James, and Daniel Komer, 1983. "Rainforests and the hamburger society." *Environment* 24 (3): 12–20.

Nations, James, and H. Jeffrey Leonard, 1986. "Grounds of conflict in Central America," pp. 55–100 in Janet Welsh Brown (ed.), *Bordering on Trouble: Resources and Politics in Latin America.* Bethesda, MD: Adler & Adler.

OAS (Organization of American States), 1974. El Salvador: *Zonificación agrícola, fase 1.* Washington, DC.

O'Connor, James, 1987. *The Meaning of Crisis: A Theoretical Introduction.* New York: Basil Blackwell.

1988. "Capitalism, nature, socialism: a theoretical introduction." *Capitalism, Nature, Socialism: A Journal of Socialist Ecology* 1 (Fall): 11–38.

Paige, Jeffery M., 1984. "Cotton and revolution in Nicaragua." Paper presented at the Eighth Conference on the Political Economy of the World System, Brown University, RI.

Painter, James, 1987. *Guatemala: False Hope, False Freedom.* London: Latin America Bureau.

Pearce, Jenny, 1986. *Promised Land: Peasant Rebellion in Chalatenango, El Salvador.* London: Latin America Bureau.

Place, Susan E., 1981. "Ecological and social consequences of export beef production in Guanacaste Province, Costa Rica." Ph.D. dissertation, University of California, Los Angeles.

Rice, Robert A., 1989. "A casualty of war: the Nicaraguan environment." *Technology Review* 91 (May/June).

Swezey, Sean, and Daniel Faber, 1988. "Disarticulated accumulation, agroexport, and ecological crisis in Nicaragua: the case of cotton." *Capitalism, Nature, Socialism: A Journal of Socialist Ecology* 1 (Fall): 47–68.

Swezey, Sean L., Douglas L. Murray, and Rainer G. Daxl, 1986. "Nicaragua's revolution in pesticide policy." *Environment* 28 (1): 6–36.

Szymanski, Albert, 1981. *The Logic of Imperialism.* New York: Praeger.

Taylor, J. Edward, 1980. "Peripheral capitalism and rural-urban migration: a study of population movements in Costa Rica." *Latin American Perspectives* 7 (2–3): 75–90.

Thrupp, Lori Ann, 1988. "The political ecology of pesticide use in developing countries: dilemmas in the banana sector of Costa Rica." Ph.D. dissertation, University of Sussex.

USAID-Costa Rica I, 1982. *Costa Rica: Country Environmental Profile.* Prepared by Gary Hartshorn et al., San José, Costa Rica: Tropical Science Center.

USAID-El Salvador I, 1982. *Environmental Profile of El Salvador.* Compiled by Steven L. Hilty, Tucson: Arid Lands Information Center, University of Arizona.

USAID-Guatemala I, 1981. *Draft Environmental Profile on Guatemala.* Athens: Institute of Ecology, University of Georgia.

USAID-Guatemala II, 1984. *Perfíl ambiental de la República de Guatemala,* Guatemala City: Universidad Rafael Landivar.

USAID-Honduras II, 1982. *Honduras: Country Environmental Profile,* Mclean, VA: JRB Associates.

USAID-Nicaragua I, 1981. *Environmental Profile of Nicaragua.* Prepared by Steven L. Hilty. Tucson: Arid Lands Information Center, University of Arizona.

USAID-Panama II, 1980. *Panama: State of the Environment and Natural Resources.* Washington, DC: International Science and Technology Institute.

van Buten, Ariane, 1988. "An analysis of the commercial woodfuel system in Nicaragua." Ph.D. dissertation (draft), University of Sussex.

Webb, Michael A., 1985. "Economic opportunity and labor markets in Central America," in Kenneth M. Coleman and George C. Herring (eds.), *The Central American Crisis: Sources of Conflict and the Failure of U.S. Policy,* Wilmington, DE: Scholarly Resources Inc.

Weeks, John, 1985. The Economies of Central America, New York: Holmes & Meier.

Whelan, Tensie, 1987. "Rebuilding a tropical forest." *Environmental Action* 17 (November/December).

Wieberdink, Ange, and Arjen van Katel, 1988. "Institutionalization of an environmental program in a Third World country: the establishment of an environmental institute in Nicaragua." *Development and Change* 19: 139–157.

Williams, Robert, 1986. *Export Agriculture and the Crisis in Central America.* Chapel Hill: University of North Carolina Press.

WOLA (Washington Office on Latin America), 1985. *Guatemala: The Roots of Revolution.* Washington, DC: Author.

Wolterding, Martin, 1981. "The poisoning of Central America." *Sierra* 66 (September/October): 6–36.

One of the most dramatic transformations of the planet in the name of progress and trade has been the construction of the Panama Canal. The Panama Canal comprises not only the manmade passage from the Pacific to the Atlantic oceans but also two manmade lakes: Gatún and Alhajuela, created in 1913 and 1934 respectively. This article explores the water demands on these lakes, particularly Alhajuela. It explores the effects on the ever deteriorating ecosystem, deforestation and pollution, as well as the increasing demands that population growth and ship transit place on these lakes. Deforestation in particular presents a great threat since it is a source of soil erosion and sedimentation that also affects the operational dimension of this waterway. Furthermore, the author lists population growth, mining, industrialization, urbanization and road construction as the most important sources of the deterioration of the Canal's ecosystem.

Impact of Development on the Panama Canal Environment

Stanley Heckadon Moreno

The Importance of the Canal Basin

The historical Chagres River Basin, which serves as the basin for the Panama Canal, extends some 3,260 kilometers in length and is not only the most important river basin in Panama but also one of the most strategic river basins in the world. Its two major lakes—Gatún and Alhajuela—function as reservoirs for the water needed to operate the inter-oceanic canal as well as to supply the water requirements of both Panamá City and Colón, urban concentrations that contain more than half the country's population.

Gatún Lake was created in 1913, when the Chagres River was closed off at its Atlantic outlet, while the Alhajuela was created in 1934 by damming up the Madden River in the high, mountainous part of the country.

Ecologically, the sub-basin of Alhajuela Lake is the more critical of the two since it is the source of (1) almost half the water of the ecosystem, as well as (2) the entire water supply for the city of Panamá. Finally, the major part of the vital protective forests that still survive are located around the headwaters of the Chagres River (Wadsworth, 1976: 22–24).

The amount of water extracted from this basin is astronomical: some 2,800 million gallons daily. Of this, about 58% (1,624 million gallons) are released through sluices to the sea, thus enabling about 32 ships, on average, to transit the waterway daily; in other words, it takes about 52 million gallons of fresh water for each ship transiting the Canal, from one ocean to the other. Of the remainder, about 33% goes to generate hydroelectric power, another 4% is lost in the form of preventive release to prevent the sluices from overflowing, leaving only about 6% to be consumed as municipal drinking water. However, the demand for water has been increasing at a rapid rate, so much so that it has been projected that, by the year 2000, almost 4,000 million gallons per day will have to be extracted from the river basin (Grupo de Trabajo sobre la Cuenca del Canal de Panamá, 1986).

Because economic growth in the basin has been both haphazard and unplanned over the last 40 years, it has seriously undermined, and led to the deterioration of, its fragile ecosystem. It is a process which threatens the very ability of the ecosystem to continue to produce and store fresh water in sufficient quantity and quality to meet the enormous demands that will increasingly be placed upon it as we approach the year 2000 when the Canal is scheduled to pass into Panamanian hands. One of the greater challenges facing Panama as this moment draws near is how to bring into some kind of compatibility the competing needs of economic development on the one hand with the need to protect this vital tropical ecosystem on the other.

Fragility of the Ecosystem

The importance of the basin lies in its function as a natural system which produces and stores sweet water and which, by its very geographical nature, can be easily degraded or destroyed.

The Canal basin is situated in a region given to heavy, if not excessive, precipitation, with an annual rainfall estimated to range anywhere from 2,800 to 3,900 millimeters (110–153 inches). Most of this rain falls, with torrential violence, during a brief period of just a few months (Alvarado, 1985). The land itself is vulnerable: though over 63% of its terrain is made up of hills which may rise no more than 1,000 meters (3280 feet), many of these have slopes of up to 45 degrees. Terrain in the Alhajuela area is even more precipitous, with almost 94% of the terrain consisting of hills with slopes steeper than 45 degrees (Larson, 1979).

The land is poor, of a reddish, clay-like soil that erodes easily and is rendered hard and compact once its protective vegetation has been removed or destroyed. For the most part, the soil is poor and typical of that found in tropical forests, of which perhaps only 3% may be suitable for agriculture (Jonas and Ponce, 1986).

The Ecosystem Crisis

The most serious problem to threaten the ecosystem is deforestation. As recently as 1952, some 85% of the basin was covered by forests (Wadsworth, 1976); by 1983, that ratio had dropped to only 30%, so quickly has this process advanced (Robinson, 1985). It has been estimated that, from the early 1950s to the present, over 180,000 hectares (444,870 acres) have been stripped of their forest cover (Isaza, 1986). However, there are no reliable figures on the rate of deforestation, though estimates range anywhere from 3–10,000 hectares annually, which would be the equivalent of from 7,000 to 24,000 acres (Larson and Albertin, 1984).[1] Nevertheless, both rates are cause for concern since, if they continue at the present rate, the forests of the basin will disappear by the year 2000. The rate of deforestation presages dire consequences for the future of the Canal in other ways: deforestation fosters erosion of soil and contributes to the build-up of sediment in the lakes. Increased sedimentation will make the Canal less competitive as a route for world trade.

According to the studies of both Larson (1979) and Alvarado (1984), the sedimentation of the lakes has been increasing rapidly and becoming more severe. Over the last 15 years, Lake Alhajuela has lost 5% of its storage capacity, though Larson (the more pessimistic of the two) predicts that this percentage could rise to 23% by the end of the 1990s.

Another cause for concern is the decline in water quality due to increased pollution, visible in the murkiness or darkened color of the water and confirmed by the presence of bacteria and other organisms injurious to human health (Hutchinson, 1986).

Causes of Ecosystem Deterioration

The Canal Basin owes the progressive deterioration of its environment to 5 principal developments: (1) population growth, (2) mining, (3) industrialization, (4) urbanization, and (5) road construction.

While the most immediate dangers derive from the fallout from deforestation, i.e. soil erosion and sedimentation, the greater threat, in the long run, comes from water pollution, which has risen in direct proportion to the continuous increase of both urbanization and industrialization.

1. Population Growth

A number of researchers and historians—like A. McKay (1977), O. Jaén (1981) and D. Lecompte (1984)—have found that the presence of human inhabitants in the Canal basin is of long standing. However, the impact of these earlier inhabitants on the environment was minimal since they tended not only to be few in number but to limit their occupancy to that narrow strip of land which has long served as the primary passage between the two oceans. Up until the middle of the 20th century, almost the entire region was covered by dense forests.

During the colonial period, the population never rose above 1,500 inhabitants who lived, clustered in small communities, along the banks of the Chagres River and made their living from agriculture and the transport of passengers and cargo, by mule and small boat, across the Isthmus.[2] In the second half of the 19th century, the population began to grow: first, in response to the construction of the interoceanic railroad (1850–1855) and then to the work of the French in attempting to build a canal (1880–1890). By the end of the century, the area probably numbered about 20,000 inhabitants (Jaén, 1981). Despite the amount of activity which these works inspired, changes to the environment were confined to the immediate surroundings of the towns and camps which sprang up along the railroad line or near the excavations for the canal.

When the United States became engaged in building the Canal (1904–1914), the population rose to over 40,000 persons, most of whom were foreign workers. After completion of the Canal, the population dwindled as a result of two major events: (1) the United States created the Canal Zone, displacing most of the previous Panamanian population, and (2) Lakes Gatún and Alhajuela were created, which involved the flooding of some 480 kilometers and more than 50 small towns. By the end of the 1930s, there were no more than 8,000 inhabitants remaining in the basin.[3]

In the wake of World War II, a veritable population explosion took place which resulted in the growth of the area's population from about 20,000 (in 1950) to more than 100,000 (by 1980). About 66% of this increase has been centered in Alhajuela, where the population doubles every 10 years and still grows at 6% per annum (García, Bern and Morán, n.d.; Cortez, 1978). Initially, the major increase came from immigration: both that of peasants as well as a consequence of the outward thrust of urban dwellers from the cities of Panamá and Colón, which began to expand and extend into the basin along the path of the cross-isthmus highway. This highway, which crosses the isthmus alongside the Canal and the railroad, was completed in 1947, whereupon it became the axis along which the urbanization and industrialization of the basin proceeded. At present, the natural increase of the local population provides the major source of its demographic growth.

For the purpose of this work, however, the most important implication of demographic growth on the environment comes from the migration of the *campesino* into the Canal Basin, since it is the systems of production which they bring with them that have been the primary cause behind most of the deforestation. Here it is necessary to stress that beneath the label of *campesino* is hidden a most complex and little studied social development.[4]

The Peasant Migration and Its Impact on the Systems of Production. In this century, the Canal Basin has been converted into the rural zone of the greatest ethnic, cultural, and economic complexity in Panama. To this area have come peasants from the provinces of Coclé, Veraguas, Chiriquí, Los Santos, Darién and Herrera, as well as indigenous *chocoes,* West Indians, Chinese, and Colombians.

What attracts the peasantry to this area? On the one hand, there is its proximity to the metropolitan region, the largest market of the country; on the other, they are also pushed by the crisis of the countryside in their regions of origin.

Each of these groups has come at different times, and each group has brought with it its own social institutions, methods of production, and cultural values. In this way, the peasant migrants have been able to preserve, to a great extent, their own ways of perceiving and interpreting the world around them.

In more recent times, the first wave of immigrants was made up of the farmers displaced from the old towns located along either "the line" or the River Chagres, which had been flooded in the process of creating Lake Gatún and now lay under its waters. Many of those families sought refuge either on higher ground or along the banks of the new lake system. Ethnically and culturally, these people were Afromestizos, growers of tubers and other perennials, whose main income came from the cultivation of bananas.[5]

Another group which established itself early on came from the West Indies. This population was made up of workers—black, English-speaking, and Protestant—who had opted to remain on the isthmus after construction on the Canal was completed rather than return to their densely populated islands of origin. The town of New Providence (*Nueva Providencia*) was founded in 1916 on the banks of Lake Gatún by workers from Barbados.[6]

Two waves of migration came from Colombia: the first wave came in response to the intensive lumbering industry which had existed in the area prior to creating Lake Gatún, while the second wave came, mostly from the departments of Chocó and Bolívar, to work on building the dam across the Madden.

For thirty years (1920–1950), the rural economy was oriented to producing bananas for the US market, until several factors—primitive means of production, impoverishment of soil, and inability to control plant disease—combined to lead to a rapid decline in production and, ultimately, to destruction of the industry. Plantations were profitable for only 4–5 years, whereupon they would be abandoned and other areas of the forest sought out and demolished in order to plant *guineos* (small bananas).

Because the banana front was always moving, in just a few years it soon penetrated several kilometers inland, which then contributed to the raising of prices almost prohibitively due to the cost of transporting the fruit to the loading platforms on Lake Gatún.

At the heighth of the "banana boom," as this stage of economic prosperity was termed, the migration of *cholos* from the Coclé sierra accelerated. These peasants, latinized descendents of the indigenous Guaymas, had been slowly migrating toward the Chagres River basin ever since the 19th century (Panamá, 1916).

Initially, migration from the Coclé ran in cycles. The peasants worked on the plantations for brief periods to earn money and then returned to the mountains. Eventually, many remained and settled in the river basin, forming such settlements as *Cerro Cama, Lagartera,* and *Lagarterita.* The economy of the Coclé people was based on both a "slash and burn" as well as on a farming (*finca*) type of agriculture. Raising livestock never played a major role.

Though the region was still heavily forested at the beginning of the 1950s, the arrival of newcomers from the interior—peasants from the extremely dry plains on the western Pacific side of Panama—gave impetus to the destruction of the forests. As these groups colonized the area, deforestation accelerated at an unusually rapid rate. This was due to their extensive cattle-raising, for which thousands of hectares of forest were razed and transformed into pasture for grazing. These *campesinos* in particular, mostly from the Azuero peninsula, are the most numerous and have had the greatest impact on land use and landholding.

During the 1960s and 1970s, peasant settlement continued and intensified. Almost all the basin area that surrounds Lake Gatún, plus the western section of Alhajuela, has been stripped of forests. Migration is now directed toward the last of the basin's forest reserves, which are located along the upper reaches of the Chagres River (Heckadon Moreno, 1981).

The crux of the problem posed by peasant migration to the area comes from their introduction, and employ, of traditional agricultural methods that make extensive use of natural resources—and which have a deleterious, if not disastrous, impact on the new environment.

The economy of these peasant households can be likened to a table supported by four legs: one leg is provided by agriculture, another by livestock, a third by wage labor, and the last leg by fishing. It is the first two "legs" which cause the most damage to the environment.[7]

Agriculture, probably the most important activity, is based on one or the other of two basic methods: either (1) a slash-and-burn type of cultivation or (2) that of the *finca*. The first type requires that a different part of the forest be destroyed and burned each year in order to clear enough land to grow the basic grains and tubers which make up the bulk of the family diet. Though the rice and corn are raised primarily for domestic consumption, the corn makes it possible to raise poultry and pigs for market as well, albeit on a small scale.

Finca-type agriculture, on the other hand, relies on a more permanent type of cultivation, in which a number of different crops are rotated and intermingled, some for family consumption and the rest for sale. Although this system is better adapted to the fragile nature of the land, it is now becoming less and less common for a number of reasons: lack of credit and technical assistance, the high cost of transportation, and the low prices that farmers receive from middlemen. While *finca* agriculture is drying up for lack of incentives, the slash-and-burn method is also declining in tandem with the disappearance of the forests.

In order to obtain its minimum supply of food, each family must have access to at least 1–2 hectares of forest, which then must be cleared for planting. Clearing practices rely on primitive measures, such as fire, and the use of rudimentary tools, like the axe and machete. Generally, these plots remain productive for about a year, after which the yield quickly falls off due to the poor soil, whose fertility is rapidly depleted in the absence of either fertilizers (to replenish nutrients) or herbicides (to control/ combat insects and plant diseases). Very seldom do these plots yield a surplus which can be sold.

Ecologically, slash-and-burn agriculture constitutes a rational system of land use where the population is small and forests are plentiful. However, several factors have intervened over the last 30 years to upset the balance which this system must maintain with nature. One factor has been a constant increase in the peasant population. Another factor is the *campesino's* need for cash money. Third, and unlike the situation in the past, the slash-and-burn plots have not been allowed to lie fallow in order to give the forest time to regenerate before sowing again. Thus the extinction of the forests is hastened.

Another aggravating factor has been caused by the introduction of government regulations designed to protect the forest, which have contributed to the growing scarcity of forest land available to slash-and-burn cultivators. According to the 1977 Torrijos-Carter Treaties, Panama promised to guarantee that sufficient water would be available to operate the Canal. In order to carry out this pledge, it was necessary to establish a corps of forest rangers to protect the forests of the basin and to regulate, by means of licenses, the practice of slash-and-burn agriculture. In 1987, destruction of virgin forest was forbidden on a permanent basis. However, the government did continue to allow use of slash-and-burn techniques, though only in second-growth forests, for the next 5 years. At the end of that time, the prohibition of slash-and-burn was extended to second-growth areas as well. In essence, the government decided that, in order to save the Canal, the forests had to be protected from the machetes of the farmers.

This means that it is very difficult for peasant farmers to obtain parcels of primary forest for slash-and-burn type agriculture. The shrinking of the forest area, the prohibition against cutting trees, and the decreasing yields from crops have brought about a shortage of basic grains which is forcing a growing number of families to buy these foodstuffs from stores. Before this combination of forces, the peasants felt insecure, frustrated, and at the mercy of destructive forces beyond their control. Not being able to feed their families through their own efforts creates anguish and resentment among the peoples so affected.

As a result and understandably, political dissatisfaction is widespread throughout the region, making the task of those officials responsible for carrying out the laws to protect the environment just that much more difficult.

At the present time, 90% of the land formerly covered by forests is now devoted to the raising of cattle. This is unfortunate and one of the worst alternatives for development given the high rainfall, hilly terrain, and impoverished soil. Nevertheless, this is the economic activity that has received the most stimulus from institutions, both public and private, in order to incorporate the forest regions into the economy of the country. Almost 98% of the farm loans granted by the state development bank have gone to the cattle industry in the Canal basin (García, 1986).

This support for the cattle industry is essentially a response to the demand for meat in the urban markets of the metropolitan areas. However, the cattle industry is technologically unsophisticated; as a result, it not only causes serious damage to the environment but its overall productivity is quite low.

The principal grasses are the *fragua* and the *indiana*. In the dry season, the pasture is burned, which leaves the soil exposed to the impact of the heavy rains and the wear and tear of the cattle's hooves as they go up and down the steep hillsides. As the rains wash away the soil, eroding the landscape, great gullies and deep ditches are carved in the pastures. Another detrimental practice is that of maintaining more cattle than the pasturage can support. The surplus of animals leads to overgrazing, with the result that the vegetation that they spurn soon becomes dominant. When the combination of erosion and inedible growth finally destroy the pasturage, the fields become "lost," as the saying goes, and are abandoned. This destructive process is gradually extending further and further throughout the basin.

Although, in the beginning, it took one hectare of grass to support one head of cattle, eventually two hectares were required, then three, up til four hectares per head. The cattle industry, on a small or medium scale, is barely profitable.

Extending the cattle industry further and further across the land not only results in the expulsion of men from the land but it generates little employment and leads to ever larger concentrations of land-holding. Right now, in the basin, there is a marked tendency for land to become concentrated in the hands of a few large landowners. Although, in the first stage, ranchers displaced the peasant farmers, in the second stage, the small and mid-sized ranchers sold their *fincas* to other ranchers, who became transformed into large landed proprietors in the process. However, despite the fact that these thousands of peasant families have been the main agents of the deforestation, they will still have to be an essential part of the solution if the Canal basin is to be saved.

Let us close this part of the discussion by emphasizing the dilemma of the peasant economy, whose crisis has been aggravated by the government's decision to protect the forests in order to insure that there is sufficient water for the Canal and for the metropolitan population. In effect, the government decided to eliminate—in just 5 years—all slash-and-burn agriculture, a period in which there should have been offered, and disseminated among the peasantry, new methods of production that would be economically, ecologically, and socially viable. It is urgent that peasant methods of production be modernized. This will require that the farmer have access to low-interest loans, effective and timely technical assistance, means for penetrating the market, and just prices for his products. In the basin, these vital support services for production have been either deficient or non-existent.

While the peasant economy is in decline, there are other economic areas which also have a great impact on the environment.

2. Mining

There are two sorts of mining. At the artisan level this involves panning for gold in the streams and shallows of the rivers, a hard task to which hundreds of humble peasants devote themselves in order to obtain cash. However, it is the large-scale, mechanical extraction of primary materials for the construction industry which places the greatest burden on, and has the greatest repercussions for, the environment.

The construction industries of Panama City and Colón have been exhausting their sources of stone, gravel, sand, lime, etc., located in the vicinity of those metropolitan areas. In consequence, each year those companies must go farther afield in pursuit of the necessary raw materials, which must then be transported across ever-increasing distances, a situation which not only adds to their cost but is also a factor in creating frequent shortages. For this reason, the ownership and control of those sources of supply closest to the metropolitan area have turned into an issue of major economic importance. This has forced an increase in the number of mining companies extending their interests across the basin. There are presently some 22,000 mining concessions listed and another 17,000 under negotiation (Mérida, 1986).

The mining industry thus presents us with another dilemma regarding the appropriate tradeoffs between development and conservation. Mining cannot be prohibited because that would be too serious a blow for the construction industry, a major source of employment in the urban areas. However, it is necessary to try to strike a balance by establishing where, and under what conditions, this activity should be carried out.

3. Industrialization

Thirty years ago, there was only one plant—a cement factory—located within the basin area. Today, there are many factories, turning out plastic products, glass, paper, lubricants, soaps, pesticides, pharmaceuticals, foundries, sawmills, and the like. Besides the manufacturing plants, there are others engaged in the large-scale raising, and processing, of poultry and pigs.

The number of such plants is bound to increase even more in the future since the region offers a number of conditions favorable to industry: good highways and transportation services, a railroad, water, and proximity to both the country's largest markets as well as to the best ports and international airports. Not only that, but the land is cheaper than in the cities of Panamá and Colón.

Factories, however, are great generators of waste material in the form of garbage, polluted water, and smoke. At the same time, industrialization has brought an increase in the population, with all the accompanying impact on the environment which that implies.

The process of industrialization is an anarchic one, with environmental controls and regulations almost non-existent. This situation offers cause for alarm given the fact that some of the plants process highly toxic substances. Another worrying effect of industrialization is that it has brought with it an increase in contaminated water. Factories discharge their waste water directly onto the banks and into the rivers that feed the lakes, a practice which threatens the water quality of those sources that supply municipal drinking water to the cities of Panamá and Colón.

Panama, a poor country with a high level of unemployment, needs to broaden its industrial base and to depend less on a service economy. However, this process should not come at the expense of its natural environment, nor risk deterioration in the health and quality of life of its population. How can this dilemma be reconciled? It is important to ask such questions as: what kind of factories should be permitted within the basin and which not? Where should they be established and where not? And, above all, how—and who—should set the standards on pollution?

4. Urbanization

The basin of the Panama Canal is one of the regions of greatest urban growth in the country. This growth is a consequence of two major developments. The first is the expansion of the two terminal cities at either end: e.g., the city of Colón, which has been moving southward from one end, and the other, Panamá City, moving northward, following the trans-isthmian trajectory. It is possible that, by the year 2000, both cities will find themselves connected by an elongated corridor of houses. The other contributor to growth has come from the increased industrialization, which has generated much employment and brought better services to the area.

Many factors that make the area favorable for industrialization also encourage its urbanization. For example, not only is land cheaper outside than inside the cities of Panamá and Colón, but there is also a good public transporation system. In addition to the expansion of the cities, other settlements have sprung up in the rural areas around the lakes, and in the mountains surrounding the basin.

Increasing urbanization carries problems along with growth, most having to do with pollution. Families produce garbage and waste water. The traditional practice has been to discharge water and waste material into the streams and rivers, which then empty into the lakes.

It thus becomes an urgent matter to reconcile the process of increasing urbanization with sufficient protection of the environment in order to ensure that the quality of the water delivered to the metropolitan region remains sufficiently high that it does not constitute a threat to public health.

5. Road Construction

The increase in population goes hand in hand with intensive construction of roads and highways. Because this activity is unregulated also, it has become a major factor in land erosion and contributor to the silting up of water courses.

At the same time, secondary roads, often built at the instigation, and for the convenience, of lumber and mining companies, lead off the main highways to which they are tied and into remote areas, thus facilitating and serving to encourage settlement there.

Practically anyone with any authority feels entitled to sanction the building of roads: local authorities, public institutions, the army, and private businesses. Such thoroughfares are usually built without any concern for their impact on the environment. The majority turn out to be the well-known "summer short-cuts," poorly done and without provision for their subsequent maintenance. Tractors cut trails in the summer which are left to deteriorate in the winter, subject to the coming and going of animals and vehicles which turn the soil into a muddy morass that later, under the impact of the heavy rains, becomes washed away into rivers and streams.

While it is difficult, if not impossible, to bring road construction to a halt, some criteria must be established to define who can build roads, where they can (or cannot) be built, and under what technical conditions.

The environmental impact of the economic processes analyzed above is aggravated by the presence of non-economic factors.

Problems: Administrative, Legal, and Cultural

Even though the basin makes up a geographical entity, Panamanians are unaccustomed to looking at, and analyzing, its problems as a whole. This is due, in part, to the fragmentation of its administration. The basin area is divided into two provinces, seven districts, and

30 *corregimientos* (districts under the jurisdiction of a *corregidor*). Furthermore, these also correspond to areas of the old Canal Zone, which is divided up into a variety of civil and military jurisdictions for administrative purposes.

Another area of concern is the number of public and private institutions which operate with little or no coordination with one another. The administrative situation resembles an orchestra in which each musician follows a separate score. Not only does this often result in a duplication of effort, but also, at times, the pursuit of opposing goals. Neither is there any one single management plan or strategy that would be acceptable to all the different institutions involved.

Laws to protect the environment present another sticky situation. There are a great number of decrees, laws, and standards established which are designed to protect the environment. However, on the whole, this body of law is obsolete and there is no relation between the punishment and the crime from the standpoint of the kind and/or magnitude of damage done. In Panama, those who destroy or pollute the environment do not have to "pay the piper."

Given the negative view which the Panamanians have of natural resources, it is not at all easy either to apply the laws or to take steps to protect the environment. Regardless of class or level of education, Panamanians consider their natural resources to be inexhaustible. This is a dangerous myth. To save the basin will require a change in both cultural values and the outlook of the people, a change in which a variety of forces—the educational system (both formal and informal), the media, and civic groups—will have to play a key role.

Halting the deterioration of the Panama Canal basin will also require a high degree of administrative efficiency, political will, the participation of civilian groups, and economic resources. From whence will these resources come, given the present crisis in which Panama and the rest of Latin America finds itself?

An Economic Proposal to Save the Canal Basin

The Panama Canal basin, as we have seen, is a marvelous system for the production and storage of fresh water. Ironically, neither the users nor the beneficiaries of this system—international trade and the inhabitants of Panamá City and Colón—contribute anything towards protecting that vital water resource. The urban consumer pays only a small fee to cover the cost of making the water potable. Neither does the Panama Canal Commission, which is controlled by the United States and which uses 94% of the water, pay anything for this resource since, according to the Torrijos-Carter Treaties of 1977, Panama must provide all the water, free of charge, required to operate the Canal up to the year 2000. Ships transiting the Canal pay a tariff of $1.76 per ton to the Canal Commission, a fee which nets the Canal Commission more than $400 million per year according to its own report. Nevertheless, not one cent of this fee is allocated for the critical task of protecting the Canal basin.

Up to the present time, Panama has assumed the cost of programs to protect the basin by means of international loans, granted, more specifically, by the US Agency for International Development (US-AID). For this reason, there is no way that Panama, already burdened by a gigantic foreign debt, can continue to add to this indebtedness by bearing all the costs of protecting this vital ecosystem, whose major beneficiary is the international community. Therefore, it is imperative to increase the present fee for using the Canal by some 3 cents per ton. Each cent by which the fee is raised will represent an annual increase of income of about $3 million. Increasing the tariff by 3 cents will represent a sum on the order of $9 million, which could be allocated to the task of safeguarding this vital artery of international communication and progress.

Notes

1. See also Isaza (1986).
2. An interesting book on life in the Chagres River basin during the colonial period and, above all, in the 19th century, is that of Easter Minter (1948).
3. Displacing Panamanian *campesinos* fron the Canal Zone in the early decades of the 20th century is the main subject of a monograph by Gonifacio Pereira Jiménez (n.d.).
4. One of the few researchers who have touched on the issue of the peasantry of the Canal basin is Francisco Herrera (see his two studies).
5. In his novel entitled *Pueblos Perdidos,* Gil Blas Tejeira captures the trauma suffered by the farmers who lived in the towns along the Chagres when Gatún Lake was created.
6. According to Omar Jaén Suárez (1978: 309–318), the export of bananas from the Chagres River basin to the markets of the United States was initiated at the beginning of 1857, thanks to the inter-ocean railroad and the advent of the steamship.
7. Information on *campesino* systems of production described here are provided by Heckadon Moreno (1981).

References

Alvarado K., L. (1985) "Final Report on Sedimentation in Madden Reservoir." Panamá, República de Panamá: Panama Canal Commission, Meteorological and Hydrographic Branch.

Cortez, R. (1978) "La población de la cuenca," pp. 45–52 in S. Heckadon Moreno (ed.). La cuenca del Canal de Panamá: actas de los seminarios talleres. Panamá, R. de Panamá: Grupo de Trabajo sobre la Cuenca del Canal de Panamá.

Easter Minter, J. (1948) The Chagres River of Westward Passage. New York, NY: Rinehart and Co.

Garcia, M. (1986) "El crédito agropecuario," pp. 159–166 in S. Heckadon Moreno (ed.). La Cuenca del Canal de Panamá: actas de los seminarios talleres. Panamá, R. de Panamá: Grupo de Trabajo sobre la cuenca del Canal de Panamá.

Garcia, A., G. Bern and G. Moran (n.d.). "Algunas características de la población en el area de la cuenca del Canal de Panamá." Panamá, R. de Panamá: Ministerio de Planificación y Dirección de Recursos Naturales Renovables.

Grupo de Trabajo sobre la Cuenca del Canal de Panamá (1986) "Informe del Grupo de Trabajo sobre la cuenca del Canal del Panamá" (Executive Summary). Panamá, R. de Panamá: Grupo de Trabajo sobre la Cuenca del Canal de Panamá.

Heckadon Moreno, S. (1981) "Los sistemas de producción campesinos y los recursos naturales en la Cuenca del Canal de Panamá." Panamá, R. de Panamá: Dirección de Recursos Naturales Renovables y Agencia para el Desarrollo Internacional (AID).

Herrera, F. (n.d.) "Estudio socio-económico de tres comunidades en el sector oeste de la Cuenca del Canal." Panamá, R. de Panamá: Smithsonian Institute of Tropical Research.

_____. (n.d.) "Análisis de factibilidad social de la Cuenca del Canal." Panamá, R. de Panamá: US Agency for International Development (US-AID).

Hutchinson, R. (1986) "Calidad y demanda de agua para la población de la región metropolitana," pp. 87–108 in S. Heckadon Moreno (ed.) La Cuenca del Canal de Panamá: actas de los seminarios talleres. Panamá, R. de Panamá: Grupo de Trabajo sobre la Cuenca del Canal de Panamá.

Isaza, C. (1986) "Análisis de los factores que influyen en la erosión de la cuenca," pp. 121–141 in S. Heckadon Moreno (ed.). La Cuenca del Canal de Panamá: actas de los seminarios talleres. Panamá, R. de Panamá: Grupo de Trabajo sobre la Cuenca del Canal de Panamá.

Jaen Suarez, O. (1981) "La creación de una franja pionera en las riberas del Canal de Panamá," pp. 121–151 in Smithsonian Institute of Tropical Research (ed.). Hombres y ecología en Panamá. Panamá, Panamá: Editorial Universitaria.

_____. (1978) La población del Istmo de Panamá del siglo XVI al siglo XX. Panamá, República de Panamá: n.p.

Jonas, J. And V. Ponce (1986) "Los tipos de suelo y limitaciones para su uso," pp. 109–120 in S. Heckadon Moreno (ed.). La Cuenca del Canal de Panamá: actas de los seminarios talleres. Panamá, R. de Panamá: Grupo de Trabajo sobre la Cuenca del Canal de Panamá.

Larson, C. (1979) "Erosion and Sediment Yield as Affected by Land Use and Slope in the Panama Canal Watershed," pp. 1086–1095 in Part III of the Proceedings of the II World Congress on Water Resources, sponsored by the International Water Resources Association, in México (DF), México.

Larson, C. and W. Albertin (1984) "Controlling Deforestation, erosion and sedimentation in the Panama Canal Watershed" (Paper presented at the International Workshop on the Management of River and Reservoir Sedimentation). Hawaii: Environmental Policy Institute.

Lecompte, D. (1984) "Transformación del medio geográfico en la región canalera," pp. 57–76 in Tierra y Hombre (Revista del Departamento de Geografía). Panamá, R. de Panamá: Universidad de Panamá, Departamento de Geografía.

Mckay, A. (1977) "Salud comunitaria y colonización rural en Panamá: el caso de Cerro Cama." pp. 50–75 in S. Heckadon Moreno and A. McKay (eds.). Colonización y destrucción de bosques de Panamá. Panamá, R. de Panamá: Asociación Panameña de Antropología.

Merida, J. (1986) "El potencial minero de la cuenca del Canal," pp. 193–200 in S. Heckadon Moreno (ed.) La Cuenca del Canal de Panamá: actas de los seminarios talleres. Panamá, R, de Panamá: Grupo de Trabajo sobre la Cuenca del Canal de Panamá.

Panamá. (1916) "Informe del Gobernador de la Provincia de Colón," p.42 in Memoria de Gobierno y Justicia. Panamá: Tipografía Diario de Panamá.

Pereira Jimenez, G. (n.d.) "Biografía del Río Chagres" (monograph). Panamá, R. de Panamá: Imprenta Nacional.

Robinson, F. (1985) A Report on the Panama Canal Rainforests. Panamá, R. de Panamá: Panama Canal Commission, Meterological and Hydrographic Branch.

Wadsworth, F. (1976/77) "Deforestation: Death to the Panama Canal" (Paper presented at US Conference on Tropical Deforestation). Washington, DC: US Department of State and Agency for International Development (AID).

In October 1998 Category 5 Hurricane Mitch hit the Pacific Coast of Central America leaving devastation and death. One of the most affected regions was the Department of Choluteca along the southern Pacific Coast of Honduras. The Choluteca River reached a disproportionate size and destroyed the central area of the capital city of Tegucigalpa, leaving thousands homeless and several dead. As the river moved towards the Pacific, rain continued to pour, further increasing the size of the river. By the time it reached the town of Choluteca, the river buried most of the town under the mud, killing hundreds and leaving thousands destitute. This article by Jeff Boyer and Aaron Pell explores the reasons for the destruction left by Mitch, particularly the toll it took on the poorest populations of both Tegucigalpa and Choluteca. The authors explore the not-so-natural reasons behind the devastation left by Mitch particularly on the poor by looking at the living conditions of those who dwell in poor and makeshift housing; by discussing forced migrations to urban centers due to peasant encroachment, pesticide use and extensive cattle ranching; and by analyzing neoliberal policies that drove the Honduran government and multinational companies such as Chiquita to pour their resources into the reconstruction of the export economy's infrastructure.

Mitch in Honduras

A Disaster Waiting to Happen

The tragic tale of Honduras strongly suggests that decades of unsustainable development and the physical impacts of this terrible hurricane have fallen most heavily on the poor.

Jeff Boyer and Aaron Pell

The winding Choluteca River connects the wide and fertile valleys of Honduras' central mountains with the southern mountains along the Pacific slope. This watershed links Tegucigalpa, once a tiny colonial mining town in the central mountains and now a hustling capital city of 800,000 inhabitants, to Choluteca, the major city on the southern coastal plain with a population of over 110,000.

When Hurricane Mitch hit Honduras last October, the Choluteca River, engorged by the heavy rainfall, became a raging monster that took out Tegucigalpa's bridges, hospitals, factories and prisons. As the river widened, it poured into Fourth Avenue, rechanneling itself through low-lying downtown districts. Cars, buses and refrigerators were swept away by the torrent. Mud and rock slides either buried or slid out from under a dozen poor neighborhoods on the bare hillsides surrounding the downtown area, sending hundreds

"Mitch in Honduras: A Disaster Waiting to Happen," by J. Boyer and Aaron Pell, *NACLA Report on the Americas*, 33, No. 2, September/October 1999, pp. 36-43.

of people to their death. Over 150,000 displaced people from 80 neighborhoods crowded schools, hospitals, churches and makeshift shelters.[1] With power, streets and bridges out, the usual half-hour trip across town was taking half a day if it could be made at all.

The raging Choluteca River continued on, picking up still more rainwater in its deadly rampage to the Pacific Gulf. In the northeastern highlands of the department of Choluteca, it ripped out 60 houses in Duyure and destroyed the entire town of Morolica before descending upon Choluteca's capital. There it widened to six times its normal size, burying many mostly poor neighborhoods and part of the commercial center in mud. The city reported only 102 deaths and 78 missing, but the displaced numbered 38,814, more than a third of its inhabitants.[2]

In many ways, Tegucigalpa and Choluteca were accidents waiting to happen. While Tegucigalpa and southern Honduras managed to resist world development pressures until mid-century, the subsequent urbanization and economic expansion took off at a furious if utterly unplanned pace in a fitful attempt to catch up with the country's industrial North Coast, which has been dominated by the U.S. fruit companies since the early 1900s. Displaced by agribusiness and steady population growth in the central and southern hinterlands, peasants have flocked to these two cities, doubling the country's urban population from 20 to 40% over the past 50 years. Given the lack of affordable housing, new urban dwellers established squatter settlements on Tegucigalpa's hillsides and out along Choluteca's river banks in the south, a process which has left the hills surrounding the capital devoid of vegetation. Successive neoliberal governments of the 1990s have served to accelerate the polarization of urban space. In Tegucigalpa, the many crowded, impoverished neighborhoods with poorly constructed houses and few services contrast sharply with new well-constructed residential areas for the small middle and upper classes with their shiny new shopping malls, banks and U.S. retail chains like K-Mart, Burger King and Radio Shack.[3]

The tragic tale of these two cities strongly suggests that decades of maldevelopment and the physical impacts of this Class 5 hurricane have fallen most heavily on the poor.[4] With shoddier housing, usually located on highly vulnerable areas, the poor of Tegucigalpa and Choluteca were more exposed to the damage caused by Mitch. The grassroots response to the hurricane was impressive. Emergency neighborhood committees sprang up overnight to counter looting and to organize the search for food, water and medicine, while nongovernmental organizations (NGOs) worked side-byside with local groups and international agencies to coordinate relief efforts. Grassroots communities and local NGOs are working to rebuild their lives with a more palpable awareness of the historical patterns of environmental degradation that Mitch has served to compound. But the immediate and long-term damage is devastating. Nearly a year after the hurricane hit, some 10,000 people who lost their homes due to Mitch remain in large temporary shelters. With well over 100,000 people unemployed, the south since Mitch is a region of acute crisis.

Mitch also laid bare the unsustainable nature of Honduras' export-oriented development model. The challenges of reconstruction are daunting given that Honduras' natural resource base has long suffered the demands of global capitalist development.[5] But the government has given few indications it will seek to take the storm's destruction as a point of departure for building a more sustainable development model.

Honduras' southern region, which consists of the departments of Choluteca and Valle, presents a classic, well-documented case of both failed and contested export development.[6] The region's colonial land-use pattern generally consisted of cattle ranches occupying the coastal plains and a few peasant communities in the highlands to the north and east. Having attracted peasant settlement from Nicaragua and central Honduras from 1880 to 1930, the southern highlands began to fill up. Together, peasant slash-and-burn agriculture and slowly expanding pasture land had reduced the region's forest cover to less than 40% by mid-century. But with the growth of the U.S. fast-food industry and investments in new packing plants and container trucks in Honduras, and with multilateral investments in the new highway system to the north coast ports, cattlemen, greedy for more pasture land, began to enclose and evict the peasants. By 1974 land in pasture had increased to 61% of the south's land area. The region's remaining stands of deciduous and pine forests were cut to 13%.[7]

From a human perspective, the south's reliance on this U.S.-backed export development model—first beef, cotton and sugar and, since the late 1970s, melons and gourmet shrimp—has led to rural landlessness, chronic unemployment and steady outmigration. The jobs these agro-industries created never kept pace with the numbers of peasant farmers they displaced. This model has also contributed to a decline in basic food production and the loss of traditional skills for future sustainability. From a health perspective it has not only generated widespread malnutrition, but also, thanks to the cotton and melon industries, to one of the highest levels of pesticide poisoning in Latin America. From an environmental perspective it has wrought massive deforestation, soil erosion and the pesticide contamination of soil, water, plants and animals. And the shrimp industry has brought about significant species loss. Even before the hurricane, the south was already Honduras' poorest and most denuded regions.[8]

But southerners have consistently challenged the export agriculture model. Since the late 1950s, peasants have protested land enclosures by cattlemen and, in coordination with peasants in other regions, they organized one of the largest land reform movements in the isthmus. Indigenous fisher families have bitterly protested their own displacement from the coastal estuary and the environmental destruction of mangroves by the shrimp corporations. While neither the peasants nor the fishermen succeeded in breaking the dominant power of local cattlemen nor of U.S. agribusinesses in the two industries, they both remain active in the struggle to find more autonomous and sustainable alternatives to this largely imposed model of development.[9]

Mitch hit the eastern Choluteca highlands equally hard. On the fateful night of October 30, 1998, when the storm was at its height, the mountain's steep slopes and narrow valleys put people between crashing boulders and trees from above and flash flooding from below. "People heard a whirring noise," said Venancio Montoya, manager of the United Communities (CU) and president of a peasant cooperative, "Some thought it was a relief helicopter and stepped outside in the night, only to be buried under the rock and debris of the collapsing hillside above them."[10] Forty seven died and 785 houses were damaged or destroyed in El Corpus and Concepción de María.[11] Virtually the entire harvest for maize, sorghum and beans was destroyed. The campesino farmers of the area call the scarred hillsides, left bare by thousands of rock slides that evening, the "devil's claw marks."

Just as it recarved the physical landscape, Mitch seems to have carved a fundamental sense of vulnerability deeply into people's psyches. "We were like islands! For two weeks we were cut off from the city of Choluteca," said Juana Laínez, a school teacher in El Corpus, as she recounted the isolation of the hillside communities after the hurricane hit. "And now with the rains returning," she said, anticipating even heavier rains from September to mid-November, "we are becoming islands once again."[12]

In addition to the anguish of the isolation imposed by the disaster, peasants are hesitant to plant new crops for fear of more rock slides during this rainy season or even of another "La Niña" superstorm. The irony of this bizarre post-Mitch year is that the necessary shipments of emergency foods often lower grain prices, adding another disincentive to plant.

Usually it is drought and usurious grain merchants called *coyotes,* often financially linked to cattlemen capital, that have directly undermined production and, ultimately, peasant livelihood itself. A needy peasant will sell his crop before harvest at a low price to a *coyote,* who sells the grain later for as much as a 600% markup. Several years of low harvests and indebtedness often forces peasants to sell their land, often to cattlemen ready to convert the farmland to a pasture.

Over the past decade, the farmers involved with United Communities have helped each other secure their production of maize, sorghum and beans. They have also promoted the replanting of native subsistence crops for local consumption and to preserve these now perilously scarce genetic materials.[13] With the help of outside technical assistance, often from NGOs or religious organizations, it is possible for the peasants to reduce or end their need to presell their crops to *coyotes.* If subsistence production can be maintained or even surpluses achieved, then peasant families can hold their own against the encroaching cattlemen, still eager for more pasture.

A savvy peasant farmer named Ignacio "Nacho" Espinal took us on a morning walk behind the long, curved horseshoe-shaped ridge of Potreritos, his remote highland community of 74 households in Concepción de María. Nacho, a tall and wiry man who appears younger than his 58 years, learned to read in the 1960s through Catholic Radio Schools and is something of the community scribe and news analyst. He is the president of "The Eleven," now a group of 16 Potreritos households who farm cooperatively, and one of the founders of the CU. At home with the curved blade mountain machete in his *milpa,* the traditional plot of interplanted maize, beans and sorghum, Nacho has cautiously introduced elements of the new permaculture promoted by a Church-run peasant agriculture program.

Nacho took us into a grove of older hardwoods that adjoined a stand of scrubtrees below. "The Eleven" will let the old trees stand, as Nacho put it, "to keep nature's vegetation." The scrub trees would be cut next year for the *milpa,* especially for Potreritos' prized red beans. Crossing the property line, we entered an open, overgrazed pasture, with eroded gullies. "Look over here," he said, pointing to a nearby flat area on the hillside. The land once belonged to an absentee cattlewoman who let them cultivate this hillside in exchange for clearing pasture below. They could follow the slash-and-burn cycle for two years and then fallow it for three or four years, allowing secondary growth to return. But the land was sold to a cattleman who decided to turn the whole slope into pasture by burning every year, eliminating any growth but pasture grasses. "It's no good for *milpa* now," said Nacho, "with all this grass and erosion."

As we passed hundreds of "devil's claw marks" on the mountains before us, I asked Nacho if there had been more rock slides on the pasture land or on farm land. "Mitch dumped a lot of rain all at once; we got in eight days what we usually get in a year," he said. "There are steep places with forest cover up to the ridge top that slumped and started a slide. I think the ground got so heavy and sodden that it just gave way." He paused. "But wherever the ground was open or eroded, the heavy rains opened it up even more. Plowed land is the most likely to erode, but the thin, steep pasture lands can erode more quickly than the *milpa,* especially if the farmer leaves some vegetation on the farmland."[14]

Looking across the mountains and valleys in the foreground, we estimated that approximately 6 to 8% of it had stands of older growth trees. Approximately twothirds of the hillsides and valleys in front of us were eroding cattle pasture. Environmental destruction—mostly cattlemen-induced deforestation—and its foreclosure on so much human opportunity was well under way here before Mitch.

For at least the past 20 years in this area, most families have had insufficient lands on which to produce at subsistence levels. Steady population growth has been one causal factor; these southern highlands have the highest rural densities in Honduras. Yet large families will remain a rational response to poverty as long as the government denies any real social security for the elderly of this poor nation.[15]

Nacho took us to the farm of a neighbor, Mamerto Guillén, who has transformed his farm into a model for mountain permaculture. The slopes are terraced on the contour, both with stone walls and perennials with large root systems. In the beds, *milpa* crops are inter-planted with a variety of fruits, vegetables and medicinal plants. We walked around to a shady slope to see Mamerto's cultivation of spiny cedar, native to Honduras and much valued for fine furniture-making. As we returned to Nacho's home under the midday sun, he talked about Mamerto's farm in hopeful terms as a viable alternative for highland farmers. A recent study by World Neighbors/Honduras has confirmed that this type of hillside permaculture retained more soil and sustained fewer landslides than conventional hillside farms during Hurricane Mitch.[16] But Nacho also questioned both the initial labor costs needed to establish the terraces and the yields, especially compared to his traditional second planting of monocropped beans.

Such questions cry out for continued applied research. Moving regions like southern Honduras back from the deep human and environmental crisis that has beset the country requires government dedication to implementing sound environmental and agriculturally sustainable policies. Such policies must guarantee a modicum of land security for peasant farmers and be accompanied by sustainable practices. They must also promote the production of healthy food for Honduras instead of using its limited land in export production.

The great Sula Valley, on Honduras' north coast, was once a lush tropical ecosystem with small, self-sustaining peasant communities. It is now an agro-industrial landscape, transformed by the predominance of United Fruit and Standard Fruit since 1915, when these two U.S.-based companies consolidated their banana holdings in the region. The land was made to produce an enormous genetic homogeneity, typically bananas or, more recently, palm oil trees. It also became one of the plantation world's first pesticide treadmills. Oriented toward the technical ends of mass production, the Sula Valley now accounts for 60% of the country's gross domestic product (GDP).[17] In this hurricane region, fields are frequently flooded and they must be periodically reclaimed from deposited mud and rock.

Peasants from the north coast became banana workers, losing their cultural ties to small-scale peasant agriculture and to nature itself. Yet they struggled against fruit company exploitation and in 1954 won the right to unionize. Later, they helped peasants in other regions organize for land reform. Agriculture-based industries now coexist with hundreds of newer finishing plants for the global assembly line, mostly U.S. and South Korean maquilas that employ 50,000 women at non-union wages. The older system of railroads and newer highway networks link the banana and palm oil plantations to ports, and to the major industrial city of San Pedro Sula and the traditional centers of fruit company operations, the towns of La Lima and El Progreso.[18]

Mitch's initial winds prevented the northern rivers from discharging as it simultaneously dumped heavy rains. The massive flooding drowned countless people and stranded thousands of workers on the tin rooftops of their scattered banana camps for days without food or drinking water. The Jesuits of El Progreso report that emergency neighborhood committees, not the political or military authorities, constituted the only initial force to stop looting. The government of President Carlos Flores was more concerned with restoring the highway connecting Tegucigalpa to San Pedro Sula and then north to Puerto Cortes—its national "export artery"—which it did within a week with support from the U.S. military.

The government could blame its absence to the urgency of other priorities. But Chiquita Brands—the old United Fruit Company—had helicopters and a fleet of four-wheel drive trucks yet did nothing to rescue thousands of their stranded workers from the rooftops when the banana fields were flooded. To add insult to injury, Chiquita laid off 7,500 employees a week later. The transnational claimed that their fields had been totally ruined from the debris that had washed down from the surrounding mountains. Yet they later hired a smaller number of non-union workers to clean up many fields. Had the mayor of El Progreso not turned over the emergency food distribution to the Jesuits and neighborhood committees a week after Chiquita's callous firing of hungry workers, there probably would have been food riots.[19]

In contrast to this commercialized landscape, a bit of natural green remains in the Jeanette Kawas National Park, west of Tela on the Caribbean coast. It has beautiful coral reefs, marine and lagoon ecosystems and tropical forests in the background and is home to Garífuna villagers of African and Carib descent. Formerly Punta Sal, the park was renamed in 1995 when its namesake was murdered for defending it from timber and palm oil interests backed by the military. Kawas' martyrdom helped spark Honduras' environmental movement and the creation of a private nonprofit organization charged with protecting the park. Rather than encourage these conservation efforts, the government is supporting the construction of a large petroleum storage and shipping facility for the entire country in Tela. Brenda Avila, a park technician, said that the first pipes that the government installed were washed to sea by Mitch's heavy rains. Had there been oil in those pipes, they certainly would have ruined the park's botanical gardens, coral reefs and beaches. Despite the danger, the Flores Administration appears willing to risk this natural treasure, as well as Tela's growing ecotourism industry and one of Honduras' most popular beaches, in order to benefit corporate industrial interests.[20]

Other regions of Honduras share the telltale scars of global capitalism's misuse of Honduras' natural resources. La Mosquitia, the vast eastern Caribbean lowlands, once held one of the world's significant rainforests, where Honduran mahogany was in abundant supply. By the 1980s the timber industry, cattle ranching and peasant colonization were reducing these forests at an annual rate of nearly 4%. An 80-year-old Misquito compared Mitch's mud-filled floodwaters with the clearwater flooding of another hurricane 70 years ago, testimony to the erosion-producing deforestation that has resulted from the heavy logging and agricultural activity of recent years.[21] The government, apparently tied down with the disasters in central Honduras, left the stranded coastal and inland communities along the Patuca River to fend for themselves.[22]

From the north-central region of Yoro, Ines Fuentes, a national leader of the peasant land reform movement spoke of another kind of environmental maldevelopment. Fuentes is the founder of a multiple service cooperative that supports 14 cooperatives with tractors and other equipment on the rich soils of the Negrito Valley. He reported that Mitch destroyed over 100 acres, covering them in rock, with one small cooperative losing all of its land.[23] Part of the problem, he says, was too great an emphasis in the 1970s and 1980s government agrarian reform program on rapid mechanization and not on longer-term sustainable practices. Even the national peasant movement often seemed ready to abandon the more environmentally sensitive elements and scale of traditional agriculture in the rush to become modern.[24]

Mitch's destruction would surely have taxed the resources of any government. In June the Flores Administration reported a 5.8% reduction in GDP and a 30% reduction in tax revenues this year compared to 1998. At Stockholm's recent International Summit for Central American Reconstruction, President Flores secured $2.7 billion in loans and grants. Since January, however, the government has put the total cost of reconstruction at $5.2 billion, which means that only half of the reconstruction bill has been financed—assuming that these new funds are prudently spent.[25]

Then there is the question of priorities. In January, Flores argued that since it would take four years of the national budget to rebuild the entire economy, the government must concentrate on the infrastructure for the nation's productive plant—the main structures of power, transport and communications for agribusiness and industry. The tasks of "human development," he said, must fall to the 297 municipalities and to the NGO and the international communities—meaning scant help for secondary roads and bridges, rebuilding water systems, clinics, schools, houses and reclaiming small farmsteads.[26] Part of Juana Laínez's frustration at becoming an island again is that she knows that the bridges linking the El Corpus highlands to Choluteca will not be rebuilt anytime soon.

Since Stockholm, Flores has softened the rhetoric about funding priorities and has given some support to the Municipal Emergency Committees and the Honduran Fund for Social Investment (FHIS). But he is quite adroit at using both institutions and some favored NGOs to manage staged public forums and undermine genuine participation while stifling criticism. This official subterfuge notwithstanding, Mitch has made the government's priorities abundantly clear: to support large, corporate interests that generate foreign exchange for debt repayment and for ever-greater consumption for the wealthy. Responding to the basic human needs and aspirations of the poor and working majority is simply not a priority.

The environmental negligence of Flores and previous neoliberal governments precedes Mitch. They have turned a blind eye to the illegal burning of many thousands of acres of forests each year, which is rapidly turning Honduras' forest reserves and biodiversity into fragmented remnants.[27] Scavenger loggers are officially allowed to sell the semi-damaged timber after a burn. Cattlemen burn for pasture, while peasants burn off public lands, often frustrated by landlessness and by the more powerful loggers and ranchers who seem to have no trouble securing access to public forests.

The government also refuses to look to the long-term and fund reforestation projects or the three large bioreserve projects it gave to the National Institute for Environment and Development (INADES) to manage.[28] It frequently runs "scare" articles in the national tabloids on "ecoterrorism" to divide the environmental movement.[29] Its new cabinet-level environmental ministry is underfunded and rarely consulted. This is, of course, the environmental side of what has been called the savagery of contemporary neoliberalism.[30]

In the weeks immediately following the hurricane, there was palpable optimism across Honduras that somehow this great disaster would catalyze widespread rethinking about the dominant development model and that sensible alternatives would emerge. Mitch has given environmentalism an urgency that was missing in the earlier peasant movement, and there is evidence of sustainable innovations at the grassroots throughout the country. But unfortunately, the optimism about Mitch's silver lining seems to have eroded as the government directs its energies toward the engineering of big highways and away from any sort of cogent social policy.

Social disintegration and anomie, like the physical isolation of communities after Mitch, is a growing danger. But the post-Mitch world is only intensifying global capitalism's 20 years of imposed atomization of Honduras' traditional bonds of families and communities. As many NGO leaders told us, history is not destiny, and a more authentically Honduran development is possible. A network of 28 environmental NGOs is organizing a national forum to devise strategies to challenge the Flores government's anti-environmental policies and demand support for a participatory, sustainable plan for reconstruction.

Writing from Costa Rica in the late 1980s about the environmental destruction occurring throughout Latin America, Ingemar Hedstrom attempted to answer the provocative question posed in his book's title: "When will the swallows return?"[31] As he and so many Hondurans reminded us, the dominant neoliberal policies, corporate practices and consumer patterns of the United States must also change before Central American governments feel compelled to change. Only then might the swallows return to Honduras and the isthmus.

NOTES

1. *New York Times,* November 9, 1998, p A8; *La Tribuna* (Tegucigalpa), January 3, 1999, p. 2.
2. *New York Times,* November 9, 1998; p. A9; Choluteca municipal data collected by Pedro Corrales, July, 1999.
3. United Nations Development Program, *Informe sobre desarrollo humano, Honduras 1998* (Tegucigalpa: UNDP), pp. 49, 182, The neoliberal governments of the 1990s were led by Presidents Rafael Callejas of the Nationalist Party (1990–94), and Liberals Carlos Roberto Reina (1994–98) and Carlos Roberto Flores (1998–present).
4. "1998: Hurricane Mitch (Category 5)," Intellecast at <http://www.intellicast.com/>, June 4, 1999.
5. See also Susan Stonich, "Development, Rural Impoverishment and Environmental Destruction in Honduras," in Michael Painter and William Durham, eds, *The Social Causes of Environmental Destruction in Latin America* (Ann Arbor: University of Michigan Press, 1995), pp. 63–70.
6. For economic and environmental assessments of Central Americas export-led model of development, see Robert Williams, *Export Agriculture and the Crisis in Central America* (Chapel Hill: University of North Carolina Press, 1986); H. Jeftrey Leonard, *Natural Resources and Economic Development in Central America* (New Brunswick: Transaction Books, 1987); and Michael Conroy, Douglas Murray and Peter Rosset, *A Cautionary Tale: Failed Development Policy in Central America* (Boulder: Lynne Rienner/Food First, 1996). For analyses of southern Honduras see Jeff Boyer, "From Peasant *Economia* to Capitalist Social Relations in Southern Honduras," *South Eastern Latin Americanist,* Vol 27, No. 4 (1984), pp. 1–22; Boyer, "Capitalism, Campesinos and Calories in Southern Honduras," in Jack Rollwagen, ed. *Directions in the Anthropological Study of Latin America: A Reassessment* (Albany: State University of New York Press, 1987); and Susan Stonich, "The Political Economy of Environmental Destruction: Food Security in Southern Honduras," in Scott Whiteford and Anne Ferguson, eds. *Harvest of Want: Hunger and Food Security in Central and Mexico* (Boulder: Westview Press, 1991), pp. 45–74,
7. See Boyer, "From Peasant *Economia* to Capitalist Social Relations," pp. 8–11; and Stonich, "Development, Rural Impoverishment and Environmental Destruction," pp. 74–75.
8. On peasant malnutrition see Boyer, "Capitalism, Campesinos and Calories"; and Stonich, "The Politcal Economy of Environmental Destruction." On heavy pesticide use, poisonings and contamination in the cotton and melon industries, see Stonich, "Development, Rural Impoverishment and Environmental Destruction"; and Conroy et. al., *A Cautionary Tale.* Omar Lainez collected the preand post-Mitch data on the shrimp industry, June 1999.
9. On agrarian politics and resistance, see Boyer, "Peasant Leaders and Allies Speak: Land, *Economia* and Democracy in Honduras," Paper presented at the XXI Conference of the Latin American Studies Association, Chicago, September 1998, and Boyer, "Charisma, Martyrdom

and Liberation in Southern Honduras," *Comparative Social Research,* No. 1 (1990), pp. 115–159. Stonich, "Development, Rural Impoverishment and Environmental Destruction," discusses the environmental politics surrounding the gourmet shrimp industry.

10. Authors' interview, Venancio Montoya, El Corpus, Choluteca, January 1999.
11. Data from both municipalities collected by Pedro Corrales, July 1999.
12. Authors' interview, Juana Lainez, El Corpus, June 1999.
13. For a broader discussion of these issues, see Boyer, "Capitalism, Campesinos and Calories."
14. Authors' interview, Ignacio Espinal, Potreritos, Concepción de Maria, June 1999.
15. Rural densities here are now above the 310 inhabitants per square mile cited in Boyer, "From Peasant *Economia* to Capitalist Social Relations." Honduras' current average density is 119 inhabitants per square mile. See *informe sobre el dessarrollo humano, Honduras 1998,* p. 43.
16. See the Honduran Network for Sustainable Development at < http://www.rds.org.hn/ >.
17. "Global Review," *New York Times Business Supplement,* December 8, 1998, p. 1.
18. For a history of the north coast, see Victor Meza, *Historia del Movimiento Obrero* (Tegucigalpa: Centro de Documentación de Honduras (CEDOH), 1991). See also *Informe sobre el desarrollo humano, Honduras 1998,* p. 57. Information also provided by Jack Warner, S.J. (personal correspondence), November 6, 1998.
19. Using their radio station "Radio Progreso" to keep people in touch, the Jesuits worked closely with the neighborhood committees that formed to control looting and distrubute the food aid. Jack Warner, S.J. (personal correspondence), November 7–20, 1999. See also Gary MacEoin "Honduras: Corruption Hinders Hurricane Recovery," *National Catholic Reporter,* April 30, 1999.
20. Authors' interview, Brenda Avila, PROLANSATE official, Tegucigalpa, June, 1999.
21. The national area in forest cover shrunk from 44% in 1970 to 36% in 1980. The Mosquitia, with Honduras' largest forest, sustained very high rates of loss in the 1980s, possibly higher than the cited figures. See Leonard, *Natural Resources and Economic Development in Central America,* pp, 117–121.
22. Authors' interview, Angela Rivas de Rosenzweig, Howard Rosenzweig and Susan Van der Linden, II Sagni Relief Poject, Copán Ruinas, June 1999. See also Howard Rosenzweig, "II Sagni Relief Project Conducts Survey in La Mosquitia," *Honduras This Week* (Tegucigalpa), January 9, 1999.
23. Authors' interview, Ines Fuentes, Tegucigalpa, June 1999.
24. Authors' interview, Ines Fuentes, June 1999. See Jeff Boyer, "Peasant Leaders and Allies Speak."
25. *El Heraldo* (Tegucigalpa), June 14, 1999; See also MacEoin, "Honduras."
26. *La Prensa* (San Pedro Sula), January 5, 1999.
27. *La Tribuna* (Tegucigalpa), May. 13 and April 1, 1998.
28. Authors' interview, Roberto Vallejo, director of INADES, Tegucigalpa, May 1996 and May 1999.
29. See, for example, "Los Ecoterroristas," *La Tribuna* (Tegucigalpa), January 3, 1999.
30. Marc Edelman, "Reconceptualizing and Reconstituting Peasant Struggles: A New Social Movement in Central America," *Radical History Review,* Vol. 65 (1996), p. 43.
31. See Ingernar Hedstrom, *Volverán Las Golandrinas?* (San Jose: Departarmento Ecuménico de Investigaciones, 1990).

This article introduces us to the particularities of postwar development in Central America. It looks into the policies instituted by the World Bank and the new administrative efforts to re-direct the process of modernization under the banner of the Puebla to Panama Plan, known as PPP or Mesoamerican Project. It shows the neo-discursive practices that argue for a mythical concern for the environment while developing megaprojects and modern corridors that are impacting communities, nature, and land tenure.

Excerpt from Road Mapping: Megaprojects and Land Grabs in the Northern Guatemalan Lowlands

Liza Grandia

Introduction: Roads to Development

Analysts in the development field have long treated immobility and poverty as equivalents (Hilling, 1996). While the appropriate sequencing of infrastructure and development remains a lively topic of debate, most planners — following Rostow's (1960) teleological stages of economic growth — presume that infrastructure, especially roads, are a necessary and sufficient precondition for economic 'take-off' and, therefore, an appropriate indicator of progress. Hence, following cautious loans to rebuild war-torn Europe after World War II, the World Bank shifted its focus to the restoration of colonial infrastructure (Goldman, 2004) and high modernist projects (Scott, 1998) in the Third World, devoting some 40 per cent of its budget in the 1960s to transport projects (Hilling, 1996). Much of the World Bank's thirteen-fold increase in lending under Robert McNamara (1968–1981) was from loans for infrastructure that poor nations still have difficulty repaying (Danaher, 1994).[1]

Despite the international debt crisis in the 1980s and 1990s, and notwithstanding substantial criticism from academics and citizens about the environmental and social problems associated with trans-forest highways, pipelines, hydroelectric dams, etc., 'infrastructuromics' is experiencing a rebirth among the planning elite. By this, I refer to the assumption that investments in 'gargantuan' (to borrow Scott's 1998 terminology) infrastructure will ineluctably produce economic growth. As the Guatemalan Roads

"Road Mapping: Megaprojects and Land Grabs in the Northern Guatemalan Lowlands" by Liza Grandia, in *Development and Change*, March 15, 2013, pp. 233–259.

Department grandiosely claims, 'Every nation in the world cements its economic, political and social structure into its highways' (Caminos, 2002: section D.1.1).

There are historical continuities in the intimate links between infrastructure and state power. Since medieval times, states have invested in roads as 'distance demolishing technologies' (Scott, 2009). Coupled with land surveys and population censuses, roads serve to incorporate peripheral regions into the formal (and taxable) economy. Symbolically, as well, they connect frontier populations with the 'imagined community' of the nation state (Anderson, 1983). During the Cold War, they were politically important in establishing state presence in regions thought to be vulnerable to communism (or capitalism, depending on one's point of view). Contemporary threats of convergent food, energy and financial crises (Borras et al., 2011) are once again focusing the attention of states and their donors on the integration of national hinterlands.

Across the Americas, governments and international development banks are co-financing new waves of megaprojects to support corporate trade and commerce. From south to north these ambitious planning frameworks include the Initiative for the Integration of Regional Infrastructure in South America (IIRSA), the Puebla to Panama Plan (PPP) in Central America and Mexico, and, more recently, recession stimulus plans in the United States and Canada. While a sustained comparison of these plans is beyond the scope of this article, both IIRSA and the PPP originated (in 2000 and 2001, respectively) as brainchildren of the Inter-American Development Bank (IDB). Reflecting a close alignment between states and corporations, these contested plans aimed to accelerate regional economic integration by leveraging multi-billions in hybrid public–private capital for a dazzling number of new infrastructure projects—mostly roads, but also port development, electric grids, hydroelectric dams and telecommunications upgrades—in tandem with legal initiatives to facilitate transnational business (such as more standardized customs procedures).[2]

In addition to infrastructure planning, governments and international donors also typically regard a legible property system as a pre-condition for development and capital investment. Since the late 1990s, the World Bank has unfurled a global initiative to encourage countries to realign their land governance systems according to neoliberal principles (Deininger and Binswanger, 1999), through 'market-assisted agrarian reform' later euphemized as 'land administration'. The Bank portrayed states as incapable of managing land distribution and therefore recommended that governments should limit their agrarian interventions to facilitating transactions between 'willing buyer/willing seller' in an otherwise unfettered land market. Projects essentially aimed to 'depoliticize' territorial governance structures by promoting investment in the technical infrastructure of land administration (cadastral mapping and registration) and streamlined land titling processes (Borras et al., 2012). Many of the World Bank's early projects focused on Latin America (Rosset et al., 2006), in tandem with the IDB's megaproject planning.

In Guatemala, the country focus of this essay, the World Bank alone has lent the government US$ 93 million since 1998 for two land administration projects in the northern lowlands (see Figure 1), also a highly targeted region for infrastructure development under the PPP. Project designers hypothesized that this 'territorial ordering'[3] of Guatemala's northern lowlands would resolve latent and active agrarian conflicts and that enhanced tenure security would stimulate improved agricultural practices and sustainable intensification of land use. Contrary to expectations, a third to half of smallholders who participated in land survey and titling projects in Guatemala's northernmost department of Petén — especially those located along upgraded roads — are now selling (or being forced to sell) their plots to African-palm planters, cattle ranchers, narco traffickers and other investors. In a country where just 2 per cent of the population still controls two-thirds of arable land, this rapid agrarian concentration is troubling. The Petén was Guatemala's last

FIGURE 1. Political Map of Guatemala with Historic Colonization Zones.
Source: David Eitelberg and Liza Grandia.

frontier where indigenous and other landless peasants could claim parcels large enough for robust subsistence, and become 'yeomayan' farmers, as it were.

In some ways, Petén's 'land deal politics' echoes a familiar imperial pattern, in which transportation networks have long facilitated the plunder of native lands. Yet, while much of the literature rightly focuses on *transnational* transactions (Zoomers, 2010), land grabbing is not always a neat neo-colonial story. As in much of Latin America, the panoply of actors responsible for Petén's land grabbing include: 'trans-Latin American companies, often in alliance with international capital' (Borras et al., 2012: 845), national elites who are acquiring land as intermediaries or for subsequent business alliances with foreign corporations (Cotula, 2012), and domestic individuals and families increasingly connected to transnational cartels. Although forms of agrarian transformation in Guatemala once clustered neatly along traditional class lines, distinctions among 'labour control grabbing' by landed elites (Li, 2011), 'green grabbing' by transnational interests (Fairhead et al., 2012), and 'violence grabbing' by illicit actors (Grajales, 2011), as well as their relations with the Guatemalan state and its military shadow, are increasingly blurred.

Based upon seven years of ethnographic fieldwork between 1993 and 2012, this study explores how the convergence of the PPP and World Bank land administration efforts are reconfiguring this strategic lowland territory for the benefit of these interconnected 'elites'. Echoing the Spanish term employed widely in Petén ('élites'), I refer here to the messily imbricated dominant classes profiting from this frontier, which include privileged groups within Guatemala that took advantage of their family and political connections to claim parcels in excess of official policies during Petén's formal frontier settlement programme (1959–89) (Schwartz, 1990). Hence, for poor and middle-class Peteneros alike, the labelling of 'elites' can refer to wealthy locals or *capitalinos* (people from the capital) as often as it does to foreigners. Q'eqchi' Maya people in Petén describe all these groups simply as *aj b'iomeb'* (rich people), whose power is enhanced by *aj puub'* (soldiers, literally those with guns).

As critiqued in the Introductory essay to this volume, World Bank officials in Guatemala and elsewhere are quick to attribute land grabs as a problem of weak states (Deininger et al., 2011). While attention must be paid to the rising salience of corporate power in processes of agrarian concentration, 'muscle-bound' states (Scott, 1998: 4) and their donors have hardly been 'relegated . . . . to the dustbin of history' (Chase-Dunn and Lawrence, 2008: 78). Albeit presented in 'well-intentioned' terms of development, state violence remains a continuing force in globalization and internal territorialization — defined here as contested efforts to re-orient the social, ecological and economic relationships of a region for the purposes of capital accumulation. As Corson (2011: 707) notes, territorialization may alter 'not only human–environment relations, but also power relations among social groups'. As this analysis will show, the Guatemalan military may be a shadow beneficiary of new power assemblages emerging from narco/cattle/industrial/military land grabbing occurring in Petén.

To give a 'road-map' of the logic of the paper, I begin with a contextual analysis of continuities in Petén's frontier development from colonization efforts of the 1960s–80s through its more recent alliterative trajectory from *conservación* (conservation) to *catastros* (land surveys) and *carreteras* (highways). The next section 'unbundles' the mix of land grabbing actors in Petén with an emphasis on their relationship to infrastructure and land administration projects, and their imbrications with one other. Against the academic tendency to insinuate that neoliberal projects are conspiratorially interconnected, I then attempt to document the actual crossings and conjunctures of the PPP with the World Bank's land administration project, as well as their contradictions, and the implications of these elite vectors for Guatemalan civil society more broadly.

Surveying the Petén

At almost 36,000 km^2, Guatemala's northernmost and largest department, the Petén, occupies a third of national territory. It covers a zone of strategic resources — biodiversity, forestry/carbon values, transportation corridors, hydroelectric energy and petroleum — all of which, of course, depend upon the control of the land underneath. Once isolated from Guatemala, the Petén is undergoing swift integration and economic change, making it a compelling context for witnessing the unfolding of new regional/national/international power networks, as well as continuities from the past. Almost entirely covered by semi-tropical woods, swamps and savannahs until the 1960s, accumulation in Petén was historically based on forest resource exploitation, the control of land for cattle ranching in the department's fertile central grasslands, and trade with Mexico. Petén's most prominent families are descendants of the original colonial families who settled after the relatively late Spanish subjugation of the region in 1697 and who became loggers, ranchers, shopkeepers/contractors who commissioned and provisioned camps for extracting non-timber forest products (chicly-gum resin, allspice berries and palm fronds for export) (Schwartz, 1990). Many kept ties with relatives in Guatemala City, sending their children there to be educated as doctors, lawyers and engineers. Some are also rumoured to have enhanced their fortunes through archaeological smuggling (Anon, 2011).

Petén was, until very recently, a distant backwater in the national imaginary that required at least two days to traverse by land, but which can now be comfortably travelled in a long afternoon. With most of the population concentrated around Lake Petén Itza in north-central Petén and twelve sparsely settled municipal seats, ground travel across the department was limited to footpaths, mule trails and limited roads. Not until 1933 was a Guatemalan president able to visit Petén, when Jorge Ubico inaugurated its first airstrip (Schwartz, 1990). The region's first all-weather road to the capital was not built until 1970 as part of a colonization effort led by a semi-autonomous government body called FYDEP ([Agency for the] Foment of Petén's Development). A 64 km paved road was then opened in 1982 between a new airport adjacent to the department capital and the Maya archaeological attraction of Tikal. In 2000, the region was finally connected by asphalt to the rest of the country.

Prior to construction of the 1970 overland dirt road to Guatemala City, the region was home to fewer than 5,000 people. As landless peasants and ranchers flocked to Petén, its population grew by 8–10 per cent annually, reaching the current estimated three-quarters of a million inhabitants. As on many Latin American frontiers, roads facilitated deforestation and land settlement. In turn, taxes from logging and land adjudication sales financed more second and third-class roads (roughly 100 km per year) (Schwartz, 1990). Land sales did occur during the colonization period, but then settlers could claim new parcels further north along an expanding road network. During Guatemala's three-decade civil war (1960s–1996, at its apex in the early 1980s), roads were also vectors of military violence. As late as the mid-1990s, travelling by bus was a risky undertaking; buses were stopped and searched at military checkpoints and any civilians suspected of being leftist insurgents and caught travelling without national identification papers could be arrested and thereafter 'disappear'.

Above the 17'10° parallel (roughly the northern third of Petén), the military kept the forests relatively free of roads and settlements, utilizing this zone as a private fiefdom for industrial timber and petroleum concessions, border defence manoeuvres against Mexico and (according to rumours) for their own trafficking in marijuana. When *National Geographic* published satellite photos showing deforestation in this military reserve from Mexican logging incursions along the Usumacinta River (Garrett and Garrett, 1989), key international conservation leaders were able to convince Vinicio Cerezo, Guatemala's first democratic president in decades, to establish the 1.6 million ha Maya Biosphere Reserve that would be connected to reserves in Mexico and Belize as a kind of tri-national peace park or 'Maya Forest' (Nations, 2006).

In the post-peace context, civil society was anxious to complete land titling and reclaim the freedom to travel. Many of Petén's elites invested in bus companies, opening new services and routes in the 1990s and diversifying into more customized mini-van transportation in the 2000s. At a time when many civic groups were demanding accountability, truth commissions and agrarian reform after the signing of the 1996 Peace Accords, Guatemala's leading political party tapped into populist transportation sentiment with the campaign slogan *Obras, no Palabras* ('Works not Words') and boosted Petén's road network to 1,033 km by 2004 (fieldnotes). Petén's unique combination of archaeological attractions, conservation and colonization programmes made it an easy target for two development-bank plans: the IDB's PPP and the World Bank's land administration projects, described below.

The PPP

With a projected budget of US$ 25 billion in public–private partnerships, the PPP represented an audacious infrastructure plan unparalleled in Central America and Mexico since the 1930s construction of the Pan-American Highway.[4] At a 2001 summit convened by Mexican President Vicente Fox, signatory nations made a loose preliminary agreement to increase regional trade and investment. In response to civil society opposition, the PPP was eventually renamed in 2008 as the 'Mesoamerican Integration and Development Project' (or Mesoamerica Project, for short),[5] but the logic of the plan remains essentially unchanged despite its new name. Hence, like many Guatemalan leaders, I continue to refer to it as the PPP. Organized into eight sectors headed by each of the seven original members, plus Belize, transport and energy dominated the original PPP budget (Table 1; see also AVANSCO and SERJUS, 2003) and continue to be the main features of the Mesoamerica Project today (Altmann, 2007), for a simple geopolitical reason.

The world's cheapest labour markets in Asia, especially China, are located half a planet away from its largest consumer base living along the densely populated east coast of the United States (Hansen, 2004). With use of the Panama Canal at a saturation point, and with the high cost of shipment via land across the US, North American-based corporations face a shipping bottleneck.[6] To create a third alternative, the PPP aimed to build and upgrade inter-oceanic highways that would connect the most proximate Atlantic and Pacific ports in Central America as 'dry canals', allowing intermodal containers to be transferred from ocean vessels to trucks, shipped via land across the narrowest parts of the isthmus, and then reloaded onto ocean vessels.

As illustrated in Figure 2, there are plans to add several east–west corridors to the International Network of Mesoamerican Highways,[7] as well as upgrading two north–south corridors along the Pacific and Atlantic coasts to speed transportation of commercial freight between Central America and Mexico. Other miscellaneous linkages are planned to connect the above routes with major cities, economic zones and tourist attractions (Baraquí, 2003; Zunino, 2010). Additional energy and infrastructure projects are intended to facilitate corporate investment. Indeed, the website www.investinguatemala.org features a revealing interactive map which allows the viewer to overlay roads and PPP transportation corridors with oil and mining contracts, electrical transmission networks and power generation points.[8]

TABLE 1. PPP Budgets by Sector

PPP Budget		2003	2007
Total (US$)		4.23 billion	5.45 billion
Sectors	**Coordinator country**	**Percent of overall budget**	
Transport	Costa Rica	84.0%	74.4%
Energy	Guatemala	9.6%	8.8%
Telecommunications	El Salvador	2.4%	1.1%
Sustainable development	Nicaragua	1.4%	4.1%
Human development	Mexico	1.0%	10.9%
Disaster prevention and response	Panama	0.6%	0.3%
Tourism	Belize	0.9%	0.0%
Competitiveness and trade facilitation	Honduras	0.2%	0.4%

Source: Created by author, based on AVANSCO and SERJUS (2003) and Altmann (2007).

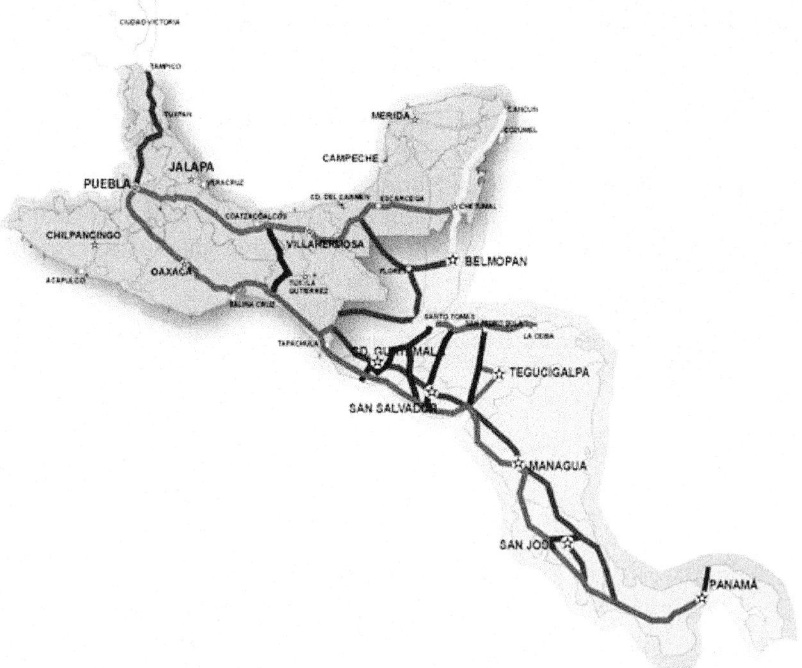

FIGURE 2. PPP Transportation Corridors.
Source: Inter-American Development Bank.

With nearly 800 km of unconnected international borders with Chiapas, the Yucatán Peninsula and Belize, and with proximity to Atlantic shipping ports, the Petén was an obvious target of early PPP transportation planning. This included a new connection to Chiapas; an upgrade to the existing overland route to Belize; the addition of a new road through south-eastern Petén, asphalting the route from Flores south through Sayaxché to the Franja Transversal highway; continued improvement of the highway to Guatemala City; and a highly controversial road through the Maya Biosphere Reserve into Campeche or Quintana Roo.

Notes

1. Clearly influenced by McNamara's emphasis on infrastructure as the means to development, the UN declared a Transport Decade (1978–88) following the World Development Decade (1968–78) (Hilling, 1996).
2. Although IIRSA was launched slightly earlier, anti-PPP activism via Central America's strongly integrated indigenous, peasant, human-rights networks peaked faster. See Pieck (2011) on IIRSA and Grandia (2007) on the PPP and related Mesoamerican Biological Corridor.
3. Guatemalans use synonymously the terms 'land administration' and *ordenamiento territorial* [territorial ordering].

4. The Pan-American Highway was proposed at the fifth International Conference of American States in Santiago, Chile, in 1923. Construction of the Guatemala portion, named after Franklin Delano Roosevelt, began in 1944 (López, 1981).
5. Official PPP members include: Mexico, Guatemala, Honduras, El Salvador, Nicaragua, Costa Rica and Panamá; Belize is involved informally; and Colombia, the Dominican Republic and Ecuador participate as observers. Sensing possible benefits to United States corporations, Governor Jeb Bush once proposed that Florida should also join (Barreda, 2004).
6. Nonetheless, through a US$ 5.15 billion project supported by loans, the Panamanian government is upgrading its Canal to support longer and wider ships that can carry two to three times the current cargo limit (Fountain, 2011).
7. Red International de Carreteras Mesoamericanas (RICAM).
8. Thanks to L. Solano for bringing this map to my attention (Solano, 2012).

Water releases, holding metals, acidic materials, excessive use of water, topsoil destruction, and sickness to the population are some of the effects of mining in El Salvador. The author traced back the damage inflicted upon the Salvadoran communities of Cabañas, the resistance of the organized movement, and the violence against community leaders of the opposition to gold mining. It also addresses the work between the organized community, NGOs, and government to ban the exploitation of gold in El Salvador.

A Mining Ban in El Salvador?

Emily Achtenberg

Will Tiny El Salvador, where two thirds of the population lives on less than $2 a day; become the first nation on the planet to legally ban gold mining? On June 28, President Mauricio Funes reaffirmed his campaign promise that no metals mining would be permitted in El Salvador during his administration. Despite the potential relief that mining revenues could offer his cash-strapped government, Funes said, "I will not put the public health of the population at risk in exchange for some additional income that we might receive."

> The average metallic mine uses 24,000 gallons of water per hour, or what a typical Salvadoran family consumes in 20 years. Toxic runoff, leaks, or spills could cause contamination, and the Cabañas region is prone to earthquakes and torrential rains, heightening safety concerns.

The National Roundtable Against Mining (known as the Mesa), a coalition of community, environmental, and human rights organizations that has led the anti-mining struggle, wants the government to go one step further—by passing a bill sponsored by Funes's party, the Farabundo Marti Liberation Front (FMLN), that would permanently ban metals mining. They note that even conservative ex-president Tony Saca declared his opposition to mining in 2008, in response to public pressure. What's needed, they say, is for the ban to be legally codified, rather than leaving mining policy to the discretion of each successive president.

The growing resistance to mining in El Salvador has focused on Pacific Rim, a Canada-based transnational that received a permit in 2002 to begin exploratory work on a massive gold mine in the north-central department of Cabañas. The mine is located in the basin of the country's largest river, the Lempa, which is one of the few remaining uncontaminated water sources in El Salvador, supplying nearly half the country, including the capital, San Salvador. After Pacific Rim was granted its exploratory permit, a surge of applications by other mining companies followed, as gold prices sky-rocketed and opportunities for private investment increased under the Dominican Republic–Central American Free Trade Agreement (DR-CAFTA).

The Mesa argues that the water-intensive cyanide ore process used by mining companies like Pacific Rim will undermine rural farming and fishing economies, and deplete drinking-water supplies—the average metallic mine uses 24,000 gallons of water per hour, or about what a typical Salvadoran family consumes in 20 years. Toxic runoff, leaks, or spills could cause widespread contamination, and Cabañas is prone to earthquakes and torrential rains, further heightening public health and safety concerns. Such problems would add to the many environmental challenges already facing El Salvador, which is arguably the second-most environmentally degraded country in the Americas (after Haiti).

Although Pacific Rim and other mining companies promise jobs and tax revenues to benefit affected communities, the Mesa says few local residents have the technical skills to qualify for a permanent position. Under existing law, only 3% of mining profits would be paid to the Salvadoran government for potential reinvestment in social and economic programs. In any case, the projected operational life of Pacific Rim's Cabañas mine is just six years.

Mining has also caused social conflict and violence in communities still struggling to overcome the effects of El Salvador's civil war (1980–92). Pacific Rim targets funds for scholarships, schools, and other benefits to municipalities (and mayors) not directly impacted by mining, creating friction with those communities that are affected. In this context of mounting tension, four anti-mining activists in Cabañas have been killed since 2009 in what the Mesa describes as targeted assassinations. Dozens more, including environmental leaders, priests, and community radio journalists, have received death threats, which the company blames on "internal feuds"—that is, the very conflicts that its presence has created.

While some of those who carried out the murders have been convicted, the "intellectual authors" of these crimes have never been prosecuted. For anti-mining activists, the persistence of this climate of impunity evokes bitter memories of the civil war, with communities once again facing the threat of displacement and the loss of land and natural resources that they fought and died to protect.

In 2007, more than two thirds of those polled by the San Salvador–based Central American University agreed that the mining of precious metals should be banned in El Salvador. Faced with growing opposition from civil society, the Catholic Church, and even from the Saca government, Pacific Rim failed to complete the technical steps required to secure its permit for mining operations. In 2008, the company ceased all exploratory activities.

Pacific Rim then sued the Salvadoran government for $77 million under DR-CAFTA, alleging that the government's failure to approve an extraction permit had violated its investors' rights. The case, which is pending in a World Bank court, represents the first challenge to a sovereign government's environmental policy under DR-CAFTA. A subsequent lawsuit filed by another gold-mining company in the same court was dismissed on a technicality in March, but only after the Salvadoran government spent $800,000 defending its claim.

The DR-CAFTA lawsuit was clearly on the mind of Environmental Minister Hermán Rosa Chávez when he met with a delegation from the Cambridge–El Salvador Sister Cities project in June, just a few days before Funes announced that no mining would take place during his administration. According to Rosa Chávez, a critical tool in formulating the administration's new mining policy and legislative proposal will be the strategic environmental assessment that Funes commissioned from a Spanish consulting firm in 2010. The study, which is in its final stages, will evaluate the costs and benefits of metals mining in El Salvador. Both transnational mining companies and anti-mining activists are eagerly anticipating the results.

The Mesa, however, is concerned that the study's highly technical framework may obscure what should be a foregone conclusion. "Instead of wasting money on this consulting project," says Francisco Pineda, a farmer who was recently awarded the Goldman Environmental Price for his anti-mining work in Cabañas, "we should be studying how to help the communities most affected by the environmental damage" caused by mining.

But a major goal, according to Rosa Chávez, is to insulate the Funes government from legal challenges by Pacific Rim and other mining transnational. With 26 active exploration permits inherited from past governments and 73 pending applications, the government's potential legal exposure is enormous. The study will also help to build consensus within the government, including the legislature, which has diverse views on mining. (The FMLN has the largest voting bloc, but not a majority.)

For these reasons, Rosa Chávez says, the study must weigh alternative scenarios, ranging from selectively promoting certain types of mining to a partial or complete ban. "We are the government now," he explains. "We have to play by the formal rules."

Rosa Chávez believes that metallic mining, especially gold mining, is difficult to justify under current conditions in El Salvador. He's confident that the blue ribbon commission he hand-picked to oversee the environmental study will come to the same conclusion. And if mining is not appropriate for Cabañas, Rosa Chávez said, Funes will want to know what alternative regional development strategies the government should support—such as the sustainable farming initiatives that local communities are already developing.

The Mesa recognizes that renouncing gold mining would be an epic decision for El Salvador, with significant global implications. Though the stakes are high, it may be easier for El Salvador to ban mining than for countries already heavily dependent on mining export revenues—including those with left-leaning governments, like Bolivia and Ecuador. If Funes recommends a ban, the Mesa believes that popular pressure will force the legislature to support it, especially with local and congressional elections coming up next year.

But at the end of the day, Rosa Chávez stresses, governments and public officials should never be trusted. On that point, the Mesa fully agrees.

CHAPTER SIX

DIVERSE ETHNIC AND CULTURAL PRACTICES

As we have discussed earlier, Central America is a region of multiple ethnic and cultural identities and practices. In this chapter, we are particularly interested in conveying not only this diversity, but also the exchanges that take place among different communities and groups in the region today. As a result, our interest is not to present a sample of these identities, nor to attempt to define any group or community from an *essentialist* perspective. To the contrary, we will pay particular attention to the intersection between race, class, ethnicity, gender and culture, as well as to the exchanges that take place between Western and non-Western ways of understanding culture, economy, prosperity, religion, history, and the concept of the nation in general.

Identities are malleable, and the interactions and exchanges of a community with alternative perspectives and worldviews transform them. They are constructed both with historical and cultural links to a community's own past and within the historical, economic, social and political context in which they exist today.

One of the most important aspects to take into consideration as we explore diversity in Central America is the fact that the modern construction of Central American national identities disseminated the idea that national identity should be homogeneous for each individual nation in the region. As a result, throughout the modern history of Central American nations, many have often perceived diversity as an obstacle for progress. In contrast, a homogeneous *Ladino/Mestizo* national identity has been presented as the ideal for the national subject in order to implement modernity and to bring progress to these nations. As we explored in Chapter 3, this obsession with the homogenization of Central American national identities has also played an important role in the justification of numerous human rights violations in an attempt to erase diversity from the actual landscape of these nations or from the cultural panorama built throughout the modern period in the region.

In examining diversity in Central America it is unavoidable to address and problematize the issues of racism, the politics of race and the racialization of cultural practices. Since the arrival of the first Europeans, these issues have permeated and defined identities and have hierarchically classified cultural practices. Based on biological notions of superiority the early Spanish colonizers established a legal and political order that has ensured the dominance of their descendants until today. Although these biological ideas have been discredited they continue to support modern and contemporary arguments on socio-political, economic and religious practices. Furthermore, this biological narrative has produced political agendas that have transformed some components of that rich diversity that still exists in Central America today. However, the imposition of this narrative has also produced alternative discursive practices of resistance and challenge to this process of homogeneity.

Indigenous and Afro-Caribbean cultural identities have resisted a violent and copious attack by the modern nation that has had great implications for their daily life, subsistence, access to basic needs, political oppression and cultural exclusion. Cultural and ethnic diversity exists in contention to the cultural and political dynamics imposed by the Central American modern nations. We can gather examples to illustrate this dynamic from colonial times, as a whole taxonomy or classification of peoples was defined in order to establish a social hierarchy. We can also gather them from the time of independence, as equality and the end of slavery were announced at the same time national citizenship was defined in Eurocentric terms with Spanish as the national language for most Central American nations. We can gather them as well from the period of the liberal reforms that enabled the privatization of the land while often excluding Indigenous communities from owning land based on their cultural practices. Examples are also available from the more contemporary use of Black and Indigenous labor for the production of coffee and bananas, the two products that enabled Central America to participate in the world economy; from the contemporary efforts to question Indigenous and Black participation in national politics; and from the implementation of neoliberal economic policies.

This chapter includes four articles that discuss three main issues. On the one hand, the first two articles discuss the links between the definition of ethnic and cultural identities and the legal claim for land rights within the modern nations for two separate cultural groups, the Garifunas in Honduras and Indigenous and Black communities in the Atlantic coast of Nicaragua. On the other hand, the third article in the chapter discusses the syncretic experience of Catholicism and contemporary Indigenous practices in El Salvador. Furthermore, it examines one of the traditional forms of organizing for the Cacaopera Indigenous community in contemporary El Salvador. Finally, the last article in this chapter explores cultural resistance and cultural visibility in the changing cultural landscape of Costa Rica.

Eva T. Thorne's article documents the problematic relationship between the recognition of a cultural identity within the context of the nation and the negotiation of land rights for Garífuna communities in Honduras. Garífuna people emerged after the mixing of Indigenous communities and a group of shipwrecked African slaves on the island of Saint Vincent in the seventeenth century. From there they were forced to migrate to other locations, including the island of Roatán, close to the Atlantic coast of Honduras. They eventually moved on to populate that region as well as parts of the Atlantic coast of Guatemala and Belize. In more recent years, a number of them have migrated to the north, and a Garífuna community has settled in Southern California. However, the largest Garífuna population continues to live in Honduras. While forced migration has impacted their background, they have lived within a gray area between the recognition of their Afro-Caribbean identity and their status as an Indigenous group in the Honduran nation.

Because of the way in which the context of the modern nation of Honduras defines Indigenous and Afro-descendant identities, Indigenous peoples' land rights have been recognized in some contexts, while Afro-descendants do not have access to those same rights. In the case of Garífuna peoples, the gray area of the definition of their identity—that is, their Indigenous roots and their arrival to the Central American region prior to the formation of the modern nations—has allowed them to qualify as an Indigenous community in Honduras. In order to do so, this community has been forced to document through oral traditions and memory their historical presence in the region prior to independence, their background as descendants of escaped slaves and their traditional use of the lands. However, these rights are relative as Thorne illustrates in her discussion the ways in which the tourist industry and neoliberal economic policies in Honduras today continue encroaching upon the Garífuna communities in spite of the recognition of their land rights.

Land Rights and Garífuna Identity

EVA T. THORNE

The history of the Garífuna people has long been tied to land. The Garífuna originate from the 17th century when, on the windward Caribbean island of St. Vincent, the island's indigenous Arawak-Caribs integrated runaway and shipwrecked African slaves into their communities. European colonists first referred to their progeny as "Black Caribs" and later "Garífuna," as they are still known. When the English pushed out the French settlers of St. Vincent and sought possession of the island, they encountered fierce resistance from the Garífuna. The conflict erupted into a yearlong war in 1772, ending in a treaty considered by most accounts to be the first signed between the British and an indigenous Caribbean population.

A second war broke out over the failure of the British to honor the terms of the treaty, but this time the overpowered Garífuna surrendered on British terms. The entire population was imprisoned for a year in a camp on a nearby island, where more than half perished. The survivors were then loaded onto the *H.M.S. Experiment,* no less, and transported thousands of miles away to the Honduran island of Roatán. From there, they fanned out throughout the Caribbean coast of Central America. Garífuna communities now ring the coast from Belize and Guatemala to Honduras and Nicaragua.

Honduras currently has the largest population of Garifuna at 250,000, according to the country's Special Office on Ethnicity and Cultural Heritage. Their communities reside, as they have for generations, along the northern coast of the country and La Mosquitia in the east. There, they have managed to preserve their language and many cultural practices, including unique musical, culinary and religious forms. The high degree of coherence and continuity that characterizes their cultural identity and residency patterns has become central to their renewed struggles to secure land.

In fact, the increasingly powerful Garífuna community in Honduras leads one of the more successful Afro-descendant land rights movements in Latin America. As part of their political mobilization, they have affirmed their racial and ethnic identity to strengthen their collective territorial claims. Indeed, the partial victories of the land rights struggles of Honduras' Garífuna cannot be understood without taking into account the ways in which this community has successfully politicized and linked identity and land, and forced the Honduran government to recognize this linkage.

Land conflicts have occurred regularly In Latin American societies for centuries, and they continue to do so despite the regional trend toward rapid urbanization. Access to land has long been documented to play a vital role in reducing rural poverty and remains an important political and policy issue in the region. Most Afro-descendant communities in Latin America are still heavily reliant on access to land for their cultural, economic, environmental and social security. In recent years, these communities have asserted collective claim to the lands they have inhabited since the colonial era, pressuring national governments to provide them formal title.

As a central element of this struggle, rural blacks across Latin America are demanding recognition as distinct ethnic groups with group-specific rights, including to land and territory. Here, the distinction between race and ethnicity is important. In the juridical context of most countries of the region, historically derived ethnicity, and not race *per se,* forms the legal basis for collective claims to a distinct territory. Not all rural black communities can successfully claim such rights: only those able to document their history as communities founded by escaped slaves. Thus, most Afro-descendant groups pursuing collective land rights have begun their struggles for land by first upholding a set of claims relating to ethnic lineage and historic residency. Typically, these groups first seek legitimation based on social memories of their battles, dating from the colonial era, against racial oppression. They also affirm their distinct ethnic identity and link this to longstanding occupation of a given territory, dating from before the founding of the independent Latin American nation state. These claims confer upon them indigenous-like legal status.

This strategy stems from the constitutional reforms that became an integral part of the Latin American political landscape as democratization swept the region in the 1980s. While these reforms often legally enshrined authoritarian enclaves that shaped the emerging democratic regimes, they also contained elements of promise for the promotion of popular interests. In particular they allowed for land reform, one category of which was ethnic-specific, introduced to address Afro-descendant and indigenous land claims. These reforms reflected increasing governmental acknowledgment of the pluricultural and multiethnic character of the region's populations.

As a result, in some Latin American countries rural Afro-descendant communities are now legally recognized as having a distinct ethnicity and as commanding the right to collective and communal land title. In 1988, the Brazilian Constitution adopted Transitory Article 68, which recognized the land claims of descendants of the country's escaped slave communities, known as *quilombos.* In Colombia, the land rights of blacks on the Pacific coast gained constitutional recognition in 1991 with Transitory Article 55, which was implemented with the 1993 approval of Law 70.[2] Article 83 of the 1998 Constitution of Ecuador granted Afro-Ecuadorians collective rights to ancestral lands.

Indigenous groups have often been granted additional rights not afforded to Afro-descendant groups. In Colombia, for example, indigenous communities were granted not only rights over land but also political, jurisdictional autonomy, so that local, indigenous-led governments now govern their own territories. In sharp distinction, no such privileges have been granted Afro-descendant communities.

The legal logic behind ethnically based land claims can be both empowering and exclusionary. It is empowering insofar as it accepts the legitimacy of deeply rooted, ethnically distinct community identities. It is exclusionary to the extent it demands strict ethnohistorical "proof" that draws potentially controversial boundaries within and between communities, excluding those unable to generate acceptable documentation. In the notable cases of Brazil, Colombia and Ecuador, for example, to be eligible to claim land rights a community must be able to clearly demarcate the territory linked to its historically rooted identity. In Honduras and Nicaragua, groups must show that they have traditionally used their lands. Such requirements imply the prerequisite of cultural or ethnic distinctiveness.

Although some Afro-descendant communities define themselves in ethnic terms, the dominant societies in which they exist insist upon viewing them still as strictly racial groups, negating these communities' diverse self-conceptions.[3] Their social and political marginalization partly stems from their identification as racially Other and, complicating matters further, in some instances the communities themselves claim both ethnic and racial identities.[4] These issues of racial and ethnic identity further overlap with land titling and natural resource use and require better integration, both analytically and practically.

These complicated issues are all at play in the land struggles of Honduras' Garífuna. The Garífuna are one of nine recognized ethnic groups in Honduras, which collectively represent about 13% of the country's population. The Garífuna alone account for approximately 2%.

Among those practices that distinguish the Garífuna as a separate ethnic group are a particular set of subsistence activities and a related gendered division of labor. Garífuna men engage in non-commercial, low-intensity fishing in both the ocean and rivers. They also hunt, mainly deer and iguana. In agricultural production, men are usually responsible for soil preparation as well as slashing and burning, while both men and women are involved in the sowing, harvesting and storage of the crop. Women cultivate and grate yucca, dry it, and then bake it over hot coals into the finished product, cassava bread, some of which is reserved for local market consumption. Women are also responsible for the sale of surplus fish and agricultural products. (With massive male migration abroad from Garífuna communities, a growing non-traditional male subsistence role is the provision of remittances, while women increasingly assume the formerly male responsibilities of property transactions and maintenance.)

The Garífuna maintain other unique cultural practices such as the Garífuna language, a particular set of religious beliefs and associated practices, as well as culturally specific festivals. Many of these practices are inextricably linked to the group's conceptions of land and territory: Community festivals mark the planting and harvest seasons and particular fishing activities, for example, and Garífuna cosmology invokes very specific notions about the land and how it is to be treated.

With respect to land rights, the Garífuna occupy a complex position. Legal and constitutional instruments are often too narrow to acknowledge the diverse ways in which Garífuna self-perceive and position themselves externally. Although they have been racialized within the categories of *negro* (black) and *moreno* (dark-skinned), the Garífuna see themselves, and are seen, as both a racial and an ethnic group. As a group, they have experienced high levels of discrimination ever since their arrival in Honduras, characterized by the denial of social and civil rights. Historic indicators of their exclusion include their concentration in low-wage labor positions and their lack of access to public spaces and higher learning, In these ways, their experience recalls that of blacks in the United States during the Jim Crow era. Their "blackness" has also excluded them from Honduran national identity, which, as in most Latin American countries, is characterized as mestizo. This concept incorporates a mix of European and indigenous qualities, but largely ignores and/or marginalizes Honduran society's African legacy. This exclusion from the hegemonic understanding of national belonging previously undermined the ability of the Garífuna to make group-specific claims. Active political mobilization, however, has largely attenuated the Latin American myth of the mestizo nation.

To the extent that the reality of cultural difference has been acknowledged and addressed in conceptions of national identity, legal frameworks and public policies in Honduras, this largely has been the accomplishment of indigenous people. These groups have successfully commanded official recognition as distinct, collective subjects with specific languages, cosmologies, and relationships to land and territory. Moreover, they have won special legal status by virtue of their pre-European presence in Honduras.

It is within this rubric of "the indigenous" that the Garífuna have gained political leverage. First, the Garífuna originated from a mixing of Africans with an indigenous

Caribbean population. Significant elements of their language are Amerindian in origin, as are other elements of their unique, indigenous-like identity. For example, they organize their communities communally, especially with respect to land tenure and agricultural practices, much like their indigenous counterparts. Second, they are "indigenous" to Honduras in that they arrived before the republic won independence from Spain in the 1800s.

Garífuna leaders have used this indigenous framework to promote their case with the Honduran state. They have also reached out for international points of leverage, taking advantage of the overarching institutional framework characteristic of this era of globalization. For instance, they successfully pressured the Honduran state to recognize the applicability to their status of International Labor Organization Convention 169 on indigenous peoples. They have also gained considerable ground through analogous policies within multilateral development banks, such as the World Bank and the Inter-American Development Bank. These legal instruments and institutional policies, with their provisions for group land rights, have offered the Garífuna a critical foothold by which to proceed with their claims. Ironically, however, the same international bodies are also indirectly undermining Garífuna gains. The World Bank has provided the government of Honduras with a loan for coastal and tourism development, which may have profoundly negative consequences for Garífuna communities and their struggle for land.[5]

Since Garífuna communities are located along the country's spectacular northern beaches, the growth of tourism imperils their land claim efforts. Tourism has become Honduras' second largest source of foreign exchange. According to the National Tourism Institute, in 2001 tourism generated $256.2 million from 483,300 tourists—the majority from neighboring Central American countries, about a third from the United States. The government projects a more than 5% annual increase in tourism and anticipates Honduras will attract one million foreign tourists and generate 30,000 direct and 40,000 indirect jobs over the next four years.[6]

Honduras' tourism plan centers on a combination of six attractions: archaeology, colonial cities, nature and adventure, beaches and *culturas vivas* (living cultures). As the centerpiece of the country's tourism effort, its ecotourism program offers an extensive system of national parks and protected areas created over the past 20 years. Through the coordination of the Honduras Tourism Institute and the Ministry of the Environment (SEDA), the government has made a concerted effort to attract foreign investment to the industry.

Foreign investment in the tourism sector necessitates clarity around existing land ownership. Honduran constitutional recognition of Garífuna land rights puts valuable lands under a communal titling regime that is, at least theoretically, immune to market logic. The representative political institutions of Garífuna communities, known as *patronatos,* hold the communal land titles. These titles grant the community rights to a given area in perpetuity. They may not sell the land or transfer its ownership outside the community. Improvements, such as houses and other buildings, can be bought and sold within the community, but the land remains inalienable.

Meanwhile, the tourism boom of recent years and the consequent demand for valuable beachfront property has created incentives for land invasions and intimidation, as well as bribery and outright violence against Garífuna communities. While other commercial interests have historically threatened encroachment on Garífuna lands, tourism has greatly amplified the intensity and dimensions of this threat. Some community members have responded by illegally selling their land to outsiders, often fearing they will lose their land without financial compensation if they refuse to sell. Some patronatos have also engaged in illegal land sales to outsiders. Because of such sales, and because Honduran political and legal institutions are often ineffective and corrupt, nearly all Garífuna territories suffer from multiple ownership claims. This has made foreign investment in coastal tourism contentious and difficult to manage.

These threats to Garífuna land have generated a massive grassroots political response. Since the late 1980s, a number of Garífuna-led organizations have arisen. Two are especially prominent: the Black Fraternal Organization of Honduras (OFRANEH) and the Ethnic Community Development Organization (ODECO), both of which have offices in La Ceiba, on the Atlantic coast. OFRANEH is a grassroots support organization. ODECO, the more powerful of the two nongovernmental organizations (NGOs) in terms of its international reach and funding, serves as an intermediary between international aid agencies and Garífuna communities. Both have played a key role in pressuring the Honduran government to honor its constitutional commitment to title Garífuna land. They are active in public education and consciousness-raising, political advocacy and lobbying, community organizing, development work and fundraising.

Until 1992 all the Garífuna communities in Honduras, with the exception of those of Cristales and Río Negro, possessed only *títulos de ocupación* (titles of occupation) for their lands. These titles acknowledged the community's presence on the land but not its right to full and legal ownership. In 1996, Garífuna NGOs and patronatos united under the umbrella of the National Coordinator of Black Organizations of Honduras (CNONH) to mobilize more than five thousand people for the "First Grand Peaceful March of the Black People of Honduras." This demonstration sought to pressure the Honduran government into addressing *titulación* (titling), *ampliación* (enlargement) and *saneamiento* (dealing with third parties) in Garífuna communities. The *Coordinadora,* as the coalition was known, succeeded in securing a meeting with a presidential commission, which resulted in an agreement to set aside the equivalent of $227,000 for the National Agrarian Institute to title Garífuna lands.

Between 1997 and 2002, most Garífuna communities received formal ownership titles to a significant portion of land. This major accomplishment reflects the Garífuna's success in pressing for the recognition of their ethnic distinctness and their linking of this identity to lands of traditional occupation. In most cases, however, the titles are limited and apply only to the *casco urbano* of the community. In other words, communal titles have generally been granted only to areas where Garífuna houses are actually located, leaving untitled areas where the communities' agricultural activities take place. Yet these areas—in addition to those used historically by the community for hunting, fishing and other activities—comprise the majority of Garífunas' territorial claims. Mestizo cattle ranchers, real estate speculators, large businesses and foreigners target these territories for invasions. Powerful Honduran military, business and political actors hold land in these areas and have sponsored a number of legislative efforts designed to reduce the size of Garífuna territory. Although several Garífuna agricultural cooperatives did surmount these powerful competing interests and receive title in 1998, the struggle is clearly unfinished and the obstacles remain substantial.

Notes

1. See Coordenação Estadual dos Quilombos Maranhenses, CCN, SMDDH, PVN, "Documento Referente as Chamadas Terras de Preto no Estado do Maranhão," São Luis-Maranhão May, 1996; O Estado do Maranhão, "Comunidades Negras: Terras e cultural preservadas," São Luis Maranhão, May 21, 1996.
2. For more on blacks in Colombia, see Jaime Arocha, "Afro-Colombia Denied," *NACLA Report on the Americas,* 25(4), pp 28–31; Alexander Cifuentes, "Propuesta de desarrollo legislativo: del Articulo Transitorio 55 de la Constitución Política de Colombia," in A. Cifuentes, Al. Mauricio and J. Velasquez, editors. *La Nueva Constitución y La Territorialidad en El Pacífico Colombiano* (Cali: Corporación SOS Colombia, 1993). For more on land titling of black lands in Chocó, see Ministerio del Medio Ambiente and Instituto Colombiano de la Reforma Agraria—INCORA, *La Capacitación y la Titulación Colectiva en los Territorios Afrocolombianos.* For a grassroots activist's perspective, see Vicente Murrain, "Securing Legal Rights for AfroColombians: A Grassroots Organizer's View," in Margaret H. Frondorf, editor, *Local People and Lawyers: Building Alliances for Policy Change* (Washington, DC: Paul H. Nitze School of Advanced International Studies Program on Social Change and Development, The Johns Hopkins University), pp. 15–24.
3. For example, in Chocó, Colombia, residents refer to themselves as Afro-Colombian and view themselves as an ethnic group. Quilombos in Brazil often see themselves racially, however. In Honduras, some Garífuna see themselves as both racial and ethnic, depending on context.
4. In Panama, Colombia, Nicaragua, and elsewhere, mixed black/indigenous identities are common.
5. In July of 2001 the World Bank's soft loan window, International Development Association, approved a $5 million, interest-free credit for The Sustainable Coastal Tourism Project. See, http://wbln0018.worldbank.org/MesoAm/UmbpubHP.nsf/917d9f0f503e647e8525677c007e0ab8/aa7c3cbbf399e7ee8525682c006f1889?OpenDocument.
6. Edmund T. Gordon, "San Juan: A Case Study," unpublished manuscript, written for a World Bank-funded study on Garífuna and Miskito land rights, October 2002.

This article discusses land rights of Indigenous, Garífuna and Afro-descendant or Creole communities living on the Atlantic coast of Nicaragua. It explains these communities' contention that the Nicaraguan state does not have legitimate authority over their territories. It also argues that Nicaraguan national rights do not apply to their lands, particularly based on their occupation of these lands prior to the formation of the modern Nicaraguan state as well as the historical background of the region as part of the British colonial territories. This article traces the historical background of the conflict from the formation of the nation and *Ladino/Mestizo* efforts to establish their governments in the region. It also explores Sandinista claims that national sovereignty had precedence over Indigenous, Garifuna and Creole communities positioning as a threat to national sovereignty. Furthermore, it examines the implementation and recognition of autonomous governance for the region, inaugurated in 1990.

In addition, this article documents the experience of fieldwork by a team of three anthropologists in the coastal region of Nicaragua, both with the support of the World Bank and the support of the Indigenous and Creole communities. Their objective was to answer two main questions: What land did each of the 133 communities claim as its own? And: How did they justify their claims?

The article documents the training of community-based investigators as well as the researchers' own experience creating maps for their land claims. While this effort required active community participation, lengthy discussions, questions about land claim overlap by different communities and other obstacles, it also empowered these communities.

Rights, Resources, and the Social Memory of Struggle

Reflections on a Study of Indigenous and Black Community Land Rights on Nicaragua's Atlantic Coast

EDMUND T. GORDON, GALIO C. GURDIÁN, AND CHARLES R. HALE

Since the electoral defeat of the Sandinistas in 1990, political relations within Nicaragua's Atlantic Coast region, and between the region and various external actors, have been exceedingly volatile. More often than not, rights to land and resources have stood at the

"Rights, Resources, and the Social Memory of Struggle: Reflections on a Study of Indigenous and Black Community Land Rights on Nicaragua's Atlantic Coast," by Edmond T. Gordon et al., *Human Organization*, 62.4, Winter 2003, pp. 369–381. Reprinted by permission of the Society for Applied Anthropology.

center of this volatility. Here we report and reflect on a study of indigenous and Afro-Nicaraguan, or "Creole," land rights financed by the World Bank. This study emerged from, and was carried out within, a dense thicket of contradictions.

While research and media reports have focused mainly on conflicts between the region and the central government, and between coast communities and transnational companies, the role of multilateral development institutions such as the World Bank has been generally neglected. Yet the bank has exerted a powerful influence in questions of land tenure and rights to resources among coast communities, all the more important because the thrust of this influence at first glance appears counterintuitive. According to standard accounts, the World Bank defends and promotes neoliberal economic development policies, which give precedence to the logic of the capitalist market and tolerate cultural rights only if they do not contravene these first principles. Yet in Nicaragua and elsewhere, especially since the internal reforms of 1991, World Bank policies have provided substantive support for indigenous rights initiatives that appear to challenge aspects of that neoliberal economic framework. (For an analysis of these bank reforms, see Treakle 1998 and Gray 1998.)

Not only did World Bank funds support a research and social process that stood in tension with its own mandate, but the study formed part of a broader effort to nudge the Nicaraguan government toward a more tolerant stance on indigenous cultural and resource rights. The government reluctantly agreed to the study only after being threatened with the freezing of bank funds for other projects. Moreover, the specific bank-funded project—Tecnología Agropecuaria y Ordenamiento de la Propiedad Agraria (Agricultural and Livestock Technology and the Regulation of Agricultural Property)—from which funding for the study originated had the principal objective of "agricultural modernization" and was undertaken in collaboration with the (now defunct) Nicaraguan government entity called the Instituto Nicaraguense de Reforma Agraria (Institute for Agrarian Reform [INRA]). Yet most indigenous and Creole peoples considered INRA, which has provided individual land titles to many rural Mestizos in disputed areas, to be one of their principal adversaries in the struggle for land and resources. The Ministero del Ambiente y los Recursos Naturales de Nicaragua (Nicaraguan Ministry of Environment and Natural Resources [MARENA]) is viewed in a similar way.

Within regional coast politics, opposition to the study came not only from predictable sources—threatened powerful interests—but also from an enigmatic and influential indigenous organization called the Consejo de Ancianos (Council of Elders). This group held that any study of *individual* community land rights would undermine the legitimacy of their *territorial* claims to the entire region. Strangely enough, the consejo itself recently received World Bank funding as part of a broader effort to encourage the participation of "civil society" organizations in bank development initiatives.

Three anthropologists, all of whom worked during the Sandinista decade with the Centro de Investigaciones y Documentación de la Costa Atlántica (Center for the Investigation and Documentation of the Atlantic Coast [CIDCA]), coordinated the study. While CIDCA consistently and strongly supported indigenous and Creole land rights during that period, we also worked from a position of critical support for the Sandinista revolution and deep opposition to the imperialist intervention of the United States in Nicaragua. To be offered, much less to accept, World Bank funding for our research during the 1980s would have been inconceivable. (Reports on that research can be found in Gordon 1998; Hale 1994; and Gurdián 2001.)

Contradictions notwithstanding, the opportunity to carry out this study opened an important space, which we could not pass up. It offered financial support for what we viewed as a crucial step in the ongoing struggles of coast peoples for legally validated rights to their lands. More generally, it was the main type of space within which progressive political initiatives in Nicaragua currently occur; that is, opportunities to pursue incremental, negotiated change from within, pushing at the limits of what is conceded from above, while avoiding all-out mobilizations for utopian transformations. The study itself was conceived as a *diagnóstico* (research and analysis) of 128 coast communities, focused primarily on each community's claims for land and resources and their own justifications for these claims. We also carried out research on the history of the "land rights question" on the coast generally and the specific history of each community claim.

The World Bank contracted through INRA with the Central American and Caribbean Research Council (CACRC) to coordinate the diagnóstico. We direct CACRC, based in Austin, Texas, which is devoted to activist research and pedagogy on issues of racial justice, cultural rights, and the distribution of resources. Once the contract was signed in early 1997, CACRC quickly established a close collaborative relationship with CIDCA, whose personnel—all coast natives (*costeños*)—carried out much of the field research under our direction.

We knew from the outset that the research would produce meaningful results only if community members participated actively in the collection and validation of the data on which the diagnóstico's analysis would be based. In addition to methodological feasibility, this principle of participatory action research had a broader ethical and political grounding. We assumed the collective process of identifying community land claims, recounting to diagnóstico researchers the justifications for these claims, and assessing the results of the research would clarify and strengthen their long-standing efforts to achieve legal recognition of their claims. This assumption was amply borne out.

The participatory process yielded answers to the immediate research question: What lands and resources do community members claim as their own? These answers can be summarized as follows:

1. Community members throughout the coast have well-elaborated justifications for their land claims, which are grounded in reference to political institutions that existed in the region before the advent of Nicaraguan state sovereignty.
2. Community members also vigorously deny the validity of the concept of "national lands," from which derives the Nicaraguan government's claim to a priori dominion over untitled territory and its ability to grant land rights in the first place.

3. Although many costeños have an expansive notion of territorial rights, they also have very specific ideas of the land and resources that they occupy and use and that therefore belong to their own community. In most cases, community spokespeople now articulate these claims as "multicommunity blocs" (*bloques*), which are the product of prior agreements among two or more communities to pool their community land to create one aggregate claim.

4. These bloques, taken together, cover approximately 24,650 square kilometers and are contiguous throughout the area of study, which reiterates the community members' contention that "national lands" do not exist. Figures 1 and 2 are maps of the Región Autónoma Atlántico Sur (Autonomous Region of the South Atlantic [RAAS]) and the Región Autónoma Atlántico Norte (Autonomous Region of the North Atlantic [RAAN]) respectively, with outline maps of black and indigenous communal land claims drawn in. These autonomous regions cover the entire length of Nicaragua's Caribbean coastline. The maps graphically demonstrate how the multicommunal claims of the region's indigenous and afro-descended peoples overlap and contest the existence of unoccupied "national" lands between them.

5. Although many of the bloques are in a state of evolution, and in some cases were constituted in the course of the diagnóstico research process itself, they also have deep historical antecedents—in prior grants of community titles, in shared occupation and use, and in long-standing patterns of interaction, cooperation, and collective identity formation.

While we expected the diagnóstico to yield empirical results of this sort, we did not anticipate this research method would be so rich and revelatory in theoretical terms as well. In particular, the research helped advance our analysis of this broader concern: How to analyze indigenous and Creole identities in ways that affirm their variable, fluid, and constructed character, while simultaneously giving appropriate weight to the continuities—in collective self-representation, relations with others, and in relation to space and territory—on which that identity rests? This question takes on particular urgency in discussions of land rights because phrases like "continuous occupancy" and "areas of traditional use" are so easily converted into a litmus test for juridical legitimacy. Yet notions of "rights to the land," like identity itself, are multifaceted at any point in time and historically variable. How, then, do we talk about processes of identity formation and assertions of land rights, giving due consideration to how they are made, while rejecting the counterargument that they have been simply "made up"?

Rather than merely summarize the diagnóstico, we take the process itself as our subject of analysis in the pages that follow. First, we provide a brief historical backdrop for the study, noting four episodes—each centered around access to land and resources—that occupy a central role in costeños' collective memory. The final episode—land demands and ethnopolitical conflict in the Sandinista era—brings us to the 1990s. A second section begins with a brief analysis of Atlantic Coast politics in this

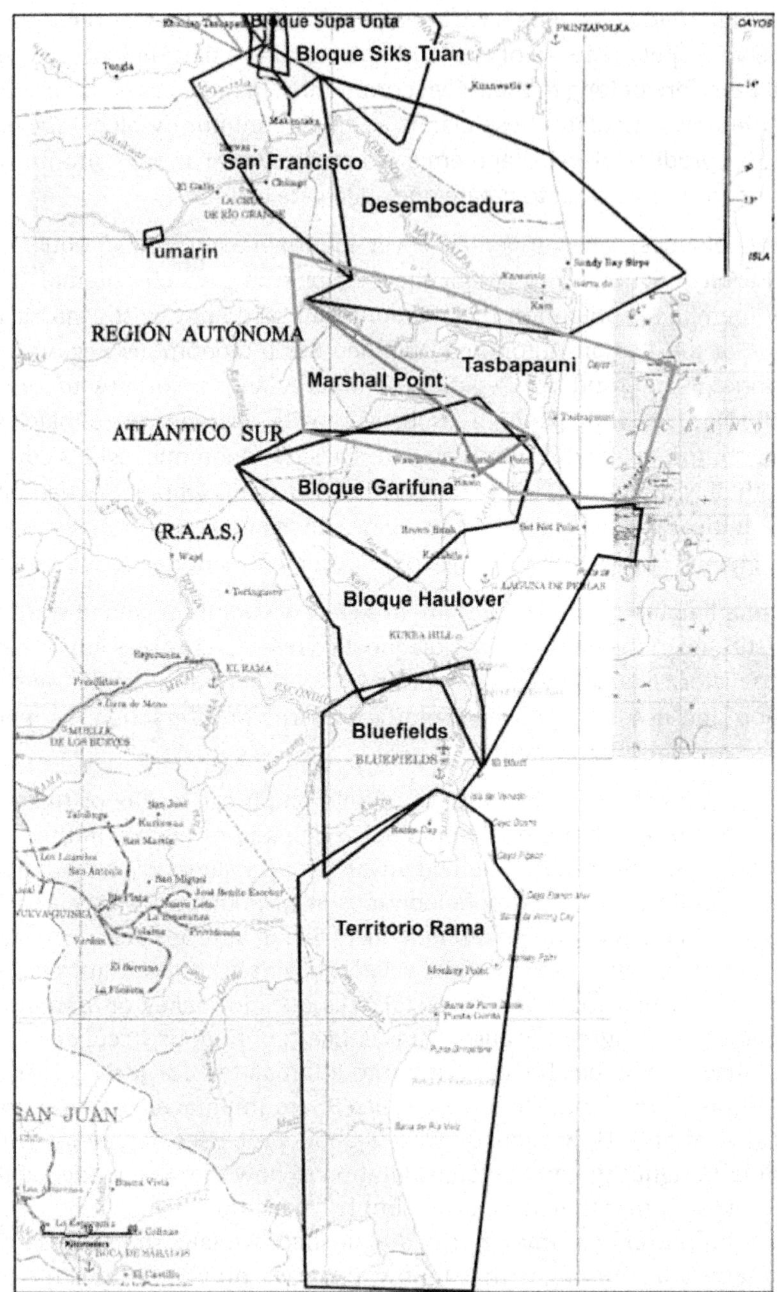

FIGURE 1. Consolidated Map of the Autonomous Region of the South Atlantic (Región Autónoma Atlántico Sur [RAAS]).
Rights, Resources, and the Social Memory of Struggle: Reflections on a Study of Indigenous and Black Community Land Rights on Nicaragua's Atlantic Coast," by Edmond T. Gordon et al., *Human Organization*, 62.4, Winter 2003, pp. 3690381. Reprinted by permission of the Society for Applied Anthropoloby.

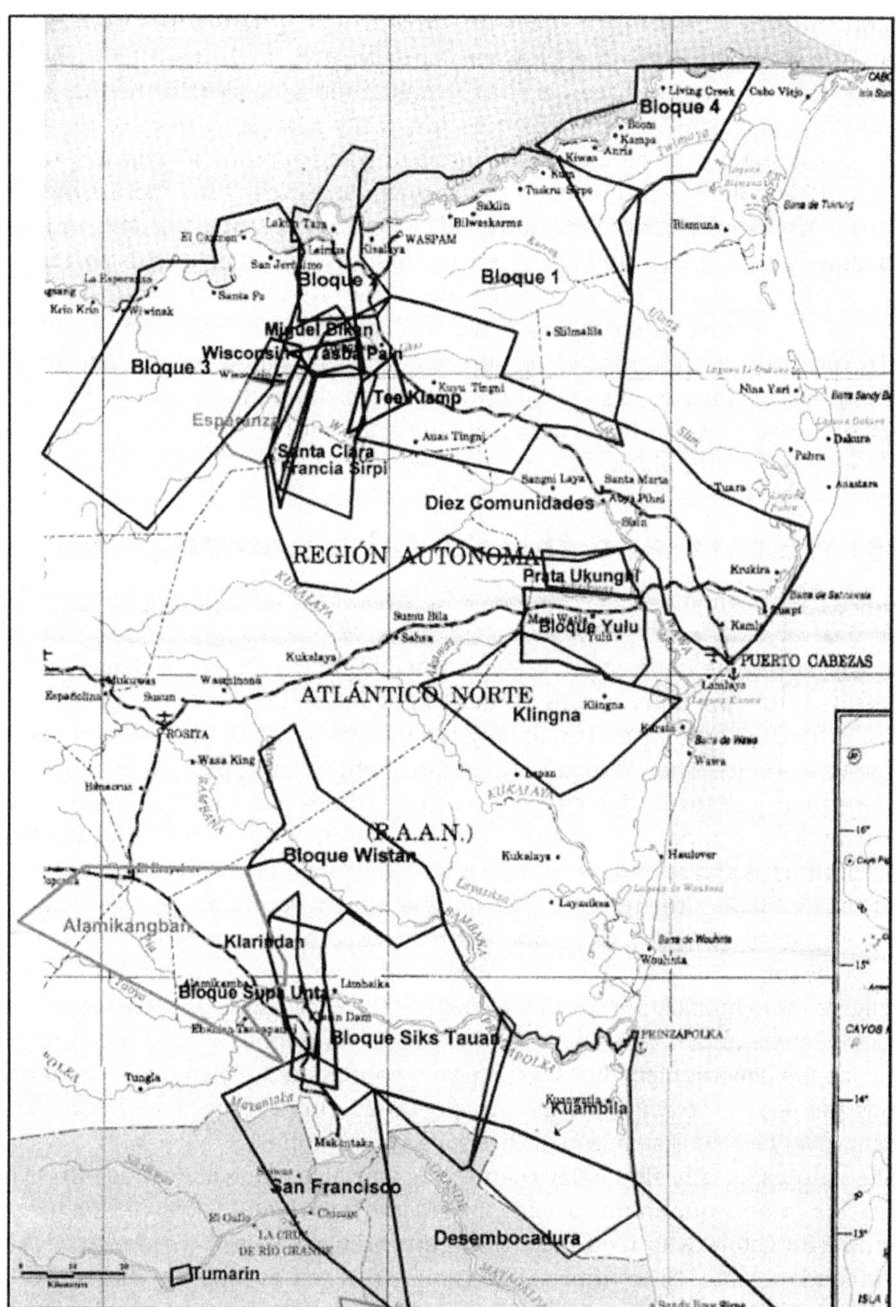

FIGURE 2. Consolidated Map of the Autonomous Region of the North Atlantic (Región Autónoma Atlántico Norte [RAAN]).
Rights, Resources, and the Social Memory of Struggle: Reflections on a Study of Indigenous and Black Community Land Rights on Nicaragua's Atlantic Coast," by Edmond T. Gordon et al., *Human Organization*, 62.4, Winter 2003, pp. 3690381. Reprinted by permission of the Society for Applied Anthropoloby.

neoliberal era, as a means to introduce the project, its contradictory origins and development, and its implementation between January 1997 and July 1998. Our analysis here emphasizes how the research both documented and transformed its subject of study. The specific transformation in question is the *bloque,* or multicommunity land claim. We explain how the bloques came into being and explore how diagnóstico participants could formulate their claims in this way while avoiding the morass of "invented traditions." Their assertions of "traditional" occupancy and cultural continuity are grounded, we suggest, in a cumulative social memory of struggle. This social memory downplays the question—"Have you been there from time immemorial?"—and instead emphasizes the history of struggle against the oppression of outsiders and for rights to self-government and control of resources based on shared culture and history. An assessment of this idea brings us full circle back to the contradictions of World Bank support for indigenous and black rights and the search for progressive politics in the era of neoliberal multiculturalism.

Coast History and the Social Memory of Struggle

In February 1894, when General Rigoberto Cabezas marched into Bluefields with a contingent of soldiers and orders from President Zelaya to "re-incorporate" the coast into the Nicaraguan nation, he confronted a deeply divided region. To some degree, these divisions resulted from previous actions of the Nicaraguan state.

The process of eroding and encircling the reserve began in earnest in 1860 with the Zeledón-Wyke Treaty. The "Mosquito Kingdom," which had operated as a semiautonomous dependency of the British crown, was reorganized—it became a "reserve," reduced substantially in size and political authority. Over the next 30 years the Nicaraguan state made a continuous and relentless effort to isolate the Mosquito Reserve and take it over. In the two decades before the military overthrow of the Mosquito Reserve government, the Nicaraguan state established three districts—Siquia, Rio Grande, and Prinzapolka—and two *comarcas* (regions)—Cabo Gracias and Rio San Juan—each with their corresponding civil, religious, and military authorities, to civilize, "protect," and convert ("nicaraguanize") the Indians in the area surrounding the reserve. Land politics played a key role in this effort, since the new municipalities were legally entitled to the ownership of the communal lands and *terrenos baldíos* (literally "empty lands"; in practice, a euphemism for land used extensively for subsistence by indigenous communities).

The state, especially after Zelaya came to power, also made concerted efforts to draw coast leaders from communities outside the reserve into the fold. Even inside the reserve, some powerful actors who read the writing on the walls were poised to pledge loyalty to the ascendant state. Other internal divisions emerged as well. By the 1860s Creoles already held most key positions in the reserve council; the government seat had moved southward toward the Creole towns of Bluefields and Pearl Lagoon; and by this time successive Mosquito kings (a hereditary position) had developed primary cultural affinities as Creole. Some observers spoke of active Miskitu "alienation" from the government that bore their name. Although this conclusion may have been exaggerated (or tainted by self-interest), it does seem clear that an important shift was underway. Creoles were making increasingly forceful claims to control of the Mosquito government and bolstering these claims with a protonationalist assertion of "Mosquitian" identity (Gordon 1998). Inhabitants of Miskitu communities, in turn, had a diminished voice in reserve government affairs, which probably helps to explain their limited mobilization to repel Cabezas' military intervention.

Despite these divisions, conditions of Nicaraguan state presence in the Mosquitia over the following two decades generated a remarkably unified and powerful social memory of "king times." The "Reincorporation" brought about a profound transformation of the regional political-economic hierarchy, with Mestizos from the west now displacing costeños and joining foreigners in key positions of dominance. To bolster their authority these Mestizos could draw on a dense network of ties to national-level power holders. The costeños' loss of material privilege came paired with cultural-racial oppression, since the new ruling class assumed the task of hispanicization with great zeal and justified its policies with a combination of assumed superiority of the national culture and blatantly racist denigration of its black and indigenous citizens (Gordon 1998).

This "invasion" of powerful Mestizos posed a direct threat to the resources and livelihood of less privileged costeños—the majority of whom were rural Miskitu. Political conditions within the newly created Nicaraguan territory made it relatively easy for Mestizos to take legal control of valuable coast lands; state imposed taxation, even in minimal and rudimentary forms, added insult to injury. Costeños quickly began to frame their discontent with Mestizo dominance and state authority around a stark contrast between oppression "now" and political autonomy "then" under the Mosquito king. Divisions among costeños did not fade; contradictions inherent in this emergent political consciousness—especially the way costeños' desire for autonomy included deep affinities with the Anglo American world—were not reconciled. But experiences of cultural-political oppression in the present produced powerful social memories of the Reincorporation as the crowning act of usurpation. Alternative historical terminology helped to cement these meanings in place. To this day Miskitu remember the protagonists of the Reincorporation as *ispail kunin kira* (liar Spaniards), while in Creole English the event is known simply as "the Overthrow."

Coast history from the Overthrow to the installation of the Somoza dictatorship (1936) is filled with cases of individual and collective resistance against Mestizo state rule. None are as important for politics then, and for the remainder of the century, as the struggle for titles to community lands, which culminated in the *Comisión Tituladora* (Title Commission) of 1910–1916. Conflicts and general unrest over Mestizo usurpation of community lands had become so intense that even the central government grew interested in a legal settlement that would quell dissent and establish a framework for governance. Costeños vigorously disputed the legitimacy of the state's role as mediator of a conflict in which it was also the principal antagonist. In a move that would have profound political resonance for years to come, the state implicitly sustained that objection and agreed to the formation of a land-titling commission under the authority of the British Crown. British government officials assumed this role as a means to discharge obligations acquired with their negotiated withdrawal from the coast, which entailed little or no commitment to the notions of land rights that animated the costeños' mobilization. Indeed, the comisión implemented the minimalist formula stipulated in the Harrison-Altamirano Treaty of 1906 (8–12 *manzanas* per family, with one manzana, a colonial land block measurement, equal to 0.7 or 1.5 acres). At the end of the process, most established indigenous and Creole communities inside the former reserve had communal titles. But they had been granted a paltry amount of land that did not correspond to their land use patterns or the communities' own perceptions of what belonged to them. Moreover, there were no provisions for population growth or systematic protection of the ecosystem in which these lands were embedded. More important still, the titling process left vast expanses of coast territory under the rubric "national lands," essentially freed up for legalized state and private primitive accumulation.

In costeño memories of the Comisión Tituladora and its outcome, however, these troubling limitations fall almost completely out of the picture. The titles themselves, and the official correspondence surrounding the process, take on a symbolic power that completely transcends the practical details of how much land was granted and, even in many cases, the precise location of these legal boundaries. A tattered sheet of official stationary with the imprimatur of the British Crown; references to a "treaty," which evokes negotiations among sovereign nations; a relatively recent process in which the British and the costeños worked together, with Nicaraguan state officials on the sidelines—these are the images that persist and retain salience. Memories of the process also affirm the costeño belief that the Nicaraguan state has no legitimate authority to resolve conflicts over land rights; British involvement stands as proof that costeños' rights originate in a time before Nicaraguan state sovereignty in the region. In a detached historical reading, one could plausibly interpret the Comisión Tituladora process as the definitive British withdrawal and endorsement of Nicaraguan state sovereignty on the coast. Such a reading, however, would miss the point. At least since the 1930s, costeño intellectuals and activists have mined these events for alternative meanings, which ended up reinforcing precisely the opposite conclusion. This experience of struggle for community land rights added another element to the cumulative social memories of a time when costeño dominion in the region was secure, free from intervention by the "Spanish" state.

Pressures on community members' control over resources continued in various forms over subsequent decades, and comisión land titles did little to ameliorate the problem. On the one hand, communities outside the former reserve had little access to the symbolic power that the title conferred on its holder; at times, this difference between those who held titles and those who did not exacerbated intercommunity conflict. This was the case in the strained relations between the "Diez comunidades," which received a multicommunal title from the comisión, and the Wangki communities to the north, which did not (Hale, Gordon, and Gurdián 1998).

Even for those inside the former reserve, the community's actual land and resource use extended well beyond the boundaries stipulated in the comisión titles, which rendered the titles next to useless in strictly legal terms. Private companies—at times Nicaraguan, but more often transnational—exerted much of this pressure. Whether in lumber, bananas, rubber or mining—or later in cattle, seafood, and tourism—the conditions were fundamentally the same. Economic activity made use of land and resources that costeños claim as their own, with no prior negotiation or even vague promise of compensation. Costeños provided the unskilled labor for these activities and received wages that allowed unprecedented access to Western consumer goods. But even these benefits were transitory. The companies left behind depleted resources and very little of lasting value for the communities. By the 1970s, the principal legacy of "company times" were deforested grasslands and wistful memories of consumer goods and diversions that people no longer had the money to buy.

Costeño social and political mobilization dissipated during the 1930s and 1940s. It acquired new strength by the 1960s, but now in a different register. Whereas protest in the previous period tended to come from an imagined space outside state sovereignty, posing a fundamental challenge to state presence and prerogatives (e.g., taxation), organization now tended to revolve around the goals of collective cultural affirmation, antiracism, and equal citizenship rights. This was especially true among Creoles in the south who, with more education and resources, had achieved a greater voice in the national political arena. However, it held also for the first Miskitu farmers' organizations in the northern Río Coco area, called ACARIC, which had emerged around opposition to the marketing practices of Chinese and Mestizo intermediaries and general discontent with the Mestizo-controlled municipal and provincial authorities and the national government. As the process of collective cultural affirmation advanced, articulations with social memories of "king times" grew stronger. Especially for the Miskitu, a transnational notion of Indian identity and rights bolstered these associations and helped to put the land-territory question back at the center of the political agenda. It is ironic, if understandable in historical terms, that this growing militancy did not include a critique of U.S. companies or of the Anglo American presence in the region. Social memories had been predicated on a sharp dichotomy between "Spanish" violation of, and Anglo support for, costeño self-rule; this dichotomy may even have helped to protect Somoza dictatorship from more sustained criticism (see Chapter 5 in Hale 1994). Somoza was, after all, a close ally of the U.S. government, which costeños tended to view as a "friendly" power. As costeño organizing gained strength through the 1970s, opposition to Somoza did begin to build. Still, the further irony is that this mobilization remained moderate under Somoza, only to burst forth a few years later in an explosive grassroots social movement against the Sandinistas, who came to power in 1979 promising "liberation" for all poor and oppressed Nicaraguans.

Even with the sobering distance of 10 years of post-Sandinista governments, it is difficult for us to view the revolutionary decade as "one more phase" of coast politics. We lived that decade as a period of epic struggle, from which the answers to a series of monumental questions would emerge. Could a small, impoverished country strike out on its own path, defy the most powerful government on the globe, and survive? Would a national-popular government, with a zealous and at times arrogantly Mestizocentric notion of "liberation" learn quickly enough to embrace an antiracist politics and open a space for costeños within their revolution? Would costeños find a way to transpose the historically constituted dichotomy between "Spanish" enemies and Anglo American friends, so "Spaniard" Sandinistas could be reimagined as allies? And a final question, equally important to us, if considerably less monumental: Would the activist research of two North American and one Nicaraguan anthropologists—one African American, one Mestizo, and one white, and all strongly aligned with both costeño struggles and with the broader principles of the revolution—end up being more constructive than contradictory? The short answer to all these questions has turned out to be "no." But even so, they inevitably form the lens through which we view the Sandinista decade, which leads us to downplay continuities with what came before and with what followed.

Costeño participants in the diagnóstico in the late 1990s pushed us toward a different perspective. Their memories of armed struggle against the Sandinistas are still relatively fresh; ex-combatants often command greater moral authority for having given the best years oftheir lives to the cause; many continue to express great bitterness over the loss of loved ones, displacement, and military occupation of the region; the coast branch of the National Sandinista Liberation Front (FSLN), though present and "costeño" in composition, still has great difficulty moving out from under the weight of their debacle of the 1980s. Yet in many of these participants' minds, bitterness surrounding the "broken promises" of the two post-Sandinista governments is equally strong; a number of sharp conflicts in recent times, some involving minor incidents of armed conflict, reinforce a sense of distrust for "Spanish" governments in general. Even more important, given our central argument here, is the blurring of boundaries between "Sandinista times" and all that came before. Memories of the massive anti-Sandinista mobilization have not faded. They have taken their place in the cumulative social memory of struggle, fitting neatly within the notion that a cluster of rights—to autonomy, control over resources, cultural recognition—have been repeatedly asserted and denied since the Overthrow of 1894.

Viewed from this perspective, which emphasizes continuity rather than rupture, which reduces the Sandinistas' utopian vision to little more than a smokescreen for the same (or worse!) oppressive practices toward costeños, the legacy of the Sandinista decade for the land question is threefold. First, the early to mid-1980s were a period of the most widespread and sustained political mobilization in recorded costeño history. As time passes, the ideological affinities of the adversaries matters less than the fact that they held state power and used it to violate costeño rights. This recent experience of mobilization, regardless of the unique conditions that made it possible, gives subsequent costeño political discourse on the land question an added credibility and a sharp critical edge. In meetings held for the diagnóstico research, Miskitu community leaders often ended speeches with the resolve to "rise up in arms again" if their land rights could not be achieved through legal means.

The second legacy is a shift in political sensibilities with regard to the Anglo American world, and especially, the U.S. government. While costeños did enjoy a brief moment of abundant U.S. support and material aid for their struggles, this solidarity turned to disapproval when it became clear that most costeños were willing to negotiate rights to autonomy within the Sandinista revolution. The limits to "solidarity" grew more evident still when the Sandinistas were voted out of power: disapproval turned to utter disinterest and abandonment. Although facets of Anglo ideology surely persist, gone are the deep political affinities with the Anglo American world and the illusion that costeños have powerful "American" allies who care about their political fate.

The third legacy is autonomy—a monumental achievement that has evolved into something of a mixed blessing. Costeños achieved an autonomous government, codified in its own legal statute and affirmed in the Nicaraguan Constitution. Throughout the armed conflict in the early 1980s, the summary explanation for what animated costeños' struggles always revolved around the term "autonomy." Negotiations for autonomy, together with other related Sandinista initiatives, did indeed put an end to most of the fighting. Since the autonomous governments were not elected and inaugurated until 1990, however, we can only speculate how the Sandinistas would have managed the new political relationship. We do know that the experience under the subsequent governments of Violeta Chamorro and Arnoldo Alemán has been a source of disillusionment, so much so that many costeños now associate the very term "autonomy" as much with the corrupt and oppressive practices of the "Spanish" central government as with their own collective political aspirations. This disillusionment and intraregional political fragmentation, in turn, are the epitomizing signs of the neoliberal times.

Land Rights in the Neoliberal Era

The near unanimity of indigenous and Creole mobilization against the Sandinista government in the previous era has long since passed. Some organizations—most notably the *Consejo de Ancianos* (Council of Elders)—have carried on the ideological mantle of that mobilization, making control over a vast indigenous "territory" a nonnegotiable demand around which political struggle should proceed. A few have cast their lot with the autonomous government, which has operated with minimal funding and efficacy since it was inaugurated in 1990. Still others have sought—often with the backing of one or another national political party—to gain control over Coast *municipios* (municipalities), the lower administrative units of rising political importance in recent years, which in turn has created a tense relationship with the autonomous governments. These mayors are subjected to powerful external interests—lumber companies and merchants, drug traffickers, and political parties—and often fall victim to the corruption associated with them. Many of these mayors have become alienated from the communities in which they were raised, as the values of individualism and personal enrichment—encouraged by neoliberalism—overcome those of communal solidarity.

Finally, many who live in rural communities appear to be fed up with extralocal politics of all varieties, and they level bitter critiques against corruption and unresponsiveness of municipal, autonomous, and central government authorities alike. The depth of community-level opposition to the autonomous governments is most noteworthy, since demands for autonomy have animated the anti-Sandinista mobilization and served as a common thread in Miskitu social memories of struggle since the last century.

The Diagnóstico and Its Principal Findings

Diagnóstico research began in earnest in mid-1997, in the midst of this contradictory political environment, and we felt the contradictions immediately. On the one hand, the diagnóstico's mandated emphasis on community-based land claims coincided nicely with the predominant political sensibilities in many indigenous and Creole communities: mistrustful of their own regional leaders; determined to achieve local control over land and resources; inclined to leave larger questions of coastwide political institutions and relations with central government for later. On the other hand, this individual community focus also fit within the blueprint for neoliberal governance and economic development, echoing the "classic liberal" solution of Comisión Tituladora some 80 years before: recognize small "islands" of community lands, as a means both to defuse political opposition and to free up the immense "sea" of territory around these islands for exploitation at the discretion of state functionaries and their private-sector partners. Leaders of the Consejo de Ancianos and other such organizations denounced this convergence, insisting that the diagnóstico's communitycentric conception be abandoned. Officials of the autonomous governments voiced parallel objections, propelled by the fears that a state-endorsed regime of individual community land rights would further undermine their authority, and eliminate any chance for the devolution of control over coast territory from the central government to the autonomous region.[1] To make matters worse, fieldwork for the diagnóstico coincided with the beginning of the 1998 autonomous governments' electoral campaign, which provided extra impetus for politicians to find "hot-button" issues that could arouse costeños' interest and garner their votes.

To confront these multiple strands of questioning, and at times outright opposition, our diagnóstico research team proceeded according to two key methodological principles. First, we made great efforts to explain the purpose of the study to all interested parties, to elicit cooperation, and also to make it very clear that communities could opt not to participate. Such meetings of an informational character were held with all important regional political actors, from the Moravian Church to the Consejo de Ancianos, as well as with assemblies in every community that would be included in the diagnóstico universe. Second, we emphasized our role as technical experts. We made it clear we had no intention of taking a position on, much less dictating the results of, the contentious question of how land claims should ultimately be conceived and pursued. Our overriding interest was to document answers to two simple questions: (1) What land and resources does each of the 133 communities in our study "universe" claim as its own?; and (2) How do they justify these claims?

The centerpiece of our methodology was a hand-held Global Positioning System (GPS) receiver, with a retail value of less than $200, which anyone with a basic education could quickly learn to use. Employing the GPS, researchers worked together with community representatives to find key landmarks that form the boundaries of their land, register the coordinates of these landmarks in a notebook, and then have the coordinates plotted on the appropriate scale computer-generated map. These "ethnomaps" were generated in Austin using 1:50,000 scale base maps, under the direction of Dr. Peter Dana, an expert on Geographic Information Systems (GIS) and computer cartography.

This methodology was "democratic" in that we taught community-based investigators to use the GPS, and even more important, we prefaced research in every community with extensive discussions in open meetings, where we explained in detail the diagnóstico's purpose and invited all present to participate. At these meetings a communal team for locating community boundaries and using the GPS was elected to work directly with the researchers from CIDCA. Although straightforward to explain, this basic data collection process was never easy. The mere logistics of travel to outlying locations were at times daunting, generally requiring days of trekking by foot or dugout canoe deep into the rain forest. In one extreme case this involved a trip of two weeks simply to reach the outlying boundary post. Discussions about where the community boundaries actually lie often erupted into heated disagreements, which had to be patiently mediated. Questions of the relationship between one community's boundaries and another had to be handled with great care. Our firm methodological position was to desist from any discussion of "overlaps" and from any attempt to mediate overlapping claims. We attempted solely to document what each community claimed as its own, fully aware that the next step of the process would necessarily entail mediation among communities. Although a viable position, which in general worked fairly well, it was far from conflict free, especially in the final phase, when preliminary maps were taken back to the communities for validation.[2]

After a preliminary map was created the research team returned to the community to present the results, ask for further input or modifications, and then to carry out the second facet of the project. This involved further research focused on achieving a brief ethnographic description of the community, an explanation of how the land they claim is used, and a full rationale for the claim that the land and resources belongs to them. Diagnóstico researchers recorded this information both in narrative form in a community ethnography and in graphic form, as a symbol that would appear in the final draft of the map representing the community land claim. The legend for the symbols was bilingual in Miskitu and Spanish.

The visual impact of the draft version of the map was enormous. It engendered a deep sense of empowerment, which comes from having long-denied claims etched onto the "official" medium of national survey maps. And it made the process appear much more concrete, dramatizing the direct connection between long treks in the jungle to locate boundary markers and the cartographic product. Once we presented the draft maps to community members, the final task of validation and recording ethnographic and environmental details fell quickly into place. It is perhaps a measure of the success of this methodology, as well as the urgently felt character of the issue, that only two or three of the 133 communities in our universe chose not to participate in the diagnóstico. By the end of the study, as awareness of the results were coming to be generally known, communities in zones excluded from the original universe began clamoring to be included.

The questions of cultural continuity, and the politicized character of the land rights, both reasserted themselves as soon as the research began. Although our methodology stipulated that we document land claims on an individual, community-by-community basis, that same principle instructed us to shift to multicommunity claims if this reflected the mutual consensus of individual communities. In the end, the vast majority of communities choose this alternative. When the diagnóstico was complete, 128 communities had formulated a total of 29 claims, of which 17 were multicommunity or bloques (including a total of 116 communities), while only 12 were claims by individual communities. To opt for a bloque in no sense meant that community members abandoned concern for community-specific boundaries. To the contrary, throughout the process individual communities retained their role as fundamental building blocks in the affirmation of identity, the exercise of political representation, and the assertion of rights. The collective decision to put forth bloque claims corresponded to a different, complementary set of rationales, which combined "real politick" strategy with broader visions of costeño identity and rights.

The real politick reasoning followed a straightforward argument for strength in numbers. Community members immediately (and correctly) understood the diagnóstico as a preliminary step in what was sure to be a difficult, protracted struggle for legal recognition by the Nicaraguan state. In one community meeting after another, discussion turned to scenarios of subsequent legal struggle, which galvanized a consensus view that: "we should band together to get the title and leave internal boundaries within the bloque for later, for decisions that we can make among ourselves."

The second rationale revolved around broader visions of costeño rights, which covered the entire coast territory that indigenous and black communities historically had controlled. The bloque, according to this reasoning, made it easier to piece together this larger claim, making sure that each bloque was contiguous with the next, leaving no space in between for "national lands." This "historic rights" argument, in turn, merged with a third rationale, which focused on preexisting boundaries of sectoral divisions within larger identity groups. For example, four Garífuna communities put forth claims to a bloque that would represent all Garífuna people; a long-standing division between river- (Wangki) and seacoast-dwelling (Sal) Miskitu in the northeast became a bloque boundary. The five communities at the mouth of the Río Grande de Matagalpa (encompassing three different ethnic/racial groups), which had long worked together as a single administrative unit, also decided to demarcate a single bloque claim.

The predominance of bloque demands gave the diagnóstico a politicized edge because together they produced an aggregate territorial claim the state has been loathe to address, much less recognize. But in this form, the claim was even harder for the state to deny because it was championed not by one entity but by 29. This aggregate territorial claim also reintroduced the question of cultural continuity: the bloque demands built upon long-standing patterns of intercommunity relations and upon a broader vision of territorial rights for coast peoples. Yet they also in some sense could be considered new, in that most had not functioned as stable cultural or political units before the diagnóstico and some resulted from negotiations among communities during the research process itself. Was this a case, then, of "invented tradition"?

Theoretical Implications

This notion of "invented," or as we prefer in this case "reconstructed," traditions is the touchstone in a broader theoretical quandary that has surrounded the analysis of identity politics and claims to rights grounded in cultural difference, for some time (Hobsbawm 1983). The quandary boils down to two key questions. How can we make the case for a special regimen of rights without recourse to an "essentialism" that limits political options and brings about negative (at times unintended) consequences for the people in question? And conversely, how can we affirm the dynamic, changing character of indigenous and black identities without endorsing a "constructivism" that undermines their claims to rights?

Some measure of essentialism is inherent in all efforts to affirm and defend a given identity. The danger arises when a particular feature—an expression of aboriginality, for example—acquires special status, which creates distinctions in relation to others who do not exhibit this feature, but who also make claims grounded in cultural difference. Distinctions of this sort emerged between indigenous and black costeños in the process of diagnóstico research. Some Creoles even shifted to greater emphasis of their indigenous cultural affinities as a counterweight to the assumed deficit in legitimacy of the African diasporic "routes" versus aboriginal "roots." This was especially striking, given that black costeños generally occupy a higher position in the coast socioeconomic hierarchy than indigenous peoples.

A second set of dangers—associated with constructivism that undermines claims to cultural rights—are even greater. In Nicaragua, and throughout Latin America, political and economic power holders stand poised to seize any opportunity within their reach to delegitimize indigenous rights, and constructivist theories of identity can be powerful arms in their arsenal. If identity is constructed and tradition is invented, then both can be relegated to the sullied realm of political maneuver and machination, which places indigenous and black people at an inherent disadvantage with respect to the powerful state institutions they oppose.

Participants in the diagnóstico charted a path between these twin dangers with considerable ease and pointed toward a distinct third position. The arguments of Miskitu and Creole participants did not focus primarily on the "time immemorial" occupation of traditional lands and persistence of key cultural traits as the foundational justification for their land claims. Outside intervention has been too massive; culture change too extensive. Whatever realm of cultural practice one chooses to scrutinize, one finds hybridity through and through. Instead, they made a persuasive case for continuity by emphasizing not only where people live, or what cultural practices they share, but what memories they have in common, and how these memories form a narrative of the past they claim as their own. Cultural continuity in rights to land lies in the resonance of the claim "this belongs to us," and this resonance, in turn, is grounded in a shared understanding of their history. In this sense, continuity depends more on having the resources—both symbolic and material—to connect with others and develop a common narrative of the past than on substantive cultural material passed from one generation to the next. These assertions of continuity are "constructed," drawing on conditions in the present, but they also are always genuine and real, as long as the assertions resonate and the people in question continue to defend their version of the past in the face of those who seek a fundamentally different narration.

The diagnóstico research methodology did encourage, and even depend on, a constructivist approach to land rights—but within limits. Community-level discussion often proceeded with the participants' full understanding that the mapping of their land claims was a unique opportunity that required not a passive rendition of existing boundaries, but, rather, an audacious and creative process that might allow them, finally, to achieve their due. Community leaders conferred, negotiated, and strategized in an effort to "get their claims right" and to take the claims of neighboring communities into account. Positions at times shifted during the research process; in some cases community members insisted on going back and mapping their lands a second time. The limits to this fluidity were equally clear. People always had an argument, a rationale, that grounded their claims in past experiences, both relations with the physical environment and interactions with others. In justifying the formation of a given bloque, for example, some key factor always made this particular configuration compelling: whether a notion of extended kinship, memories of cooperative economic practices, collective participation in religious activities, or some legal-political precedent, such as a previously granted multicommunity title. These factors were not the only ones people could have mustered from their repertoire, nor were the particular bloque configurations the diagnóstico documented the only ones that could possibly have emerged. But the range of possible outcomes was limited by the specifics of the historical experiences and cumulative social memories of costeño participants. The bloques were constructed in the heat of the moment, but participants made them drawing on a finite reservoir of memories to which they had access because they had lived on the coast, learned from prior generations what was rightfully theirs, and learned what those before them had struggled to defend. This reservoir of knowledge and memories, in turn, had become deeply entwined with their identities as costeño.

Both these practical responses to the questions raised by the notion of reconstructed tradition bring the issue of access to resources to the fore. In a much-cited essay that reviews and reiterates the constructivist approach to identity politics, Gupta and Ferguson (1992) challenge the assumed "isomorphism" between "place" and "identity." Such assumptions, they argue, reinforce an image of the bounded subject, which makes it difficult for one to affirm identity while moving around, downplays connections among groups across these boundaries, and freezes in place "traditional" hierarchies. Much of this critique is salutary, especially in relation to conventional wisdom about indigenous politics, which often posits an intrinsic connection between indigenous cosmology and nature and then makes this connection the central rationale for indigenous rights to land. Yet in their zeal to deconstruct this orthodoxy, Gupta and Ferguson (1992) ultimately leave the problem of access to resources underspecified. While it is certainly true that one does not have to be tied to the land or fixed in a "traditional" place to be Miskitu, Mayangna, or Creole, it is certainly the case that access to and use of the land have been important bases of the power to construct themselves as such in a positive and sustaining way.

Moreover, in the future, without access to resources they may not be able to make any case at all for cultural integrity. While the resources in question would not have to be the land and waters of the coastal region, in practical reality few other options exist. Without access to land, coast peoples lack the power to affirm connections with their chosen narrative of the past. Without this assertion of cultural continuity, they lack the impetus for collective action to improve their lot.

The constructivist critique of the link between place and identity, in sum, misses the importance of resources to any given construction of identity. A serious predicament follows. To achieve legal recognition for their community lands, costeños need to be able to make a strong and persuasive case for cultural continuity; that is, a historical account which emphasizes their presence and political dominion before the rise of the Nicaraguan nation-state. The key ingredient for making this case persuasive, however, is access to resources that would put symbolic and material power behind this narrative. As costeños lose access to land that once was theirs, they also lose the basis to make the case effectively for getting it back.

The World Bank: Opening and Contradictions

The World Bank has thrust itself right into the center of this predicament with promises of support for indigenous rights, but with results severely limited by the ambivalence of its own institutional position. It is crucial to acknowledge the substantive change that has occurred. In keeping with a broader general trend of neoliberal governance, the bank has explicitly endorsed a policy of cultural pluralism. Indigenous cultures are to be recognized, their way of life preserved. The new mandate even extends to "indigenous land tenure," which the bank now takes action to respect. The diagnóstico emerged from such a mandate and produced maps and accompanying analysis that documented extensive costeño territorial claims and the cumulative social memory of struggle that would serve as these claims' most persuasive rationale. In the case of this diagnóstico, bank resources were redirected in support of the costeño cause, or at least one popular version of that cause. But the financial magnitude of this redirection was tiny and its duration brief. The Nicaraguan government apparently suppressed the report, and anonymous state officials referred to its contents as "defamatory." There was no serious follow-up on the report's many recommendations, even though its contents apparently were widely read and at least selectively used by all those involved.[3] The immediate barrier to such follow-up was that a member-state, Nicaragua, had policies toward the coast that were far less open to cultural rights than those of the bank itself. This was enough to prevent the *diagnóstico* from having an impact, or generating further action in the official channels from which it originated.

A deeper and more insuperable barrier comes into focus with a closer look at the internal contradictions of this new bank policy itself. The central thrust of these reform initiatives will always be to endorse and promote cultural rights of "recognition," without a parallel endorsement of demands for a redistribution of resources. This means that bilingual education, culturally appropriate health delivery systems, cultural-religious tolerance, and strict compliance with the principle of nondiscrimination are "in," while direct financial support for the faltering autonomous governments is "out." In the arena of rights to land the same dichotomy applies. Legislative reform that recognizes culturally specific forms of land tenure is in; "regularization" of the status quo, such that communities have titles to what they currently hold, is a logical next step. But this initiative stops short of systematic reallocation of resources, such that communities could document and justify an alternative notion of land rights based on cumulative social memories of struggle that have persisted as a subterranean counterpoint to the official history. This last step would cross the line. The crucial transgression would not be in the specific claims themselves, but in the "defamatory" alternative narrative that would be legitimated and, even more importantly, the further reallocation of resources that this narrative would prescribe.

The final irony of this impasse is that the diagnóstico followed, to the letter of the law, a research methodology explicitly endorsed by the World Bank and the Nicaraguan state. This research then produced an aggregate vision—a coast territory divided up into contiguous bloques, each controlled by a cluster of communities that would use the resources therein for their own benefit—which neither the state nor the bank could even begin to accept. At a critical juncture in the study, we insisted upon full implementation of the research methodology, which prescribed a devolution of initiative from "researcher" to "subject." If we had restricted the unit of analysis to individual communities and refused the move to form bloques, the official plan for small islands of community land rights in a sea of neoliberal development may well have emerged strengthened. The formulation of demands in bloques, by contrast, allowed a full articulation between community lands and costeños' broader vision of collective political rights. A more cautious team of bank consultants, with one eye on the present job and another on the next contract, might not have allowed this vision to emerge. As it happened, for a brief moment, bank resources went in direct support of a narrative of costeño identity, history, and cultural continuity that the Nicaraguan state has vehemently opposed since its inception at the beginning of the 19th century. Whether or not the communities can turn this moment of support into long-term advantage is an open question. Either way, in the absence of a remotely plausible alternative vision of political transformation, this search for momentary openings, for contradictory spaces of struggle from within, may be the best we can do.

Conclusions

If the diagnóstico had been carried out in the previous era of coastwide mobilization for autonomy and territorial rights, the figure of the bloque might never have emerged. Both the broader vision of coastwide rights to territory and the real politick rationale of strength in numbers could have fit nicely within the notion of an autonomous government for and by costeños, with the same corollary that "once we get those territorial rights, we can decide the specific community boundaries among ourselves." Sectoral divisions would not have disappeared but just diminished in importance in relation to the broader struggle to wrest concessions from the central government. But by the late 1990s this vision of territorial autonomy had lost much of its symbolic power, precisely because the autonomous government, in existence for nearly 10 years, had produced so little. The bloques emerged as an alternative means for participants to respond to the specific research question of "what lands do you claim as your own?", while still linking their answer to a broader notion of historic rights. The process of demarcating and then justifying the bloques brought historical narrations of "king times" to the fore, reemphasized the great divide between costeños and the oppressive "Spanish" state, and reiterated the principle of costeño political control over the entire expanse of coast territory. The coastwide mosaic of bloque demands created a bridge between community-specific demands and the broader social memory of struggle.

By insisting on land claims as bloques, community members became agents of transformation of the very phenomenon—community land claims—that we set out to study. This dual character of knowledge production—where the process of gathering the data transforms the object of study—is inherent to any research methodology that requires active participation of subjects. It emerged in especially stark relief here because the participants cared so deeply about the content of the knowledge they helped to produce. This unusually intense connection between the production of knowledge and transformation of the object of that knowledge enhanced the results of the research in three important ways. First, and foremost, it gave the diagnóstico an ethical grounding, a greater assurance that the results would be responsive to the interests and aspirations of the participants themselves. Second, it bolstered the study's feasibility: community members made it clear from the start that they would only participate in the data collection if they felt they had a stake in the outcome. Without ample community-based cooperation, in turn, the study would have been impossible. Finally, this participatory methodology yielded privileged insight into the theoretical quandary of so-called invented traditions.

Strangely enough, a prime example of this understanding of tradition can be found in the writings of Eric Hobsbawm (1983), the scholar who coined the phrase "invented traditions." His argument stems from an observation about what happens to the politics of culture in the face of rapid social change: an authentic bedrock of tradition breaks down, established social relations enter into flux, movements emerge in the midst of the resulting turmoil and invoke "tradition" to legitimate an inherently and necessarily "new" political project. "The strength and adaptability of genuine traditions," Hobsbawm (1983:8) emphasizes, "is not to be confused with the 'invention of tradition.' Where old ways are alive, traditions need be neither revived nor invented." This distinction between genuine versus spurious traditions, which maps directly onto the broader dichotomy between tradition and modernity, has dangerous implications for indigenous and Creole struggles. One could surely argue that indigenous political assertion arises from "genuine" tradition, an ancestral culture, which stands in sharp contrast with the invented traditions that nation-states deploy to justify territorial sovereignty. Hobsbawm might even agree. But the dichotomy leaves indigenous peoples positioned on the far side of a chasm that divides tradition from modernity, with rights tied to their status as tradition-bound wards of the modern state.

Collective identities congeal, and claims for rights associated with a given identity become powerful, when group members are able to weave their memories into a coherent, persuasive, and widely resonant narrative of the past, and when they possess the symbolic and material resources necessary to constitute and sustain it. The reservoir of memories on which people may draw to affirm these connections is vast, but it is not infinite; just as the range of interpretations of a given historical event is wide, but limited by the materiality of history itself (Trouillot 1995).

This reference to materiality, in turn, signals the second key dimension of our alternative formulation: the emphasis on access to resources. The research project allowed for a devolution of resources toward indigenous and black communities of the coast as they participated in efforts to define and document their land claims. The concrete results of this study—28 ethnomaps and accompanying texts in the hands of the community members—are the most tangible evidence that such a redistribution actually occurred. Moreover, the diagnóstico results substantiate the broader political vision of costeños for primary control of coast resources, showing how that vision is both historically justified and widely held among coast people themselves.

Yet these achievements are relatively small in relation to the tasks that remain and the barriers that this work is sure to confront. The ethnomaps must be used as the basis for creating bloque-specific resource management plans and for generating further documentation in anticipation of the legal title demarcation process. Widespread political mobilization will be necessary to exert pressure on the state, both to begin that process and to assure that it doesn't stop with the palliative solutions of times past. In the meantime, communities and bloques must engage in some form of "autodemarcation," which carries forward from the grassroots the myriad tasks that land demarcation entails, without waiting for the central government to respond favorably to these demands. Some progress toward these ends already has been achieved in the northern region of the Bosawas International Biosphere Reserve,[4] which can be a source of guidance and encouragement for these efforts. But the Bosawas case should also serve as a sobering reminder: even under the least threatening conditions, with a highly favorable degree of support from the international community, it has not been possible to achieve legal recognition of indigenous community lands from the state. A corollary surely follows: when push comes to shove, the World Bank can be expected to side with its member state.

Despite the many obstacles, for more than a century coast peoples have demonstrated both the resilience and the creativity needed to continue the struggle for social justice, as they understand it. From this tradition and shared memory of struggle, as well as the power that emanates from their historical relationship with the land and its resources, costeños have forged many of the elements necessary to overcome present obstacles and complete the many tasks that remain in pursuit of their rights. The diagnóstico has helped to document this process, and in so doing we hope also to have made a contribution in support of the struggles that lie ahead.

NOTES

1. Some intellectuals associated with the autonomy experiment, since its inception 1990, had argued for the idea that coast territory in its entirety be considered "patrimony" of the autonomous governments, which would effectively eliminate the category "national lands" and transfer full authority for adjudication of community land claims from the central to the regional governments. This seemed, to us at least, to be a highly coherent and convincing position in theory. Yet it had so little practical political viability that it played only a minor role in the day-to-day implementation of the diagnóstico.
2. In a few cases where logistical or technical problems made the GPS recording of a given boundary marker impossible to achieve, we made recourse to a best estimate and recorded the coordinates as such.
3. In a case being tried at the Inter-American Human Rights Court, involving the demands of the Mayangna community of Awas Tingni against the Nicaraguan government, the latter has cited the diagnóstico, both as evidence of good faith toward resolving indigenous community land rights and as proof that the Awas Tingni claim lacks validity.
4. Bosawas is a nature reserve in the northwestern part of the RAAN that the Nicaraguan government created with the cooperation of the Mayagna people. The word "Bosawas" is commonly used in place of the acronym "BOSAWAS," which is formed from the first letters of the place names that comprise the Bosawas International Biosphere Reserve: Bocay River, Saslaya National Park, and Waspuk River. The Bosawas International Biosphere Reserve is commonly referred to as "Bosawas" or "Bosawas Reserve." There are a number of Mayagna settlements in the reserve and the Mayagna claim the bulk of its territory as communal lands. Community members played an active role in mapping the boundaries of their lands and those of the reserve. They also played a role in the development of resource management plans for the area, nevertheless, the state still has not granted official title to Mayagna lands within Bosawas.

REFERENCES CITED

Gordon, Edmund T. 1998. Disparate Diasporas: Identity and Politics in an African-Nicaraguan Community. Austin: University of Texas Press.

Gray, Andrew. 1998. Development Policy, Development Protest: The World Bank, Indigenous Peoples, and NGOs. *In* The Struggle for Accountability: The World Bank, NGOs, and Grassroots Movements. Jonathan A. Fox and L. David Brown, eds. pp. 266–300. Cambridge, Mass.: MIT Press.

Gupta, Akhil, and James Ferguson. 1992. Beyond "Culture": Space, Identity and the Politics of Difference. Cultural Anthropology 7:6–22.

Gurdián, Galio. 2001. Mito y memoria en la construcción de la fisonomía de la comunidad de Alamikangban. Ph.D. dissertation, Department of Anthropology. University of Texas at Austin.

Hale, Charles R. 1994. Resistance and Contradiction: Miskitu Indians and the Nicaraguan State, 1894–1987. Stanford, Calif.: Stanford University Press.

Hale, Charles R., Edmund T. Gordon, and Galio Gurdián. 1998. Diagnóstico general sobre la tenencia de la tierra en las comunidades indígenas de la Costa Atlantica. Bluefields y Puerto Cabezas, Nicaragua: Central American and Caribbean Research Council.

Hobsbawm, Eric. 1983. Introduction: Inventing Traditions. *In* The Invention of Tradition. Eric J. Hobsbawm and Terence Ranger, eds. pp. 1–15. Cambridge, Mass.: Cambridge University Press.

Treakle, Kay. 1998. Ecuador: Structural Adjustment and Indigenous and Environmentalist Resistance. *In* The Struggle for Accountability: The World Bank, NGOs, and Grassroots Movements. Jonathan A. Fox and L. David Brown. eds. pp. 219–264. Cambridge, Mass.: MIT Press.

Trouillot, Michel-Rolph. 1995. Silencing the Past. Power and the Production of History. Boston: Beacon Press.

In this article, Douglas Carranza Mena analyzes the syncretic religious and cultural practices that take place within the Cacaopera Indigenous community of eastern El Salvador. He pays attention to the forms of association and organization within this Indigenous community, particularly the *cofradías*. The *cofradías* are a medieval form of organization within the Catholic Church imposed during the colonial period in places such as Cacaopera, and the Indigenous community uses them as a form of resistance in modern times. One of the rituals performed annually by the Indigenous people there is called *el lavado de ropa* (the washing of the clothes). Although, the Catholic Church has banned this practice, every year the Indigenous community of Cacaopera and its *cofradía* organize this celebration. The celebration of *el lavado de ropa* requires each member to participate and invest time, money and other forms of cooperation for the celebration, without the expectation of financial rewards. The Indigenous people of the *cofradía* are interested mainly in local issues affecting its membership and their Indigenous community. Among such issues is their participation in the local political contestation for their rights, such as the right to have a good road from their *cantones* (small villages) to the town of Cacaopera, access to electricity and potable water. These practices have produced ideas of collective sharing, responsibility and communal solidarity that have united these communities for years in their struggle for survival.

The Washing of the Clothes: Spirituality and Resistance in Cacaopera, El Salvador

Douglas Carranza Mena

The municipality of Cacaopera is located 12 kilometers to the north of the departmental capital of San Francisco Gotera, in the Central American republic of El Salvador. The landscape of this region is steep and rocky, formed by hills and *quebradas* (rocky streams) of volcanic origin. Travel from San Francisco Gotera to Cacaopera requires an arduous bus ride on an unpaved road that in the dry season can take up to an hour. The road is nearly blocked during the rainy season when streams turn into virtual torrents and the dirt road turns to mud.

In terms of its cultural history, studies indicate that the Indigenous communities in this area are descendants from pre-Hispanic migrants from Honduras and Nicaragua. According to Mac Chapin (1990), both archaeological and anthropological investigations indicate that to the east of the Lempa River the Pre-Columbian Indigenous population was quite diverse, composed of Lenca, Xinca, and Matagalpa speakers. With the Spanish invasions and the subsequent process of colonization the Indigenous population was decimated through genocide, disease, exposure, forced labor and assimilation (Las Casas 1992; Anderson 1982; Dominguez 1984). Today the residents of Cacaopera are monolingual speakers of Spanish, although their Indigenous language was associated with the

Matagalpa group, a member of the Misumalpan family, which includes Miskito and Sumu (Campbell 1976). Sisal production and the related craft industry of hammock making is a major source of employment for Cacaoperans outside of farming. Corn and beans are the basic components in their Indigenous diet. Although the majority of Indigenous households have relied on sisal production during and after the civil war, they have experienced increasing socio-economic and cultural vulnerability due to the introduction of non-natural fibers in hammock making at a national level and to their lack of access to financial credit.

In my research, I examined the forms of association within the Indigenous community of Cacaopera. I was particularly interested in their *cofradías,* which are a medieval form of organization within the Catholic Church that was imposed during colonial times in places such as Cacaopera by the Spaniards. Between the late 1800s and the early 1900s, *cofradías* (sodalities) were hierarchical religious and political organizations whose main function was to establish a service structure and a power system within local communities (Cardenal 200–219). *Cofradías* provided religious service through personal and communal contributions (in kind, cash, participation and organizing) to support Catholic rituals including priest fees, ritual expenses, and organization (Chance and Taylor 8). Their political influence has faded, at least in Cacaopera, but in the past, they were able to influence the political power structure of the community by naming the Mayor (*alcalde mayor*) and his council (*cabildo*). The *cargo* system attached to the *cofradía* instituted a hierarchical order where only adult males could aspire to hold religious and political offices that were in charge of ordering communal life (Cancian 1967). Religious cargos, including the *mayordomía* (*mayordomo*), were assigned hierarchically according to the time in service; the chain of command was related to the prominence of the image of the saint they were serving. The end of the nineteenth-century was an important period for the modern (secular) republics of Central America as they were in the process of implementing and executing liberal policies such as the privatization of land, the development of the agro-export economy and the banking system (Lauria-Santiago 1999, Torres Rivas 1993). The deployment of these new political and social ideas forced the Catholic Church to change the nature of its landholding interests that were closely linked to the *cofradías* to a more private notion of land tenure. As a result, the Catholic Church sold many of its properties and demanded an immediate administrative overhaul of the *cofradías.* However, the Indigenous communities and municipal authorities affiliated with the *cofradías* that were in charge of the financial, spiritual, and ritual affairs resisted the changes and maintained a local power structure, despite the pressure from the ecclesiastic institution.

When I visited Cacaopera (1999–2000), the Indigenous community was still organized following the *cofradía* model, which, while it had undergone modifications over time, retained some cultural continuity with the practices of the past. Nonetheless, this community was also practicing other forms of religious association, including *Comunidades*

Eclesiales de Base (Christian Base Communities) informed by liberation theology starting in the early 1970s (Rodríguez and Lara 2000:15).

Every year the Indigenous community of Cacaopera and its *cofradía* organize a celebration called *el lavado de ropa* (the washing of clothes). The celebration of *el lavado de ropa* requires each member to participate and invest time, money, and other forms of cooperation for the celebration, without expecting financial rewards. As I observed in February 1999, the organization of the celebration, and in particular the actual *lavado de ropa* of the statues of the Virgin Mary, (the Lord) Jesus, and the Saints, differed greatly from modern and urban Catholic practices. During this experience, I realized that the Cacaopera *cofradía* had forms of organizing festivities and celebrations that did not require written agendas with specific points to be addressed and a moderator in the modern sense. Rather, they have alternative ways of organizing such events that rely on the oral transmission and memorization of the task to be implemented; of course, tradition and repetition play an important role in knowing the assignment at hand.

In fact, there was no leader or particular individual responsible for the organizing teams; everything was done collectively by virtue of personal responsibility. The organization of this ceremony surprised me because of its complexity. Not only did it include the mobilization of more than 350 people to attend the ceremony, but it also required the preparation of enough food to feed all the participants and the delegation of tasks, which included washing the clothes. All these rituals, ceremonies and celebrations were performed in order to thank the Virgin Mary, Jesus, and the Saints for the blessings that they had given the community during the previous year and for those they would be giving in the future, such as good crops. Meanwhile, it is important to note that in the nineteenth-century, the Catholic Church condemned this ceremony and its accompanying rituals as practices that according to the Church abused the saintly images of Jesus and the Virgin Mary (Cardenal 209).

The Washing of the Clothes: 120 Years Later . . .

Santiago Chalchuapa, Santa Ana, February 25–March 1st, 1880.

"Among the customs that the priest was not able to suppress were the nocturnal processions, which were very well attended and orderly. On Holy Thursday, for instance, the procession of the Cofradía of the Cross took place, [with] approximately 200 men in underwear [walking] through the streets lashing their backs with small whips. The parish priest was also displeased by the custom of washing Jesus' clothes in the river on Holy Friday, 'they do ridiculous things like that, this ceremony resembles an idolatry, they respect the Lord's old clothes more than God himself, all this is quite ridiculous.' "[1]

—Cited by Rodolfo Cardenal, 209

Cacaopera, Morazán, February 4, 1999

On February 4, 1999 I went to Cacaopera to learn more about the two Indigenous associations that I had contacted in this area. First, I contacted the Indigenous association called by some Salvadoran scholars *traditionalist* because this Indigenous association is still working within the framework of the *cofradías* associated in some way to the medieval structures of the Catholic Church. As I previously described, the *cofradía* was a colonial hierarchical organization interested in creating a power system within the community and a service force that fulfilled the Church's and the municipal needs in the community. On February 3, 1999, Antonio, the *Mayordomo* principal invited me to a special ceremony to be held in Cacaopera on February 4 and 5. I asked what kind of ceremony was going to take place. He told me it was the "*Lavado de ropa de los Santos*" (the washing of the Saints' clothes) in the Río Torola, and he gave a brief description of the celebration.

I was supposed to find Antonio at the old convent of the Church, but he was not there—he was doing some chores for the next day's celebration. Instead, I found Teresa, his wife, and other women members of the *cofradía;* few men were there. I embraced Teresa and the other women came and talked to me (I already knew some of them). Teresa told me about their illnesses and the difficulties of their lives; she looked older and had a runny nose. The other women kept working and, once in a while, looked at me, smiled, and moved their heads in a welcoming gesture. I asked Teresa what they were doing and she replied: "We are cooking *tamales pisques* for tomorrow's celebration, the *lavado the ropa* (the washing of the clothes), you know. They (making a head gesture toward a group of women) belong to the *Cuadrilla del Señor.* We are in the *Cuadrilla de la Virgen.*"

In Cacaopera, at least when I visited, the *cofradía* was divided into two groups called *cuadrillas,* each with its own *mayordomo principal* and helpers that included their wives, relatives and other members of the community. Officially, only the men are members in this *cofradía,* as the Catholic tradition mandates. Nevertheless, despite this exclusion in terms of membership, women also participate in the decision-making processes and in the food preparation. Although the standard practice is that men are in charge, there are several instances where women participate to different degrees, including the holding of official responsibilities. In her study on the *cargo* system in the Mexican community of San Miguel, H. Mathews argues that according to her data, the responsibilities are distributed by household (Mathews 285–301). In other words, instead of pinpointing and saying he or she is the *mayordoma/o,* Mathews observed that the household unit is entrusted with that responsibility. The sharing of responsibilities (for example: developing meetings, activities, food preparation and ceremonial performances) also goes beyond the household unit and may encompass those household units that are closely associated with the family in charge. The community assigns the sponsorship of religious ceremonies to those members or households that not only have a religious commitment, but also the willingness to spend material and social wealth. In Cacaopera, the only religious *cargo* system is the *cofradía,* which runs the operation of the Catholic Church in the town. Its responsibilities include the care of the Church and Saints, the performance of ceremonies, and administrative duties associated with the Church. Although the position of *mayordomo* is awarded to men, my observations agreed with Mathews' research in Mexico; it is Antonio, Teresa, and their family who bear the responsibility of the *cargo* (or *carga,* as they say in Cacaopera). This is significant because the Indigenous community has been able to put its own cultural imprint on the idea of sharing responsibilities at the spiritual and financial level. In other words, the original purpose of holding a position within the *cofradía* was to exercise influence within the municipal and religious spaces. Nevertheless, today such power has diminished considerably. As a result, the position held by Antonio is not an award, on the contrary, it represents a financial burden, as Antonio previously expressed. Thus, this position is not one of power, but an obligation in order to secure the well being of the Indigenous community.

The women were using large clay pots to make the *tamales pisques.* These tamales are made of a type of corn called *pisque,* which is boiled with ash. After the corn is washed, and ground, the dough is wrapped with banana leaves. Afterwards, the tamales are steamed until they gain a firm consistency and are then ready to be served. As Teresa explained the process, we stood in the smoke produced by the *cocina de leña* (wood burning hearth), a very common custom in the rural areas of El Salvador where electrical and gas stoves are not affordable. At that moment Antonio showed up and started to tell me about the responsibilities that he has been bearing as a *mayordomo* for almost 14 years. Usually that responsibility lasts for one year and after that the *mayordomo* sends letters to the members of the community who are eligible to assume the responsibility for the following period. However, in this case, no other member of the community has been willing to accept the *carga.* This *carga,* according to Antonio, implies giving priority to the things of the Lord instead of one's personal needs. His investment is financial and also costly in terms of time in the *asuntos* (things) of the Lord. He told me that he needs to do something in order to solve this situation because he also needs to provide for his family, but the problem is that no one else is willing to make that kind of sacrifice (material and spiritual) for the *cofradía. Cargas* are public in the sense that most of the responsibilities deal with activities and performances that are open to public view. In some instances, both Antonio and Teresa visit other members of the community in order to develop and strengthen the network for future members and to ease their burden by asking them to collaborate financially:

> "Look brother, today is not like in the past. Our people used to ask for the *carga,* and every year we had new *mayordomos,* but the situation has changed. My house is crumbling because of [my involvement in] these things, the cornfield needs attention, and there isn't time."[2]

In the early period, the institution of the *cofradía* helped the Catholic Church and the colonial authorities to administer the emerging colonial settlements. The exploitative nature of these institutions and their individual and collective funding of events are still a subject of debate among scholars and social activists of Indigenous rights (Chance and

Taylor 1–26). In anthropology, the scholarly arguments on the *cofradías* and the *cargo* system have been guided by different anthropological approaches to the study of these institutions and the *cargo* system. Points of view differ on the functional nature of non-secular organizations: one is that the *cofradías* serve as a protective device against external forces and create conditions for economic equilibrium within the community. In other words, these spaces create a social engineering control for the Indigenous communities; such spaces gain importance in the administration of colonial life.

February 5, 1999

The *lavado de ropa de los Santos* (the washing of the Saints' clothes) started around 4:00 A.M. At that time a group of women and men left for the Torola River with the food (tamales *pisques*) to prepare the following:

* To arrange the hearths for reheating the tamales and making other food;
* To prepare the chicken and rice soup, rice pudding and coffee;
* To construct the special clotheslines;
* To tend the special dining table for the washers to eat afterwards.

In addition to the *tamales,* they also brought *guineos majonchos* and *pericos* (two different types of local bananas), bread, tortillas and clay plates. All the food was provided and prepared by women and men belonging to the *cuadrillas de la Virgen* and *del Señor* (the Virgin and the Lord). Another group of women and men belonging to the same *cuadrillas* stayed in the *vieja casa del convento* (old convent house) waiting until 7:00 A.M. to arrange the four sets (bundles) of the Saints' clothes. Around that hour, they went to the Church to pick up the clothes, where a ceremony took place. The clothes were already arranged in front of the main altar, which is dedicated to the Virgen del Tránsito (Virgin of Assumption). Antonio and others had arranged the clothes the night prior to the ceremony. The prayers took place in front of the main altar under the direction of a woman who was leading the prayer with a group of about 12 women that only responded. Simultaneously, a group of men started to perform a ritual (moving in the four cardinal directions as a human block), but only one of them was praying. Their movement toward the four cardinal directions—literally facing them every 5 minutes—was done with precision and following the prayer by the leading man. The prayers directed by the woman and the old man were different in structure and rhythm and were recited simultaneously. These prayers were recited in Spanish, although it was some sort of archaic Spanish mixed with their native language that had survived and had been incorporated into the spoken language of the region. Incense was used to purify and bless the attendants surrounding the Saints' clothes. After 40 minutes of ritual, we left for the Torola River to wash the clothes. During the three-mile walk, I was able to interact with several people who did not ask me who I was. I assumed that I was familiar to some, and for others, my relation to those who knew me made them comfortable.

One of the most important aspects of the ceremony was the level of organization required for the development of the whole celebration of the *lavado de ropa*. Despite the complexity of the celebration, there was no written program or agenda.

Several days later, I asked Antonio how they were able to accomplish this level of success. He said:

> "Look brother, we prepare this with time on our favor, besides we have been doing this for years. During the war (the so called civil war, 1980–1992) we were unable to do certain things, and so we had to make changes. The *cofradía* organizes everything, the *Cuadrilla de la Virgen* and the *Cuadrilla del Señor*, both *cuadrillas* are in charge of the entire celebration. If some people are not able to participate, others will do it, we do not get upset, there are no bosses, not like in José Pedro's organization (the head of the non traditional Indigenous Association). We do not force people, if they can not help us right away, they join us later."[3]

Antonio often brought into the conversation the difference between their Indigenous community and the organization led by José Pedro. José Pedro is a selfproclaimed Maya priest who has organized a Lenca Indigenous association that receives support from international organizations, including NGOs. Some Indigenous members of the community belong to José Pedro's organization, but for the most part, the latter's membership consists of young people affiliated with the governmental *Casa de la Cultura* who are interested in knowing about the culture of Cacaopera. Antonio's continuous reference to the distinction between them goes back to the time when José Pedro was in charge of the *Casa de la Cultura*. Later on he became the leader of Antonio's Indigenous association, but conflicts regarding their personal interaction forced José Pedro to abandon this organization and to move on, becoming a Maya priest. Their mutual animosity and jealousy is based on the question of cultural representation, José Pedro considers that Antonio's Indigenous association is controlled by the Catholic Church. Antonio, on the other hand, has criticized José Pedro for his *Ladino* roots and for bringing a foreign [Maya] spirituality to the Cacaopera culture. As I mentioned above, Cacaoperans arrived from Nicaragua hundreds of years ago and they are affiliated to the Misumalpan language family, and in no way are they related to Maya traditions. For his part, José Pedro claims that his Indigenous community belongs to the Lenca family, a contention based on the cultural dominance of the Lenca in the area.

Two weeks after the ceremony of the *lavado de ropa* José Pedro's association organized a festivity to honor the *Lord of Cacao* or *Aw Kakaw*, a Maya symbol of life and prosperity promoted by José Pedro. However, none of the members of Antonio's association participated in this ceremony. In contrast to the ceremony of the *lavado de ropa* that the *cofradía* organized, the festivity that José Pedro organized was widely reported in El Salvador's most distributed newspaper, *La Prensa Gráfica*, in its Sunday edition. In the past, José Pedro had been a student in a Catholic seminary; nevertheless, the rituals performed by his association were not related to any ritual of the Catholic Church. Contrary to the way the ceremony of the washing of the clothes is attended by the community without the need of a formal invitation, in the case of José Pedro's association, an official invitation was circulated days before the festivity began. Although José Pedro's ritual ceremony was intended to celebrate the Lord of Cacao, it was also a performance that would bring attention to his association in order to reaffirm its cultural representativeness of the region and secure future funding from national and international institutions. José Pedro's spiritual approach combines mostly Maya rituals with Nahua and Lenca features, foreign elements that have created uneasiness in terms of spiritual identity among the Indigenous members the *cofradía*. As a result, the invitation included the official program for the four days that the festivity would last.

In contrast, the *cofradía* that organizes the *lavado de ropa* lacks financial support from NGOs or transnational Indigenous associations, a modern sophisticated organizational structure; it even lacks support from the hierarchy of the Catholic Church. Nevertheless, it is compensated by the support received from the Indigenous community itself. However, most of them live below the poverty line in relation to other rural inhabitants of the Salvadoran countryside. After my conversation with Antonio during the walk to the Río Torola to wash the clothes, I was able to interact with other members of the community. Almost all of them said that they have been participating in this ceremony since they were kids; they said their parents were members of the *cuadrillas*. They also agreed that more people attended in previous years, people also donated more food and other necessary things. Like Antonio, they said that people do not want cargas anymore, that the civil war made these kinds of meetings impossible due to the state distrust, the implementation of martial law, and other state security measures. They also said that common crime and delinquency has lately hampered their trust, especially for women who are the subject of attacks by common delinquents.

During our procession, we made a stop 500 meters before we got to the riverbank; a group of women and men who were at the river came to meet us to pray again for 20 minutes. They lighted candles and burned incense in front of the four women carrying the four bundles of clothes. However, this time only the man who had led the previous set of prayers was in charge of praying. The procession then continued to the riverbank. There were eight *fogones* (hearths) being used by each of the two *cuadrillas*, and each contained coffee, milk and rice, rice and chicken soup, and tamales *pisques*.

Each *cuadrilla* also had its own supply of sweet bread and bananas to feed 300 people or more. When we arrived the first thing that took place was another round of prayers for 20 minutes led by the same man. However, this time he included the same kind of ritual performed at the Church, facing the four cardinal points (José Pedro's association also performed this ritual of the cardinal points two weeks later in the *Lord of Cacao* festivity). More than 250 people were assembled at the riverbank, most of them came for the ceremony and to eat and participate. Some people were clearly *Ladinos* (non-Indigenous), but they were observing the ceremony from a distance. After the brief prayer ceremony, the members of the *cuadrillas* distributed the food under the direction of the women supervising each *fogón*. There was a specific order in the way the food was distributed, first, important guests, second, people that provided services, and then the general public.

During the ceremony and food distribution, Antonio was in charge of the *Cuadrilla de la Virgen* and Catarino of the *Cuadrilla del Señor,* and the leading prayer man was in charge of setting up the bundles of clothes to be distributed later. The distribution of clothes was performed randomly by some members of the *cuadrillas* at the edge of the riverbank and near the *tendederos* (clotheslines), the latter were made out of tree branches and sisal cords. The washing was done by men and women, but mostly women, and it was done at the point of convergence of the *Río Torola* and a smaller stream, called *El encuentro* (the meeting point). During this process, the food was distributed in large and double portions one from each *cuadrilla.* After the four bundles of clothes were distributed and washed, they were hung on the *tendederos.* The washers sat at the special table—where the clothes were set previously for distribution—to eat their meals after a short prayer. The *lavado de ropa* is a ceremony that takes place on a yearly basis and that has created a sense of communal solidarity among the Ulúa Indigenous people of Cacaopera despite the obstacles, prohibitions and political harassment from those who want changes in their way of seeing Indigenousness.

Even 120 years after the priest of Santiago Chalchuapa condemned the practice of the *lavado de ropa* as a ridiculous ritual, the Indigenous community of Cacaopera continues its spiritual practices. The *cofradía,* as an organizing tool for Indigenous people in Cacaopera, has been able to overcome the Catholic prohibitions and sanctions of the nineteenth-century, the modernization of Catholic practices for organizing under the ideas promoted by liberation theology during the 1980s, and today, they resist competing Indigenous associations with other views about how to organize the community. The critiques against their practices during the nineteenth-century were aimed at finishing the evangelizing project initiated in the sixteenth-century. The rudimentary goals of the nineteenth-century were coupled with the need to reform the Church for the advent of the next century where the demands for more control were the result of a more complex mode of governing. It was a mode of governing that experienced the dilemmas encountered in the emergent liberalism after decades of internal strife against the conservatives. Likewise, liberation theology and the emergence of the Christian Base Communities attempted to dislodge the unity of the *cofradía* during the civil war in El Salvador. Those Indigenous people that resisted further changes were accused of collaboration with the *status quo* of the old hierarchical Church, even if that same Church one hundred years earlier had tried to remove and prohibit this Indigenous mode of organizing because it worked against *the good morals* of the Christian faith. Also, the new and modified evangelizing project of the Catholic Church and other Christian denominations has redrawn the space for Indigenous participation within their institutions. In El Salvador, Indigenous theology is considered valid only if it is performed according to the signs of modern times and the practices of NGOs, or if other international institutions lend their support to these new initiatives. José Pedro's initiatives fall within these expectations of transnational spirituality and solidarity, the redrawing of this transnational *space* of Indigenous spirituality is washing away the old vestiges of resistance of the Indigenous people of Cacaopera. Novel forms of organizing Indigenous communities are emerging within this modern *space,* however, these modern forms may not represent the aspiration of these communities that for more than 500 years have resisted the imposition and appropriation of identity and culture respectively.

The practice of the ritual of the washing of the clothes shows the hybridity of spiritual practices of the Indigenous community of Cacaopera that I summarize as follows:

* Use of ritual paraphernalia such as copal (Indigenous incense) and traditional Catholic incense;
* Prayer performance, the use of the Catholic rosary combined with the movement of people facing the four cardinal points (sacred to the Indigenous communities of the entire region of Mesoamerica);
* The use of the private striated space of the Catholic Temple to initiate the ceremonies, which end in the open space of the riverbank with the washing of the clothes;
* Although men are the ones assigned the responsibility (within the *cofradía*) of practicing the rituals, women also participate as leading prayer individuals;
* Organizationally the previous points are reflected on the overall development of the celebration of the washing of the clothes.

Conclusion cannot be made regarding these ongoing cultural practices, but based on my observations I would like to make the following comments that I hope will generate a better understanding of the complexity of contemporary Salvadoran society, despite the state's argument of cultural homogeneity.

1. The Indigenous association of Cacaopera working within the *cofradía* structure does not depend on the cultural movement developed after the Peace agreements of 1992—such is the case of José Pedro's association and other similar Indigenous associations—in order to provide economic sustainability to these communities.
2. The Indigenous people belonging to the *cofradía* do not see the importance of publicly revealing their cultural practices because their primary concern is the maintenance of their traditions within the community. A different case is seen in José Pedro's association where there is a clear politico-cultural motivation to "recover" Indigenous cultural rights and other important goals for the revival of the Indigenous culture such as identity as is understood within the limits imposed by the state.
3. The Indigenous people of the *cofradía* are interested mainly in local issues affecting its membership or their Indigenous community. Among such issues is their participation in the local political contestation for particular rights, for example, right to have a good road from their *cantones* to the town of Cacaopera, access to electricity and potable water. However, their political power is not as great as that

of José Pedro's association. The latter ties with the regional Lenca movement (an Indigenous movement that originally emerged in Honduras), NGOs (national and foreign), and other national cultural institutions, which make him the political and cultural broker *par excellence* in Cacaopera.

The use of the concept of the social within Indigenous communities arrived to these communities with liberation theology, among others, because of its concern with socio-political and economic issues. The Indigenous people associated with the *cofradía* do not emphasize the "social" in the way the Christian Base Communities or José Pedro's association have for the past eight years. This situation has generated an image that tends to be interpreted by others as one of indifference on the part of the *cofradía* and, in some cases, others have even singled them out as government collaborators. Nevertheless, their presence in local politics makes the Indigenous community associated with the Church an important socio-political asset to be persuaded when there is a need for support of local and regional policies. Despite their greater financial and institutional resources NGOs, the Church, and the government cannot produce the ideas of collective sharing, responsibility and communal solidarity that for years have maintained these communities together in their struggle for survival.

Works Cited

Anderson, Thomas R. *El Salvador* 1932. Trans. Juan Mario Castellanos. San José: Editorial Universitaria Centroamericana, 1982.

Cancian, Frank. *Political and Religious Organizations.* Ithaca, N.Y.: Cornell University Press, 1967.

Campbell, Lyle Richard. "The Last Lenca." *International Journal of American Linguistics* 42.1 (1976): 73–78.

Cardenal, Rodolfo. *El Poder Eclesiástico en El Salvador.* San Salvador: Dirección de Publicaciones e Impresos, 2001.

Chance, J. K. and Taylor, W. B. "Cofradías and Cargos: An Historical Perspective on the Mesoamerican Civil-Religious Hierarchy." *American Ethnologist* 12.1 (1985): 1–26.

Chapin, Mac. *La Población Indígena de El Salvador.* San Salvador: Dirección de Publicaciones e Impresos del Ministerio de Educación, 1990.

De las Casas, Bartolomé. *A Short Account of the Destruction of the Indies.* London: Penguin Books, 1992.

The Devastation of the Indies: A Brief Account. Translated from *Tratados I de Fray Bartolome de las Casas 1965.* Fondo de Cultura Económica, Mexico. London: The John Hopkins University Press, 1992.

Dominguez Sosa, Julio Alberto. Las Tribus Nonualcas y su Caudillo Anastasio Aquino. San Jose: Editorial Universitaria Centroamericana, 1984.

Lauria-Santiago, Aldo A. *An Agrarian Republic: Commercial Agriculture and the Politics of Peasant Communities in El Salvador, 1823–1914.* Pittsburgh: University of Pittsburgh Press, 1999.

Mathews, Holly F. "We Are Mayordomo: A Reinterpretation of Women's Role in the Mexican Cargo System". *American Ethnologist* 12 (1985): 285–301.

Rodríguez, América and Lara, Carlos B. "Las Perspectivas de la Globalización: Identidades Indígenas de Izalco y Cacaopera." Conference presentation. San Salvador: V Congreso Centroamericano de Historia. 2000.

Torres Rivas, Edelberto. *History and Society in Central America.* Trans. Douglas Sullivan-Gonzalez. Austin: University of Texas Press, 1993.

NOTES

1. Santiago Chalchuapa, Santa Ana, 25 de febrero–1° de marzo de 1880: "Entre las costumbres que el cura no pudo suprimir estaban las procesiones nocturnas, las cuales eran muy concurridas y ordenadas. El Jueves santo, por ejemplo, tenía lugar la procesión de la *cofradía* de la Cruz, aproximadamente 200 hombres en calzoncillos por las calles pegándose en las espaldas con pequeños látigos. También disgustó al párroco la costumbre de lavar la ropa de Jesús en el río el viernes santo, 'hacen ridiculeces, parece esa ceremonia una idolatría, más respetan los trapos viejos del Señor, que al mismo Dios, todo esto es muy ridículo' (Citado por R. Cardenal, 209).
2. "Mire hermano, hoy ya no es como antes. Nuestra gente buscaba la carga, y cada año teníamos nuevos mayordomos, pero la situación ha cambiado. A mí se me está cayendo la casa por andar en estas cosas, la siembra necesita atención y no queda tiempo."
3. "Mire hermano, nosotros preparamos esto con tiempo, además hemos estado haciendo esto por años. Durante la guerra (la llamada guerra civil, 1980–1992) si ya no pudimos hacer algunas cosas y tuvimos que cambiarlas. La cofradía organiza todo, la cuadrilla de la Virgen y la cuadrilla del Señor, las dos cuadrillas están a cargo de toda la celebración. Si alguna gente no puede participar, otros lo hacen, nosotros no nos enojamos, no hay jefes como en la organización de José Pedro (el responsable de la asociación Indígena no tradicional). Nosotros no obligamos a la gente, si ellos no pueden ayudarnos en ese momento, ellos vienen más tarde."

This article is the conclusion of the book titled *Place, Language, and Identity in Afro-Costa Rican Literature.* In this book, Dorothy Mosby examines the literary and intellectual contributions of Afro-Caribbean authors in Costa Rica. She explores their history of migration, their political marginalization, the racism that they have to face on a daily basis, and their participation in local and national social movements. In addition, she examines the richness of their literary practices, the multicultural dimension of their artistic production, and their sense of belonging to both, the nation, and the African diaspora.

Becoming Costa Rican

DOROTHY MOSBY

From the literary contributions of black writers of Afro–West Indian descent in Costa Rica, it becomes clear that the expression of cultural identity is constituted by the convergence of history, political and social movements, and location. The generations of writers who witnessed the post-1948 political interest in the enfranchisement of the Afro–West Indian population articulate a common concern, as do the generations born well after the event. The unifying conflict for all black writers studied in this volume is the great tension regarding the expressed desire to belong to Costa Rica, which often becomes, as Ian Smart asserts, "more of a desired goal than an achieved one" (*CAW,* 41). Certainly, this tension between cultural difference and prevailing national ideologies is not unique to Afro–Costa Rican writing. Most notably, this "double-consciousness" has been explored by several generations of black writers in different locations in the African diaspora. First articulated by African American intellectual W. E. B. DuBois in *The Souls of Black Folk,* double-consciousness describes the condition of U.S. blacks in the post-Reconstruction period. DuBois claims, "One ever feels his two-ness—an American, a Negro; two souls, two thoughts, two unreconciled strivings; two warring ideals in dark body." British cultural critic Paul Gilroy examines DuBois's ideas as a response to modernity and deploys the concept of double-consciousness to verbalize the complex of nation, "race," ethnicity, and language in the black (North) Atlantic. In *The Black Atlantic,* Gilroy observes: "Striving to be both European and black requires some specific forms of double consciousness . . . where, racist, nationalist, or ethnically absolutist discourses orchestrate political relationships so that these identities appear to be mutually exclusive, occupying the space between them or trying to demonstrate their continuity has been viewed as a provocative and even oppositional act of political insubordination."[1] In spite of Gilroy's geographic concentration on transatlantic movements and communication among diaspora blacks in England, the United States, and the Anglophone Caribbean (particularly Jamaica and Guyana), the concepts he explores may be applied to the "Other America" in the black

South Atlantic and to migrations to nonmetropolitan centers such as Costa Rica, Panama, and Nicaragua. The settlement of migrant subjects in nonmetropolitan sites presents an oppositional engagement with a national discourse that negates the possibility of being black and a citizen of the nation-state. This is even more pronounced for the fourth generation that has no old home in the West Indies or Limón to which to anchor their cultural identity; Costa Rica is their only home.

Double-consciousness in Afro–Costa Rican writing reveals this struggle to be Costa Rican and black, which is characterized by a difficult negotiation of difference and national identity. However, Afro–Costa Rican writing stands not only between "two great cultural assemblages" of ethnic identity and national identity as an expression of diaspora double-consciousness, but also between other cultural sites.[2] It is the product of complex migrations and transmigrations: the transatlantic passage of African slaves to the West Indies and the dispersal of Caribbean peoples all over the world. Afro–Costa Rican identity emerges as the result of migration of a colonized population who were once the ethnic majority at "home" to a situation as a neocolonized, ethnic minority population in a country with its own distinct cultural identity. These multiple dispersals constitute and inform the expression of this identity in literature. In the case of works by writers of Afro-West Indian descent, the desire to be Costa Rican and express ethnic difference figures prominently in the literature.

Revisiting the Limonese Creole saying "me navel-string bury dere," we can observe that this is not an easy proclamation or a simple symbolic gesture for the generations of blacks of West Indian descent born in Costa Rica. As presented in the literature by several generations of writers, the struggle to declare that their "navel-string is buried there" is an act that sets in motion the emergence of an Afro-Costa Rican cultural identity by claiming home for a former immigrant identity. Home is refigured and reimagined from the memory of what was in the West Indies of the first generation, the bridging of two worlds in the second and third generations, and eventually the hope of the future offered by the fourth generation. The literature written by blacks of West Indian descent demonstrates that cultural identity transforms over time and "is a matter of 'becoming' as well as 'being'" and that it "belongs to the future as much as the past."[3]

In the process of becoming Afro–Costa Rican, which is also a process of being ethnically and culturally different while being "at home," the concepts of home and nation are recodified over time. Black writers in Costa Rica articulate the ability of a people to configure their cultural identity by "reconstructing old homes and imagining new ones."[4] This practice is reflected in the historical shifts in attitude toward place, language, and nation. These shifts mark transformative moments in the configuration of cultural identity in Afro–Costa Rican literature, particularly the destabilization of the naturalized homologous association of home and identity. The first generation as literary precursors (including storytellers, calypsonians, Alderman Johnson Roden, and Dolores Joseph) demonstrates a British West Indian immigrant identity situated in the islands of origin in spite of displacement in Costa Rica. Bilingual second- and third-generation writers Eulalia Bernard and Quince Duncan represent an ambiguous position between the islands of their parents and grandparents and the country of their birth. Like their predecessors of the first generation, there are "reflections" on the condition of exile of the immigrant identity. However, Bernard and Duncan reveal a continuous play of tensions between an affinity for West Indian culture and their national allegiance to Costa Rica. Both writers display these tensions through the incorporation of ancestral history and the English language in their texts—either in its entirety, in the case of Bernard, or as phonetically transcribed phrases, in the work of Duncan. Both Bernard and Duncan use Spanish and English to talk about the "new" home.

Eulalia Bernard negotiates between the cultural spaces of the West Indies and Jamaica and supports an embrace of both worlds by challenging the latter to accommodate the former. She holds the myths and contradictions of Costa Rica before her nation like a mirror. She subversively addresses the polemic by turning those same myths of ethnic homogeneity and erasure of blackness (both in the present and in the colonial past) against themselves. In her poetry, she explores language and how it shapes and constructs cultural identity through a mixture of languages, registers, humor, protest, West Indian cultural traditions, mimicry, and parody. She assaults traditional constructs of poetry through a valorization of the Afro-West Indian oral tradition and "playing" with the limits of language. Bernard and other Afra-Hispanic writers "deal seriously and imaginatively with linguistic, ontological, and epistemical issues."[5]

Quince Duncan values his West Indian heritage and cultural difference. He proposes a position that can be described as integrationist, but like Bernard is not assimilationist. Duncan negotiates the so-called third space or in-between space where two cultures meet. Like Eulalia Bernard, whose poetry straddles the desired outcome of her vision of a harmonious multiculturalism and the reality impeding this Utopian desire, Duncan presents in his narrative a negotiation that is "neither assimilation nor collaboration" that "makes possible the emergence of an 'interstitial' agency that refuses the binary representation of social antagonism."[6]

The perspectives of Bernard and Duncan on Costa Rica as home and nation contrast with younger writers Shirley Campbell and Delia McDonald. Their poetry does not resonate with the echoes of the preoccupations of locating and claiming home of the immigrant identity. In Spanish, they affirm "home" is Costa Rica, and their culture is a not-so-harmonious integration of the West Indian past and the dominant Hispanic culture. They explore the difficulty of affirming their blackness in a country that clings to the national myths of homogeneity. where blackness still denotes an element of "foreignness." The two younger poets present a shift in the Afro-Costa Rican cultural identity by representing a movement away from a West Indian cultural identity toward one that can be termed as more Afro-Hispanic or Afro-Latin American with a diaspora consciousness. This shift can be described as such because determining the location "home" is not an issue for this generation of writers; their concern is with making the land of their birth recognize their two-ness—their blackness and their Costa Ricanness. The literary preoccupations of Campbell and McDonald are rooted in a difference that no longer adheres to their ancestors' islands of origins. Although acknowledging certain West Indian cultural retentions (such as foods, carnival, and obeah) and the history of the earlier West Indian immigrants through the motifs of the train and the imagery of plantations, their concern is not finding and claiming place—rather, they want to assert it. As part of a new generation, their concern is with how to be black and Costa Rican when the national dominant discourse signals that the two positions are mutually exclusive. In their poetic vision, the West Indies as well as Africa are mythic and imagined places. The poets lack the intensity of a cultural affinity with the West Indies that is present in the works of Alderman Johnson Roden, Dolores Joseph, Eulalia Bernard, and Quince Duncan. Nor do they demonstrate the problematic "mascon" elements that Ian Smart (via Stephen Henderson) describes as terms that "evoke with naked directness the primordial sense of belonging to the ethno-linguistic minority group" (*CAW*, 42).

It is evident from such a reductive view that Smart did not take into consideration the possibility of the transformation of cultural identity over time. He did not factor in the possibility of writers such as Shirley Campbell and Delia McDonald. He did not examine the possibility of change owing to the increased cultural contact and integration into the dominant culture or the preference of the younger generations of Afro-Costa Ricans for Spanish—not only for commercial reasons (work, education, and publication), but also because it is their first and sometimes only language. The fourth generation is distanced from the West Indies and assimilated into Hispanic culture in childhood. They speak Spanish as their first language, and it is their language of choice; therefore, they can no longer be identified by the "mascon" elements they are able to recognize. Although the fourth generation is a minority, it is no longer part of a separate ethno-linguistic group. In comparison to Eulalia Bernard and Quince Duncan, Shirley Campbell and Delia McDonald do not adhere to an imaginary psychic attachment to the West Indies. They turn away from the islands of their forebears and look inward to the place they call home and attempt to force it to face their blackness and accept difference. More so in Campbell, there is an effort to bridge to the wider community of blacks in the Americas and the diaspora. Both Shirley Campbell and Delia McDonald honor this diaspora consciousness by recalling historical and literary figures (such as Nicolás Guillén, Aimé Césaire, and Claude McKay) and through the images of a continuum of black women as givers of life and guardians of culture. Instead of seeking a home or forging in the imagination a connection to the now distant West Indies, the later generation of writers seeks a cultural citizenship and not the political citizenship of previous generations. According to Aihwa Ong, "[C]ultural citizenship is the demand of disadvantaged subjects for full citizenship in spite of their cultural differences from mainstream society."[7] The younger writers define a new history and a new landscape without returning to the West Indies, but make a link with their foremothers and the motherland, Costa Rica.

Afro-Costa Rican cultural identity has transformed over time as a result of social, historical, and political events and contact with dominant society, and this transformation is articulated in the literature. Generations of writers express different sentiments of belonging to Costa Rica as a part of this cultural identity. For the generations that witnessed the post-civil war enfranchisement of the Afro-West Indian population, citizenship was granted by the governing junta. However, from the legal act of "nationalizing" the Afro-West Indians, questions emerged, particularly in works by Eulalia Bernard and

Quince Duncan, about the struggle to find meaning in "belonging" to the nation-state that previously excluded their forebears. However, these expressions and dilemmas of belonging to Costa Rica are addressed in the writings of all generations. Cultural identity is rooted in a territory, but needs to foster a sense of belonging in an alien culture. This difficult negotiation raises issues of ethnicity and language in the process of affirming place and nation. In the process of combating imagery that blacks in Costa Rica are "foreign," Afro–Costa Rican writers refute myths of ethnic and linguistic homogeneity through the expression of their cultural identity in literature.

There remains much work to be done in the recovery of texts written by blacks of West Indian descent, particularly the older "foundational" texts. As Miriam DeCosta-Willis affirms, "[I]t is possible that the recovery of lost and forgotten texts will permit the archeological reconstruction of a discursive tradition, however fragmentary and discontinuous."[8] Though this comment specifically refers to the situation of a tradition of women's writing in Afra-Hispanic literary studies, it can be applied to the general situation of "emerging" literatures. This study has attempted to establish a context and a frame to build a more complete literary history of Afro–Costa Rican writing in English, Creole, and Spanish.

In the field of Afro–Costa Rican literary criticism, Ian Smart, Richard Jackson, Donald Gordon, Janet Jones Hampton, and Paulette Ramsay have done important and pioneering work, and Dellita Martin–Ogunsola added the important translation of Duncans short stories. Whereas these and other scholars have made significant contributions, which serve as a foundation for this investigation, I have attempted here to expand the scope and depth of Afro-Costa Rican literary studies.

Notes

1. DuBois, *Souls of Black Folk,* 5; Gilroy, *The Black Atlantic: Modernity and Double Consciousness,* 1. I agree with the pitfalls of Gilroy's study addressed by Lourdes Martínez-Echázabal. She asserts that Gilroy's "Anglocentric gaze" in *The Black Atlantic* should have prompted him to name his book *The Black North Atlantic.* She accurately observes, "Gilroy, like other British and US cultural critics, seems only to pay lip service to African Latin America. . . . [T]his oversight is due to a metonymic reading of the Americas, one that privileges some places (the US and Jamaica), and treats them as if they constitute and, consequently could stand for the whole of the Americas" ("Hybridity and Diasporization in the 'Black Atlantic': The Cases of *Chombo,"* 121).
2. Gilroy, *Black Atlantic,* 1.
3. Hall, "Cultural Identity," 70.
4. Roy, "Postcoloniality and Politics of Identity," 102.
5. DeCosta-Willis, "Afra-Hispanic Writers," 215.
6. Homi K. Bhabha, "Culture's In-Between," 58.
7. Aihwa Ong, "Cultural Citizenship," 264.
8. DeCosta-Willis, "Afra-Hispanic Writers," 204.

CHAPTER SEVEN

IMMIGRATION

Central American peoples have settled in the United States throughout the twentieth century. However, they have done so in massive numbers starting with the 1980s, particularly as a result of the civil conflicts in El Salvador and Guatemala. While the conservative sector and some racist perspectives on American society consider these migratory trends damaging to the fabric and resources of the U.S., there is a certain collective responsibility that we all have in U.S. society for the arrival of these immigrants. On the one hand, our own lifestyles have played a role in the destruction of the Central American environment and the exploitation of Central American workers. Also, our collective indifference made it possible for foreign policies during the Reagan and Bush Sr. administrations to grant financial and military support to the military regimes in Central America during the 1980s. As we discussed in Chapters 3 and 5, the price paid by Central American peoples was extremely high, since they had to endure massacres and human rights violations such as torture and illegal imprisonment, and they were forced to flee their towns and countries and start the trek north in search of a place to live under different conditions.

In spite of this, large numbers of immigrants from Central America live today at the margins of U.S. society because they lack the documents to gain access to basic rights such as healthcare, job security and political participation. Instead, they are part of an informal U.S. economy that very much replicates the lives of slaves in the not so distant but dark past of this nation. While there are conservative groups that continue to strive for the expulsion of these immigrants, the fact is that they are here to stay. Combined with other Latin American immigrant populations they outnumber other minorities, and they have become a necessary part of the fabric of this society. They clean the parks and streets where we walk and the homes of the middle and upper class; they care for their children, and they produce many of the agricultural products that keep this nation's economy going.

Unfortunately for Central American peoples—particularly those of Guatemala and El Salvador—their countries of origin have an interest in the continued export of a percentage of their populations. Their living in the north ensures that they will be sending copious remittances to their relatives, radically boosting the national economy, taking part of the responsibility for social services and so forth.

However, there are many other effects of immigration, many within the realm of culture. These include the transnationalization of citizenship, the emergence of alternative forms of organizing, and the traumatic displacement of peoples in the global panorama as war refugees, survivors and newly adopted members of non-Central American families. As a result, there are many positive consequences to this immigration, particularly, the visibility that Central American cultural and ethnic diversity has in the diaspora, and the emergence of a regional Central American identity and culture that is not possible in contemporary times in the isthmus but that is quite real and palpable in U.S. cities where Central American populations have settled. In addition, is the activism of young Central Americans that are part of diverse local chapters and a national network of DREAMers that seek access to education and labor opportunities for Central American and other immigrants that came to the United States at a young age.

Today Central Americans have positioned themselves as socio-political and cultural players in the places where they have settled since the 1980s. In the United States, they continue to be a force in their struggle for human rights and dignity. That continued activism has gained relevance as new immigrants from Central America face massive raids in their workplaces along with deportation and other humiliating treatment. This includes such cases as the criminalization of their immigrant status that has led to the use of electronic devises to control their movements on the part of the Immigration and Customs Enforcement Office (ICE).

The Central American immigrant experience includes a continued cultural production that reflects not only this population's place of origin, but the cultural practices created throughout its process of interaction with their new cultural space. Central Americans have impacted U.S. urban settings by moving into those spaces, but, most importantly, by participating in the urban experience, challenging cultural traditions and establishing cultural bridges that bring together not only the Central American communities but others that face similar challenges as immigrants as well. Today our economy is also propelled by small entrepreneurs, including transnational Central American business leaders. Immigrants from the isthmus teach in our schools, work in the health care system, are politically engaged, and are constantly moving through and impacting diverse cultural spaces.

The Central American experience as a transnational community has challenged the traditional nationalistic agendas promoted both by the country of origin and by the new place of settlement. It has created the need for an academic, institutional and legal overhaul in the way we think about immigrant communities. As a result of war, economic displacement, and violence from the 1980s until today, Central Americans in the United States today face challenges that combine the traditional views that an immigrant community must be integrated to the national culture or to larger Latino communities that seek to overpower them, and the innovative perspectives of this transnational community that is part of a new global ordering.

On the other hand, there are also negative consequences to immigration, particularly as immigrants are marginalized and excluded and as they face high levels of violence that easily compare to the violence that they or their parents escaped during the civil wars in Central America. In the 1980s immigrant children from Central America faced physical threats and endured cultural isolation in their schools and neighborhoods. These bullying conditions prompted a reaction that gave birth to gangs, which became not only a permanent presence in US society, but also turned into a transnational social phenomena that extended its reach into Central America, Mexico, and beyond. Gang threats and violence have also caused a massive migration from Central America to the US and neighboring countries. Despite the physical threats, the difficult logistical conditions of migrating through Mexico, and the massive deportations since 2008, Central Americans continue migrating in large numbers. In addition, the effects of the global recession at the end of the first decade of the new millennium have increased the total number of Central Americans looking for better economic conditions in the US. Today, Central American migrants continue to argue for a comprehensive immigration reform that will allow them to live under dignified conditions and to unify their families.

Before moving on to the readings included in this chapter, we would like to mention that the experience of immigration in Central America is not limited to the displacement of populations to the north, but it is also quite evident internally. Large segments of the population move from the rural areas to the cities in all the Central American nations in an effort to find jobs as part of the service economy that neoliberal policies have institutionalized in the region. But others also move from one country to another in search of the means to survive. The most important and visible group among them is the population of Nicaraguan immigrants that have settled in the last two decades in Costa Rica. For further reading on the issue, we would like to suggest the book *Threatening Others: Nicaraguans and the Formation of National Identities in Costa Rica* by Carlos Sandoval-García.

Beth Baker-Cristales, an anthropologist and activist in Los Angeles, wrote the first article in this chapter. This article is part of her book-length study *Salvadoran Migration to Southern California*. In it she examines the modern history of El Salvador in search for explanations to the migration patterns of Salvadorans to the United States, particularly to Southern California.

The author moves through the history of Central America and its labor practices, the abolishment of communal lands and the privatization of these lands for the cultivation of coffee, sugar, cotton and other crops as some of the sources for poverty and economic dependence in El Salvador. She also explores the militarization of the rural areas, at first as part of the liberal reforms meant to establish coffee as the national product of export, and later on during the military dictatorships and the civil war (1980–1992).

As Baker-Cristales explains, "[s]mall numbers of Salvadorans came to the United States throughout the 1940s and 1950s" (41). While their numbers increased during the 1960s and 1970s, it wasn't until the 1980s that Salvadorans, both documented and undocumented, came in massive numbers to the United States. However, as the author explains, the numbers of documented immigrants from El Salvador decreased by the end of the civil war. However, it is merely impossible to obtain precise data about the numbers of undocumented Salvadorans that migrate every year to the United States nowadays, as they escape from economic and social oppression, extreme poverty and the lack of resources, education, healthcare and opportunities in their home country.

The Genesis of Salvadoran Migration to the United States

BETH BAKER-CRISTALES

The majority of Salvadorans in the United States today came here during the decade of the 1980s, a time of war and economic hardship. The war lasted from approximately 1980 to 1992, but was preceded by decades of brutality and widespread impoverishment. And while the war provided the immediate impetus for people to flee their homeland, Salvadorans had long participated in migratory movements before the war; and migration to the United States emerged as an extension of these migratory patterns. El Salvador's political economy, based on a centuries-old agroexport economy controlled by a small group of powerful landowners, is the immediate cause of both the war and the virtual expulsion of people from El Salvador. The peace accords signed in 1992 put an end to the war, but migration to the United States has continued apace as Salvadorans confront the limitations of a dependent economy focused on the generation of profits rather than on

"The Genesis of Salvadoran Migration to the United States," *Salvadoran Migration to Southern California: Redefining El Hermano Lejano* by Beth Baker-Cristales, 2004. Gainesville: University Press of Florida, 2004, pp. 31–46. Reprinted with permission of the University Press of Florida.

the satisfaction of human needs. This chapter reviews the history of El Salvador with an eye towards explicating the reasons for Salvadoran migration to the United States.

The Legacy of Colonialism

When the Spanish settlers arrived in Central America in the early 1500s, they encountered a complex mix of ethnic groups interconnected by political affiliations and economic exchange. In El Salvador, there were three main indigenous groups: the Pipil, who spoke a dialect of Nahuatl; the Pokoman, who spoke a Mayan dialect; and the Lenca, who spoke their own language. Subsistence was based upon the cultivation of maize, beans, squash, chiles, and a variety of other vegetables and fruits. Individual ownership of parcels of land was largely unknown, and land use was based upon membership in a corporate group and upon need.

Central America did not provide the European explorers and settlers with the gold and silver that Mexico and Peru did. Instead, they came to depend upon the cultivation and export of agricultural products in demand in Europe at the time—cacao, balsam, and later indigo. The indigenous populations found themselves victim to forced labor in the form of *repartimiento*, a requirement that the men of the communities provide labor for the Spanish. They were also subjected to outright slavery, the forced payment of tribute to the Spanish crown, and to European diseases to which they had no immunity. Indigenous forms of self-governance were sublimated to the Spanish crown and the administrative control of the vice-royalty of New Spain.

It was only later that the European settlers began to claim their own parcels of land, first through grants from the Spanish crown and later through claiming title to lands previously controlled by indigenous communities. These communities were progressively pushed into more marginal agricultural lands, with communal land holdings occupying progressively less and less territory. The process of privatization of and was well advanced by the end of the nineteenth century, with only 40 percent of the territory of El Salvador remaining in the form of indigenous, communal land holdings by 1875 (Menjívar 1980:99). Indian resistance to these measures was strong throughout the colonial and early republican period. Despite the repressive measures enacted to controll the rural population, there were at least five uprisings between the years of 1872 and 1898 in the coffee growing regions of El Salvador (Durham 1988:64).

From Independence to Dependence

When Mexico declared its independence from Spain in 1821, Central America joined the newly independent state, but later seceded and formed the Central American Federation, which lasted from 1824 to 1839. Competition between conservatives in Guatemala and liberals in the southern provinces caused the breakup of the United Provinces of Central America, leading to the formation of the five independent countries we know today. It was about this time that coffee cultivation spread throughout Central America, and the newly formed countries would forever be shaped by the distinct landowning patterns and social relations that coffee production engendered. In El Salvador, land tenure patterns were extremely skewed, and political power rested in the hands of a small class of land-owning elite. Political independence was compromised by international relations of economic dependence.

The nineteenth century brought increased competition for land for cultivation of coffee for export, as creole (the American-born descendants of European settlers) and mestizo (mixed indigenous and Spanish) farmers fought to expand their private land holdings. Communal land holdings were banned outright through decrees issued in 1881 and 1882. The abolition of communal lands led to the expulsion of large numbers of peasants from their traditional communities, reinforcing the well-established pattern of the concentration of land ownership. The large haciendas grew much more quickly in the fertile lands in the western half of the country, because these lands were the most suitable for the cultivation of coffee—a crop of increasing value in global markets. Coffee continues to be El Salvador's most important traditional agricultural export today. Sugar and cotton also grew in importance as export crops, though they are of less importance today. The newly landless peasants helped form a reserve army of laborers that the large landowners exploited to their benefit.

The peasants were disciplined to accept wage labor and poverty by the crudest and most overtly violent methods, a precursor to the modern period in El Salvador. For instance, in the very same year communal land holdings were abolished, the Salvadoran government also instituted a rural vagrancy law effectively outlawing unemployment and forcing agricultural workers to accept low paid work on large haciendas. If caught wandering the countryside without work, a rural laborer would be punished with a period of forced, unpaid labor on a local hacienda. After completing the terms of his punishment, he would he forced to accept employment in haciendas where labor was most needed. This law was followed in 1859 by the establishment of a rural mounted police force in the coffee growing regions. Rural workers who did not present the members of this force with proof of employment on a hacienda were subject to intimidation, violence, and forced labor (Menjívar 1980:150).

The expanding coffee-growing economy set in motion a series of changes in the rural subsistence economy that tended to promote different patterns of population movement. The expropriation of communal lands throughout the nineteenth century led to the virtual expulsion of many peasants from their land. These newly landless peasants contributed to seasonal labor migrations within El Salvador, especially to the large coffee plantations in the western region of the country. When not working in the coffee harvest—roughly during the months of November, December, and January—peasants and rural laborers tended their own small plots of land or searched for work elsewhere, leading to rural-rural migration and later, rural-urban migration. During this period, Salvadorans began crossing the border into Honduras, a country with a lower population density, more available land, and a growing demand for labor in its own agroexport sector (Durham 1988:80). As Cecilia Menjívar (2000) notes, this pattern of seasonal migration led to high rates of free unions, out-of-wedlock births, female heads of household, and female labor force participation. These characteristics persist into the modern period.

After World War I, the countries of Central America increasingly directed their trade toward the United States. At the same time, U.S. direct investment in Central America increased, and by the end of World War II, the United States dominated all trade with Central America. By the 1940s, the United States was buying 84.7 percent of El Salvador's coffee exports, while coffee accounted for 90 percent of all exports (Torres Rivas 1993:59, 65). El Salvador's economy became dependent upon coffee and upon the economy of the United States. This penetration of U.S. capital into El Salvador had repercussions—the beginning of U.S.-bound migration. Salvadorans followed the U.S. shipping lines to San Francisco, looking for work in shipping and coffee processing (Menjívar 2000).

Dependence on coffee exports also had repercussions. Beginning in 1928, international coffee prices began to decline, leading to a 62 percent decline overall by 1932 (Menjívar 2000:39). The declining coffee prices resulted in increased rural and urban unemployment and the abandonment of rural lands (Torres Rivas 1993:60). The world economic crisis of this period further exacerbated economic problems in El Salvador. Rural and urban workers were faced with increasing unemployment and underemployment and growing misery. The power of the coffee oligarchy was compromised, and a reformist, Arturo Araujo, was elected president in January 1931 with the support of labor unions and progressive intellectuals. Fiscal crisis and fear of reform prompted the military to seize power in a coup in December 1931, making General Maximiliano Hernández Martínez president. The desperate economic and political situation led to an insurrection in rural El Salvador in January 1932. The military government reacted by massacring indigenous and mestizo peasants in the countryside and urban workers and political agitators in the cities, including Agustín Farabundo Martí, founder of the Salvadoran Communist Party.[1] As many as thirty thousand people lost their lives in a period of a few weeks, and the event came to be know as the "matanza" or massacre. Many of the peasants killed were indigenous, and those not killed were quick to suppress symbols of indigenous identity, leaving a population that today identifies itself as largely mestizo. Movements to organize against the military regime and the coffee elite were for a time stifled, and the country was ruled by military dictators or military-civilian juntas until 1982.

Throughout the first half of the twentieth century, coffee, sugar, and cotton dominated the agroexport economy of El Salvador. During the second half of the century, sugar and cotton declined in importance, though coffee retained its position as the most important export crop. At the same time, local and international capitalists began to invest in industrial production. Foreign direct investment increased and in the 1950s, local leaders made gestures towards creating a regional common market, resulting in the formation of the Central American Common Market (MERCOMUN) in 1960. The model of development championed at the time was import-substitution-industrialization (ISI), which promoted the production of goods for regional markets. Regional consumers, however, did not command much disposable income, and the processes of production initiated were capital intensive, failing to provide jobs for displaced and underemployed workers. Regional integration during this period provided for some economic growth in El Salvador and created a regional labor market, but it did little to provide employment for those displaced by these changes (Pérez Sáinz 1999). During the 1960s, manufacturing production grew 7.9 percent, but employment only grew 2.6 percent (Dunkerley 1983, cited in Byrne 1996:20). At the same time, El Salvador was experiencing a demographic explosion and, as agricultural producers began investing in new crops for export, there was intensified competition for land (Pérez 1999).

Rural-urban migration and migration to Honduras increased during this period. Many Salvadorans found work in the banana plantations and in industrial production and small-scale farming in Hunduras. By 1969, it is estimated that there were between 300,000 and 350,000 Salvadorans living in Honduras (Richter 1980:126). The growing cattle and sugar industries in Honduras were vying for land with poor peasants, many of them Salvadoran settlers. There were growing tensions between countries in the newly formed MERCOMUN, especially between El Salvador and Honduras, because Honduras suffered from unfavorable terms of trade. Honduras voiced increasing dis-satisfaction over the volume of Salvadoran migration and the terms of trade between the two countries. In 1969, Honduras expelled some twenty-five thousand Salvadorans from Honduran territory. In reaction to both the Honduran expulsion of Salvadorans from its territory and the disagreements between the two countries over trade relations, El Salvador invaded Honduras, initiating a short but bloody war.[2] After the cessation of violence, Salvadorans still living on Honduran territory were either expelled or fled Honduras for El Salvador. As a result of this massive influx of returning Salvadorans, 1969 is the only year in Salvadoran history in which El Salvador had a positive net influx of migrants.

The economic and social crisis brought on by the agroexport economy intensified during the 1970s, a decade marked by high unemployment and underemployment, growing disparities in the distribution of land and wealth, and exasperation with a series of fraudulent presidential elections. According to 1971 census figures, 1 percent of the farms (the largest) monopolized 41 percent of the farmland, while 71 percent of the farms (the smallest) occupied only 10 percent of the available farmland (Barry 1987). As the amount of land devoted to export crops such as coffee, sugar, and cotton has grown, the amount of land devoted to the production of agricultural crops for domestic consumption has decreased, leading to increasing dependence upon more expensive imported food items (Barry 1987; Durham 1988). Jenny Pearce concludes that, "There is a direct relationship between migration patterns in El Salvador and land scarcity" (1986:31). The best land had been monopolized for the cultivation of agricultural export products, limiting the land available for subsistence agriculture or for agricultural products destined for national consumption. At the same time, the growing manufacturing sector provided relatively few jobs. Despite the disparate distribution of land, by 1972 agriculture still accounted for 53 percent of full-time employment, and open unemployment was an astounding 20 percent (Pearce 1986:33). Fifty percent of urban dwellers lived in poverty (Briones 1992). The informal sector, composed mostly of self-employed merchants and day laborers, grew throughout Central America as industrialization and agricultural diversification proved unable to absorb available labor.

The Civil War

The 1960s and 1970s was a time of change in Latin America. When Fidel Castro, Ernesto "Che" Guevara, and the 26th of July Movement swept into Havana on the heels of a fleeing Fulgencio Batista in 1959, the reverberations echoed around the world. For almost a century, Marxists and communist party ideologues had argued that revolution was possible only when the objective conditions existed—in particular, complete proletarianization of the populace. The Cuban revolution demonstrated the viability of guerrilla warfare and of revolution in societies with large peasant populations. While most countries in Latin America were experiencing rapid urbanization and many were undergoing industrialization, the majority of people still lived in the countryside. Rural proletarianization was well advanced in El Salvador, where by 1971 60 percent of the rural population was landless (Barry 1987:9), the highest rate of rural landlessness in Central America. Even so, the population of El Salvador was far from proletarian. What, then, were the factors promoting the tendency towards revolutionary self-organization in El Salvador? The example of the Cuban revolution animated young, urban intellectuals and students, many of whom went on to organize guerrilla armies. In time, these guerrilla armies penetrated the countryside and found limited support among residents there. Peasants and the rural landless, however, were more conservative than the middle-class revolutionaries and faced more pervasive economic and social oppression. Many peasants found their inspiration elsewhere—the Catholic Church.

During the 1960s and 1970s, peasants began organizing to demand land reform and democratization of the political system. Encouraged by progressive sectors of the Catholic Church, they formed cooperatives and agricultural workers' unions in the countryside. In the mid-to late-1960s, many priests and nuns in Latin America had become radicalized through a movement towards progressive theology, which later came to be known as liberation theology. Promoting a "preferential option for the poor," seeking to work with poor parishioners and for their benefit, these priests and nuns began to organize base communities and train lay practitioners to help people interpret the bible in a way that shed light on their own poverty and disenfranchisement (Berryman 1987). In El Salvador, progressive clergy worked with peasant organizations, legitimizing their claims to economic resources and protection from the rapacious military forces. The combined activities of religious activists, guerrilla forces, and local teachers helped prompt what Hugh Byrne calls a "transformation of peasant consciousness" (1996:26). Peasants came to believe that their oppression was not inevitable and that they could struggle for change.

Another factor that contributed to the radicalization of peasants and the urban poor was the wave of repression unleashed on peasant, student, guerrilla, and religious organizers in the 1970s and 1980s. The powerful landowning families resisted even the most moderate reforms and formed paramilitary organizations that threatened and killed those pushing for change. For example, in 1976 then President General Arturo Armando Molina proposed a land redistribution plan to benefit peasants. Although he planned to redistribute less than four percent of the country's agricultural land, wealthy landowners opposed the plan and generated a wave of clandestine violence against peasant organizers, leading

Molina to abandon his attempts at land reform. In 1977, a fraudulent election brought General Humberto Romero to power, and he unleashed a wave of violence against progressive and radical organizations. Violence against religious leaders escalated with the arrest, torture, and murder of several priests. A 1979 coup brought an end to the Romero regime, and a military-civilian junta took power. Human rights violations continued, though, and in 1980 most of the members of the cabinet resigned in protest. The Christian Democrats took power, and the military and paramilitary organizations continued with their repressive and violent tactics unhampered. Peaceful protestors and peasants were commonly arrested and killed. The numbers of those who disappeared grew. The year 1980 witnessed new levels of violence. Thousands of peasants fled the countryside, some going to the cities, others to refugee camps, and some even leaving the country altogether. A vocal critic of military repression, Archbishop Oscar Romero was assassinated while giving mass, shortly after delivering a radio homily admonishing the members of the military to follow their conscience and refrain from killing. During 1980, the military and paramilitary organizations killed over seven hundred noncombatants per month (Berryman 1985:39). These extreme levels of violence and repression had the effect of mobilizing large sectors of the population to oppose the government and the military.

Organized resistance grew and consolidated its following. In 1980, five of the guerrilla armies that had been organizing over the last several decades came together to form a unified front, the FMLN (see introduction). These five groups now began to coordinate their military operations. Each group had its own leadership, philosophical tendencies, and style of military operation. And each was associated with a nonmilitary, popular organization that worked with the civilian population to coordinate mass peaceful demonstrations, strikes, and organizing campaigns. Less militant elements of the opposition formed the Revolutionary Democratic Front (FDR). These groups were encouraged by the 1979 success of the Sandinista Front for National Liberation (FSLN) in Nicaragua.

During the early 1980s, a series of governing juntas, largely under the control of the wealthy landowners and the military, waged an increasing more violent war against the FMLN and the popular organizations of the opposition. Elections beginning in 1982 brought ARENA to power, and the repression of the civilian population continued at a steady pace, subjecting activists and nonactivists alike to widespread terror. Anyone suspected of sympathizing with the guerrillas was at risk of torture and assassination. Whole villages were burnt to the ground, their residents massacred. Corpses were placed in public places to increase the level of fear, and violence and uncertainty became a part of everyday life. Schools and the National University were occupied and closed in an attempt to curtail student activism. Peasants, students, labor leaders and union activists, and progressive religious figures were all targeted in a desperate attempt to head off the death of the old order. The generalized violence and terror of the war affected millions of Salvadorans, even those who were not active in political campaigns.

The 1980s were a decade of stagnation and economic decline all over Latin America, but in war-torn countries such as El Salvador, the economic effects were compounded and the results were devastating. Petroleum prices increased in 1973 and again in 1979, depressing international markets. Latin American governments found themselves saddled with debt from loans from international institutions. War in El Salvador led to increased levels of capital flight, a problem even before the war. Production levels declined, as did per capita income. In 1980, open unemployment was 16.1 percent, while underemployment was 55 percent (Pérez Sáinz 1999:77). Unemployment. underemployment, and a decline in real wages continued to plague El Salvador throughout the decade of the 1980s. Economic decline intensified the misery that the majority of Salvadoran families were experiencing and contributed to the flow of people fleeing the country.

Towards the end of the 1980s, it was clear that neither side in the war was going to win. The FMLN had made inroads against the Salvadoran military, but with direct and indirect aid from the U.S. government totaling over $6 billion, the military was able to maintain an uncomfortable detente. Foreign and domestic pressure for a negotiated end to the conflict increased. In 1990, U.N.-negotiated talks began, and in January of 1992 the FMLN-FDR and the government signed a final peace agreement. The FMLN was demobilized and converted into a legal political party, and the security forces were reorganized with quotas for participation by members of the FMLN. The agreement fell short, however, of modifying the economic system that had for centuries caused the great differentials between rich and poor.

Approximately seventy-five thousand people died during the twelve years of civil war (Tojeira 1996), most of the deaths attributable to the activities of the government forces and the clandestine death squads associated with them (Comisión de la Verdad 1993). The violence displaced large sectors of the rural and urban population, most of them civilians. According to Socorro Jurídico Cristiano, a human rights organization founded by the Catholic Church, 11,903 Salvadorans died as a result of the war in 1980 alone, and another 16,266 in 1981 (Comisión de In Verdad 1993:24). In response, the number of officially registered displaced persons also rose, from two thousand in January 1980 to 197,199 by January 1981 (Pearce 1986:198). Many of the displaced were sent to settlement camps in El Salvador or to refugee camps in Honduras, but Salvadorans also began fleeing the country for Mexico, the United States, Canada and other countries in increasing numbers.

Migration

International migration is usually a selective process. Those who are able to migrate must have the resources to do so, and they must perceive a motivation, indeed the necessity, to leave their home country. The poor are usually unable to make the trip, while the wealthy do not need to migrate for the purpose of seeking work. They enjoy the luxury of travel and the opportunity to study abroad, but they do not need to work in order to help family and friends at home. So international migrants often occupy a middle strata—those unable to find satisfactory employment in their home countries, but those with sufficient resources to invest in a long and costly trip. In the case of war-torn countries, migration becomes less selective, as poor individuals make extraordinary sacrifices to finance migration or to reduce its costs and as wealthier individuals flee violence and the loss of economic resources.

In the case of El Salvador, migratory patterns had become well established before the war and would likely have generated increasing levels of international migration even if the war had not occurred. The war, however, pushed many Salvadorans who otherwise might not have migrated to flee their country in search of a safe haven. The war, then, must be seen as a moment, however extreme, in the political-economic history of El Salvador, a centuries-old process by which Salvadorans were literally expelled from their land to make way for commercial agriculture and manufacturing. Resistance to this process has always been strong: beginning with Indian rebellions of the colonial and early independence periods; followed by peasant and worker organizing in the early 1900s; and leading to the armed military resistance of the 1970s through the early 1990s. Resistance has always been met with extreme levels of government-sponsored violence, reinforcing the incentives to leave El Salvador. International migration also tends to be self-perpetuating, and once a migratory circuit is established, it tends to create the conditions for continued migration, including the generation of the economic and social capital that migrants need to travel and establish themselves in the receiving society. Thus migration from El Salvador did not cease with the signing of peace accords in 1992, but continues to draw Salvadorans to the United States.

Small numbers of Salvadorans came to the United States throughout the 1940s and 1950s, filling the expanding needs of the U.S. labor market. As a result of the changing conditions in El Salvador, migration to the United States increased slightly during the 1960s and 1970s. But the 1980s witnessed a massive increase in the number of Salvadorans coming to the United States, obviously in reaction to the increased levels of violence associated with the war. U.S. immigration statistics provide one measure of this migration. As Figure 1 illustrates, legal immigration to the United States was negligible until the 1980s. During the period 1931 to 1940, only 673 Salvadorans officially immigrated to the United States. During the period 1941 to 1950, over five thousand Salvadorans officially immigrated to the United States, some attracted by the availability of work in factories

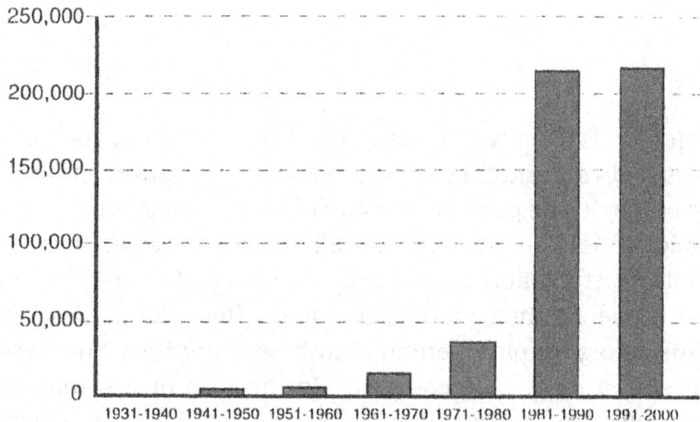

FIGURE 1. Salvadoran immigration to the United States, 1930–2000, from U.S. Citizenship and Immigration Services, *Fiscal Year 2002 Yearbook of Immigration Statistics*.

supporting the U.S. war effort. During the period 1951 to 1960, Salvadoran immigration stayed fairly constant, with another 5,895 Salvadorans entering the country legally. That number almost tripled in the period between 1961 and 1970, with close to fifteen thousand Salvadorans immigrating to the United States, perhaps due to the increase in state-sponsored violence in El Salvador during that time. During the period 1971 to 1980, the number of Salvadorans officially immigrating to the United States more than doubled, reaching 34,436. During the period of the civil war, the numbers increased dramatically, with 213,539 Salvadorans officially immigrating to the United States from 1981 to 1990. These statistics, however, fail to capture the reality El Salvadoran migration to the United States. On the one hand, the high number of Salvadorans legalizing themselves during the 1980s was due not only to increased numbers of entrants, but also to the expansion of legal options for Salvadorans during that period (see chapter five). On the other hand, these statistics do not account for the growing numbers of undocumented migrants who entered the country unable to pursue documentation.

The official statistics for emigration from El Salvador provide another partial representation of Salvadoran migration. They show a marked increase in 1980, when the violence began to escalate. From 1977 to 1979, the official rate of emigration remained close to twenty thousand per year, but in 1980, it jumped to 104,628 per year and in 1981 to 214,128 per year (Bureau of the Census, *International Data Base* 2003). These increases reflect the increase in violence during those two years. The levels of violence dropped in 1982 and 1983, and so did the number of Salvadorans officially leaving El Salvador. These figures represent the number of Salvadorans leaving the country after obtaining an exit visa. However, many Salvadorans fled their country clandestinely, especially those who feared the Salvadoran government. So these figures undercount Salvadoran emigration. Even so, they indicate a sharp rise in emigration rates during the most violent periods of the civil war.

Many of the Salvadorans who migrated during the war state that their motivation was to avoid violence and persecution. William Stanley (1987) tried to measure the role of political violence versus economic factors in the migration of Salvadorans to the United States between 1979 and 1984. He concluded that "fear of political violence appears to be the dominant motive (or Salvadoran migration during the period covered by this analysis" (Stanley 1987:144). Salvadoran sociologist Segundo Montes did a landmark survey of Salvadorans in the United States and of their family members in El Salvador (Montes 1987). He found that of the Salvadorans surveyed in the United States, those who migrated before the war were more likely to cite economic motivations for migration, while those who came during the war were more likely to mention political reasons for fleeing El Salvador.[3] In total, the percentage of Montes's sample claiming that the political situation in El Salvador motivated them to come to the United States jumped from 18.6 percent among the pre-1980 cohort to 49.1 percent among the 1980–1987 cohort. However, economic hardship and political repression had the same roots in a skewed distribution of resources and power, and they were often experienced as one set of desperate circumstances. Cecilia Menjívar (2000) found that the participants in her study had difficulty distinguishing between economic factors and fear of violence.

After the signing of the peace accords in 1992, the numbers of Salvadorans officially immigrating to the United States declined somewhat, from 46,923 in 1991 to 26,794 in 1993, to 11,670 in 1995. However official statistics are not representative of the true scope of the phenomenom. These numbers account for Salvadorans who have been able to obtain legal residence status or citizenship, leaving out those who have temporary legal status or who lack official documentation altogether. Unfortunately, in the absence of other more reliable indicators, this data stands as an imperfect measure of Salvadoran migration to the United States.

Other estimates indicate that today there are close to two million Salvadorans residing in the United States (Andrade-Eekhoff 2001:ii). They constitute the second largest group of undocumented immigrants in the United States, following Mexicans. The U.S. Citizenship and Immigration Services estimates that in the year 2000 there were approximately 189,000 Salvadorans residing in the United States without documentation (2003:225). Thus the migration rates of Salvadorans, including documented and undocumented migration, are significantly higher than official U.S. statistics admit. According to the attorney general for human rights in El Salvador, approximately 59 percent of the Salvadorans living in the United States lack documentation ("Reducción de Remesas" 1997). The difficulty Salvadorans face in acquiring a stable legal status in the United States has important implications for identity formation, patterns of incorporation in the United States, political representation in both countries, and economic development in El Salvador—themes that I explore in later chapters.

Why has migration from El Salvador continued despite the end of the war? There are several reasons. For one, conditions in El Salvador continue to compel people to leave in search of economic opportunity. The end of the war was followed by a rebound period of economic growth, but the last few years have seen the Salvadoran economy stagnate. The annual rate of growth of the gross domestic product jumped from less than 4 percent in 1991 to almost 8 percent in 1992 (ECLAC 2001:206). Since then, it has declined to wartime levels and in 1999 was only 2.6 percent (ECLAC 2001:206). Growth in per capita private consumption has been negative or less than 1 percent since 1996 (ECLAC 2001:67). Real minimum wages have not grown since 1990 (ECLAC 2001:205). In 1998, the official rate of unemployment was 7.6 percent (Direción General de Promoción y Relaciones Económicas 1998), but nongovernmental organizations contend that 60 percent of the economically active population was either unemployed or underemployed ("*Reducción de Remesas*" 1997). As of 1997, it was estimated that 48 percent of Salvadoran families lived in poverty, with 12 percent in conditions of extreme poverty; these rates climb in rural areas, where 62 percent lived in poverty and 28 percent lived in conditions of extreme poverty (ECLAC 2001:64). For many Salvadoran families, then, migration constitutes the only alternative to crushing poverty.

The opportunities for employment that do exist are extremely limiting. The productive sector of the economy that has shown the most growth is the maquila industry located in the free trade zones that first began appearing in the 1970s and today number five. In El Salvador, the most common product is clothing, assembled from imported components and produced for export. This industry tends to rely on young, single, female labor and benefits from low wages (the minimum wage is sixty cents per hour in El Salvador). It is marked by widespread use of forced overtime, low levels of employment security, and no unionization. The maquila industry grew rapidly in the mid-1990s, reaching a 35 percent rate of growth; however; the rate of growth for 1999 was only 3.7 percent, suggesting a decline in the ability of this sector to absorb labor (ECLAC 2001:212). Another fast-growing sector of the economy is the nontraditional agricultural sector. But agriculture accounted for only 21 percent of employment in 2000 (FUNDE 2003), and the agricultural sector has been severely hampered by a drop in international coffee prices, a devastating hurricane in 1998, and a drought in the eastern portions of the country between 2001 and 2002. Finally, it should be noted that about half of the urban population is employed in the informal sector, usually marked by low pay and difficult working conditions. Although the particularities of the labor market have changed with time, its general inability to provide adequate employment has not changed. The results are the virtual expulsion of labor in search of survival.

A circumscribed labor market is not the only difficulty facing Salvadorans. In the first two months of 2001, the country experienced a series of devastating earthquakes that left 1.5 million people homeless, approximately one quarter of the population. Violence still plagues the country, though now it takes the form of petty crime. For example, the average annual rate of crime-related homicide between 1994 and 1996 was 8,300, more than twenty-two per day in a country approximately the size of Massachusetts (Cuéllar 1997). Another important factor influencing U.S.-bound migration is the degree to which U.S.-style consumer culture has spread in El Salvador along with the growing importance of migrant remittances. Migrant remittances are the single largest source of income for the Salvadoran economy. As I will detail in the conclusion to this book, migrant remittances allow the Salvadoran economy to absorb many more imports than would otherwise be possible, allowing Salvadoran families to indulge in small luxuries such as televisions, VCRs, video games, and washing machines, as well as the latest fashions, music, and films from the United States. The growing prevalence of these consumer goods creates the expectation that future consumption will continue, an expectation that can only be satisfied with continued remittances. Migration is seen by many young people as one of the few avenues open to them to help their families and to pursue their dreams.

Migration, once started, tends to be self-perpetuating. In part, this is due to the growth of social networks in which migrants help finance the migration and resettlement of friends and family (Massey et al. 1987; Portes and Walton 1981). In the case of El Salvador, migration has become so pervasive that almost everyone knows someone in the United States. The informal networks so important to international migration have long been established. As Segundo Montes (1990) and Juan José García (1994) point out, the existence of these personal networks explains in part why those departments of El Salvador which suffered from high rates of violence during the war and high levels of poverty in general, have low rates of emigration, while other departments that have a more established history of emigration but enjoy more secure economic conditions continue to have higher rates of emigration.[4] And while these networks may not serve migrants well after they have arrived, most recent arrivals come with the help of relatives or friends already here (Menjívar 2000). But networks in and of themselves are insufficient to generate migration; they can only help facilitate and channel it. Most significantly, the motivations for migration continue to exist in El Salvador—a stagnant economy wracked by high levels of unemployment and underemployment; a high rate of poverty; and declining living conditions exacerbated by a series of devastating natural disasters. The desperation with which Salvadorans confront these conditions has become more acute as they also struggle with increased expectations and expanded consumer tastes promoted by the remittance economy. The combined effect of massive emigration and remittance dependency means that for many Salvadorans economic security, self-fulfillment, family, and career success all lie outside the boundaries of their country, in the United States. The next chapter describes some of the institutions and practices that Salvadorans in Los Angeles have created as they straddle two social, political, and economic worlds, El Salvador and the United States.

In this article, Beatriz Cortez explores the politics and practices of hometown associations, that is, Salvadoran associations based on the idea of the local space of the city of origin of its members and not on the idea of the nation. These associations in the Los Angeles area illustrate a change in organizational practices among Central American immigrants in the United States since the end of the armed conflicts in their countries of origin. These associations present a challenge to the traditional construction of national identity because of their transnational character and their emphasis upon the local space of their towns and municipalities.

On the other hand, Cortez discusses the ways in which international organizations, such as the United Nation's Development Program, NGOs and the Central American national governments, have developed plans to co-opt and take credit for the work and contributions of hometown associations through the publication of reports that show absolute indifference to the conditions in which Central American immigrants live in order to obtain the personal and collective remittances that they send back home. The governmental efforts to manage and direct the contributions of these organizations have become evident through the formation of institutions such as the *Fondo de Inversión Social para el Desarrollo Local,* or FISDL. Furthermore, national culture continues to promote immigration through spaces such as Departamento 15, a publication by the Salvadoran daily newspaper *La Prensa Gráfica*. In sum, the export of people continues to be one of the most profitable enterprises for Central American nations such as El Salvador.

Hometown Associations

Salvadoran Organizations in Los Angeles Challenge the National Imaginary[1]

BEATRIZ CORTEZ

The waves of Salvadoran immigrants that arrived to the United States increased considerably during the 1980s due to the pervasive levels of violence that characterized the civil war in El Salvador. Large numbers of these Salvadorans established themselves in Los Angeles and generated a solidarity movement that allowed them to give meaning to their work through a discourse of liberation that had as its foundation the national imaginary (of course, in relation to their home country, El Salvador). However, as the civil war ended and as consequence of the growth of the Salvadoran immigrant population in Los Angeles, the need to re-conceptualize Salvadoran identity and this population's idea of the nation slowly became unavoidable. There are two fundamental differences between the solidarity movement in Los Angeles in the 1980s and the emerging organizations of Salvadoran immigrants in this city since the 1990s. On the one hand, the fact that more than one-fourth of the Salvadoran population currently lives outside El Salvador has made it necessary to reconsider the link between the concept of the nation for this country and the national territory. As a result, the concept of the nation that circulated in the 1980s among Salvadoran immigrants has been transformed. On the other hand, the signing of the Peace Accords in January 1992 generated new cultural and organizational dynamics among Salvadoran immigrants, which changed the way identity is conceived for this group of immigrants. In other words, the idea of identity for this group of immigrants is no longer defined solely in terms of its relationship with the nation (El Salvador), but also in terms of the region (Central America), as well as in terms of local space, or the municipality of origin, that is, the town where those immigrants originally came from.

As a result, the organizations of Salvadorans that emerged in the 1980s as part of the solidarity movement that was linked to the civil war in El Salvador, have experienced a process of reinvention. To illustrate this process we may take as an example CARECEN, which during the civil war stood for the Central American Refugee Center, and that after the signing of the Peace Accords in El Salvador was transformed into the Central American Resource Center. The projects and initiatives of the CARECEN office in Los Angeles are also examples for this process, since, currently, CARECEN offers programs that reflect the needs of Salvadoran and Central American immigrants in Los Angeles today: legal aid, immigration and legalization assistance, training and educational workshops, as well as spaces that have turned this organization into a true cultural center for Central Americans. In a similar pattern, other Central American and Salvadoran organizations in Los Angeles define their objectives in ways that reflect the contemporary moment and the current needs of the population that they serve. The Salvadoran American Leadership and Educational Fund, SALEF, for instance, has as the center of its activities the promotion of educational programs and scholarships, as well as internships designed to encourage youth to reach their educational goals. Furthermore, SALEF has played an active role in the elaboration of a committee linking the two cities with the largest population of Salvadorans: San Salvador and Los Angeles. This Sister City Program is significant, among other things, because it organizes groups of Salvadorans residing in Los Angeles to work on projects that have their focus on the city of San Salvador. As a result, these programs present an option for them to re-elaborate their identity based on local space and the imaginary of their city of origin, instead of that of the nation.

For the rest of the population of Salvadoran immigrants, particularly for those who were born in other spaces within that country, one type of organizations that emerged after the end of the civil war in El Salvador is the Hometown Association, that is, associations of Salvadoran immigrants who work for the benefit and local development of their municipalities of origin. In this way, the traditional concept of the nation conceived as a territory, and therefore, whether immigrants are or are not national subjects, is further problematized since, through their participation in these organizations, their identity is constructed rather in terms of the locality of their origin and not of the nation. Even when these organizations have proliferated throughout all of the United States, Los Angeles is, of course, one of the points of greater concentration of Hometown Associations. It is enough to remember the marches of March 25 and May 1, 2006 to have an idea not only of their numbers, but also of the visibility that this population has reached within the general conglomeration of Latinos in the city. Since my arrival to Los Angeles in August, 2000, I have had the opportunity to see the growth and to actively participate in the activities and projects of the Hometown Associations. My objective for this essay is, therefore, to analyze the way in which Salvadoran immigrants organize nowadays taking as a point of departure their local imaginary, and following a dynamic that contributes to the deterritorialization of the nation, and that questions its more traditional definition.

A Country That Never Was

I want to approach the discussion about the topic of immigration and the experience of Salvadorans in the City of Los Angeles taking as a point of departure one of the affirmations that is made repeatedly in the Human Development Report for El Salvador, 2005. *A Look at the New 'Us.' The Impact of Migration,* published by the United Nations Development Program office in El Salvador. That is, the idea that "migration has contributed to create a yet unknown El Salvador. Meanwhile, people still carry out assessments and make plans for a country that has ceased to exist" (9). It seems to me that it is important to pay close attention to the way this idea was constructed, particularly, since it takes several things for granted. First, it takes for granted that the concept of the nation that has circulated through national discourse has in fact existed in the past, and that it has been through the recent migrations that it has ceased to exist as such, that it has become unknown. It is important to consider this idea from a critical perspective since, in fact, the country that was constructed and disseminated through the discourse linked to the independence movement did not exist either: it was not a nation that was defined by the diverse ethnic groups of the diverse cultures that were part of its heritage, it was not a nation that reflected the daily practices of its population. Fundamentally, it was a nation that reflected the liberal ideology of quite a reduced sector of the population, whose cultural affiliation in fact was foreign. It was a nation whose ideological heart was in Europe.

Second, it assumes that there is a new nation that does in fact exist and that we must get to know. For the case of immigrants, the report offers institutional options to access the knowledge required to understand this nation, such as the program "Conoce tu país" ("Know Your Country"). It is an El Salvador that, in spite of its transnational character, is defined in a rigid manner through institutionalized programs implemented by the State. On the other hand, this country that, according to the report, must be known is expected to form and reflect the new national subject, a subject that will also be defined in a rigid and fixed way. In the report, this subject is labeled "el nuevo nosotros" ("the new us"). This proposal not only demonstrates a certain anxiety in face of the ways in which immigrants challenge the definition of the nation, both through their displacement to other places and through their link to their nation of origin and their continued support of the national economy via their remittances. Furthermore, it is also a proposal far removed from reality. In contrast to this idea, the contemporary cultural production of Salvadorans living abroad provides a space where we are able to find evidence of the impossibility of fixing identity in such rigid way and of the multiple and malleable borders that transform it constantly.

Finally, the idea under discussion shows a lack of recognition of the way in which the project of building a fixed and rigid national identity has culturally eradicated from the space of visibility within the nation all signs of cultural and ethnic diversity. That is, there is a melancholic expression of identity: it is an identity that is based on the loss of the other, but it is a loss that is denied, that is not acknowledged. And it is also a loss that is silenced through the actual discourse of openness and nominal plurality. It is only through the fleeting spaces of ambivalence, in the brief moments in which the incoherence of national identity is made visible, that this diversity can be recognized. The ambivalence in face of national identity that immigration generates is significant, therefore, because outside the borders of the national territory, it provides visibility to the cultural difference and diverse ethnic groups that live within the nation. This can only happen at the margins of the normativity and uniformity established by the traditional version of national identity, such as it has been defined by through the parameters of modernity and state policies where diversity has been incorporated to the contemporary discourse of the nation only in a nominal way: it is visible in the discourse of the representation of subjectivity, but ironically it is visible in such a way that it makes diversity invisible and contributes to the re-institutionalization of a modern version of national identity as the only possible version. That is what takes place in this report. It is a perspective on national identity and the definition of the nation that is even more marginalizing than the previous one because it now represents itself as an inclusive space that is in fact interested in immigration.

As I have pointed out elsewhere, the incoherent quality of the national subject for El Salvador is not only exposed through the ambiguous quality of the subjectivity that it produces, but also through its melancholic character. The national subject exists in the absence of the Other. Be it the Indigenous subject or the "hermano lejano" ("distant brother"). As a result, the national subject for the case of El Salvador is a subject that is nurtured by its own melancholy. In El Salvador today, not only cultural and ethnic diversity brings out the problematic lack of coherence of the national subject, but also the process of de-territorialization of the nation that the massive displacement of the population has brought about since the 1980s. In the city of Los Angeles, where I live, there is a rich cultural and literary production that is rarely taken into account both in Central America and in the United States. It is the literary and cultural production of the so-called "hermanos lejanos" ("distant brothers"), the 1.5 generation, the Salvadoran immigrant population.

The Local-Transnational Displaces the National

The cultural dynamics of the Salvadoran diaspora do not follow the mandate of the nation, but rather, they function through alternative dynamics of a transnational character. Let's take as an example the case of Salvadoran immigrant organizations known as Hometown Associations. These associations generate a space for identity and a cultural imaginary based on local dynamics and not on the traditional idea of national identity as a referent. This change of focus has moved the space of definition of national identity—and, therefore, the relevance of the capital city of San Salvador—to a local space with the interior of the nation, but understood in a transnational way. Nevertheless, it is important to note that the nation in this case is no longer defined through the limits established by the national territory. It is, rather, about the nation understood from a transnational perspective, from a perspective that requires the de-territorialization of identity. In the experience of the hometown associations, the space through which identity is generated is the local space, the municipality. Therefore, the nation is displaced, since it is no longer the one that generates the points of contact for the community that gets together outside the national territory. As an example, I would like to bring out my own experience. I am from San Salvador, however, I participate in an association of *cojutepecanos,* that is, immigrants who were born and raised in Cojutepeque, and their children born in Los Angeles. I frequently find *cojutepecanos* working at the hospital in Los Angeles, at the stores, in several spaces that we have in common. And when I talk to them, it is always possible to quickly establish a point in common: "Do you know such and such person?" or "How's your mom?" or "Did you see that someone stole Monsignor Romero's bust at the entrance of the town? It is such a shame! But fortunately the Municipality placed it back on its pedestal . . ."

The information among *cojutepecanos* circulates rapidly in a transnational way, through email, phone calls, international trips and conversations. And it is possible for the members of that community, both those who live in Cojutepeque, and those who reside outside of Cojutepeque, to find points of coincidence and connection. On the other hand, for those of us who are originally from San Salvador, the experience is different and much more impersonal. While immigrants from the capital city of San Salvador can identify and collaborate in projects such as the Sister Cities San Salvador-Los Angeles initiatives, when we find in the city of Los Angeles other people who are also form the capital city of San Salvador and that we have not met before, our conversations are about generalities:

—Are you from San Salvador?

—Yes, and you?

—Yes. I am from Colonia Miramonte.

—I grew up close to there, in the Pasaje Los Angeles, next to the Gabriela Mistral, by the Boulevard de los Héroes.

—Ah, yes, I have gone through there. It is close to Metrocentro.

—Yes. Well, nice to meet you. Bye.

—Nice to meet you. Goodbye.

Taking as a point of departure only the fact of being from San Salvador, those of us who come from the capital city have a harder time finding a point of coincidence that might allow us to create community based on our place of origin, in the abstract. As a result, I am interested in considering the way in which the hometown associations generate a space that, because it is based in the imaginary of the local space, present an important alternative to the perspective of the nation for the construction of identity.

The Industry of Nostalgia

As many of us know, being an immigrant is not easy. In order to turn our place of residence into our home, we often try to recreate around us our place of origin: we plant tropical plants in our garden, we fill our house, and even our refrigerator, of nostalgic products that when we lived in El Salvador, we rarely consumed. Soon, we begin to see everything through the lens of nostalgia, which, of course, while idealized, is also dark. This can at once be a generating force and a paralyzing one.

As many of the studies on the consumption of Salvadoran products by Salvadoran immigrants in the United States will show (see Batres-Márquez, et al., and Figueroa Hernández et al., as well as reports published by the Ministry of Economy in El Salvador, for instance), nostalgia does not only feed our own feelings regarding our place of origin, it has also become an important industry. The Industry of Nostalgia informs the sales of hundreds of products, particularly, the consumption of certain food items such as *queso duro-blandito, loroco, horchata, alhuashte, frijol de seda* and others. And even if it might sound comical, it seems too me that our eating these items of nostalgic consumption should not be taken lightly, particularly since had it not had the importance that it has, the Salvadoran government would not have given priority to this issue during the negotiations of the Central American Free Trade Agreement (CAFTA). According to the Ministry of Economy of El Salvador, already in 2001, the exports of these products represented at least 10% of the total exports from El Salvador to the United States. That is, at the time, about $450 million per year.

A place where the Industry of Nostalgia is generated, encouraged, and consumed is in the section titled Departamento 15 (Department 15, in reference to the 14 departments or states in El Salvador, and the 15th representing the population outside the national territory), in the online version of the daily Salvadoran newspaper *La Prensa Gráfica*. In this space, nostalgia is promoted in such a way that the discussions about immigration rarely emphasize in a sustained or permanent way the difficulties of the trip to the North, the dangers that those who make the long trip through Mexico face, their possible encounters with the Mara Salvatrucha when crossing the Guatemala-México border or with the anti-immigrant militia the Minutemen when crossing the Mexico-United States border, or the possible encounters with the National Guard of the United States in the Southwest. Even though with some frequency some of these news pop up in Departamento 15, they circulate briefly and quickly disappear. What is emphasized and has permanence in Departamento 15 are the stories of success of the better established immigrants in the United States. A number of professional immigrants receive often invitations by Departamento 15 to become part of this catalog of success stories (I have received such an invitation at least once) that illustrate the success of immigration and that sell to potential immigrants the idea of the trip to the north. Within this context, the experience generated by the hometown associations presents the possibility of directing nostalgia beyond the consumption of these products, and to generate a space in which as immigrants, we are able to participate in the daily life of our towns of origin or of our country, and we are able to reproduce and re-elaborate the cultural identity of our community, both here in the United States and in El Salvador.

Hometown Associations

In the association to which I belong, Cojutepecanos Pro-Cultura y Educación (*Cojutepecanos* Pro-Culture and Education, COPROCE), collective work has given place to quite a complex dynamic that requires, among other things, the division of labor and of the responsibilities according to the area of specialization or to the particular qualities of the different members of the Association. During the years in which I have participated in the activities of this association, I have witnessed a process of professionalization of the work that the members of the Association carry out. This process has based itself on the experience of the work that the members of the association have acquired and that has included the elaboration of videos, of photographic posters, the participation in conference calls, the preparation of speeches in representation of the association in front of the media, the participation in interviews with the press, and so forth.

My work in this Association generally is in the area of publicity, particularly in the production of newsletters and in the preparation of the grant proposals to foundations and other possible donors. However, when there is a party, my responsibility is the elaboration of the entrance tickets, which are sold several days before the event. That is, generally, on the day when a "*tardeada*" or a get-together takes place, my responsibilities are limited to selling to food or drink tickets. But I know that on that very morning Herbert, Jesús and Pedro have gone to get the ice and the drinks, and that Esperanza and Claudia have organized the menu and the food and that Raúl, with Claudia's and my help might have decorated the place, including making beautiful and professional-looking posters that will inform the community about COPROCE's projects. I know also that Esperanza has negotiated with the lady who will come to make the *pupusas* and that Claudia has gotten the cheese and the corn flour. I also know that Douglas has gone shopping for other ingredients and has taken them in his pick-up with the tables and the grill needed to make several hundred *pupusas*. For sure he has set up several tables so that all may be comfortable. Possibly Noy or don Toño will have prepared their homes. And I know as well that all of us will bring our friends and family to the "*tardeada*" or to the party. Many times I have wondered, most of them out loud, What would happen if someone forgot their responsibilities for the event? But the fact is that up to the moment it has never happened, and each time COPROCE's membership has become more and more specialized and professional in its division or labor and the distribution of responsibilities for the association.

Even though I do not know the inner workings nor the inside organizing processes of the other organizations and their events, I have attended many of them in Los Angeles and I have been able to see also their efficient teams at work. So I think it is important to take into account the cultural identity that these associations have generated through their work in their places of residence in the United States. This will allow these associations to maintain their necessary autonomy in order to continue defining their projects and directing their participatory goals in the local development of their municipalities. Above all, it will allow them to continue elaborating a definition of their own identity, of their destiny, of the way in which they want to dream their communities in El Salvador, without the limitations established by other actors. Particularly, it is important to keep in mind, as Beth Baker-Cristales points out, that the neoliberal ideology of the free market orders the reduction of the expenses and services of the state in the name of competitivity and efficiency. As a result, the concept of efficiency, as it happened before with the concept of progress, runs the risk of turning into a double edged weapon: in its name the cultural processes that the dynamic that the associations generate could be sacrificed. The question is not if the hometown associations will be able to be more efficient if they become more professional or if they associate with other instances. The question is, seems to me, if by doing this they will necessarily have to stop being who they are, if in that process of institutionalization they will have to renounce also the space and the cultural identity that they have built for themselves through years of work.

Ironically, in the national public discourse of El Salvador, immigrants who send remittances have often been accused of generating unemployment and lack of initiative. This in a country where historically demographics have dictated patterns of relation with labor based on exploitation and made possible by the excess of available workers. That is, the excess of workers has guaranteed that their mistreatment will not diminish the demand for jobs, since there would always be a person willing to take the job—their need and competition would force them to—that someone else would not want. Even worse, as we know, often there have been workers willing to say: "I will work for less, if you want, I will work more hours in worse conditions. Please, I need the job." the culture of remittances can give a worker the privilege of saying "no more," not because he or she is lazy or because he or she wants to be unemployed, but because the options and working conditions in the country do not seem to be appropriate form them. Without a doubt it is difficult and uncomfortable for a country where historically this has been the dynamic, to face new options generated by remittances for the workers sector.

In fact, the postwar has given way to a dynamic that has transferred the responsibilities for the well-being of the population from the national state to the recently inaugurated civil society. In this sense, I think that organizations such as the hometown associations face difficult circumstances. In their recent history they have been excluded from the national panorama in their countries or origin and of residence; they live in poverty but at the same time their members are labeled as philanthropists; they carry out projects of local development that benefit their communities and municipalities until they are faced with means, particularly by the national government to regulate their work through projects such as the *Programa Unidos por la Solidaridad* (United for Solidarity Program) by the *Fondo de Inversión Social para el Desarrollo Local,* FISDL (Social Investment Fund for Local

Development). These projects make it possible to carry out plans of greater size than those that they associations are able to carry out independently, but they also impose prerequisites for the financial assistance that associations would receive and, as a result, they regulate in some way the work of the hometown associations. Baker-Cristales is quite clear when speaking about this point: "these programs allow the governments to encourage certain types of projects by offering funding for them, while discouraging other kinds of projects. The government can also use its support of hometown associations for political benefit, encouraging migrants and their families to vote for one or another party or administration. And the government can lay some claim to the development work that hometown associations are doing" (158).

Specially, I would like to emphasize that the work of the hometown associations inaugurates the possibility to generate a cultural process and an identity that function as alternatives to those defined by the national project. And even if we don't have time here to discuss in depth the origins of this project, let it be enough to remember that the nation in El Salvador has been, since its beginnings defined through processes of exclusion that have given way to a history of marginalization both through financial privilege and through the legacy of the ethnic hierarchies inherited since colonial times. Besides, this project of the nation was not defined by the great majority of the inhabitants, nor by a representative group of its ethnic and cultural diversity, but by a *Criollo* minority (Spaniards born in the Americas during the Spanish colonial period) seeking to maintain their own privileges. This imaginary of the nation with a *Criollo* legacy never did recognize the relevance, for instance, to manual labor or to rural space, nor to the needs of workers within this nation, much less to the cultural and identitarian needs of the different ethnic groups that also are part of its population. On the contrary, their efforts have been oriented towards the uniformity of the national subject and to move against diversity. Within this context, the strengthening of the local identity in which the hometown associations participate and invest in collaboration with the municipal governments, can gain relevance because it contributes to the decentralization of the processes of institutionalization led by the State. And the collaborative work on local development (in opposition to the development of the nation in general) presents important alternatives for decentralization. It seems to me then that this opportunity is important, as long as each of the participants is able to take part as a subject in the cultural and identitarian processes generated by their work and is enrich and continues to be defined in their own terms. In sum, as long as their local and collective identities are not sacrificed in the name of efficiency.

Note

1. An earlier version of this article was published in Spanish in *Estudios Centroamericanos* (ECA) 62.703–704 (2007): 467–474. Originally, this text was presented during the Second Bi-National Conference of Salvadoran Associations and Local Development in September, 2005 in Cojutepeque, El Salvador.

Works Cited

Baker-Cristales, Beth. *Salvadoran Migration to Southern California: Redifining El Hermano Lejano.* Gainesville, University Press of Florida, 2004.

Batres-Márquez, Patricia, Helen H. Jensen y Gary W. Brester. "Salvadoran Consumption of Ethnic Foods in the United States." Center for Agricultural and Rural Development, Iowa State University. October, 2001.

Documentos y discursos del Ministerio de Economía de El Salvador. < Http://www.minec.gob.sv/ >

Figueroa Hernández, Elsy Lizeth, et al. "Estudio de mercado de productos étnicos en Estados Unidos." Ministerio de Economía de El Salvador. Enero, 2003.

Orozco, Manuel. "The Salvadoran Diaspora: Remittances, Transnationalism and Goverment Responses." Tomás Rivera Policy Institute. Washington D.C., febrero, 2004.

Programa de las Naciones Unidas para el Desarrollo (PNUD). Informe sobre desarrollo humano El Salvador 2005. Una mirada al nuevo nosotros. El < Http://www.desarrollohumano.org.sv/ migraciones/idhes2005pdf/sinopsis.pdf >

This article presents an overview of the reasons young immigrants join gangs, as well as the violent and militarized reactions to gang violence in both Central America and the United States. It argues for ways to break the vicious cycle of violence that engulfs young immigrants upon their arrival in the poorest neighborhoods in the United States and upon their forced repatriation to nations that they hardly knew as small children and that they vaguely remember.

The majority of gang members joined a gang out of necessity, out of the sheer need to survive the violence in their neighborhoods and to belong to a community. Racial segregation in the cities and neighborhoods where they settled, as well as their isolation as children of poor immigrants, forced them to work several jobs to sustain the family. The response by Central American and the U.S. governments has not been to provide better educational and recreational opportunities for these young immigrants, but rather to deal with them as adult criminals and to approach the problem of youth violence in a militaristic manner.

Lainie Reisman discusses the ways in which the solutions are not working. Gang membership continues to increase, and imprisonment provides the means for young immigrants to continue their gang membership and gang related activities.

Breaking the Vicious Cycle: Responding to Central American Youth Gang Violence

Lainie Reisman

This article explores the relationship between gang violence, and the widely varying responses to such violence, in North and Central America. With a specific focus on transnational gangs like the Mara Salvatrucha (MS13) and 18th Street Gang (Calle 18), both of which have their roots in the United States, the author describes the cyclical nature of Central American gang activity and the inter-connectivity between the countries in the region. Emphasizing the important role of prevention programs, as a balance to coordinated rehabilitation and law enforcement efforts, the article argues for a comprehensive approach championed and implemented by the most affected countries in the region, namely the United States, El Salvador, Honduras, Guatemala, and Mexico.

Reisman, Lainie. "Breaking the Vicious Cycle: Responding to Central American Youth Gang Violence." *The SAIS Review of International Affairs* 26:2 (2006), 147–152.

Youth gang violence is a serious problem in North and Central America, threatening the basic security of residents as well as democratic processes throughout the region. The governmental responses vary greatly, but most have focused on adopting tougher law enforcement, otherwise known as suppression, efforts while assigning minimal resources to rehabilitation, reinsertion of reformed gang members into society at large, and prevention. Although international law enforcement agencies are beginning to increase coordination across borders, there is still an overall lack of recognition of the cyclical and transnational nature of the gang phenomenon. This international factor is crucial to the problem and its solution. Each country, acting in its own national self-interest, enacts policies and programs that both explicitly and implicitly impact other countries in the region, thus establishing a vicious cycle of violence that is difficult to stem. Clearly, this is an international crisis. In order to break this self-reinforcing pattern of youth violence and ineffective state responses, governments should implement cross-border initiatives that focus on prevention and intervention as a complement to existing law enforcement efforts.

While rooted in the specific realities of the countries in the region, youth gang violence is closely linked to the problems facing the Central American immigrant communities in North America. It is also a manifestation of a growing global phenomenon of youth violence. Although accurate data are hard to come by, conservative estimates indicate that there are up to 150,000 active Central American gang members in Guatemala, Honduras, El Salvador, Nicaragua, Mexico, and the United States—the majority of whom are members of the notorious *Mara Salvatrucha* (MS13) gang and the *Calle 18 (18th Street)* gang.[1] Both of these gangs established their roots in the Los Angeles area after fleeing violent Central American armed conflicts in the 1970s and 1980s. Once in Los Angeles, they established their own networks to rival the existing Mexican and African-American gangs. These gangs have flourished over the past two decades, establishing active strongholds in North and Central America alike, and proliferating in semi-urban and rural areas.

Recent policy changes have responded to the crisis. Most notably, in El Salvador, Honduras, and to some extent the United States, tough legislation has been passed targeting gang members through illicit association laws, mandatory minimum sentencing for young offenders, use of the death sentence for gang-related offenses, prosecution of juveniles as adults for gang-related crimes, and gang-racketeering laws.[2] But anti-gang initiatives have become mired in controversy. Human rights and service organizations in the region recognize that gang violence is a very serious problem but also note that gangs are now blamed for virtually all crimes leading to an increase in human rights and due process violations. In Central America, the number of arrests and detentions has increased dramatically, contributing to already overcrowded prison conditions, even though a mere fraction of detainees are actually convicted. With the perception that the justice system is unable to provide adequate solutions, self-styled vigilante justice is also commonplace as residents attempt to take matters into their own hands.

Confronting the Central American gangs at home and abroad has become a top priority within U.S. law enforcement circles, with the FBI going so far as to set up an MS13 task force in 2005 as part of its attempt to address this problem. In addition to tough legislation and prosecution, deportation has become an increasingly important tool in this battle. Deportations increased dramatically in the late 1990s as a result of immigration reform legislation that dramatically expanded the number and kinds of crimes for which non-citizens, including legal residents, could be deported. The impact of this legislation has been to increase significantly the number of Central American immigrant youth deported to their home countries, many of whom had been exposed to gang culture in the United States. More recently, the Department of Homeland Security (DHS) and more specifically Immigration and Customs Enforcement (ICE) have begun to use deportation actively and explicitly as a tool of anti-gang law enforcement, as evidenced by its recent Operation Community Shield.[3]

Although recent U.S. efforts may have led to a temporary reduction in gang membership, this targeted deportation policy has had a complex impact on the United States and its southern neighbors. Upon arrival in Central America, the deported youth—many of whom have lived in the United States for decades and some of whom do not speak Spanish—often are quickly integrated into local MS13 and 18th Street cells, thus strengthening ties between these gangs in different countries. It is not at all uncommon for a deported gang member, having benefited from newly established links to the drugs, weapons, and other criminal networks in Central America, to make his way back to the United States within a matter of months.

The law enforcement crackdowns throughout the region also have had other, less visible, results as gang activity seemingly has become more sophisticated. Gang members are no longer easily identifiable by their tattoos or clothing styles. Instead, many leaders of gang cells display no identifying traits. They are therefore able to move around easily and engage in increasingly sophisticated crimes, blurring the distinction between gangs and organized crime networks. While the U.S. Department of Justice is using the Racketeer Influenced and Corrupt Organizations Act (commonly referred to as RICO) laws to prosecute high-level gang leaders in the United States, Central American countries have neither the legislation, nor the investigative and prosecutorial capacity, to try RICO-type cases.

Indeed, the resource-strapped Central American countries have little to no capacity to deal adequately with the influx of gang members, as the justice sector—the courts, penitentiary systems, and police—are notoriously understaffed, under-funded, and unable to carry out basic mandates, let alone deal with the complex issues of youth gangs and newly arrived deportees. The juvenile justice sectors are even less equipped to provide an adequate solution to the problem, and neither adult nor juvenile detention centers have been able to incorporate rehabilitation and training programs into prison life. Rather, these countries face the problem that prisons in many cases serve as "graduate schools" or "training camps" for gang members who will be out of the streets and causing trouble once more.

Retaliation by rival gang members is also a constant threat to any past or present gang member. Luis, an MS13 gang member who has lived as a legal resident in the United States since he was 13, is currently under immigration custody in Los Angeles. When asked about the possibility of returning to his birth country of Honduras, he said, "I would rather be in custody here, than wait and die in Honduras." He has known many young men who were killed immediately upon return to their country of origin.[4] Additionally, deadly fires, riots, and murders in prisons in El Salvador, Honduras, and Guatemala, often fueled by inter-gang warfare, have become common. Because they have had to channel a disproportionate percentage of their scarce resources into security, the governments of the region have continually and consistently short-changed social investment.[5]

In seeking to answer the question of why Central American gangs have formed such a visible stronghold throughout the region, experts have pointed to armed conflicts, poverty, U.S. deportation policy, and a host of other explanatory factors. However, it is clear that no single explanation is adequate. The prevalence of Central American gangs results from a multitude of contributing factors that continually interact, as well as a lack of coordination in efforts to respond. Figure 1 is a simplified representation of this cycle of violent gang activity.

The precarious socio-economic conditions confronting young people throughout the region pose a serious challenge. With limited access to education and job opportunities, young people often look to gang life as a way to gain much-needed financial resources through lucrative criminal activities. Furthermore, gang life often provides a sense of belonging that many young people do not obtain from their families and communities.

Three additional contributing factors underpin the cycle of gang activity. The first is the media, which have a strong tendency to sensationalize their coverage of gang activity, often displaying images of tattooed young men being arrested or bloody shots of injured victims and corpses.

This media coverage has contributed to a culture of fear that encourages government suppression, with little public support for a more balanced approach. A second factor is the use of the widely publicized gang threat as a tool for political campaigning. For example, in Honduras, the highly publicized anti-gang policy of President Maduro (whose son was murdered in gang-related violence in 1996) was a major pillar of his election campaign in 2002. In the 2006 elections, President Maduro's preferred candidate to succeed him in office lost to liberal President Manuel Zelaya, who promoted a more balanced approach to dealing with youth violence. Many argue that the ineffectiveness of the Maduro anti-gang and security strategy was a major factor in the outcome of this election. Finally, the easy availability of weapons and drugs provides gang members with both a currency for doing business and a link to international trafficking networks that stretch throughout the hemisphere.

In the face of the challenges outlined above, the governments of North and Central America have undertaken several initiatives to confront the problem of youth gangs.[6] However, despite these efforts, it has become increasingly clear that no single sector, institution, or country can tackle this issue on its own. The problem requires a comprehensive, regional strategy of cooperation within and among the countries of Central and North America.

As a contribution to this process, a conference titled "Voices from the Field" convened in February 2005. My organization, the Inter-American Coalition for the Prevention of Violence (IACPV),[7] was one of the sponsors. Also sponsoring the conference were the

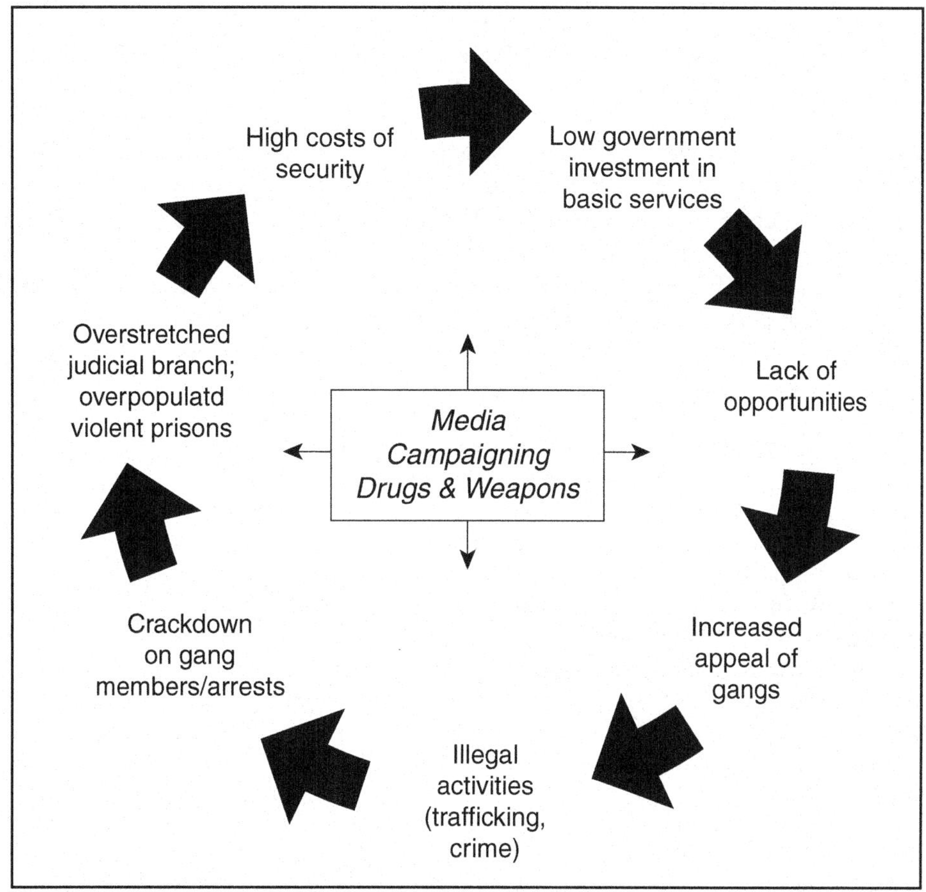

FIGURE 1. Circular Nature of Central American Gangs.

Pan-American Health Organization (PAHO), the Washington Office on Latin America (WOLA), and the Due Process of Law Foundation (DPLF). These four institutions come to the gang violence problem from very different perspectives, with diverse backgrounds in public security, human rights, due process, rule of law, public health and prevention, and education and youth work. With more than 250 attendees, the conference was an important step forward.[8] As a direct result of this event, a group of Central American practitioners formed the Central American Coalition for the Prevention of Youth Violence (CCPYV).[9] With representatives from national governments, NGOs, police forces, and academic institutions, the CCPYV initiative is the first of its kind to bring together diverse actors to promote prevention as an important complement to more traditional approaches to youth violence, The first regional conference on youth violence prevention in Central America convened in Managua in June 2005, with a follow-up event held in Honduras in May 2006.

These initiatives are based on the strong belief that only by bringing together the different key sectors, including the private sector, will it be possible to design and implement an effective response to the Central American gang problem. They recognize that youth violence is multi-faceted and closely linked to transnational developments. They concede that youth and gang violence, and the response to this problem, constitute a continued threat to public security and democracy in the region. They acknowledge that no individual sector, nor country, can independently solve this regional problem, which must be addressed in a comprehensive and carefully nuanced way. They are a tentative first step in the right direction, but much more work is needed to overcome the threat that these youth gangs pose to public safety in Central and North America.

Notes

1. USAID Central America and Mexico Gang Assessment, 2006.
2. This passage refers to the *Mano Dura* and *Super Mano Dura* laws in El Salvador, the *Leyes Anti-Maras* passed under the Maduro Administration in Honduras, and a compendium of U.S. legislation, including the Violent Crime Control and Law Enforcement Act of 1994 (P.L. 103-322) and the Gang Deterrence and Community Protection Act of 2005, popularly known as the "Gangbusters Bill," (H.R. 1279) passed by the U.S. House of Representatives in May 2005.
3. For more details see *www.ice.gov.*
4. The interviewee requested that his last name be withheld.
5. As an example, in El Salvador, the United Nations Development Program estimates the annual cost of violence to be as much as 12 percent of GDP. This amount represents double the combined annual budget of the Ministries of Health and Education. *¿Cuánto cuesta la violencia a El Salvador?, 2003.*
6. A comprehensive list is not available, but promising initiatives include the OAS/CICAD Conference and Declaration (Tapachula, Mexico, June 2005), the Summit meeting of the Presidents of the Central American countries (Tegucigalpa, Honduras, April 2005), as well as various international studies and conferences.
7. Membership in the IACPV includes the Inter-American Development Bank (IDB), Organization of American States (OAS), Pan American Health Organization/World Health Organization (PAHO/WHO), United Nations Educational, Scientific, and Cultural Organization (UNESCO), United States Agency for International Development (USAID), United States Centers for Disease Control and Prevention (CDC), and the World Bank Group (WB).
8. More details on the Voices from the Field Conference can be found at *www.wola.org.*
9. The founding member organizations of the CCPYV include the Association for Crime Prevention (APREDE, a Guatemalan NGO), the Institute of Public Opinion of the University of Central America (IUDOP/UCA, a regional university based in El Salvador), the National Police of Nicaragua (Juvenile Affairs Unit), and Honduran Youth Forward, Advancing Together (JHAJA, a Honduras NGO).

The author examines the history of immigration policy and immigration reform in the United States, and particularly the way in which it impacts the lives of Mexican and Central American workers. Hundreds of thousands of people are deported annually from the United States to other parts of the world. This, in turn, has a serious impact on the life of migrant families, who are often divided by borders, vulnerable, and lacking basic human rights. This article discusses the role of corporate interests and trade agreements such as NAFTA and CAFTA in the massive migration of workers from Mexico and Central America. In addition, it compares the civil rights movement that was able to pass the Voting Rights Act and to fight for equality and the end of segregation in the United States during the 20th-century, with the contemporary social movements that fight for immigrant workers' rights today.

Immigrant Labor, Immigrant Rights

DAVID BACON

In the late 1970s, the U.S. Congress began to debate the bills that eventually resulted in the 1986 immigration Reform and Control Act (IRCA)—still the touchstone for ongoing battles over immigration policy. The long congressional debate set in place the basic dividing line in the modern immigrant rights movement.

IRCA contained three elements. It reinstituted a guest worker program by setting up the H2-A visa category; it penalized employers who hired undocumented workers and required them to check the immigration status of every worker; and it set up a one-time amnesty process for undocumented workers who were in the country before 1982. Guest workers (i.e. workers whose immigrant status was tied to temporary, specific jobs), employer sanctions, and some form of legalization still occupy the main floor of the debate.

The AFL-CIO supported sanctions, believing they would stop undocumented immigration (and therefore, presumably, job competition with citizen or legal resident workers). Employers wanted guest workers. The Catholic Church and a variety of Washington DC liberals supported amnesty and were willing to agree to guest workers and enforcement as a tradeoff. Organized immigrant communities and leftist immigrant rights advocates opposed the bill, as did local labor leaders and activists, but they were not strong enough to change organized labor's position nationally. The Washington-based coalition produced the votes in Congress, and on November 6, 1986, Ronald Reagan signed the bill into law.

Once the bill had passed, many of the local organizations that had opposed it set up community-based coalitions to deal with the bill's impact. In Los Angeles, with the country's largest concentration of undocumented Mexican and Central American workers, pro-immigrant labor activists set up centers to help people apply for amnesty. That effort, together with earlier, mostly left-led campaigns to organize undocumented workers, built the base

"Immigrant Labor, Immigrant Rights," by David Bacon, *NACLA Report on the Americas*, 47, No. 1, Spring 2014, pp. 64–69.

for the later upsurge of immigrant activism that changed the politics and labor movement of the city. Elsewhere, local immigrant advocates set up coalitions to look for ways to defend undocumented workers against the impact of employer sanctions. Grassroots coalitions then began helping workers set up centers for day laborers, garment workers, domestic workers, and other groups of immigrants generally ignored by established unions.

Over the years since IRCA, a general division has marked the U.S. immigrant rights movement. On one side are well-financed advocacy organizations in Washington DC, with links to the Democratic Party and the business community. They formulate and negotiate immigration reform proposals that combine labor supply programs and increased enforcement against the undocumented. On the other side are organizations based in immigrant communities, and among labor and political activists, who defend undocumented migrants, and who resist proposals for greater enforcement and labor programs with diminished rights.

In the late 1990s, when the Clinton administration acquiesced in efforts to pass repressive immigration legislation (what eventually became the Immigration Reform And Immigrant Responsibility Act), Washington lobbying groups advocated a strategy to allow measures directed at increasing deportations of the undocumented to pass (calling them "unstoppable") while mounting a defense only of legal resident immigrants. Many community-based coalitions withdrew from the Washington lobbying efforts, refusing to cast the undocumented to the wolves.

In the labor movement, the growing strength of immigrant workers, combined with a commitment to organize those industries where they were concentrated, created the base for changing labor's position. At the 1999 AFL-CIO convention in Los Angeles, the federation called for the repeal of employer sanctions, for a new amnesty, and for a strong defense of the labor rights of all workers. The federation was already opposed to guest worker programs. The AFL-CIO maintained that position, even after several unions left to form the rival Change to Win federation, until 2009. At that time, a compromise was reached between the two federations, in which they dropped their previous opposition to employer sanctions, so long as they were implemented "fairly."

Over the past decade, a succession of "comprehensive immigration reform" (CIR) bills have been introduced into Congress. At their heart are the guest worker programs proposed by employers. But while the employer lobbies wrote the first bills, they have been supported by a political coalition that includes some unions, beltway immigrant advocacy groups, and some churches. Except for the vacillating and divided position of unions, this is the same political coalition that passed IRCA in 1986. Some local immigrant rights coalitions have also supported the bills, although many others have been unwilling to agree to guest worker programs and more enforcement. Supporters of the comprehensive bills have organized a succession of high-profile lobbying efforts, which received extensive foundation support.

The structure of the bills has been basically the same from the beginning—the same three-part structure of IRCA—guest workers, enforcement, and some degree of legalization. Under the CIR proposals promoted by Washington advocacy groups for several years, people working without papers would continue to be fired and even imprisoned, while raids would increase. Vulnerability makes it harder for people to defend their rights, organize unions, and raise wages. That keeps the price of immigrant labor low.

Enforcement does not stop people from coming to the United States, but it does produce a much larger detention system. Last year over 350,000 people went through privately run prisons for undocumented immigrants, while over 409,000 were deported.

The Washington-based CIR proposals all expand guest worker programs, in which workers have few rights, and no leverage to organize for better conditions. Finally, the CIR legalization measures impose barriers making ineligible many, if not most of the 11 million people who need legal status. They condition legalization on "securing the border," which has become a Washington DC euphemism for a heavy military presence, augmenting 20,000 Border Patrol agents and creating a climate of wholesale denial of civil and human rights in border communities.

A loose network of groups has grown that has generally opposed most CIR bills and their provisions, and that has organized movements on the ground to oppose increased enforcement and repression directed against immigrant communities. Outside the Washington beltway, community coalitions, labor and immigrant rights groups are pushing for alternatives. Some of them are large-scale counters to the entire CIR framework. Others seek to win legal status for a part of the undocumented population, as a step towards larger change. Many support the call for a moratorium on deportations.

One of the alternative proposals is the DREAM (Development, Relief, and Education for Alien Minors) Act. First introduced in 2001, the bill would allow undocumented students graduating from a U.S. high school to apply for permanent residence if they complete two years of college or serve two years in the U.S. military. For seven years thousands of young "*sin papeles,*" or people without papers, marched, sat-in, wrote letters, and mastered every civil rights tactic to get their bill onto the Washington agenda.

Many of them have "come out," declaring openly their lack of legal immigration status in media interviews, defying authorities to detain them. The DREAM Act campaigners did more than get a vote in Washington. They learned to stop deportations in an era in which more people have been deported than ever since the days of the Cold War.

When it was originally written, the bill would have allowed young people to qualify for legalization with 900 hours of community service, as an alternative to attending college, which many can not afford. However, when the bill was introduced, the Pentagon pressured to substitute military for community service, though even with that change, Congress did not pass the bill. In the heat of the 2012 presidential campaign, however, "dreamers" sat in at President Obama's Chicago reelection office and demonstrated nationwide, leading Obama to issue an executive order "deferring" the deportation of DREAM Act-eligible young people. Today, many immigrant rights activists view the DREAM Act as an important step towards a more basic reform of the country's immigration laws, and also see the dreamers' strategy as proof that absent Congressional action the administration has the ability, if not the political will, to end mass deportations.

Supporting the DREAM Act and other partial protections for the undocumented are worker centers around the country. Worker centers have anchored the protests against repression in Arizona, and fought to pass laws in California, New York, and elsewhere, prohibiting police from turning people over to immigration agents. They have developed grassroots models for organizing migrants who get jobs on street corners. These projects have come together in the National Day Labor Organizing Network. The National Domestic Worker Alliance was organized in part using the experience of day labor organizing, to win rights for domestic workers, almost all of whom are women. It won passage of a domestic worker bill of rights in New York and California. Other projects organize groups with a large immigrant contingent, from taxi drivers to garment workers.

Another group advocating an alternative to CIR is the Binational Front of Indigenous Organizations (FIOB). The group has conducted a series of organized discussions among its California chapters to formulate a progressive position on immigration reform, with the unique perspective of an organization of migrants and migrant-sending communities. FIOB campaigns for the rights of migrants in the United States—for immigration amnesty and legalization for undocumented migrants—while also campaigning against proposals for guest worker programs. At the same time, comments Gaspar Rivera Salgado, FIOB's bi-national coordinator, "we need development that makes migration a choice rather than a necessity—the right to stay home. Both rights are part of the same solution. We have to change the debate from one in which immigration is presented as a problem to a debate over rights. The real problem is exploitation."

"The governments of both Mexico and the United States are dependent on the cheap labor of Mexicans. They don't say so openly, but they are," says Rufino Domínguez, former bi-national coordinator of the FIOB and now the director of the Oaxacan Institute for Attention to Migrants. "What would improve our situation is legal status for the people already here, and greater availability of visas based on family reunification. Legalization and more visas would resolve a lot of problems—not all, but it would be a big step," he says. "Walls won't stop migration, but decent wages and investing money in creating jobs in our countries of origin would decrease the pressure forcing us to leave home. Penalizing us by making it illegal for us to work won't stop migration, since it doesn't deal with why people come."

The FIOB proposal on immigration reform is similar to that advanced by the Dignity Campaign, a loose coalition of organizations around the country that has proposed an alternative to the comprehensive labor-supply-plus-enforcement bills. The Dignity Campaign brings together immigrant rights and fair trade organizations to encourage each to see the global connections between trade policy, displacement, and migration. The group also brings together unions and immigrant rights organizations to spur the growth of resistance to immigration enforcement against workers, highlighting the need to oppose the criminalization of work.

The Dignity Campaign proposal draws on previous proposals, particularly one put forward by the American Friends Service Committee called "A New Path"—a set of moral principles for changing U.S. immigration policy. Several other efforts were also made earlier by the National Network for Immigrant and Refugee Rights to define an alternative program and bring together groups around the country to support it.

The critique shared by all these organizations is that the CIR framework ignores trade agreements like NAFTA and CAFTA, which have undercut workers' bargaining power and employment opportunities in Mexico and Central America. Without changing U.S. trade policy and ending structural adjustment programs and neoliberal economic reforms, millions of displaced people will continue to migrate, no matter how many walls are built on the border.

Changing corporate trade policy and stopping neoliberal reforms is as central to immigration reform as gaining legal status for undocumented immigrants. There is a fundamental contradiction in the bipartisan policies in Congress that promotes more free trade agreements, and then criminalizes the migration of the people they displace. Instead, Congress could end the use of the free trade system as a mechanism for producing displaced workers. That would mean delinking immigration status and employment. If employers are allowed to recruit contract labor abroad, and those workers can only stay if they are continuously employed (the two essential characteristics of guest worker programs), then they will never have enforceable rights.

The root problem with migration in the global economy is that it is forced migration. A coalition for reform should fight for the right of people to choose when and how to migrate. Freedom of movement is a human right. Even in a more just world, migration will continue, because families and communities are now connected over thousands of miles and many borders. Immigration policy should therefore make movement easier.

At the same time, workers need basic rights, regardless of immigration status. Progressive immigrant rights advocates call for devoting more resources to enforcing labor standards for all workers, instead of penalizing undocumented workers for working, and employers for hiring them. "Otherwise," Domínguez says, "wages will be depressed in a race to the bottom, since if one employer has an advantage, others will seek the same thing."

To raise the low price of immigrant labor, immigrant workers have to be able to organize, an activity made easier by permanent legal status. Guest worker programs, employer sanctions, enforcement, and raids make organizing much more difficult. Today, the sector of workers with the fewest benefits and the lowest wages is expanding the fastest. Proposals to deny people rights or benefits because of immigration status make this process move even faster. A popular coalition might push back in the other direction, toward more equal status, helping to unite diverse communities.

Such a political coalition might start by seeking mutual interest among workers in a struggle for jobs and rights for everyone. It is not possible to win major changes in immigration policy without making them part of a struggle for the goals of working class communities. To end job competition, for instance, workers need Congress to adopt a full-employment policy. To gain organizing rights for immigrants, all workers need labor law reform.

Winning those demands will require an alliance among workers—immigrants and native-born, Latinos, African Americans, Asian Americans, and whites. An alliance with employers, on the other hand, giving them new guest worker programs, would only increase job competition, push wages down, and make affirmative action impossible.

The basic elements of this alternative include permanent residence visas for the undocumented and new migrants, protecting family reunification, ending the mass deportations and firings, repealing employer sanctions, ending guest worker programs, demilitarizing the border, and changing trade policies that cause forced migration.

A new era of rights and equality for migrants does not begin in Washington DC, any more than the civil rights movement did. Human rights reform is a product of the social movements of this country, especially of people on the bottom, outside the margins of power. A social movement made possible the advances in 1965 that were called unrealistic and politically impossible a decade earlier. An immigration reform proposal based on human and labor rights may not be a viable one in a congress dominated by Tea Party nativists and corporations seeking guest worker programs. But just as it took a civil rights movement to pass the Voting Rights Act, any basic change to establish the rights of immigrants will also require a social upheaval and a fundamental realignment of power.

Alternative Immigrant Demands

The Dignity Campaign, FIOB, and AFSC proposals, are not just alternative programs for changing laws and policies, but implicit strategies of alliances based on mutual interest. They advocate the following:

* Give Permanent Residence visas, or Green Cards, to undocumented people already here, and expand the number of Green Cards available for new migrants.
* Eliminate the years-long backlog in processing family reunification visas, strengthening families and communities.
* End the enforcement that has led to thousands of deportations and firings.
* Repeal employer sanctions, and enforce labor rights and worker protection laws, for all workers.
* End all guest worker programs.
* Dismantle the border wall and demilitarize the border, so fewer people die crossing it, and restore civil and human rights in border communities.
* Respond to recession and foreclosures with jobs programs to guarantee income, and remove the fear of job competition.
* Redirect the money spent on the wars in Iraq and Afghanistan to rebuild communities, refinancing mortgages, and restoring the social services needed by working families.
* Renegotiate existing trade agreements to eliminate causes of displacement and prohibit new trade agreements that displace people or lower living standards.
* Prohibit local law enforcement agencies from enforcing immigration law, end roadblocks, immigration raids and sweeps, and close detention centers.

–DB

CHAPTER EIGHT

GLOBALIZATION

For modern Central America, globalization seems to be a new chapter in a life-long history of economic dependency. The main difference between the current period and other moments of Central American history is that in current times there is a shift from an agriculture based economic model to one based on service and industrial labor. Furthermore, the current economic model demonstrates that there is greater immersion of Central America in the world market and greater foreign investment in the region.

Given the globalizing trends that have taken place worldwide, it seems to be impossible for Central America not to embark in the global capitalist enterprise. However, the question is not whether there is another alternative, the question is whether Central American nations will be able to learn from their past and to implement economic models that will also protect natural resources, help the economy of each nation grow, and improve the living conditions of the majority. Because of the neoliberal policies that have been implemented and because of the ratification of the Central American Free Trade Agreement, among other neoliberal policies, the answer to this question seems to be, *no*.

Globalization and free trade agreements are not negative programs in and of themselves. The fact is that the global economy has greatly benefited some nations by providing a global market for their products, particularly in the case of developed nations that began massively exporting their high-tech products towards the end of the twentieth century. Free trade agreements have also proven beneficial when they were implemented within a region of comparable economic and labor conditions, such as in the case of Western Europe. However, in the case of an agreement such as the Central American

Free Trade Agreement (CAFTA), not only are the conditions unequal, but the legacy of economic dependency has not been removed. For instance, Central American nations continue to this day to pay the World Bank and the International Monetary Fund (IMF) a foreign debt that was acquired by unfairly elected, often times military, long gone presidents. And the debt that they are paying has been paid many times in terms of interests, labor and the use of Central American natural resources for the benefit of foreign owned companies.

Ironically, while liberalism was the ideology closely linked to the independence of the Central American nations, its close relative, neoliberalism, is the economic ideology that has ensured a new wave of economic dependency for the region. However, it is not surprising that they are connected, since both of them are economic ideologies that strive for the implementation of technological and scientific advances at any price. In the case of liberalism, the consequences it brought to the Central American region in the end were the privatization of the communal lands and newly invented systems of slave-like labor such as those generated by the vagrancy laws. In the case of neoliberal policies, which are being implemented nowadays, not much has changed. The efforts to privatize natural resources continue in order to build high-tech digital highways and new ports and transportation routes and to develop worldclass tourist resorts. Unfortunately, what also continues is the trend of ignoring the needs of the local population, particularly its access to a means not only of survival but to a dignified livelihood. What these neoliberal policies favor is foreign investment, technological and urban developments, and tourism.

Some of the efforts to privatize natural resources in Central America are openly colonial and based on a dependency model meant to transform the Central American population into captive consumers of the privatized products that originated from their own natural resources. This is the case in the growing efforts to privatize public services, water, electricity, telephone services, medical services, and so forth. These efforts represent the interests of transnational companies that seek to replicate earlier periods of Central American-U.S. economic relations within the current global economic model.

Among the policies and agreements that have come into effect, the Central American Free Trade Agreement, or DR-CAFTA, is the most significant one. This agreement includes not only Central American nations, with the exception of Panama and Belize (Panama and the U.S. negotiated a bilateral free trade agreement in 2012, and Belize is already part of the Caribbean common market). It also includes the Dominican Republic. This agreement was modeled after its predecessor, the North American Free Trade Agreement, NAFTA. In a similar manner to its predecessor and because of the large inequalities that exist between the United States and Central American nations, CAFTA has increased the poverty in the Central American region and has negatively impacted some of the natural resources that not only maintain Central American nations but also worldwide climate patterns, among them the Central American rainforest.

Because of the great inequalities between the two regions that participate in the agreement, CAFTA represents the definite end of the agriculturally based economic period for Central America because Central American farmers are unable to compete with larger, better equipped and better supported farmers from the north. As a result, as already has begun to happen in Mexico, farmers have to abandon their farms and move to urban centers to seek labor alternatives. These alternatives are usually available in the form of sweatshop labor and as part of the service economy that maintains tourism for instance, among other industries. As a result, Central American national economies are becoming more and more dependent upon the permanence of the sweatshops and factories that foreign owned companies establish on their soil, while competing with other nations globally for those jobs. Therefore, Central America is forced to offer these companies labor conditions and salaries that compete with nations such as China and that ultimately hurt and lower the already broken living standards of Central American workers.

Furthermore, because CAFTA is a treaty based on international law and not on national law (both for the United States and for Central American nations), the agreements and regulations stipulated by CAFTA supersede national laws meant to protect the natural and human resources that these countries have to offer. As a result, one of the most damaging consequences expected from CAFTA is the destruction, pollution, contamination and irreparable disintegration of the natural resources and the Central American ecosystem. To make the situation worse, because national laws do not apply, when a foreign owned company destroys the Central American environment, it does so under the jurisdiction of CAFTA-drafted international agreements and CAFTA-related international courts. Therefore, besides the obvious damages to the environment, CAFTA also undermines the already weakened national sovereignty of Central American nations.

In the great scheme of things, Central American nations under CAFTA will continue to provide cheap labor for the benefit of foreign economies. However, this has not happened without resistance. In all of the Central American nations affected by CAFTA massive demonstrations and popular resistance to CAFTA have taken place. Even in the United States, CAFTA was approved with a relatively small majority, by a vote of 54–45 in June 2005. The greatest efforts to stop CAFTA in Central America took place in Costa Rica where the decision was made by a popular referendum on October 7, 2007. CAFTA was ratified by a narrow 51.6 percent victory.

After the ratification of CAFTA, the question still remains: How does it continue to affect the national Central American economies and the Central American population? The most immediate response has been increased immigration to the north as Central American workers seek to escape a life of exclusion where they could never gain access to the products and services that they produce in their daily jobs at sweatshops, factories or in their local tourist industry.

The readings that we have included in this chapter are meant to illustrate the effects of free trade and neoliberal policies in Central America.

This article examines the early negotiations for CAFTA under Robert Zoellick, former president of the World Bank, who served as U.S. Trade Representative. At the time, in 2003, Costa Rica was not yet part of the agreement. Although the agreement was promoted since its inception "as a chance for Central America to prosper" (8), as the author explains, it actually was designed to generate more poverty, further economic dependency and reduced social services. One of the most significant aspects of Edwards' article is that it analyzes the rhetoric and the discourse contained in this and in other agreements, such as the Plan Puebla-Panama (PPP), more recently renamed Proyecto de Integración y Desarrollo de Mesoamérica (Project for the Integration and Development of Mesoamerica) or Proyecto Mesoamérica. As the article contends, the selling of the free trade agreement had a particular audience, that is, those with the means to compete and profit from the agreement. When we compare the language of the agreement to the actual numbers that it generates, it is evident that the investment is made to benefit the transnational corporations to the detriment of the Central American workers.

Selling Free Trade in Central America

BEATRICE EDWARDS

On December 17, 2003, Robert Zoellick, the U.S. Trade Representative, announced that the United States, Guatemala, Honduras, El Salvador and Nicaragua had concluded the Central American Free Trade Agreement (CAFTA). In January, after initially holding out, Costa Rica also jumped on board. The new trade regime was greeted with hearty applause from a large number of beneficiaries who were not, actually, your average Central American. They were, instead, international banks, energy corporations, road construction firms, paper companies, advertising consultants, golf course designers and beachfront developers. In announcing the agreement, Zoellick pumped its advantage for U.S. capital: more than half of Central America-bound U.S. farm exports and 80% of industrial and consumer exports will enter the region duty-free upon ratification of the treaty. The Central American countries will, in effect, open virtually all services–including telecommunications, energy, banking, insurance, transportation and construction–to unfettered U.S. investment. As always, profits may be freely repatriated. And in awarding contracts, Central American governments can no longer provide bidding advantages to their own nationals; U.S. corporations must be treated as if they are local companies.

Labor unions, which have taken a ten-year hit from NAFTA in both the United States and Mexico, greeted the new trade agreement with dismay. The president of the AFL-CIO, John Sweeney, called CAFTA "yet another job-destroying free trade agreement that will undermine workers' rights here and around the world." For his part, Zoellick assured unions that the treaty will have a limited effect on U.S. employment or labor rights in Central America. After all, the Central American signatories, renowned for some of the highest poverty rates and lowest wages in the hemisphere, will be obliged through the agreement to "effectively enforce their own domestic labor laws," he said.

This, of course, left no one reassured. Honduras, for example, has a (largely unenforced) minimum daily wage of $3 and mandates a not-very-generous 24-hour rest period every eight days. Conservative estimates suggest that 350,000 Honduran children work illegally. In El Salvador, the minimum wage is $4.40 a day, which the U.S. State Department itself declared "insufficient to provide a decent standard of living for a worker and a family."

Nonetheless, when it is inconvenient to plug CAFTA as a boon to U.S. companies shopping for cheap labor, the agreement is promoted as a chance for Central America to prosper. This marketing strategy has a checkered history associated with the Inter-American Development Bank (IDB) and its primary CAFTA building blocks: the various initiatives of Plan Puebla-Panama (PPP). Mexican President Vicente Fox announced the PPP in September 2000. The plan was billed as a 25-year, $20 billion, road, energy and communications construction program for the southern Mexican states, Central America and Panama. Through PPP, the governments are borrowing billions from a financial consortium cobbled together by the IDB to fund the infrastructure needed for high returns on investments made through CAFTA. This approach has not made Plan Puebla-Panama very popular, despite elaborate cosmetic concoctions applied by the IDB in a vain attempt to alter the Plan's otherwise frightening appearance.

For example, PPP includes the "Mesoamerican Initiative for the Prevention and Mitigation of Natural Disasters," which one assumes would support earthquake proofing construction measures or at least emergency aid provisions. On close inspection, however, this scheme will underwrite the development of a market for "catastrophe" insurance. Similarly, a sizable chunk of the funding for the "Mesoamerican Human Development Initiative" will finance a statistical information system on migration. The disparity in funding between pro-business and pro-people projects is clear in the gross numbers: while over $4 billion will be spent to expand road and highway networks, only $34 million is slated for health care. As of August 2003, the education component of the Plan still had no specified goals, never mind a budget, because, as an IDB operative confessed, the governments were unable to think up a regional educational objective. Well, we can see why that would be a tough one.

It is lopsided priorities like these that have caused the furor around PPP, and since the Plan needs private money, public anger is a problem. To put it crudely, private investors are afraid of pissed-off Indians. Ever resourceful, the IDB went out and hired the public relations firm Fleishman-Hillard to improve the Plan's image.

The challenge for the PR experts at Fleishman-Hillard is that, no matter what they claim, this is how CAFTA and PPP are really going to work: For the sake of argument, let's suppose that you are one of the fortunate few who actually gets a steady job in, say, an underpants assembly plant between San Salvador and the airport, created as a result of new highways, modernized customs and blossoming Fruit-of-the- Loom investments. You make minimum wage, so you're hauling in $22 a week. This might have been almost enough to get by in the old days, but these days your food supply is more expensive because the eggs are from Iowa and the corn is from Nebraska. You used to get this stuff more cheaply, but your local suppliers no longer exist since mega-corporations like Monsanto, Dekalb and Walmart have replaced your entire supply chain. Also, your tax burden is a bit heavier because the government is up the wazoo in debt to the IDB and Citibank (its "live richly" motto notwithstanding). Unfortunately, to help pay the debt your government has sold off its public schools, hospitals, highways, water and power utilities to private operators, thus making education, health care, water and electricity cost more too. Even with piece-work, overtime and intensive begging, you're going to have a hard time making ends meet.

But wait, says Fleishman-Hillard. Through PPP, the IDB is funding projects to "promote activities that foster productive integration and the establishment of networks for small and medium export enterprises." You could start a small business and export to niche markets in the United States! After all, many Central American products can also enter the United States duty-free, so long as they don't compete with anything made there. "The United States is working to link aid with trade, and to partner with private groups that can promote sustainable development in the CAFTA region," says a grinning Zoellick.

To prove his point, he personally visited the premises of Shuchil, a small business operating out of the home of Matilde Carillo de Palomo in San Salvador. According to Carillo, she produces pet soaps and dog shampoos, made from traditional Mayan formulas and ingredients (presumably used to launder traditional Mayan pets). Most of the company's employees are, in fact, traditional Mayan women displaced from the rural areas outside of San Salvador by export agriculture. Now doesn't that work out nicely for everyone?

These opportunities are, of course, limited: to date only $13 million has been set aside for small businesses in the eight PPP countries. And yet, there's more. Because the poor in Central America are disproportionately indigenous people, PPP will promote their prosperity through tourism that capitalizes on their colorful costumes and intriguing rituals. As part of PPP, the IDB is promoting a new Mesoamerican vacation phenomenon: "ethnotourism." If this holiday innovation takes off in upscale tourist markets, those willing to pay can observe real Injuns for entertainment.

Needless to say, both CAFTA and PPP are in for a fight this year, despite the best efforts of Fleishman-Hillard and the IDB. One PPP project has already been repulsed by the Mixtec people of Puebla. They rejected President Fox's Proyecto Milenium, which was to include a golf course, country club, luxury residential developments and an industrial zone for maquiladoras on what had heretofore been 40 square miles of productive farmland. At around the same time, a rapid mobilization eliminated potential PPP funding for a highway through the Petén Maya Biosphere Reserve.

On the labor front, pressure from the National Association of Public Employees and other civil society groups in Costa Rica nearly kept that government out of CAFTA, because, despite what Zoellick claimed, the agreement does not address the problem of inadequate labor laws and limited enforcement. Public workers' unions in the other countries that have signed CAFTA are protesting the privatization and foreign expropriation of their jobs and services. In the United States, a coalition of unions, environmental and women's advocacy groups and other civil society organizations have vowed to fight against ratification of CAFTA, which may turn up in the U.S. Congress as early as this spring. Putting this deal over on everybody might just require more than saturated media markets and better brand positioning. The PR tactics—intended to convey that the public's interests, rather than those of big business, will be defended—haven't worked all that well so far.

This article provides an example of the ways in which current neoliberal policies affect agricultural workers in Central America. The author analyzes real life economics from the perspective of Don Ramón, a small coffee producer in Guatemala. The benefits of the trickle-down economics promised in the 1980s never arrived to the agricultural workers in this country where approximately three-fourths of the population live in poverty and are not able to meet the most basic nutritional requirements. In this case, the article takes a look at the particular situation of coffee growers in Guatemala and compares the profits made by the local growers (at the time, an estimated $0.02 for every $4 cup of caffé latté) and the coffee roasters, processors, packing companies, transporters, distributors and retailers ($3.98). Therefore, this article is critical of the current free trade policies based on the premise of exchanging goods according to what a country produces instead of generating conditions of self-sufficiency. As a result, in this process of free exchange, the policies instituted create advantages for the developed countries that are able to produce beyond their population's ability to consume. Within this context, people like Don Ramón do not have the ability to compete nor the means or the land to produce a competitive product. In other words, this article provides a window into the dynamics that make it more and more impossible each day for agricultural workers to remain in their lands producing national products for export and forcing them to join the ever growing armies of service sector workers.

The Neoliberal World Order

The View from the Highlands of Guatemala

From the perspective of poor rural Guatemalans, the current global crisis has little to do with interest rates or budget deficits. It has everything to do with the fact that policies aimed at the developing world are far removed from the needs and realities of the majority of the world's peoples.

JOHN D. ABELL

It had been a productive morning so far. The family I was helping had picked close to 200 pounds of red, ripe coffee beans and we were relaxing around a cooking fire where the women had prepared a feast of beans, tortillas and avocado. Life seemed peaceful for the moment. Bellies were full. Beautiful Lake Atitlán, the jewel of Guatemala, was glistening

"The Neoliberal World Order: The View from the Highlands of Guatemala," by John D. Abell, *NACLA Report on the Americas*, 33, No. 1, July/August 1999, pp. 8–9.

in the distance. The only serious issue that remained this day was the matter of getting a couple of 100-pound sacks of coffee two miles down the side of the Tolimán volcano to the coffee-processing plant where they would be weighed and scrutinized for leaves and stems prior to the payout.

Our discussion at lunch ranged from coffee prices to politics, focusing especially on the recent Peace Accords. Yes, everyone agreed, life had improved since the cessation of hostilities in December 1996, if only because the Guatemalan military was no longer dragging their sons off the streets and soccer fields to fight in the counterinsurgency war against the Guatemalan National Revolutionary Unity (URNG). Also, sleep came a lot easier knowing that the chances of a visit in the middle of the night from a paramilitary death squad were significantly reduced if not entirely eliminated.

Had any of the benefits of the Accords on the economy or judicial reform trickled down their way? Beyond a basic recognition that the Accords had left land-holding patterns untouched, they were not aware of many details. Their lives had remained essentially unchanged, they told me, living from day to day, eagerly awaiting the coffee harvest in hopes that it would be profitable enough this year to allow them to keep their kids in school and to pay their medical bills.

I asked if they were aware of the global economic crisis that had engulfed Asia, Russia and Brazil, and if they were concerned that Guatemala might be next. Don Ramón, the patriarch of the family, patiently explained to me that during his entire lifetime, and that of his father—indeed, he said, for nearly 500 years—Guatemala had been going through an essentially permanent economic crisis. How, he asked, could a country possibly have a healthy economy when most of its people go to bed hungry each night, and when they do not have land or any control over their lives? How could the latest problems from Asia or wherever make their lives any worse? I was thinking about this lesson in real-world economics the next day when I stumbled on an issue of *Newsweek* devoted to the global financial crisis.[1] One of the broad themes running through all the stories was that while calm was returning to financial markets, economic recovery in the developing world was slow in coming. Indeed, there is abundant evidence that poverty and suffering is widespread. In the arctic regions of Russia, for example, people whose life savings vaporized in the early days of the ruble crisis faced starvation during one of the worst winters on record. In Jakarta, fathers who were once gainfully employed have now joined their families in the garbage dumps scrounging for their next meal. For many people, life—which was never very easy— has become precarious and desperate.

Many are beginning to blame the global financial system itself for such outcomes.[2] With countries like Malaysia setting a "dangerous" example by establishing restrictions on the movement of foreign capital, there is genuine fear in the establishment that some serious backsliding may be in the offing among those countries that had so eagerly embraced the neoliberal agenda. This may help to explain why Klaus Schwab, president of the World Economic Forum, selected "Responsible Globality" as the theme of this year's conference in Davos, Switzerland. Globalization is not going away anytime soon, says Schwab. The key, therefore, for lifting people out of poverty, is an improved infrastructure—"procedural, legal and institutional mechanisms"—to help harness the global revolution. "The new dividing line between richness and poverty," he suggests, "is not between the haves and have-nots, but between the *knows* and *don't knows*. The best way to help the poor is to enable them to take advantage of a global knowledge-economy."[3]

Don Ramón's eyes would probably glaze over if I told him that there was a fellow by the name of Klaus Schwab who was of the opinion that it did not matter that he was a have-not, and that he could improve his life if he would just take advantage of the "global knowledge-economy." If Don Ramón could speak with Mr. Schwab, he would surely tell him that his knowledge of the coffee business is just fine, and that what he needs is not a fancy Internet hookup or a Web page, but rather a higher price for his coffee and more land on which to grow it.

Each of the 100-pound sacks (referred to as a *quintal*) that Don Ramón's sons carried down the mountain that day only brought the family approximately $14. They only have half an acre of coffee and, because of the age of the trees, will be lucky to harvest a total of 2,500 pounds this year. If they can avoid the thieves who prey on small producers—lying in wait to take a family's harvest at gun point—they will earn an extra $360, a nice supplement to Don Ramón's weekly income of $17, but still not yet within striking distance of Guatemala's average annual income of $1,500.

Another way to think about the Ramón family's precarious position in the global economic order is to suppose that with a bit of luck some of their coffee ended up in the inventory of an upscale U.S. coffee shop. For every $4 cup of café latté sold, Don Ramón would receive about $0.02—less than 1%. Coffee processors and exporters, transportation companies, advertising agencies, roasters, retailers and other intermediaries would take the remaining 99%.

In spite of all that, Don Ramón is one of the lucky ones. Most people have no hope of owning their own land. In Guatemala, just 2% of the population owns 80% of the land. Not coincidentally, three-quarters of Guatemalans live in poverty, with nearly 60% of the population unable to meet minimal nutritional needs. Eighty-five percent of children under age five experience malnourishment to some degree, and stunted growth affects up to 95% of non-Spanish speaking children in some regions of the country.[4]

Don Ramón is luckier still because of his steady $17 per week job as a bee keeper. For many highlands residents, however, not only is land an impossible dream, but work itself has become scarce. Many highlands families survived for generations as residential employees of the giant coffee plantations, a throwback to the days of the colonial *encomienda,* or royal land commissions, where the indigenous were expelled from their own lands and, through a variety of forced-labor laws, made to work on the estates. The Constitution ostensibly protects modern plantation workers by obligating owners to provide workers with housing, clean water, a minimum wage (currently $2.80 per day), schooling and health care—not a bad deal, on paper. In reality, many of those services are not provided, including payment of the minimum wage. More often than not, a daily wage of only $2.10–$2.60 is paid. Guatemala's own Ministry of Labor estimates that there is only 15% compliance with payment of the minimum wage in rural areas.[5]

Since workers are generally poorly educated, not aware of their legal rights, and with no local authority to whom they can turn, owners can operate with impunity. Nevertheless, there is some limited degree of security for the families in this arrangement, no matter how inequitable.

A trend begun on the coastal sugar plantations in the 1980s, which is gaining more and more acceptance on the coffee estates of the highlands, is to use seasonal or sometimes daily contract laborers instead of permanent employees. For the owners, efficiencies—i.e., cost-savings—from not having to provide year-round wages and benefits far outweigh the uncertainties associated with having to hire and supervise temporary workers. There is also a secondary financial benefit that comes from releasing hundreds of families into the labor market. Their presence in the contract labor force helps to put further downward pressure on an already distressed labor market, allowing the owner to pay wages far below the legal minimum. For the families, on the other hand, who have been kicked out of the only homes they have ever known for generation upon generation, life takes a turn for the worse. They have little choice but to join the ranks of the seasonal work force. Their wages, which were never totally adequate in the first place, get cut in half or more since seasonal work is just that—seasonal. Plus, without land, there is no means to grow one's own food. Housing, medical care and schooling become additional complicated financial matters.

With at most six months of work at the subminimum wages of approximately $2.30 a day, feeding and caring for a typical highlands family of six is nearly impossible. All hopes will be pinned on a bountiful coffee harvest. The months of January and February are the peak months and entire families will head up the mountainsides at daybreak to pick coffee for the owner. They are paid by the pound, and with all hands working feverishly they may pick 300 pounds a day. At a pay scale averaging $0.023 per pound, the family may bring home approximately $6.90 every day during this peak period. It is imperative that these two months go well for the families because nearly 70% of their annual income is earned at this time. The yields are so much lower in the month before and the month after that only 25–30 pounds per day, or $0.62 per day, can be counted on.

With some luck, the father and possibly an older son may get hired for an extra couple of months for weeding, pruning or planting on one of the plantations. Additional work could conceivably be found on one of the coastal sugar plantations, though the harvest season tends to overlap with that of coffee. At any rate, the family's income for the season will be in the vicinity of about $715, an amount that will cover only about a third of the required minimal daily caloric intake of a basic corn and beans diet.[6] In addition, housing, medical care, school and clothing will take as much as a third out of this already strained family budget. Income-earning opportunities during the rainy season for families like the Ramóns are limited. The occasional odd job—shining shoes, selling prepared foods in the market, or for the desperate, begging or prostitution— brings only a modicum of financial relief. It is not hard to see where the high statistics on malnutrition come from when so many families face similar circumstances. It is also easy to see why a plot of one's own land is so critical for survival.

To my knowledge, former U.S. Treasury Secretary Robert Rubin, the architect of U.S. neoliberal economic policies during the 1990s, and his former deputy and now successor, Lawrence Summers, never invited Don Ramón or any of the rest of the world's poor campesinos to any of their free-market strategy sessions. Nor have I seen any accounts of their visits to the countryside to share a meal and a discussion with the Don Ramóns of the world for whom the benefits of trickle-down economics are slow to arrive.

Indeed, the current global crisis has little to do with the fact that Secretary Rubin has not gotten interest rates or exchange rates right, or that the various countries' budget deficits are too high, or some other statistical imbalance. It has a lot to do with the fact that policies aimed at the developing world are far removed from the needs and realities of the majority of the world's peoples. Such policies, implemented by the rich and powerful, assume a textbook world in which producers and consumers operate at arms length, negotiating until a price and quantity are determined that clear the market and benefit both parties to the transaction. Overlooked are the more realistic scenarios whereby Don Ramón and other small producers receive take-it-or-leave-it prices from agribusiness concerns that control the world's markets.

A survey done by the Association for the Development of San Lucas Tolimán, a highlands community in the heart of the coffee-growing region, indicated that small coffee producers need to receive a price of $28.50 per 100 pounds in order to cover their production costs and to put an adequate diet on the table. But the reality is that market prices have not been that high in years.[7] You can be sure that if there is a glut of coffee on world markets—and if the powerful coffee merchants have their way, there will always be a glut—prices will fall for Don Ramón and his family. On the other hand, café latté prices will hold firmly, or possibly rise a bit at the fashionable coffee houses.

U.S. Treasury policies, which draw upon free-trade concepts first espoused by the British economist David Ricardo over 200 years ago, are supposed to work like this: Guatemala should produce those products in which it has a comparative advantage, such as coffee, sugar and bananas. The United States, its largest trading partner, should do likewise, focusing on goods like sport utility vehicles (SUVs), computers and information services. Then, by trading freely with one another, their respective national incomes will be higher than if each country attempted to be self-sufficient in the production of all goods.

So how much coffee would a landowner in Guatemala have to produce to be able to afford to purchase the latest $50,000 SUV? At an average wholesale price for topend, gourmet coffee of $100 per 100-pound sacks, the landowner would need to produce 250,000 pounds of coffee beans.[8] This would entail the use of approximately 50 acres of land.[9] The landowner would have to employ approximately 21 workers during a four-month harvest season and pay them approximately $0.23 per hour.[10] This would add up to a collective wage bill of about $5,700, or 11% percent of the cost of the SUV. If the plantation in this example happened to be among the country's largest, it might be in the vicinity of 600 acres, enabling the owner to buy a fleet of nearly 12 SUVs per year.[11]

On the other hand, suppose that one of the boss's workers also wanted to purchase a vehicle. If he were somehow able to save every single cent of his paycheck it would take him 18 years to accumulate enough money to buy a $5,000 used car. To buy an SUV he would have to share the purchase with each of his 21 coworkers and they would each have to save the entirety of their paychecks for nine years.

Such free-trade policies will be deemed successful as long as they can continue to generate 20% returns year in, year out, in the U.S. financial markets. But how long can this continue? The investment guru Peter Lynch emphasizes in his television commercials for Fidelity Investments that there is nothing magical about successful stockmarket investing. Good portfolio performance results from doing one's homework, from carefully scrutinizing those companies that have strong profit potential. What is not mentioned, however, is how those profits come about, and especially how critical the connection is to the developing world.

Profits, of course, arise when sales revenues exceed the costs of production. Don Ramón might be amazed to realize just how vital he is to the amassing of global corporate profits—he figures critically in both variables in the profit equation (revenues and costs). To the coffee merchants, his family's 2,500 pounds of coffee sold at $14 represents just another cost of doing business. The more small growers like him there are around the world, the more coffee is produced. And with more coffee comes lower production costs for the coffee multinationals. The lower coffee prices are, however, the less food Don Ramón can afford to buy for her family's meals. But that is not the concern of the coffee companies.

The Ramón family is also critical to the revenue side of the equation. Here is how that connection works. The United States produces many more goods than it is capable of consuming domestically. In certain industries such as agriculture, this imbalance is quite significant. For example, wheat production exceeds domestic consumption by as much as 50% in a given year, corn by 25%. In order for corporations to provide investors with healthy annual returns, not only do they need to hold the line on costs, but they also need to find overseas outlets for their surpluses. To follow our example, this entails finding markets for as much as 50,000,000 metric tons of wheat and corn per year.[12] Exports, therefore, represent an increasingly large share of gross domestic product (GDP), having grown from less than 6% to nearly 15% of GDP in the past ten years. Also, developing countries have become increasingly more important as destinations for U.S. surpluses during this period, increasing their share of U.S. exports from 35% to 45%.[13] In countries like Guatemala, the well-to-do have been consuming imports from the United States for years. It is people like Don Ramón and his highlands neighbors who are being called upon more and more these days to do their share.

We have created a system that generates enormous profits for a select few who sell products like soft drinks, snacks and cigarettes to the masses around the world. The glitch occurs when the masses can no longer afford to buy these things. When this happens, the system begins to grind to a halt. In other words, the system is sustainable only as long as the masses are actually able to participate in it—that is, when they are paid a living wage. And the system has limited sustainability when the people who actually have enough disposable income to buy these consumer goods number less than 10% in most countries of the developing world.

For the moment, thanks to aggressive advertising—as well as high sugar and nicotine content—Don Ramón and the remaining 90% in Guatemala who are among the have-nots are obediently consuming soft drinks, snacks and cigarettes like there is no tomorrow, much to the detriment of their health and well-being. It is not an uncommon sight to see a family that cannot afford to send its kids to school or buy them shoes spending their hard-earned *quetzales* on Coca-Cola, Chiclets, Doritos or Marlboro cigarettes. However, it seems unlikely that the means exist for the Ramóns and their neighbors to increase their purchases of these products year after year so that the companies that peddle these products can continue to expand. Amazingly though, stock market investors continue to place their bets that somehow the multinationals will continue to reach more people throughout the world with their advertising, or convince those already in their grasp to dig deeper into their pockets to buy even more.

Herein lies a core capitalist contradiction. With the goal of increasing global profits, corporations are searching all over the world for new customers like Don Ramón, promising them unlimited happiness if they would just buy their products. The corporations' hope, on the other hand, is that someone else will pay these customers a high enough wage so that they can afford the products. So far, no one appears willing to do so.

Like the global corporations, Guatemala's oligarchy also faces a contradiction. In its effort to maintain power, prestige and wealth, it refuses to treat the indigenous and campesino poor of its country humanely—to share the richness of the land. Without land, the poor are forced to work as seasonal laborers or to assemble clothes in the maquiladoras for wages that cannot put food on the table, much less buy consumer goods or luxury items. Guatemala's producers thus have no choice but to become ever more dependent on export sales. What they find, though, is that the oligarchy in nearly every other developing country is doing the same thing, from Brazil to Indonesia to Russia. Prices around the world fail as a result of the collective attempt to run trade surpluses. The people who have to tighten their belts as a result are not the landowners— they do not want to give up their SUVs and their country clubs—but rather the Don Ramóns of the world.

NOTES

1. *Newsweek International*, February 1, 1999.
2. See, for example, the four-part New York Times series "Global Contagion," February 15–18, 1999.
3. *Newsweek International*, February 1, 1999, p, 56.
4. Bread for the World, *Hunger* 1990 (Washington, D.C. Bread for the World Institute on Hunger and Development: 1990).
5. Tom Barry, *Inside Guatemala* (Albuquerque Inter-Hemispheric Education Resource Center, 1992), p. 97.
6. At current market prices for corn ($0.11 per pound) and beans ($0.54 per pound), it would take $5.20 per day to provide a family of six with the minimal daily required calories (2,900-men, 2,340-women, 1,485-children) based on figures from the National Academy of Sciences. An annual income of $715 per year covers about 38% of the cost of the basic diet.

7. In an effort to address poverty in the area, the Association pays small coffee growers who meet exacting quality standards the above market price of $28.50 per 100-pound sack. For more on this effort and other sustainable projects of the community, see John Abell. "Peace in Guatemala? The Story of San Lucas Tolimán," in J. Brauer and W.G. Gissy, eds., *Economics of Conflict Resolution and Peace* (Brookfield: Ashgate Publishing Co., 1997), pp. 150–178.
8. This assumes a ratio of five-to-one raw bean to wholesale (what is known as green coffee).
9. This asumes a yield of approximately 5,000 pounds per acre.
10. This assumes each worker can pick on average 100 pounds per day. The actual day-to-day yield will depend, of course, on the stage in the harvest.
11. Barry, *Inside Guatemala*, p. 104. The exact average is 582.
12. Agricultural data from: U.S. Department of Agriculture, USDA Economic Research Service, an online data service.
13. Guatemala has gone from essentially being self-sufficient in the production of corn, importing only a negligible amount in the 1960s, to importing 25% of its domestic needs in the 1990s from the United States and other countries. Cheap U.S. wheat has swamped the domestic wheat industry such that nearly 100% of all wheat consumed domestically is imported.

This article explores the historical impact of racist identitarian and economic policies in the Atlantic Coast of Nicaragua and the quest for national homogeneity. The author explores issues of race, autonomy, economic development and governance to explain the use of a multicultural model to promote a neoliberal economic agenda on the region.

The racist representation and control of the Costeño people of Nicaragua (Black and Indigenous) date back to the early years of Spanish and British colonization in the region. Late in the 19th century the newly created Nicaraguan state annexed the Atlantic Coast and this process included the imposition of the so-called Spanish/mestizo socio-political and economic culture. This provoked a continued resistance that was visible during the Sandinista rule (1979–1990) as a result a fragile regional autonomy was obtained during this period.

Depictions of the Costeño culture as a treat to the Mestizo nation are openly represented in the conservative media that portraits the Costeño culture and people as savages, drug dealers, and worthless as Nicaraguan citizens. The recent neoliberal developmental phase has forced the Nicaraguan government to adopt a multicultural agenda that appears to be inclusive, but has inherited the tenants of the racial discrimination of the old colonial powers and the discursive practices of homogeneity of the modern Nicaraguan nation/state.

Neoliberal Governance, Multicultural State? Race and the Politics of Regional Autonomy on the Atlantic Coast of Nicaragua

JENNIFER A. GOETT

In 1903, the Nicaraguan state named the town of Bluefields administrative seat of the Atlantic Coast Department of Zelaya. A century later, this relatively minor event in the history of Bluefields might not have warranted a national celebration had it not followed the Nicaraguan state's military annexation of the Mosquito Reserve in 1894. While nationalist accounts of history refer to annexation as "The Reincorporation," Afro-descendent Creoles from the region call it the "The Overthrow." Once enslaved by British colonists, ancestors of the contemporary Creole population formed a Maroon community at Bluefields in the 1790s. Over the course of the next century, their numbers were augmented by several waves of immigration from the Caribbean, particularly Jamaica. A former British protectorate, Creoles controlled the Mosquito Reserve at the time of Nicaraguan annexation. From their perspective, annexation marked the overthrow of an autonomous state under their stewardship and the onset of a new colonial regime characterized by virulent racism. For the Nicaraguan state, the event signaled the unification of Pacific and

Atlantic Nicaragua into one sovereign territory and the defeat of an illegitimate foreign black power on national soil.

Yet Creoles have resisted integration into the mestizo nation and I argue the contemporary state continues to be unable to imagine and construct a national identity in which Creoles legitimately figure. The Bluefields Centenary celebration provides an ethnographic lens for understanding how nationalist ideologies that promote a notion of radical black alterity continue to structure Creole encounters with the neoliberal state despite significant multicultural reforms at the national level. I suggest that multicultural policies that seem to promote the recognition and tolerance of difference instead signal a reconfiguration of racial hegemonies and exclusionary tactics in the post-revolutionary neoliberal era, resulting in an "uneasy fusion of enfranchisement and exclusion"[1] for Atlantic Coast Creoles.

After several years of armed conflict, black and indigenous people from the Atlantic Coast (also known as Costeños) won regional autonomy from the Sandinista government in 1987. But with the Sandinista electoral defeat in 1990, the Nicaraguan right inherited a political mandate that they did not embrace. Once in power the right quickly adopted a broad-based neoliberal agenda, but failed to show support for Costeño autonomy and multicultural citizenship rights. Although indigenous Costeños have been central protagonists in the struggle for regional autonomy, black Costeños are often represented as posing a greater threat to the mestizo nation. With no place in dominant constructions of mixed indo-hispanic (or mestizo) national identity due to their African origins, Creoles have been racialized as foreign, counter-national and, therefore, undeserving in Nicaragua. This historical mode of racialization is conveyed in the previous image, which was drawn by a celebrated Nicaraguan political cartoonist and published in the most popular national newspaper in 2002.

FIGURE 1. Autonomy
Courtesy Manuel Guillén, *La Prensa.*

This pointedly racist caricature of a politically active Creole holds a banner that reads "Autonomy," while declaring "The Coast is for Costeños!" To the right, stands a perplexed and apprehensive mestizo, a representative of the national majority. Here the struggle over Costeño autonomy is represented as a black-white conflict between a heavily racialized Creole with dreadlocks and Rastafarian knit cap (both associated with Jamaican origins and drug use in Nicaragua) and a white (or near white) mestizo campesino hard at work. The cartoonist has taken the black-white binary a step further by using a word play on Autonomy. The word "Auto" in bold letters flanking the Creole literally translates as "Self," while the words "No Mía" over the mestizo mean "Not Mine." Indigenous Costeños do not figure in the struggle; instead, autonomy is represented as a selfish black demand that is irrelevant and even antithetical to the interests of the national majority.

In 2001, after more than a decade of limited and poorly implemented regional autonomy, the election of Enrique Bolaños as President of Nicaragua gave many Costeños renewed hope that their political demands would be recognized by the state. A self-styled reformist, Bolaños ran on a platform of national reconciliation and won a significant majority of the black and indigenous Costeño vote. Once elected, Bolaños promised to unify a polarized nation through the promotion of a modern and transparent democratic state that functioned by rule of law. National reconciliation was to provide the foundation for a more expansive hegemony or a national identity and political culture with which Pacific and Atlantic Coast Nicaraguans (from both ends of the political spectrum) could identify. At the same time, political stability and rule of law were seen as necessary conditions for neoliberal development or Nicaragua's reinvention as a viable competitor in the global marketplace.

In response to Costeños' demands, Bolaños adopted a tentative multicultural agenda for the Coast that he promoted as a step towards national reconciliation and development. In keeping with this agenda, the state passed long-awaited legislation providing the framework for black and indigenous land titling and the more effective implementation of regional autonomy. While multicultural legislation incorporated Costeño demands into the national policy agenda, the state also worked to rearticulate their demands as *actually beneficial* to neoliberal development. For instance, the new land demarcation law was part of a nation-wide program funded by the World Bank to regulate and privatize land tenure, which is a cornerstone of the Bank's economic policy for the developing world. The resolution of land conflict on the Coast was to pave the way for international investment in the region. At the same time, regional autonomy, once so threatening to the post-revolutionary state, was recast as administrative decentralization—a neoliberal governance policy liberally funded by the Inter- American Development Bank.

The 2003 Bluefields Centenary celebration serves as a prime example of this double neoliberal multicultural agenda. A nationally televised event, the Bolaños' government organized a celebration that showcased Costeño history and cultural diversity as an integral part of national heritage and identity, even as it marketed the region to the global investment community. Heads of state and delegations of international investors attended the event, which was held in the Bluefields stadium. In an speech unprecedented for its inclusive rhetoric, the president of the national legislature gave a detailed account of Creole history that lauded the community for its contributions to the nation, even noting Creole participation in Marcus Garvey's Universal Negro Improvement Association in the early twentieth century and later the Rastafarian movement as evidence of their "*liberal cultural and intellectual tradition and great religious tolerance.*"[3] Once understood to be indications of their counter-nationalism, Creoles' participation in African Diasporic politics was now lauded by a top representative of the nation. He further recognized Costeños' rights to maintain their distinctive identity and culture without suffering state discrimination: "*To grow without losing identity is the challenge of the nation. This is a fundamental contribution of Costeños to the new nation that we are promoting, an integrated nation without legal discrimination with a face to the future, hand in hand, shoulder to shoulder.*"[4]

Despite its conciliatory tone, many prominent figures from Creole civil society boycotted the Centenary and instead organized their own alternative celebration, emphasizing Creole history, diasporic culture, and black pride —an act of protest which received considerable criticism from the mestizo community in Bluefields as divisive and exclusionary. Not only did most Creoles contest the idea that the day was indeed the one hundredth anniversary of their city, which had been a thriving urban center long before state annexation, but they felt they had been denied a space to help organize and actively participate in the celebration of their own history and culture. Although the state had included officials from the municipal and regional governments in the program, the organization of the event was a highly centralized affair tightly controlled by the Bolaños administration. A common critique of the event from the Creole community was that it looked more like "*Managua government's birthday*" than Bluefield's birthday.[5] The reluctance to relinquish control over the event, however, did not just betray a mestizo state jealously guarding its own power, but cut straight to the heart of the neoliberal project.

While it was cast as a celebration of national diversity, the state had also organized the Centenary to showcase the Coast to international investors who were in fact the featured guests of the event. This effort involved representing the region as an attractive emerging market, free of political dissent, social unrest, and crime; in other words, a sound investment opportunity. A central component of the event involved promoting the Coast as an international tourism sector. The state recognized that the Coast's appeal as a vacation destination lies in its physical beauty and Afro-Caribbean culture. As a result, a carnival-like exposition occupied the second half of the Centenary event, featuring lightly clad Creole youth dancing to Afro-Caribbean rhythms. While exotified blackness became a showpiece of the marketing campaign, Creoles themselves were not included as stakeholders in the development of their region.

In a similar vein, the Centenary marketing campaign involved cleansing the Bluefields cityscape of its usual signs of poverty and state neglect. In the weeks preceding the event, the state funded a citywide beautification project, which involved giving the decrepit town hall a fresh coat of paint, repairing the potholed thoroughfares, and collecting the festering garbage that usually lines the streets. The day of the event, the president's speech to Bluefields read like a laundry list of infrastructure development catering to the long awaited Central American Free Trade Agreement. As he announced the state's plans for the modernization of the Bluefields airport and a fiber optic network linking the coast to the rest of the world, it was unclear for whom these improvements were meant.[6]

With a multicultural agenda tailored to the needs of international capital, the Centenary celebration points to a reconfiguration of state racism towards black Costeños. While inclusive rhetoric masked Creole's exclusion from active participation, the celebration also took on more coercive manifestations of state racism. Just days before the event, Bluefields underwent a spontaneous militarization as elite squads of Nicaraguan Special Forces descended on the city. There to provide security for the national and international delegations, military forces set up watch throughout the central business district and in several Creole neighborhoods. For Creoles, the military presence was a grave racial insult that served as a painful reminder of annexation more than a hundred years before. A Creole editorialist later wrote an article that mirrored the sentiment of the community asking, "*Why visit a city of savages if they were afraid that some unfortunate act might befall the president?*"[7] Creoles in their critique had hit on an increasingly powerful mode of anti-black racism in Nicaragua. Even as their political demands are incorporated into the hegemonic project, transnational modes of racialization linking blackness, criminality, and the drug trade have begun to condition Creole-State relations.

In the 1990s, Central America became an important route for the trans-shipment of cocaine from South America to the US market. Today, trafficking networks span the region, moving the drug northward and in the process creating a secondary Central American market for cocaine and crack.[8] Today drug trafficking and consumption are prevalent throughout both Pacific and Atlantic Nicaragua. Nevertheless, Costeño communities have become the focus of national anxieties about drug related violence and the growth of organized crime. Images in the Nicaraguan press depicting crack consumption by Creoles are strikingly reminiscent of US media representations of African American men during the height of the so-called "crack epidemic" in the 1980s.

Black Costeños traveling from Bluefields to Managua complain that they are singled out for baggage searches by interdiction officers and racial profiling has become a topic of debate in the editorial pages of the national press. The week preceding the Centenary, military forces collaborated with national police and drug enforcement operatives to search private residences in Bluefields with drug sniffing dogs. The same week a sports utility vehicle labeled DEA was conspicuously parked in front of the local police station sending a silent warning that the state was on alert for any signs of criminal activity.

This next image entitled "Map of Nicaragua according to the political class" (from the same center-right newspaper as the first cartoon) shows how nationalist preoccupations with Costeño separatism are beginning to morph into a new concern that the state has lost control of the region to organized crime.

Labeled the "Black's Zone" the region is represented as a separate Atlantic Coast landmass. A protruding signpost reads, "Region ceded to narco-trafficking." Again, indigenous Costeños from the northern region are absent; while coconuts and cocaine are listed as the most important produce from the historically Creole south coast. The words

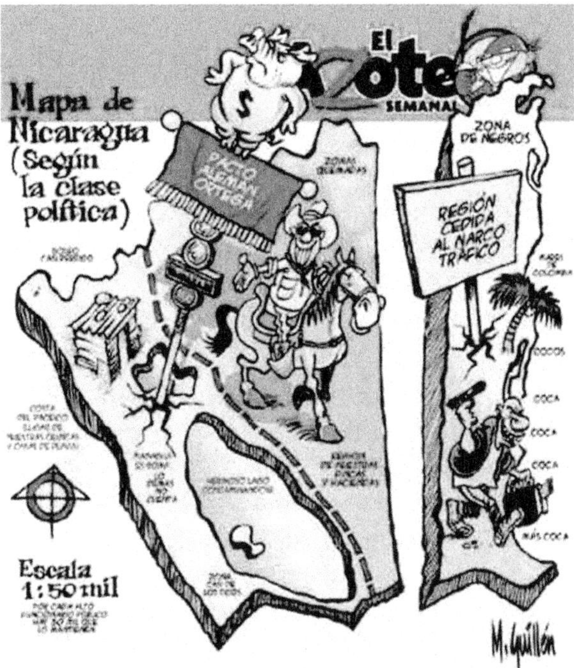

FIGURE 2. Political Map[10]
Courtesy Manuel Guillén, *La Prensa*.

"cocos" and "coca" lining the southern shore allude to a derogative mestizo term for Creoles—"come coco" or "cocoanut eater"—and suggest that Creoles have also developed a taste for cocaine. The figure of the white or mestizo drug-trafficker is not Nicaraguan, but a representative of a Colombian cocaine mafia who has found safe haven in the south coast Creole community.

To conclude, it seems that even as the state works to incorporate Creole political demands into the national agenda, it has adopted transnational modes of anti-black racism that index in new ways preexisting national panics about the place of blackness and Costeño autonomy in the Nicaraguan nation. In an era of multicultural reform, state racism is morphing into what scholars of race such as Howard Winant and Patricia Hill Collins have described as a new racial hegemony that is in some ways less recognizable than previous forms of racial domination, but equally pervasive.[11] No longer explicitly denied citizenship on the basis of their racial and cultural difference, emergent racial hegemonies in Nicaragua work to make black Costeños *implicitly* unworthy of full citizenship due to their assumed criminality, which (in its own way) has come to represent a new counter-national threat to state power and social order.

Like pre-existing myths of racial democracy and mestizo nationalism, policy agendas that seem to promote multicultural inclusion have also allowed for the denial of persisting modes of racial and material inequality.[12] In this context, Creole social movements that draw on black diasporic identity and politics in order to challenge the ongoing

FIGURE 3. Bluefields Sign[14]

manifestations of anti-black racism on the Coast are often critiqued as divisive and counterproductive to the new broadly inclusive multicultural agenda, which is now at least nominally endorsed by the state.[13] This denial is expressed in this roadside billboard erected in Bluefields in 2004.

The sign reads, "Bluefields Free of Racism," as if more than a century of entrenched state racism on the Coast has suddenly been wiped clean. Almost uncanny, the sign seems to convey a masked racial state, which embodies the new hegemonic move. Confidently, it declares racism to be a thing of the past. Yet it also issues a warning that racism as well as subaltern politics that confront racism have no place in the new Nicaragua, even as it signals their persisting power to structure the political terrain.

Notes

1. Jean Comaroff and John L. Comaroff, "Millennial Capitalism: First Thoughts on a Second Coming," in *Millennial Capitalism and the Culture of Neoliberalism,* eds. Jean Comaroff and John L. Comaroff (Durham: Duke University Press, 2001), pp. 8. Also see, Howard Winant, *The World is a Ghetto: Race and Democracy since World War II* (New York: Basic Books, 2001), pp. 305–308; Patricia Hill Collins, *Black Sexual Politics: African Americans, Gender, and the New Racism* (New York: Routledge, 2004), pp. 32–34.
2. La Prensa, Sunday, July 21, 2002.
3. Jaime José Cuadra Somarriba (Diputado-Presidente de la Asamblea Nacional), Opening Speech, Bluefields Centenary, October 11, 2003.
4. Ibid.
5. Rayfield Hodgson (Concejal-Presidente del Consejo Regional Autónomo de Atlántico Sur), Creole Radio Show "Morning Explosion," Radio Rhythm, Bluefields, Nicaragua, October 6, 2003.

6. Enrique Bolaños Geyer (Presidente de Nicaragua) Bluefields Centenary Speech, October 11, 2003.
7. Steve Hooker, Editorial, Bluefieldspulse.com, November 10, 2003.
8. See Rensselaer Lee, "Perversely Harmful Effects of Counter-Narcotics Policy in the Andes," in *The Political Economy of the Drug Industry: Latin America and the International System,* ed. Menno Vellinga (Gainesville: University Press of Florida, 2004), 187–210.
9. Image from a front-page article entitled, "Narcos Carcomen la Policía," La Prensa, May 5, 2003. The image caption reads: "This crack consumer, from the Beholden neighborhood in Bluefields, does anything he can to get drugs everyday." Beholden is one of the largest Creole neighborhoods in Bluefields and is often referred to as the "Ghetto" by both mestizo and Creole Bluefieldeños.
10. From a weekly political satire supplement entitled "El Azote," La Prensa, May 9, 2004.
11. Howard Winant (2001) The World is a Ghetto: Race and Democracy Since World War II, pp. 305–308; Patricia Hill Collins, *Black Sexual Politics: African Americans, Gender, and the New Racism* (New York: Routledge, 2004), pp. 32–34.
12. For discussions of the denial of racism in the face of persisting racial inequality see, Ariel E. Dulitzky, "A Region in Denial: Racial Discrimination and Racism in Latin America," in *Neither Enemies Nor Friends: Latinos, Blacks, Afro-Latins,* eds. Anani Dzidzienyo and Suzanne Oboler (New York: Palgrave Macmillan, 2005); João H. Costa Vargas, "The Hyperconsciousness of Race and its Negation: The Dialectic of White Supremacy in Brazil," *Identities: Global Studies in Culture and Power,* 11(4):443–470, Oct.–Dec. 2004.
13. See for instance, Juliet Hooker, "Indigenous Inclusion/Black Exclusion: Race, Ethnicity and Multicultural Citizenship in Latin America," *Journal of Latin American Studies,* 37(2):1–26; Charles R. Hale, "Rethinking Indigenous Politics in the Era of the 'Indio Permitido'" *NACLA Report on the Americas,* 38(2):16–37, Sept.–Oct. 2004.
14. Jennifer Goett, 2004.

Central American's public spaces, urban development, and the impact of globalization are examined within the urban projects in San Miguel, El Salvador and Quezaltenango, Guatemala. The urban growth is due to neoliberal policies, security issues and symbolic social status. These intermediate cities are also the recipients of migrant remittances and are populated by a small emergent middle class that dreams about living in spaces that mirror the comforts of the U.S. cities where their inhabitants have migrated. Despite their appearance as livable urban spaces, a disorderly spatial condition that threatens water supplies, skewed housing markets, social exclusion and other urban maladies has been created.

Watching the City Grow: Remittances and Sprawl in Intermediate Central American Cities

CHRISTIEN KLAUFUS

Christien Klaufus is Assistant Professor of Human Geography at CEDLA. She is trained as an architect and holds a PhD in Cultural Anthropology. Her current research projects address urbanization processes, housing and the sociocultural meanings of space, place and architecture in the Andean region and Central America. She has conducted ethnographic research in Ecuador, Guatemala, El Salvador and the Netherlands.

ABSTRACT The largest share of Latin American population lives in cities with less than half a million inhabitants. Since the publication of the Brundtland Report in the 1980s, small and intermediate cities have been regarded as places that hold out a promise for sustainable urban development. This paper explores current urbanization trends in intermediate cities in Central America. It describes the construction boom of gated communities for the middle class, in majority people with access to migrant remittances. It is argued that sustainable urbanization is challenged by the privatization of urban planning. The lack of strong governmental coordination of the housing market along with urban growth puts pressure on natural resources and on the livability of cities that used to be characterized by their human scale and rich natural environment. It is suggested that the market of existing housing should be made more attractive in order to control urban growth and prevent an oversupply of new expensive middle-class homes in the periphery, paralleled by a large number of abandoned existing houses in the urban core.

KEY WORDS housing market/intermediate cities/migration/remittances/sustainable urbanization/urban planning

Introduction

In the summer of 2008, the head of the urban planning department in Quetzaltenango, Guatemala, showed me how the urban territory was expanding. He brought me a chair, put it in front of a computer screen, clicked on Google Earth and demonstrated where recent projects had been built. Despite the relatively outdated satellite images, Google Earth was one of the few instruments available that allowed him to keep up with the growth of the city. A similar situation occurred two weeks later in San Miguel, El Salvador, where the responsible architect equally referred me to Google Earth for information he could not otherwise supply. In both cities, urban planners were proverbial bystanders in a play dominated by real estate developers. What they observed on their computer screens worried them. Urban areas were expanding in an uncontrolled fashion, with high burdens on ecological resources and existing housing markets. They lacked the means and political support to control the situation; they could only watch their cities grow.

In 1987, the Brundtland Commission asked in the report *Our Common Future* for explicit strategies to steer urbanization away from the largest cities towards smaller urban centres.(1) Although Latin America is known for its mega-cities, almost 40 per cent of the continent's population lives in cities with less than half a million inhabitants.(2) The influence of urban scale on local governance and urban development has been questioned in the literature. Yet public administration and social and environmental sustainability are believed to be more difficult to achieve in very large cities.(3) International organizations therefore suggest that smaller urban areas hold out a promise for sustainable urban growth: "*...due to their scale, [intermediate cities] constitute more balanced and sustainable systems, which have more balanced relationships with their surrounding territories.*"(4) Yet regardless of their size, many small and intermediate cities face problems with affordable housing supply, provision of basic services and poverty – problems that influence livability and sustainable urbanization, and CEPAL asserts that "*...their intermediate size does not, in and of itself, guarantee them a bright future.*"(5)

This paper addresses urban sprawl in two intermediate cities in Central America, namely Quetzaltenango in Guatemala and San Miguel in El Salvador. It explores current urbanization trends in relation to transnational migration, remittances and related manifestations of globalization. These two cities were selected as case studies based on their relatively high numbers of remittance-receiving households and their secondary positions in the national urban hierarchies. Quetzaltenango is Guatemala's second largest city, and almost 40 per cent of the population in the department where Quetzaltenango is situated receives remittances. San Miguel is El Salvador's third city, and the department of which San Miguel is part is the second largest receiver of remittances nationally, with 34 per cent of households receiving money from abroad.(6) As will be described in more detail below, sustainable urbanization in intermediate Central American cities is challenged by a combination of weak municipal planning institutions and a construction boom triggered by globalization. In recent years, many self-sufficient gated communities for a middleclass clientele have been built on the urban fringes, resulting in a rapid expansion – almost a doubling – of the urban territory. New projects continue to be built, even though the worldwide financial crisis results in stagnating sales.[7] Meanwhile, part of the existing housing stock remains unused and is falling into decline. Urban planners are only passively involved in the creation of new residential areas. Both cities lack detailed plans for urban expansion, if only because urban boundaries have never been established. The municipalities do exert control over construction permits, but detailed zoning regulations are either non-existent or are ignored. As perceived by local planners, their departments are relatively powerless compared to the private sector and central government.

This paper is organized in two parts. First, we address the nature of the urbanization processes to determine the size and pace of newly developed housing projects, and urban sprawl is described within a context of neo-liberal policies and the impact of globalization (transnational migration, remittances economy). Then, the impact of sprawl on the idea of intermediate cities as livable and sustainable systems is analyzed. Sustainable urbanization is understood as a process that comprises a social and an environmental component. The environmental component will be illustrated by describing deforestation and the use of groundwater sources for the private supply of drinking water. Social sustainability will be described by focusing on spatial segregation and skewed local housing markets. A concluding section will suggest a more integrated view of local housing markets.

Data are based on one month's fieldwork conducted in July 2008. In Quetzaltenango and Ciudad de Guatemala, six architects and three urban planners were interviewed. In San Miguel and San Salvador, nine architects/urban planners, a notary and a housing expert were interviewed. Accompanied by local architects, visits were made to new gated communities with model homes as well as to other projects constructed over the last five years. Because many of these projects were still under construction, no inhabitants were interviewed. Information about the clients is based upon conversations with lot buyers and observations in model homes, as well as information provided by the construction companies. In addition, policy documents and real estate brochures were analyzed and the websites of relevant institutions were checked regularly for updates on figures and events.

(Un)Livable Cities

Undisputed indicators of what makes a city a pleasant place to live do not exist. According to several North American authors in urban studies, intermediate Latin American cities still contrast in a positive way with American "non-place urban realms" thanks to their vibrant public life. Heterogeneous communities and accessible multi-functional public spaces are mentioned as positive qualities. Herzog mentions humanlyscaled historic centres with pedestrian areas in cities such as Querétaro, Mexico, as outstanding examples of livable places.[8] Vassoler explains the success of Curitiba by pointing out the multiple functions of the city's parks and green areas.[9] Conversely, Scarpaci argues that homogenization of the built environment in historical inner cities in Latin America reduces their vibrancy.[10] Several less optimistic studies describe Latin American cities as transforming into fragmented places, where urban and suburban ways of life are juxtaposed. Planned social housing, unplanned squatter settlements and orderly gated condominiums are increasingly situated side by side; different social groups live in each other's vicinity, yet are socially separated.[11] The nature and impact of globalization, the homogenization of the built environment, and spatial segregation have been the subject of extensive debate.[12]

Three sets of motives are mentioned in the literature to explain the fragmentation of urban space. The first set refers to an historical transformation of the socioeconomic landscape of Latin American cities since the "lost decade" of the 1980s. The introduction of neo-liberal economic models and the dominant role of the private sector in urban spatial developments resulted in a privatization of space, privileging carbased mobility and causing a homogenization of social environments. Borsdorf et al.[13] describe the general features of urban fragmentation in Chile, where middle and upper classes occupy the privatized areas in gentrifying inner-city areas and suburban locations. In their respective studies, Caldeira and Rodgers describe how selectively improved highways have contributed to the development of enclaves and segregated spatial networks in Brazil and Nicaragua.[14]

The second set of motives refers to an increase in crime levels and weak law enforcement. In many Latin American countries, crime levels have risen since the end of the civil wars of the 1970s and 1980s, especially in Guatemala and El Salvador.[15] Crime levels within cities rose and many people left the country. As a flipside of the globalization coin, informal networks for illicit trafficking across national borders generated new modes of existence for otherwise marginalized groups, and this has increased the general feeling of insecurity. Guatemala and El Salvador became transit nations for trafficking people, goods and money.

The third set of motives relates to social status symbols. Fashioned after North American examples, the construction of gated communities became an increasingly popular housing solution from the 1990s onwards. Such communities are designed as lifestyle concepts and places of leisure.[16] Living in such communities enhances a resident's social status. Marketing strategies are based on the status-generating capacity of residential qualities such as "privacy", "nature" and "pleasure". In Central America, all three have contributed to a boom in fenced-off neighbourhoods in suburban areas, not only in the capital cities but also, increasingly, in intermediary cities, where the quality of urban life is believed to be higher than in the crime-ridden capital cities. The demand for safe and comfortable housing by a middle class with access to foreign currency has spurred the construction of new real estate projects.

Globalization in Intermediate Central American Cities

With 106,000 and 158,000 residents respectively, Quetzaltenango and San Miguel are "typical" intermediate cities,[17] occupying secondary positions in the national urban hierarchies. Both are nodes in larger urban and transnational networks and both are the economic heart of a surrounding rural region, providing specialized commercial, educational and health services to the larger region. Both have a bustling atmosphere during the day but are deserted and insecure at night. In both cities, people tend to identify with their city and many are proud to live there.

Each city is shaped by a particular urban history. Quetzaltenango is situated in the western highlands of Guatemala, 200 kilometres from the capital city of Guatemala, and is part of the larger municipality, also named Quetzaltenango, that has a large indigenous population. Formal city limits have never been established. Nobody knows what territory belongs to the city and how many people live within the urban boundary. Local statistics mention 106,528 inhabitants, whereas national statistics count 120,496 urban residents.(18) The city has 25,625 housing units, of which more than 4,000 are unoccupied, in part due to out-migration.(19) Based on national census data, the annual growth rate of the urban population between 1994 and 2002 was 3.3 per cent.(20) The growth of the urban area urged Quetzaltenango and several adjacent municipalities to prepare the creation of a new administrative metropolitan area, Metrópoli de los Altos, which will become Guatemala's second metropolis after Ciudad de Guatemala.(21) In the former administrative period, Quetzaltenango had an indigenous mayor. Although ethnic–political priorities have varied in different administrative periods, they all had one thing in common: an overall lack of attention to urban planning.

San Miguel is situated in the eastern lowlands of El Salvador, 132 kilometres from San Salvador. Due to the civil war and the predominance of guerrilla forces in the region east of the River Lempa that bisects the country, San Miguel has been cut off from the capital city for a long time. San Miguel is part of a large municipality with the same name. The whole municipality has 218,410 inhabitants and 71,054 housing units, of which more than one-fifth are left empty. Unoccupied houses are a consequence of transnational migration and absentee owners.(22) As in Quetzaltenango, no official urban boundaries have been established, which makes urban population figures ambiguous. According to the 2007 census, the city had 158,136 residents. Estimates for the annual urban growth rate vary from 1.5 per cent to 2.9 per cent.(23)

Both cities have seen part of their population leave as a consequence of the civil wars in Guatemala and El Salvador. Large proportions of the population migrated to the US and, to a lesser extent, to Europe, especially since the 1990s. Transnational migration from the Quetzaltenango region started during the civil war of the 1980s. After the peace accords were signed in 1996, the economy stagnated and new forms of violence abated. Due to economic and social insecurity, the outflow of people increased substantially at the end of the twentieth century and remittances rose to unprecedented levels.(24) The amount of remittances to Guatemala tripled between 2001 and 2004, reaching almost US$ 2.7 billion in official flows. Remittances make up 10 per cent of GDP, and the incoming amount is 21 times greater than foreign direct investments, indicating the profound influence of remittances on the national economy.(25)

The department where Quetzaltenango is located has the fourth largest share of migrant families and incoming remittances in Guatemala. More than 100,000 of the department's urban population and more than 120,000 of the department's rural population receive remittances, part of which has been destined for the development of small artisanal (often textile) businesses in nearby villages.[26] Also, new houses have been constructed, and of late luxury gated communities have been built. Private construction companies target the remittance-receiving population in Quetzaltenango, in the capital city and abroad. With the remittances, people can buy a house for cash or they can make a down-payment on a mortgage that is usually offered as part of a package deal by the private developer. The nature of real estate developments – low-density, middleclass housing with communal facilities – has accelerated urban sprawl. According to the media, the new and opulent houses contribute to a visual degradation of the landscape.[27]

As San Miguel is the centre of an agricultural region, many peasants fled to the city during the civil war of the 1980s. During that decade the city expanded rapidly. Others opted to leave the country and emigration continued after the peace accords were signed in 1992. As soon as the political situation had stabilized at the end of the twentieth century, the inflow remittances to San Miguel rose substantially. Nationally, El Salvador received US$ 2.5 billion in 2004, which represented 16 per cent of GDP and was six times more than foreign direct investments.[28] Transnational migrants started to invest in real estate, which in turn attracted developers, banks and retail commerce. San Miguel revived after years of stagnation, and all sorts of small-scale commercial activities developed. However, as the city does not have a productive sector, the urban economy is sometimes called a "fictitious economy".[29] Nowadays, an estimated 35 per cent of the population within the larger department of San Miguel receives remittances. About 45 per cent of them, approximately 70,000 people, live in the municipality of San Miguel.[30] As in Quetzaltenango, people associate urban transformations primarily with the remittance economy.[31]

Over the last decade, remittances have been one of the engines of local consumption. In order to make remittances more productive, international organizations such as the IDB and the World Bank have promoted the use of remittances as investments in transnational mortgages. National housing institutes and commercial chambers in Central America have adopted the IDB programme, trying to persuade migrants to use remittances for savings and credits to finance the production of new homes. The programme is designed to stimulate financial markets and the construction sector. It also aims to empower the target group through financial literacy. Another positive aspect mentioned is that people get "more house" for their money.[32] These programmes prioritize the construction of new houses over the re-use of existing housing.

Besides transnational money flows, international development plans such as the Plan Puebla Panamá (PPP) are an impetus for urban change. Under the banner of the PPP, the harbour at Puerto de Cutuco, close to San Miguel, and an international road system are being developed. San Miguel is the principal city in the harbour's surrounding area and is well connected to the Pan-American Highway, so real estate developers anticipate a growing number of residents and visitors. A few hundred kilometres to the west, Quetzaltenango is equally close to the Pan-American Highway. Because of its tranquil atmosphere and relatively low levels of crime, combined with high standards of education and health services, real estate developers expect to attract buyers from the polluted and insecure capital city. Apart from being a gateway to provincial cities, the Pan-American Highway has also become a lifeline for illegal flows of people and products. Money generated by transborder smuggling, drug trafficking and money-laundering activities is said to contribute to the real estate business in both cities.[33] To summarize, the inflow of remittances combined with improvements in the international road system and a new harbour have stimulated urban transformation in Quetzaltenango and San Miguel over the last years.

Enclaves for a Transnational Middle Class

After the end of the civil wars in El Salvador and Guatemala, housing shortages could not be addressed by the weakened state institutions. Instead, the private sector took responsibility for a large part of social housing production, either in the form of lotizaciones (lots in serviced areas) or as urbanizaciones (turnkey houses).[34] Gradually, as private sector influence increased, profit making overruled local housing needs on their agendas. At the end of the twentieth century, intermediate urban centres were identified as apt locations for the development of new real estate projects. As a result, Quetzaltenango and San Miguel were confronted with an oversupply of relatively expensive lots and middleclass houses in gated communities. As an indication of this trend, the Construction Chamber in El Salvador noticed a decline of 35 per cent in social housing in 2005, attributed to larger investments in *proyectos de lujo* (luxury housing projects).[35]

One of the projects currently under construction on a hill in Quetzaltenango is La Nueva Ciudad de Los Altos. The name refers to the city's nickname, Ciudad de los Altos. The name New Quetzaltenango reflects the ambition of the project, namely to build a completely new city adjacent to the existing one. The plan consists of two phases. Phase one includes 436 lots with basic services in two fenced-off communities; commercial, educational, sports and medical facilities; and a new campus for a private university. During phase two, a residential area of similar size will be created, situated around a "city centre". Drinking water will be provided by a private well and an internal water supply system not connected to the public drinking water network. Outside the main entrance, two smaller housing projects with turnkey houses have already been built by another developer. Slowly, the hill that used to be a forest is turning into an urban extension of approximately 4.5 hectares, where more than 10,000 people are expected to live by 2025. By that time, the zone will occupy an area as large as the current historical centre of Quetzaltenango.[36]

La Nueva Ciudad de Los Altos is not the only large project in Quetzaltenango. Several others have been designed or are under construction, one of them a neo-colonial gated community close to the village of Cantel, called Xela Gardens (Xela is the indigenous name for Quetzaltenango). The project comprises approximately 1,200 lots. It is designed as a "fairytale community", with cobblestone streets, colonial-style buildings and nicely designed picnic areas. According to one of the lot buyers, a local architect, the clientele consists of remittance-receiving families from Quetzaltenango, migrants in the US and people making money from drug trafficking.[37] Whereas the cheapest social housing units in Guatemala cost approximately US$ 2,700,[38] the cheapest lots offered in the new urbanizations in Quetzaltenango cost more than US$ 8,000. In 2008, real estate prices in Quetzaltenango had risen to levels even higher than those in the capital city of Guatemala.[39] Still, these projects are expected to generate in-migration from the capital city and hence, population growth.

In San Miguel, similar forms of urban sprawl are taking place. New gated communities in neo-colonial style, often with more than 1,000 lots or houses, have been built on the road to San Salvador. Even in a provincial town like San Miguel, real estate developers offer condominiums with a "cosmopolitan" atmosphere and English or colonial Spanish names such as RiverSide Gardens and Hacienda San Andrés. The communities offer high levels of comfort and maximum privacy and security in fenced-off areas. RiverSide (1,500 lots and houses) on the northern side of town has a fitness school, a swimming pool with a jacuzzi, several sports fields and a picnic place. The model homes in Hacienda San Andrés (2,500 houses) on the western side of town offer an American atmosphere with cinnamonperfumed bedrooms and bathrooms decorated with flower-patterned cloth curtains. Facilities for installing a dishwasher and an ice cube maker are incorporated in the design. Inside the gates everything is designed to enable an American lifestyle. Outside the gates another world starts. On the narrow, dark and bumpy road that connects RiverSide to the city centre, extortion and robbery by criminal gangs occurs on a regular basis. The image of RiverSide as an area of wealth and luxury has created a risk factor that limits the inhabitants' freedom to travel at night. This situation differs from that in Managua where, for example, roads have been improved and are well lit in order to create what Rodgers calls "fortified networks".[40] Such networks have not yet been constructed in San Miguel.

The prices for lots and houses in San Miguel are higher than for similar units in Quetzaltenango. Prices for lots vary between US$ 20,000 and US$ 50,000, and for houses between US$ 60,000 and US$ 250,000. One explanation for these high prices is that unlike the Guatemalan companies, the Salvadoran developers try to sell directly to transnational migrants in the US, where the migrant population has become accustomed to these types of settlements and price levels. Their main clients are migrants in the US. Since 2006, the Chamber of Commerce for the Construction Sector in El Salvador, Casalco, has organized four trade fairs in different places in the US; the fourth took place in October 2008 in Los Angeles. The results of the first three fairs were promising, with sales increasing from US$ 2.6 million at the first fair to US$ 5.4 million at the third one. The fourth fair was seen as a trial because of the sub-prime crisis. USbased Salvadoran migrants have been affected by the economic recession and consequently, developers in El Salvador are having difficulties selling their properties. Some offer a refund on down-payments during the first year; others simply reduce their prices. The fifth fair, that was to have taken place in October 2009 in Washington, was cancelled.

Meanwhile, new houses continue to be built in San Miguel. The discrepancy between supply and demand on a local level is not just an economic problem. It is also a social one. Illustrative of the mismatch between housing supply and demand is the gap between the upper limit of US$ 15,000 for social housing in El Salvador and the price of new homes in San Miguel, the majority of which cost more than US$ 40,000.[41] This reflects a national trend: 70 per cent of the Salvadoran population can only afford houses under US$ 10,000.[42]

Spatial Disorder

For decades, unsustainable urban growth has been associated with the urban poor – with informal housing on inadequate land, lacking running water and sewerage. The primary challenge for Latin American planning authorities was to formalize and upgrade informal settlements. In Central American cities, where the private sector obtained a leading role in housing and urban development, commercially developed communities became a principle force of urban growth. Paradoxically, nowadays the new housing projects challenge exactly those qualities that are used to sell the properties: access to spacious green areas and proximity to a lively inner city. While they privatize urban space and denude green areas for the creation of self-sufficient communities, the advantages of the urban size and the human scale are reduced by low-density sprawl that generates car-based mobility.

Whereas real estate developers are keen to present gated communities as high quality self-sustaining areas, local professionals and authorities who made inventories of the projects associated these with spatial disorder. Municipal and independent professionals expressed their concerns about the scale of the housing projects. In December 2007, the head of the municipal land register in Quetzaltenango commented in a newspaper that the city was growing "in a disorderly way" and that the population had increased to almost one million inhabitants. He pleaded for more government control. The picture accompanying the article suggested that the problem lay in an increase in informal housing on the fringes, but quotes made it clear that the real threat to sustainable urban growth was from formal housing projects.[43] According to various professionals in both cities, local governments are incapable of directing large real estate developments because the private sector has become too powerful economically. In presenting new plans to the local authorities, real estate developers anticipate the inflow of rich consumers and the creation of local employment in the construction sector, emphasizing that the construction of new housing would benefit the city. In most cases, however, real estate developers employ specialized construction workers trained in specific design details, such as the neo-colonial woodcarvings in Xela Gardens. The companies bring in their own teams of specialists instead of training local workers on the spot, thus limiting local employment opportunities generated by the new housing projects.

Two damaging effects of a lack of urban planning were specifically mentioned in interviews: skewed housing markets and house price inflation, and the exhaustion of the hydro-geological system. In both cities, the need for cheap urban housing solutions persists. The new residential areas are not being built for local households in need of housing but for households from other cities or from abroad. Besides the increase in new housing, a part of the existing housing stock – 16 per cent in Quetzaltenango and more than 20 per cent in San Miguel – remains unused. Thus, the territory of provincial cities with vibrant and humanly-scaled city centres expands more rapidly than demographic growth requires. This contributes to spatial and aesthetic fragmentation and social segregation.

The second consequence is the exhaustion of groundwater and the destruction of natural areas. In order to solve the lack of capacity of local urban drinking water systems, project developers construct private water wells. They sell their projects as being auto-sostenible (i.e. self-sustaining). Yet in the long run and on a larger scale, the extraction of water is not environmentally sustainable. In both cities, private water supply systems have already reduced groundwater levels. Besides water extraction, deforestation also causes problems. In Quetzaltenango, deforestation of several hectares on the hill on which La Nueva Ciudad de los Altos is being constructed has caused flooding problems in the lower urban areas.(44) In San Miguel, most new communities have been constructed on the western side of town, in a volcanic area where groundwater levels are extremely vulnerable. In 1998, an international team of experts financed by the IDB wrote a masterplan called the Plamadur, with scenarios for urban growth until 2015. As part of the Plamadur, a strategic plan stressed the urgent need to consolidate the existing urban area and protect the freshwater resources.(45) In 2008, it became clear that these water resources had not been protected but, rather, had been extensively used.(46)

Ironically, this situation was triggered by the urban planning regulations themselves. Municipal control in Quetzaltenango was based on an outdated and never fully implemented urban development plan issued in 1983, and a housing law issued in 2001. There was no control regarding compliance with this law. Professionals within and outside the municipal administration stressed that there was a lack of political interest and that corruption prevented the implementation of the plans.(47) Generally, approval of a housing plan depends on the availability of sufficient basic services. Although the applicant has to deliver an environmental impact study approved by the Ministry of Environment, in everyday policy practice in-depth studies about the long-term effects of deforestation and water extraction are not required. According to the urban planners, prestigious development plans were often approved at the highest political level, overruling the advice of lower-ranking professionals, even if the environmental impact studies showed negative effects.

In San Miguel, the Plamadur, which was published more than 10 years ago, concluded that: "*In practice, the municipality... did not and does not exercise planning or control of urban development.... Political willingness and resources to strengthen the municipal administration are lacking.*"(48) In 2008, urban planners in San Miguel stated that the situation had become worse: the Plamadur was outdated and they did not have any other framework to work with.(49) Local professionals in Quetzaltenango and San Miguel have similarly stated that it is formal housing projects rather than informal housing that has put pressure on the idea of sustainable urbanization. The need for urban control has increased over the years, but the institutional instruments have weakened. Urban planners tend to be overruled by local politicians and national policy makers, who stress economic advantages. The absence of effective monitoring tools forces them to map out new urbanization in hindsight, relying on Google Earth.

Generally, it can be concluded that intermediate cities that are seen as profitable locations for new housing projects for a middle-class clientele lack the local governance structures to plan and control the construction of new residential areas. The urban planners in charge lack the political support to implement zoning plans and enforce environmental regulations on powerful – often multinational – real estate developers. The case studies show that powerless planning departments, working with outdated plans, are unable to steer urban growth and create a balanced housing market. This increases social inequality in intermediate cities. Updated regulations should be implemented and enforced to deal with new housing demands and simultaneously keep these smaller cities socially and environmentally sustainable.

To reduce the charges on natural resources and redress the balance between local housing supply and demand, better use of the existing housing stock is also needed. One reason why this has not taken place is that it is generally difficult to get a loan to buy an existing house. Besides, in the current market, houses with thematic designs and that reflect suburban lifestyles are regarded as status symbols. The lack of a tradition that makes it acceptable, even desirable, to buy an existing home has shaped consumer preferences. To complicate matters, a large number of houses with absentee owners are not even available on the housing market, as transnational migrants keep houses in El Salvador as investments or as future retirement homes.[(50)] There are, however, some incipient initiatives. In El Salvador, two government institutions provide credit to low-income families for the acquisition of existing housing. One of them, the Fondo Social para la Vivienda (FSV) offers credit to people who want to buy a house that has been recovered from a defaulter. In San Miguel, these houses cost between US$ 8,000 and US$ 14,000. Yet 58 per cent of the nationwide FSV credits are destined for the acquisition or construction of a new house.[(51)]

Apart from these programmes for the urban poor, additional programmes should be developed that encourage the middle class (in the sector should also be stimulated to take an interest in revitalizing the existing housing stock. Urban development is still predominantly understood in terms of the economic growth of the real estate and construction sector, even if this sector is now confronted by stagnating sales. To activate the market in existing housing, a change of attitude needs to be stimulated by national and international programmes to encourage loans for purchasing existing homes, and marketing strategies need to be developed that envision neighbourhood life in the urban parts of intermediate cities as pleasant, safe, comfortable and affordable. In combination with accurate planning instruments, intermediate cities can steer towards more sustainable urbanization.

Conclusions

Intermediate Central American cities face rapid urbanization on the fringes. Whereas uncontrolled urban growth used to be associated with informal self-provision of houses, suburban disorder is now attributed to fully serviced residential projects for a new middle class, built on ecologically vulnerable land. Target groups are remittance-receiving families or other people with access to foreign currency, for example from illicit trafficking that is enhanced by improved international transport systems. Consumers with access to dollars and euros prefer comfortable middle-class houses in fenced-off neighbourhoods in quiet suburban areas with a secure water supply. These gated communities are spatially segregated from the rest of the city, sometimes even designed as parallel cities. The construction of private water supply systems causes a reduction in groundwater levels, while deforestation in higher areas where urbanization projects are developed causes flooding in lower urban areas.

Local governance structures in Central America lack political continuity, legal frameworks and the financial and administrative possibilities to steer or control these processes. This is illustrated in the independent remarks by urban planners in the two cities that the only way they can keep up with the speed of urbanization is by using Google Earth. Meanwhile, the private construction sector and international organizations adhere to policies that privilege the construction of new housing over the use of the existing housing stock. The one-sided focus on the construction of new real estate projects causes urban sprawl, threatens the natural environment, causes a deterioration in the quality of existing neighbourhoods, with high numbers of abandoned houses, and sustains the deficit of affordable dwellings. Besides, the monotonous enclaves jeopardize the idea of intermediate cities as socially mixed and livable urban areas.

Although smaller cities might not be as socially segregated as San Salvador or Ciudad de Guatemala, the pace and scale of new projects challenge the idea of sustainable urbanization. I have argued that urban planners in smaller cities need political support and updated instruments to control urban sprawl and the use of natural resources, and that national and international programmes should encourage revitalization of the existing housing stock to achieve a more balanced housing market.

Notes

1. WCED (1987), *Our Common Future,* Report of the World Commission on Environment and Development, Oxford University Press, accessed March 2009 at http://www.undocuments.net/ocf-09.htm#I, Chapter 9, Part II, Article 29.
2. Satterthwaite, D (2006), *Outside the Large Cities: the Demographic Importance of Small Urban Centres and Large Villages in Africa, Asia and Latin America*, Discussion Paper Series, Urban Change 3, IIED, London, page 3.
3. Gilbert, A (1996), "The mega-city in Latin America: an introduction", in A Gilbert (editor), *The Mega-city in Latin America*, The United Nations University Press, New York, Tokyo, Paris, pages 1–24.
4. Ayuntamiento de Lleida, UNESCO, UIA and Ministerio de Asuntos Exteriores (editors) (1999), *Ciudades Intermedias y Urbanización Mundial*, Municipalidad de Lleida, accessed 3 October 2008 at http://www.unesco.org/most/ciudades.pdf, page 44; also Bolay, J C and A Rabinovich (2003), "Intermediate cities in Latin America: risk and opportunities of coherent urban development", *Cities* Vol 21, pages 407–421.
5. CEPAL (2000), *From Rapid Urbanization to the Consolidation of Human Settlements in Latin America and the Caribbean: A Territorial Perspective*, CEPAL, Santiago, page 11.
6. INE (2008), *XI Censo Nacional de Población y VI de Habitación (Censo 2002)*, accessed 7 October 2008 at www.ine.gob.gt; also IOM (2005), "Survey on remittances and microenterprises", Working Notebooks on Migration 21, Guatemala City; and UNDP (2005), *Informe sobre Desarrollo Humano El Salvador 2005: Una Mirada al Nuevo Nosotros; El Impacto de las Migraciones*, UNDP, San Salvador.

7. *El Diario de Hoy* (2009), "Venta de viviendas cae en un 70% por la crisis", 11 February, accessed 16 September 2009 at www.elsalvador.com.
8. Herzog, L (2006), *Return to the Centre: Culture, Public Space and City Building in a Global Era*, University of Texas Press, Austin, 256 pages.
9. Vassoler, I (2007), *Urban Brazil: Visions, Afflictions and Governance Lessons*, Cambria Press, Amherst, 244 pages.
10. Scarpaci, J (2005), *Plazas and Barrios: Heritage Tourism and Globalization in the Latin American Centro Histórico*, University of Arizona Press, Tucson, 267 pages.
11. Griffin, E and L Ford (1980), "A model of Latin American city structure", *Geographical Review* 70, pages 397–422; also Ribeiro, L and L Lago (1995), "Restructuring in large Brazilian cities: the centre-periphery model", *International Journal of Urban and Regional Research* 19, pages 369–382; Ford, L (1996), "A new and improved model of Latin American city structure", *Geographical Review* Vol 86, No 3, pages 437–440; Barros, J (2004), "Urban growth in Latin American cities: exploring urban dynamics through agent-based simulation", PhD thesis, University of London; and Borsdorf, A, R Hidalgo and R Sánchez (2007), "A new model of urban development in Latin America: the gated communities and fenced cities in the metropolitan areas of Santiago de Chile and Valparaíso", *Cities* Vol 24, pages 365–378.
12. Caldeira, T (2000), *City of Walls: Crime, Segregation and Citizenship in São Paulo*, University of California Press, Berkeley, 487 pages; also Lima, J (2001), "Sociospatial segregation and urban form: Belém at the end of the 1990s", *Geoforum* Vol 32, pages 493–507; Coy, M and M Pöhler (2002), "Gated communities in Latin American megacities: case studies in Brazil and Argentina", *Environment and Planning B* Vol 29, pages 355–370; Aguilar, A and P Ward (2003), "Globalization, regional development and mega-city expansion in Latin America: analyzing Mexico City's periurban hinterland", *Cities* Vol 20, pages 3–21; Fortín-Magaña, G (2003), "Low-income housing in El Salvador", *ReVista Harvard Review of Latin America*, Winter; Rodgers, D (2004), "'Disembedding' the city: crime, insecurity and spatial organization in Managua, Nicaragua", *Environment and Urbanization* Vol 16, No 2, October, pages 113–123; and Baires, S (2006), "Los barrios cerrados en el AMSS: una nueva forma de segregación residencial en la era de la globalización," *Revista ILA* Vol 288, pages XII–XIII.
13. See reference 11, Borsdorf et al. (2007)
14. See reference 12, Caldeira (2000); also see reference 12, Rodgers (2004).
15. Moser, C and C McIlwaine (2001), *Violence in a Post-Conflict Context: Urban Poor Perceptions from Guatemala*, World Bank Publications, Washington DC, 163 pages; also Moser, C (editor) (2004), "Urban violence and insecurity: an introductory roadmap", *Environment and Urbanization* Vol 16, No 2, October, pages 3–16.
16. Low, S (2004), *Behind the Gates: Life, Security and the Pursuit of Happiness in Fortress America*, Routledge, New York, 288 pages; also Leichenko, R and W Solecki (2005), "Exporting the American dream: the globalization of suburban consumption landscapes", *Regional Studies* Vol 39, No 2, pages 241–253.
17. For a description of the characteristics of intermediate cities, see reference 4, Ayuntamiento de Lleida et al. (1999), pages 43–44; also Klaufus, C (2009), *Construir la Ciudad Andina: Planificación y Autoconstrucción en Riobamba y Cuenca*, Abya Yala/FLACSO, Quito, page 17.
18. UIEP–PROINFO (2002), *Información Estadística y Social del Municipio de Quetzaltenango, 2000–2002*, Unidad de Información, Investigación Estadística y Planificación–Proyecto de Información Sociodemográficay de Salud para el Desarrollo Local, Quetzaltenango; also see reference 6, INE (2008).

19. See reference 18, UIEP–PROINFO (2002).
20. www.citypopulation.de.
21. Mancomunidad de Municipios Metrópoli de los Altos (2007), *Plan Estratégico Territorial del Valle de Quetzaltenango*, Quetzaltenango, Guatemala.
22. Digestyc (2006), "Indicadores demográficos por departamento, 2006", accessed 7 October 2008 at www.digestyc.gob.sv; also Digestyc (2008), *VI Censo de Población y V de Vivienda 2007*, Ministerio de Economía, Dirección General de Estadística y Censos, San Salvador. The same source mentions a total municipal population of 282,367 in 2006. Discrepancies in the official data show the weaknesses of statistical procedures in El Salvador.
23. See reference 22; also see reference 20.
24. IOM (2004), "Survey on the impact of family remittances on Guatemalan homes", Working Notebooks on Migration 19, Guatemala City; also Acosta, P, P Fajnzylber and J H López (2008), "How important are remittances in Latin America?", in P Fajnzylber and J H López (editors), *Remittances and Development: Lessons from Latin America*, World Bank, Washington DC, page 27; and Suro, R (2005), "A survey of remittance senders and receivers", in D Terry and S Wilson (editors), *Beyond Small Change: Making Migrant Remittances Count*, Inter-American Development Bank, Washington DC, pages 35–36.
25. Agunias, D (2006), "Remittance trends in Central America", Migration Information Source, accessed 15 October 2009 at www.migrationinformation.org.
26. See reference 6, IOM (2005); also Orozco, M (2006), *Between Hardship and Hope: Remittances and the Local Economy in Latin America*, Inter-American Development Bank, Washington DC, pages 14–15.
27. *Prensa Libre* (2006), "Remesas cambian el rostro de Cantel", 6 February, accessible at www.prensalibre.com; also *El Periodico* (2006b), "El día que las remesas dejen de llegar en Salcajá", 5 September, accessible at www.elperiodico.com.gt; and *El Periodico* (2006a), "Mi casa es como las de Estados Unidos", 3 September, accessible at www.elperiodico.com.gt.
28. See reference 25.
29. Landolt, P, L Autler and S Baires (1999), "From *hermano lejano* to *hermano mayor*: the dialectics of Salvadoran transnationalism", *Ethnic and Racial Studies* Vol 22, No 2, page 295.
30. See reference 6, UNDP (2005).
31. *El Remesero* (2008), "Las remesas impulsan la economía de la zona oriental de El Salvador", 23 April, accessible at http://elremesero.com; also *El Diario de Hoy* (2006b), "Compatriotas usan remesas en vivienda", 20 September, accessible at www.elsalvador.com.
32. See, for example, Sociedad Hipotecaria Federal (SHF) (2005), "Programa de créditos hipotecarios a migrantes", accessed 13 March 2009 at http://nuevoportal.shf.gob.mx/prensa/Paginas/Presentaciones.aspx, page 18.
33. Interviews with architects, codes EC 15/07/08 and XO 24/07/08.
34. Stein, A and I Vance (2008), "The role of housing finance in addressing the needs of the urban poor: lessons from Central America", *Environment and Urbanization* Vol 20, No 1, April, pages 13–30.
35. *El Diario de Hoy* (2006a), "El crédito para la vivienda minima disminuyó en 35 per cent", 6 January, accessible at www.elsalvador.com.
36. Interview and personal communication with architect, code HG 18/07/08.
37. Interview and personal communication with architect, code EC 16/07/08.
38. The internationally sponsored programme of the Fondo Guatemalteco para la Vivienda (FOGUAVI) provides a subsidy of 16,500 quetzales (approximately US$ 2,050). Families

have to add the equivalent of 5,000 quetzales in cash or kind (approximately US$ 620). The total cost of a house should not exceed 80,000 quetzales (approximately US$ 10,000). See *Prensa Libre* (2007a), "Vivienda, un proyecto de 20 años", 2 December, accessible at www.prensalibre.com; also FOGUAVI (2004) Programa Fortalecimiento a la demanda de Vivienda Popular, accessed 16 March 2009 at: http://www.cepal.org/pobrezaurbana/docs/minurvi/Gua/Fortaleci%20Demanda%20Vivienda%20Po.pdf.

39. See reference 36.
40. See reference 12, Rodgers (2004).
41. www.fsv.gob.sv; also interviews with notary and architect, codes RA 29/07/08 and CV 04/08/08.
42. Sorto Rivas, F (2004), "La situación del déficit habitacional en El Salvador", Digestyc, San Salvador.
43. *Prensa Libre* (2007b), "Xelajú crece sin orden", 19 December, accessible at www.prensalibre.com; this is also mentioned in interviews with architects and planners, codes EC 10/07/08, RG 14/07/08 and EY 18/07/08.
44. See reference 37.
45. PADCO–ESCO (1998), *Plan Maestro de Desarrollo Urbano de la Ciudad de San Miguel*, Consorcio PADCO-ESCO, San Miguel, page 12.
46. Interviews with architects and urban planners, codes AA 25/07/08, RO 28/07/08 and ML 29/07/08.
47. Interviews with architects and urban planners, codes CS 11/07/08, HG 17/07/08, KR 11/07/08, EC 15/07/08 and EC 16/07/08.
48. See reference 45.
49. See reference 46.
50. McBride, B (2007), "Building capital: the role of migrant remittances in housing improvement and construction in El Salvador", unpublished Master's thesis, Institute of Housing Studies, Rotterdam.
51. www.fsb.gov.sv.

References

Acosta, P, P Fajnzylber and J H López (2008), "How important are remittances in Latin America?", in P Fajnzylber and J H López (editors), *Remittances and Development: Lessons from Latin America*, World Bank, Washington DC, pages 21–49.

Aguilar, A and P Ward (2003), "Globalization, regional development and mega-city expansion in Latin America: analyzing Mexico City's peri-urban hinterland", *Cities* Vol 20, pages 3–21.

Agunias, D (2006), "Remittance trends in Central America", Migration Information Source, accessible at www.migrationinformation.org.

Ayuntamiento de Lleida, UNESCO, UIA and Ministerio de Asuntos Exteriores (editors) (1999), *Ciudades Intermedias y Urbanización Mundial*, Municipalidad de Lleida, accessible at http://www.unesco.org/most/ciudades.pdf.

Baires, S (2006), "Los barrios cerrados en el AMSS: una nueva forma de segregación residencial en la era de la globalización,", *Revista ILA* Vol 288, pages XII–XIII.

Barros, J (2004), "Urban growth in Latin American cities: exploring urban dynamics through agent-based simulation", PhD thesis, University of London.

Bolay, J C and A Rabinovich (2003), "Intermediate cities in Latin America: risk and opportunities of coherent urban development", *Cities* Vol 21, pages 407–421.

Borsdorf, A, R Hidalgo and R Sánchez (2007), "A new model of urban development in Latin America: the gated communities and fenced cities in the metropolitan areas of Santiago de Chile and Valparaíso", *Cities* Vol 24, pages 365–378.

Caldeira, T (2000), *City of Walls: Crime, Segregation and Citizenship in São Paulo*, University of California Press, Berkeley, 487 pages.

CEPAL (2000), *From Rapid Urbanization to the Consolidation of Human Settlements in Latin America and the Caribbean: A Territorial Perspective*, CEPAL, Santiago.

Coy, M and M Pöhler (2002), "Gated communities in Latin American megacities: case studies in Brazil and Argentina", *Environment and Planning B* Vol 29, pages 355–370.

Digestyc (2006), "Indicadores demográficos por departamento, 2006", accessible at www.digestyc.gob.sv.

Digestyc (2008), *VI Censo de Población y V de Vivienda 2007*, Ministerio de Economía, Dirección General de Estadística y Censos, San Salvador.

El Diario de Hoy (2006a), "El crédito para la vivienda minima disminuyó en 35 per cent", 6 January, accessible at www.elsalvador.com.

El Diario de Hoy (2006b), "Compatriotas usan remesas en vivienda", 20 September, accessible at www.elsalvador.com.

El Diario de Hoy (2009), "Venta de viviendas cae en un 70 per cent por la crisis", 11 February, accessible at www.elsalvador.com.

El Periodico (2006a), "Mi casa es como las de Estados Unidos", 3 September, accessible at www.elperiodico.com.gt.

El Periodico (2006b), "El día que las remesas dejen de llegar en Salcajá", 5 September, accessible at www.elperiodico.com.gt.

El Remesero (2008), "Las remesas impulsan la economía de la zona oriental de El Salvador", 23 April, accessible at http://elremesero.com.

FOGUAVI (2004) Programa Fortalecimiento a la DEMANDA de Vivienda Popular, accessible at http://www.cepal.org/pobrezaurbana/docs/ minurvi/Gua/Fortaleci%20Demanda%20Vivienda%20Po.pdf.

Ford, L (1996), "A new and improved model of Latin American city structure", *Geographical Review* Vol 86, No 3, pages 437–440.

Fortín-Magaña, G (2003), "Low-income housing in El Salvador", *ReVista Harvard Review of Latin America*, Winter.

Gilbert, A (1996), "The mega-city in Latin America: an introduction", in A Gilbert (editor), *The Mega-city in Latin America*, The United Nations University Press, New York, Tokyo, Paris, pages 1–24.

Griffin, E and L Ford (1980), "A model of Latin American city structure", *Geographical Review* 70, pages 397–422.

Herzog, L (2006), *Return to the Centre: Culture, Public Space and City Building in a Global Era*, University of Texas Press, Austin, 256 pages.

INE (2008), *XI Censo Nacional de Población y VI de Habitación (Censo 2002)*, accessible at www.ine.gob.gt.

IOM (2004), "Survey on the impact of family remittances on Guatemalan homes", Working Notebooks on Migration 19, Guatemala City.

IOM (2005), "Survey on remittances and microenterprises", Working Notebooks on Migration 21, Guatemala City.

Klaufus, C (2009), *Construir la Ciudad Andina: Planificación y Autoconstrucción en Riobamba y Cuenca*, Abya Yala/FLACSO, Quito.

Landolt, P, L Autler and S Baires (1999), "From *hermano lejano* to *hermano mayor*: the dialectics of Salvadoran transnationalism", *Ethnic and Racial Studies* Vol 22, No 2, pages 290–315.

Leichenko, R and W Solecki (2005), "Exporting the American dream: the globalization of suburban consumption landscapes", *Regional Studies* Vol 39, No 2, pages 241–253.

Lima, J (2001), "Sociospatial segregation and urban form: Belém at the end of the 1990s", *Geoforum* Vol 32, pages 493–507.

Low, S (2004), *Behind the Gates: Life, Security and the Pursuit of Happiness in Fortress America*, Routledge, New York, 288 pages. (2007), *Plan Estratégico Territorial del Valle de Quetzaltenango*, Quetzaltenango, Guatemala.

McBride, B (2007), "Building capital: the role of migrant remittances in housing improvement and construction in El Salvador", unpublished Master's thesis, Institute of Housing Studies, Rotterdam.

Moser, C (editor) (2004), "Urban violence and insecurity: an introductory roadmap", *Environment and Urbanization* Vol 16, No 2, October, pages 3–16.

Moser, C and C McIllwaine (2001), *Violence in a Post-Conflict Context: Urban Poor Perceptions from Guatemala,* World Bank Publications, Washington DC, 163 pages.

Orozco, M (2006), *Between Hardship and Hope: Remittances and the Local Economy in Latin America*, Inter-American Development Bank, Washington DC, 29 pages.

PADCO–ESCO (1998), *Plan Maestro de Desarrollo Urbano de la Ciudad de San Miguel*, Consorcio PADCOESCO, San Miguel.

Prensa Libre (2006), "Remesas cambian el rostro de Cantel", 6 February, accessible at www.prensalibre.com.

Prensa Libre (2007a), "Vivienda, un proyecto de 20 años", 2 December, accessible at www.prensalibre.com.

Prensa Libre (2007b), "Xelajú crece sin orden", 19 December, accessible at www.prensalibre.com.

Ribeiro, L and L Lago (1995), "Restructuring in large Brazilian cities: the centre-periphery model", *International Journal of Urban and Regional Research* 19, pages 369–382.

Rodgers, D (2004), "'Disembedding' the city: crime, insecurity and spatial organization in Managua, Nicaragua", *Environment and Urbanization* Vol 16, No 2, October, pages 113–123.

Satterthwaite, D (2006), *Outside the Large Cities: the Demographic Importance of Small Urban Centres and Large Villages in Africa, Asia and Latin America*, Discussion Paper Series, Urban Change 3, IIED, London, 28 pages. *and Globalization in the Latin American Centro Histórico*, University of Arizona Press, Tucson, 267 pages.

Sociedad Hipotecaria Federal (SHF) (2005), "Programa de créditos hipotecarios a migrantes", accessible at http://nuevoportal.shf.gob.mx/prensa Paginas/Presentaciones.aspx.

Sorto Rivas, F (2004), "La situación del déficit habitacional en El Salvador", Digestyc, San Salvador.

Stein, A and I Vance (2008), "The role of housing finance in addressing the needs of the urban poor: lessons from Central America", *Environment and Urbanization* Vol 20, No 1, April, pages 13–30.

Suro, R (2005), "A survey of remittance senders and receivers", in D Terry and S Wilson (editors), *Beyond Small Change: Making Migrant Remittances Count*, Inter-American Development Bank, Washington DC, pages 35–36.

UIEP–PROINFO (2002), *Información Estadística y Social del Municipio de Quetzaltenango, 2000–2002*, Unidad de Información, Investigación Estadística y Planificación–Proyecto de Información Sociodemográfica y de Salud para el Desarrollo Local, Quetzaltenango.

UNDP (2005), *Informe sobre Desarrollo Humano El Salvador 2005: Una Mirada al Nuevo Nosotros; El Impacto de las Migraciones*, UNDP, San Salvador.

Vassoler, I (2007), *Urban Brazil: Visions, Afflictions and Governance Lessons*, Cambria Press, Amherst, 244 pages.

WCED (1987), *Our Common Future,* Report of the World Commission on Environment and Development, Oxford University Press, accessible at http://www.un-documents.net/ocf-09.htm#I.

www.fsb.gov.sv.

www.citypopulation.de.

www.fsv.gob.sv.

CPSIA information can be obtained
at www.ICGtesting.com
Printed in the USA
FSOW04n0208231215
14799FS